THE FINDS OF ROMAN BRITAIN

Guy de la Bédoyère

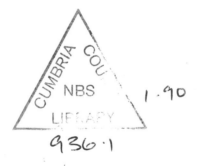
B. T. Batsford Ltd, London

Typeset by Tek-Art Ltd, Kent
and printed in Great Britain by
The Bath Press, Bath
for the Publishers B.T. Batsford Ltd
4 Fitzhardinge Street, London WIH OAH
ISBN 0 7134 6082 2

Contents

List of figures

List of colour plates

Acknowledgements

I am extremely grateful to a number of people, all experts in their various fields, for the help which they gave in the preparation of the text. No one person could possibly hope to be master of all these various aspects of Romano-British life, least of all myself, and without the assistance of the following the book could not have even been attempted. They are: Graham Webster, the long-suffering editor; Catherine Johns of the British Museum who besides helping with the bulk of the text also supplied invaluable support and assistance with some of the photographs; Miranda Green (religion); Don Bailey (lamps); Jennifer Price (glass); Richard Reece (coins); Grace Simpson and Richard Hattatt (brooches).

A number of individuals and bodies have kindly allowed me either to photograph or re-draw objects in their various collections or publications. These are too numerous to list here but I would like to make special mention of the Society of Antiquaries in London, English Heritage, the Society for the Promotion of Roman Studies, and Philip Clarkstone for his help with preparing the author's photographs. I would like to thank Peter Kemmis Betty at Batsford for his enthusiastic reception of the idea, and his subsequent assistance with its preparation. Finally I should thank my wife Rosemary for her tolerance in the months between October 1987 and August 1988 when this book was written and illustrated.

In this kind of book a number of painful decisions have had to be made about what could be omitted. The result, I hope, is a judicious selection of artefacts mainly defined by being portable. Mistakes, and unwise omissions are entirely my responsibility.

Guy de la Bédoyère, Eltham, 1988

Introduction

Several years ago I published a book concerned with a substantial deposit of Roman material from the river bed in London. The find was a chance one, the material having been removed from a modern building site and dumped. Unexpectedly launched into a serious study of Romano-British artefacts I naturally looked around for something like a general textbook. Apart from histories and coffee table books, of which there were many, there did not appear to be a single up-to-date textbook which dealt with artefacts of Roman Britain. The last few years have seen not only huge advances in archaeological techniques and understanding of artefacts but also a number of major finds. Such books as do exist are thus hopelessly out-of-date and of little use nowadays.

Having established this fact I then encountered the specialist literature concerned with Romano-British archaeology. There is a great deal of it, some of it excellent reading. But for the most part it is expensive, obscure, incomprehensible, and exceedingly difficult to find unless one lives close to a large, serious bookshop and a university library – always assuming that the would-be reader has access to the library. I was lucky on both counts but it soon appeared that these various publications have made some of the artefacts of Roman Britain into grains of driven sand.

This is one of the curious paradoxes of modern archaeology. No sooner is an excavation successfully concluded than objects, lost for centuries, are effectively re-lost in vaults and plastic bags. The lucky ones may be the subject of an article in a periodical, or feature in an excavation report which may not appear for a generation after the dig. Even then artefacts found together, and perhaps even identical in form, are dispersed amongst the pages on grounds of the material they are made of. Thus bone pins appear in the section on 'Objects of bone', bronze pins appear in the section on 'Objects of bronze (or 'copper-alloy')'. This book has been written and illustrated to make a small

redress by drawing together Romano-British objects where they share a common or associated function. Thus the book deals with the army, trades and industries, household life and so on.

This reflects the modern approach of a number of excellent museums which have displayed their material in an exciting and evocative manner – the Museum of London and the Corinium Museum in Cirencester come immediately to mind. Displays of reconstructed rooms and display cabinets concerned with particular themes do much to re-create the way of life in Roman Britain. The only weakness is that each museum can necessarily only use material from its respective area. There is no such limitation with a book: artefacts have been selected from all over Britain.

Although many readers will not need or want to trace individual artefacts some will. In order to help those who do a select, but comprehensive, bibliography has been prepared and each artefact is accompanied by appropriate references and details of scale. At an early stage of the book's preparation it was decided for the most part to use the author's drawings in favour of photographs. This has certain advantages: it makes for a certain unity of style and has vastly increased the number of artefacts illustrated. It can also be surprisingly difficult to see important detail on photographs. However, it has sometimes been necessary to use different scales for artefacts illustrated together. This has also allowed a larger number of objects to be illustrated.

Artefacts hold considerable value for archaeologists. Fashions changed in the Roman Empire, just as they do now. By charting the changes in artefacts and the different artefacts used for different jobs we can build up a picture of life in different places at different times. For some periods, particularly prehistory, an archaeological definition of the period is the lack, or small number, of objects. This is not true of Roman Britain. There is a wealth of material in the ground – a casual walk across a field which

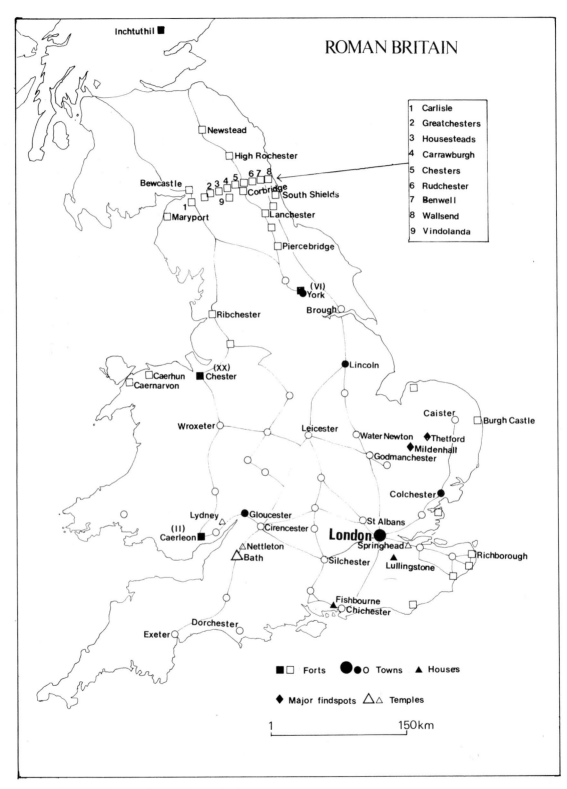

ROMAN BRITAIN

Inchtuthil

1	Carlisle
2	Greatchesters
3	Housesteads
4	Carrawburgh
5	Chesters
6	Rudchester
7	Benwell
8	Wallsend
9	Vindolanda

Newstead

High Rochester

Bewcastle

Corbridge

South Shields

Maryport

Lanchester

Piercebridge

(VI)
York

Brough

Ribchester

Caerhun
Caernarvon

(XX) Chester

Lincoln

Wroxeter

Leicester

Caister

Burgh Castle

Water Newton
Thetford
Mildenhall
Godmanchester

Colchester

Lydney
(II)
Caerleon

Gloucester
Cirencester

St Albans

London

Springhead

Richborough

Nettleton
Bath

Silchester

Lullingstone

Fishbourne
Chichester

Dorchester

Exeter

■□ Forts ● ●○ Towns ▲ Houses

◆ Major findspots △△ Temples

1   150km

1 Map of Roman Britain showing the main sites mentioned in the test.

was once the site of a Roman settlement will inevitably yield pottery, tiles, possibly coins and maybe traces of brooches. Excavations yield far more.

Despite the quantities of Roman material in Britain the subject is not overwhelmingly difficult to understand. This was a cosmopolitan society much like our own with a large range of industries catering for the extensive consumer tastes of Roman life. A few concepts separate our way of life from Roman existence, particularly the application of pressure to create motion, electronics, printing and the Arabic system of numbers. But like our world there were mass popular tastes – for example the 'crossbow' brooch which is found right across the Roman Empire of the fourth century, or the pottery flagon used throughout the period. So, while a book such as this has inevitably resulted in a great deal of selectivity, this has, I hope, not involved excluding whole categories of artefacts which were in common use in Britain in the first to fourth centuries AD.

The vagaries of archaeology and chance finds mean that a slightly cavalier approach has proved necessary towards dates. While pottery, military equipment, brooches and coins are fairly well-dated simply because of the large quantities found in association with sites of historically testified date, some are not. They are too few and too fragmentary to be teated so comprehensively. There is, as a result, a certain amount of jumping about which assumes a basic knowledge of Romano-British history. A date chart is supplied for assistance but otherwise I hope the reader will turn to some of the excellent modern histories of Roman Britain.

1

The Roman Army in Britain

Introduction

The Roman army had a dramatic effect on the material culture of Britain for a number of reasons. Firstly, a new class of artefact was introduced in the form of Roman military equipment of whatever function, such as armour, arms, and tools. Secondly, the army was made up of men who were accustomed to all the normal accessories of everyday Roman life. So these accessories were either imported or made by the army or local people working under instructions. This is especially apparent in pottery forms, for example the flagons and the mixing bowls, called *mortaria*, almost unknown in Britain before the invasion but essential for Roman cooking. Thirdly, because the soldiers were themselves paid in coin this encouraged the dispersal of cash amongst the indigenous population, and the introduction of the whole concept of currency and markets. This provided the Romano-British with the means to buy imported goods themselves. The result was that the Roman army became the main dynamic behind the phenomenon of romanisation. Even the most remote settlement might be introduced to the consumer world of Rome through the presence of a nearby minor fort and its garrison.

The most important collections of Roman military equipment have been found in other parts of the Roman Empire, mainly in Germany along the line of the frontiers, and in the East, for example at Dura-Europos on the upper Euphrates. The British climate and its soil conditions have not favoured the survival of iron, leather and bone, materials which were used for most Roman military equipment, whether armour or armaments. The student of Roman military equipment is therefore unavoidably dependent on finds elsewhere, and a number of references are included in the bibliography. However, this book is about Roman Britain and so emphasis is placed on the kind of evidence more commonly found in Britain.

Britain has produced a very large amount of Roman military equipment but the material is mostly fragmentary and in the main consists of bronze fittings, and their publication is dispersed in many different sources. These items can be difficult to identify in isolation because some of these metal components can be mistaken for jewellery. We also depend on the less direct evidence of tombstones and narrative relief sculpture for how this equipment was actually worn and the descriptions below rely heavily on these sources. However tombstones do not show soldiers in their fighting equipment; rather, soldiers are portrayed in an un-dress style appropriate to peaceable activities. Only with the tombstones of cavalrymen in their parade armour do we gain an indication of how soldiers may have fought.

This raises the interesting question of whether military artefacts in isolation necessarily represent the presence of the army. It seems to have been common for Romano-British towns to begin life as minor settlements outside forts established in the decades immediately following the conquest. However not all towns have produced evidence of early forts – Silchester is a case in point – but a fort, in all probability, did precede the Roman town. Soldiers are attested in different parts of the province in contexts which suggest a personal or administrative capacity, such as London where they were attached to the governor's staff (*RIB* 122), or Bath where they visited the spa (*RIB* 143/146).

The organisation of the army

Before looking at the equipment used by the Roman army and which survives in Britain it is worth considering how the army was organised because its strict hierarchy was reflected in the hardware used. The Roman army had two constituent types of unit: the citizen legions and the various forms of units made up of non-citizens generally known as the *auxilia*. There were exceptions but broadly speaking this was how the army was organised. It can be difficult to fully appreciate the rôle of the auxiliary units because Roman historians, particularly Tacitus on whom we depend so much for our knowledge of the events of the first century in Britain, preferred to glorify the legions. Dio Cassius, whose version of the Conquest of AD 43 is the only surviving account, includes no detail about the auxilia except to say that their total number approximately equalled that of the legions.

Legions

The legions were made up of male Roman citizens. The legion contained approximately 5,000 men divided into ten cohorts of 480 men, sub-divided into six centuries of 80 men which were divided into ten groups of eight, each called a *contubernium* (p.24). After the reign of Vespasian (AD 69-79) the first cohort was enlarged to 800 men sub-divided into five double centuries of 160. Each of the 30 or so legions in existence had a number of craftsmen legionaries who were responsible for skilled construction tasks, surveying and other maintenance tasks. There was also a small cavalry contingent for reconnaissance though the legion was primarily an infantry force.

Auxiliaries

The *cohors* and *alae* were the basic components of the Roman army. They were divided into units of about 500 or 1000, and were either infantry *cohortes peditatae*, cavalry *alae*, or mixed *cohortes equitatae*. Some units was made up of an ethnic type in order to preserve their specific skills, such as archery or stone-slinging. Their reward for 25 years' service was citizenship. There were also units of rather lower status, called *numeri* (infantry), and *cunei* (cavalry). These were first raised in the early second century for specific campaigns to support the army but they were really only loosely-organised native levies, and not 'Roman' in any sense at all, though they proved so useful that they were gradually incorporated into the army.

Command structure

The army was under the personal control of the emperor, as *Imperator*. This title belonged to the period of the Republic and was one held by a *consul*, the most senior magistrate (of which there were two, elected annually), permitting him to raise an army through the power of *imperium*. The power only lasted for a year and had to be renewed by the senate. During imperial times this had become something of a formality but the emperors continued to observe the form. Each legion was commanded by his delegate, the *legatus legionis*, of senatorial rank, and beneath him came the most senior of the six tribunes, also of senatorial rank. This tribune, known as a *tribunus laticlavius*, might eventually be promoted to a legionary command. This certainly happened to Gnaeus Julius Agricola who served in both capacities in Britain before eventually becoming provincial governor. After the *tribunus laticlavius* came the *praefectus castrorum*, who had formerly been the most senior centurion, *primus pilus*. His expertise in the practical business of soldiering and managing a legion was essential. Thereafter came the other five tribunes, of equestrian rank, who might hope eventually to command an auxiliary unit.

Each century was led by a centurion. A centurion's seniority depended on which century in which cohort he commanded. The most senior was the *primus pilus*, who led the first century of the first cohort. Within the century the centurion was assisted by an *optio* (a kind of corporal), a *tesserarius* (an administrative rôle) and the *custos armorum* (who took care of armour and equipment). Most of the auxiliary units were arranged in a similar way except that being smaller they had a more limited command structure. Each was commanded by an equestrian *praefectus*, sometimes being assisted by junior officers whose titles, *duplicarius* and *sesquiplicarius*, merely refer to the higher rates of pay received for the job.

Legionary equipment

Having seen how carefully the Roman army was sub-divided into legions and the hierarchies within each it is not surprising to learn that equipment was similarly treated. Naturally there were variations in time and in place but throughout the first two centuries the evidence suggests that in the Western Empire at least legionaries looked very much like one another. It seems that government-sponsored factories manufactured equipment, hence the similarity of military artefacts which makes them relatively easy to identify.

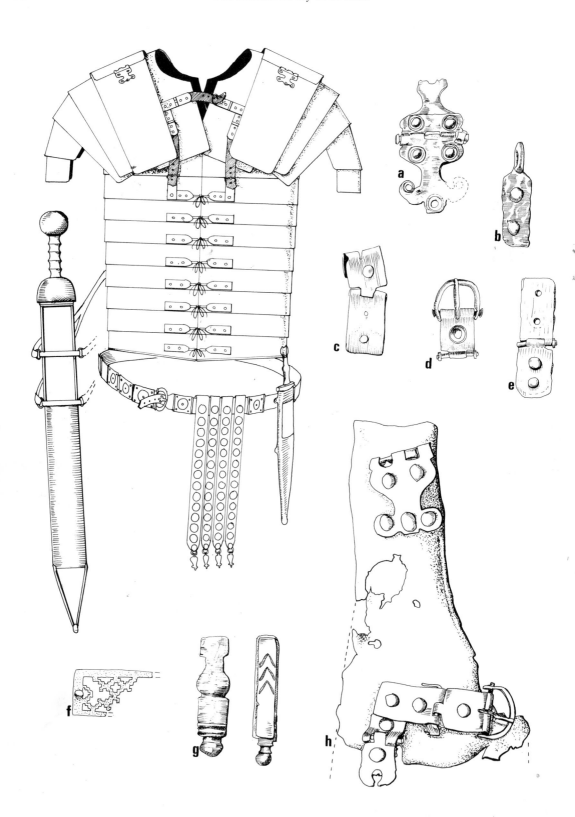

Unfortunately the general administrative disorder from the 240s on seems to have destroyed this system. In Britain there was little military activity and, in fact, a certain amount of deterioration of military structures (fig. 22 c). So we have little evidence of military equipment for this period and it is quite impossible to draw a general picture.

Legionary equipment can be considered in three categories: the soldier's actual military dress, that is, his armour; his weapons and other tools; and equipment used by the legion, such as artillery.

Legionary armour and clothing

The Roman legionary wore clothing of essentially three types: metal armour, helmet, and metal accessories; fabric undergarments; and leather shoes and accessories. Naturally it is the metal goods which tend to survive. The fabric is hardly ever found, but leather is occasionally found in waterlogged deposits.

Armour (*lorica*)

Up until around the middle of the first century BC the main type of armour in use was mail but by AD 43 legionaries were using armour made of iron strips mounted on leather straps inside and joined on the outside with bronze buckles, hooks, hinges and more leather straps. Designed to move with the body this kind of armour is now

---

2 *Lorica segmentata* and components (two-thirds actual size). *Lorica segmentata* suit of armour consisted of overlapping iron strips and bronze fittings (based on H. Russell Robinson's reconstructions)

a hinge unit from Verulamium (after Frere, 1984, 32, no. 77)

b tie-hook from Verulamium (fits to rear of suit, after Frere, *op. cit.*, no. 73)

c hinged buckle (part missing) from Verulamium (after Frere, *op. cit.*, no. 74)

d buckle from Richborough (after Cunliffe, 1968, pl. 36, no. 110)

e hinged buckle from Kingsholm (after Hurst, 1985, 28 no. 5)

f fragment of a fretted legionary belt plate from Caerleon (after Zienkiewicz, 1986, 175, no. 36)

g apron terminals. Left: from Verulamium (after Frere, *op. cit.*, no. 80); right: from Hod Hill (after Brailsford 1962, fig. 3, A46)

h section of iron neck plate for *lorica segmentata* with hinge and buckles, from the Bank of England, London

known as *lorica segmentata* or 'laminated armour'. Each suit included larger plates over the strips which protected the shoulders, chest and back. These plates were attached to the rest of the armour either with hooks and eyes or straps and buckles (fig. 2 a-e; Robinson, 1974, 174 ff.). The remains of at least six suits were found at the fort of Corbridge, packed into a box belonging to a context of *c.* AD 100 (Daniels, 1968; and Allason-Jones and Bishop, 1988). It is these metal hinges and buckles, or the hooks and eyes mentioned above, which are the most commonly found pieces of legionary armour. Iron corrodes so easily in British soil conditions that this kind of armour is known mostly from these attachments. *Lorica segmentata* presumably had the advantage of being relatively easy to repair from spare components, and thus not necessarily requiring skilled attention.

In time the iron strips used seem to have become smaller and by the later second century armour made of overlapping bronze or iron leaves, 'scale armour' (*lorica squamata*), was in use alongside revived mail armour (*lorica hamata*). Scale armour leaves, which could be anything from about 2cm^2 (0.3sq in) to over 40cm^2 (6.2sq in) in size, were individually wired together and then sewn to an undergarment made of fabric or leather (fig. 9 b; also Curle, 1911, pl. xxiv). The use of tinning or alternating bronze and iron scales enhanced the appearance of a suit (Robinson, 1975, 156). There seems to have been less homogeneity in equipment used in this period, possibly reflecting a general decline in centralisation, and the pragmatic need to use whatever was available. Centurions wore either scale or mail armour throughout the period.

The helmet (*galea or cassis*)

As important as the armour was the helmet. At the time of the invasion of Britain in AD 43 a change was taking place. The bronze 'coolus' or 'jockey cap' type (fig. 3 a; plate 1) currently in use resembled a skull cap, had attached cheek pieces, and a rearward projection. Being bronze it was softer than iron swords, moreover it lacked protection for the neck; so by about the year AD 60 it had been almost completely superseded by the 'imperial-Gallic' type (fig. 3 b). This improved type of helmet afforded protection for the neck: it was reinforced with, or made of iron and was in common use in the Western Empire. Apart from this basic design difference the

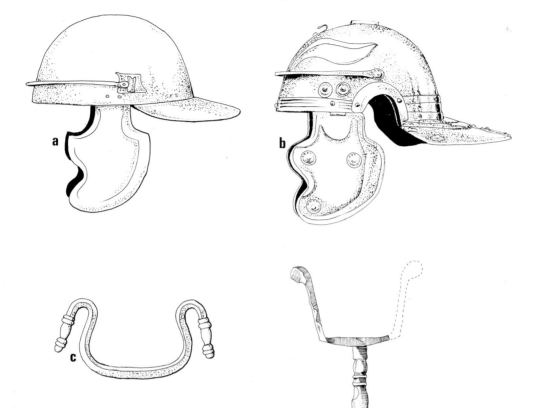

3 Helmets (first and second centuries):
a bronze 'coolus' helmet. Claudian-Neronian.
b iron imperial Gallic helmet, mid-first century on.
 Auxiliaries often wore basic versions of this type
c carrying handle from an imperial Gallic helmet,
 found at Corbridge, *Corstopitum*. Diameter 6.7cm
 (after Robinson)
d plume holder from an imperial Gallic helmet, found
 at Richborough. Height 9.4cm (after Cunliffe,
 1968, pl.34 no.90)

imperial-Gallic helmet was also decorated. In the main this took the form of 'eyebrows' on the front of the skull-cap and small circular bronze bosses. Both kinds of helmets had fittings for crest holders; these were probably only used on parade (fig.3 d). Inside they probably had leather linings which seem to have been glued on. The imperial-Gallic helmet sometimes had a handle affixed to the neck protector so that the helmet could be carried or hung (fig.3 c). In isolation these handles are easily mistaken for furniture attachments. Helmets could have long lives. An example of the 'coolus' type from London has the names of four successive owners inscribed on its rear projection. Doubtless the same considera-

tions might apply to much military equipment and this complicates dating. The best discussion of helmets is to be found in H. Russell Robinson's work on Roman armour (1975).

Accessories
The use of metal also extended to the decoration of leather belts. In the first century these were often elaborately decorated with silvering, tinning, and enamelling. In the second century patterns were made more simply by using metal plates cast in stencils with fretted patterns which exposed the leather and coloured cloth beneath (fig.2 f). On the front of the belt a kind of apron made of strips of leather was worn. These strips usually had decorative discs and terminals of tinned bronze (fig.2 g).

The evidence of tombstones and the narrative sculptures of the Columns of Trajan (fig.7) and

Marcus Aurelius in Rome indicate that the legionaries wore undergarments of linen and wool. Not surprisingly these are unlikely to occur in a context where they were identifiable and where they were certainly military undergarments. The tombstone of the *optio* Caecilius Avitus of *legio* XX at Chester shows him wearing what appears to be either a woollen or leather cloak (*RIB* 492). Fabrics are discussed in Chapter 4.

Leather was used for more than simply holding armour together. The most important leather component of clothing was footwear. Legionaries wore sandals which consisted of multi-layered soles reinforced with iron hob-nails (fig.24; and see Chapter 4). They were secured to the foot with a network of thongs which rose up the leg. These shoes, known as *caligae*, are more commonly found in the form of footprints on roofing tiles, or in the remains of the nails, than in the leather parts themselves. Leather was also used to make trousers (*bracae*) for use in cold climates. Legionaries wore belts made of leather too but the most visible parts of these were the metal decorative plates and buckles.

The officers

Senior officers wore distinctive equipment. Centurions wore equipment which was significantly more decorated than that of the legionaries, if they could afford it. They wore mail or scale armour and metal greaves on the lower legs (fig.8 a). On their helmets they wore transverse crests. The legate and his tribunes seem to have worn armour designed to individual requirements or affectations adorned with discs on the chest bearing the images of various gods. Their cuirasses were of a type now known as the 'muscle cuirass' and involved two moulded sheets of metal in the form of a muscular chest. However, no example of Roman date has survived and they are known only from sculpture and pre-Roman examples. The officers also wore necklaces, armlets and bracelets on parade, which were possibly decorations for valour. A single surviving officer's helmet, from Autun in France, serves to suggest their form (Robinson, 1975). It emulates, in a particularly outrageous and theatrical manner, helmets of Greek and Etruscan form with the addition of a neck protector and embossed acanthus leaves.

The tombstone of M. Favonius Facilis, a centurion with *legio* XX, provides an interesting portrayal of a first-century centurion (fig.8 a) stationed in Britain. Facilis was dead by AD 49, the year in which the XX left Colchester where his tombstone was found (*RIB* 200, and below, p.43). It must therefore date to between AD 43 and 49. Facilis is bare-headed (a sign of death) and therefore no information about his helmet is available. It probably bore a transverse crest as on the tombstone of T. Calidius Severus, found at Carnuntum (Webster, 1985).

Legionary arms

These include the offensive equipment such as swords and javelins, and the defensive equipment such as shields. As with the armour, it is the metal components of these items which are much more likely to be found.

Sword (*gladius*)

The legionary was an infantryman and his arms reflected this rôle. The iron sword (*gladius*), was a short weapon designed to be used with one hand for sharp thrusting in close combat (fig.4 a, b). In the early first century these weapons, around 50cm (20in) or a little longer in length, had tapering points derived from Spanish models, but by the latter part of the century a shorter point had replaced this, with blades varying around 50cm (8-10in) in length.

Sword handle-grips could be made of wood or bone (fig.4 b) and were grooved for better grip. They were kept in wooden scabbards which were strengthened with leather and bronze bands and tips. A bronze scabbard from the Thames at Fulham is decorated with scrolls and a scene of the wolf suckling Romulus and Remus (fig.5). The sword was supplemented by the dagger which was about half the length, though by the time of Trajan's Column it seems to have passed out of use. While both were in use they were attached to individual belts, or the sword could be worn slung on a baldric. A fragmentary bone grip found in the fill of a first century ditch at Aldgate in London may point to the presence of an early fort (fig.4 b).

Dagger (*pugio*)

The sword was supplemented by the dagger (*pugio*) which resembled it in shape, differing mainly in shorter blade length at about 20-25cm (8-10in) (fig.4 c). The blade is also somewhat

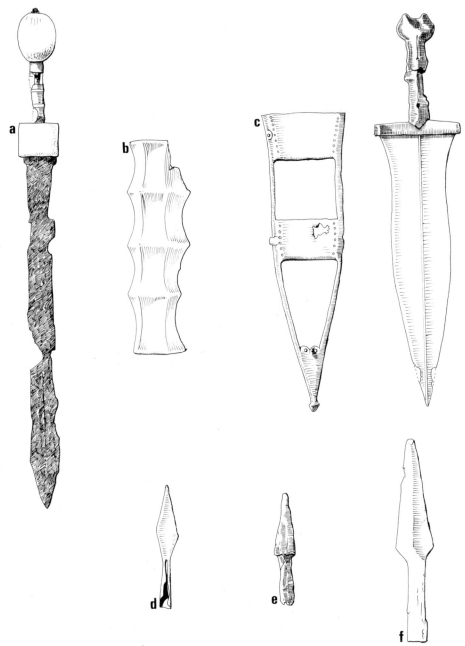

4 Arms (not to scale):
a *gladius* from Caernarvon, *Segontium*. Length 46cm
b bone handle from a *gladius*, found in a first-century
   ditch at Aldgate, London. Length 8.6cm (after
   Chapman and Johnson, 49)
c iron dagger, *pugio*, and scabbard, from Copthall
   Court, 1911, London. Length 41cm
d iron *ballista* bolt head (length 4.5cm)
e iron javelin head and spearhead (10cm long) and,
f artillery bolt (16cm long) from Vindolanda (after
   Bidwell, 1986)

more pointed. The sheath was either made
entirely of bronze or iron, sometimes decorated
with embossed silver plates, or it was made of
wood and bronze. A fine iron example of a
dagger sheath mount was found at Richborough
in association with 'Claudian pottery' (Bushe-
Fox, 1949, 123 no. 75 and pl. XXXIII). The iron
plate is decorated with a silver inlaid geometric
design. The dagger may not have remained in use
by legionaries after the end of the first century. It

does not appear on Trajan's Column but this may be because of an artistic convention in which the shield conceals the left side.

Javelin (*pilum*)

Additional offensive power came in the form of the 2m (6ft 7in) long *pilum*, or javelin. These were made of wood and had hardened iron heads of pyramidal form of a little under half the length either secured to the shaft by means of a socket, or with rivets. The purpose of the weapon was to bend on entering an enemy's shield and thus render it useless. Examples, presumably of Claudian date, are known from Hod Hill (Brailsford, 1962, 6, and pl. IIB) and Maiden Castle (Wheeler, 1943, 278), and a number of other fort sites (fig.4 d-f).

Shield (*scutum*)

The shield (*scutum*) was mainly composed of corruptible materials and only the metal fittings are usually found (but see the reconstructed example shown on fig. 6). Like the helmet there was a change in the early first century, from an oval form to a similar shape but with the top and bottom squared off (fig.6 a). Subsequently the shield, made of laminated plywood, was altered entirely to a rectangular shape (Josephus, *The Jewish War*, III, 5, writing about the years AD 66-73). Shields seem to have functioned as display items as well, bearing legionary colours and appropriate symbols of courage and bravery, such as thunderbolts. During the Second Battle of Cremona, part of the Civil War of AD 68-9, two soldiers supporting *legio* VII disguised themselves as members of *legio* XVI, whose artillery was pounding VII, by picking up the shields of two dead soldiers; this permitted them to approach a catapult and cut its ropes (Tacitus, *Histories*, III, 23).

Shields were curved so as to protect the body and were held by means of a central handle which was itself protected by a bronze or iron boss. It is this component or the bronze reinforcing strips which are most likely to be found. The shield boss could be richly decorated and an outstanding example was found in the River Tyne at Newcastle (fig.6 b). Shields were protected when not in use with a leather cover, such as an example found at Hardknott fort in the Lake District.

5 A legionary *gladius* found in the River Thames at Fulham, West London. The handle is missing but the iron blade contained within a bronze scabbard survives. The scabbard is decorated with a scroll and a panel depicting Romulus and Remus suckling from the wolf. Length 53cm (photo and copyright: the British Museum)

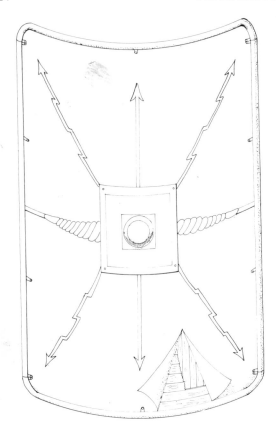

6 Shield (*scutum*):

a reconstructed *scutum* with folded-back fabric covering revealing the strips of plywood beneath

b decorated bronze boss from the shield of Junius Dubitatus, member of Iulius Magnus' century in *legio* VIII *Augusta*. Found in the Tyne at Newcastle. The boss is decorated with various divine characters including the Four Seasons, and Mars as well as a bull, an eagle and standards. On the original much of the work is performed in dots, shown here in line for clarity. Height 28cm

Other equipment

The Roman legionaries might almost be regarded as the equivalent of the modern Royal Engineers. Roman soldiers were by no means confined to purely military activities. Legionaries participated in the construction of the temporary fortifications of their overnight camps, or of their forts – more permanent structures made either of turf and timber, or turf and stone. In order to do this effectively they carried tools to assist in the movement of earth. Some of these are unlikely to be recovered from the ground, particularly the basket for carrying earth, and ropes. However, the legionary also carried a saw, bill-hook, chain, pickaxe and turf-cutter (fig.14 a-c; Josephus, *The Jewish War*, III, 5) but these are unlikely to be obviously military unless found in a military context, such as a fort ditch, or demolition pit as at Newstead (Curle, 1911). The pickaxe, *dolabrum* (fig.14 a), was made of iron but its

cutting edge was protected by a small bronze sheath with hooks at either end so that it could be slung on the soldier's belt (fig.14 b).

As we saw earlier, the smallest division of a century of soldiers was the eight-man *contubernium*. While on campaign the *contubernium*, which actually means 'tent-party', shared a tent. Surprisingly enough Britain has produced evidence for these leather tents in the form of fragments from Birdoswald and Newstead. These have allowed a reconstruction to be made (fig.14 d; Richmond and McIntyre, 1934). The tents were carried by a mule assigned to the *contubernium* .

There is no particular reason to definitively assign this sort of 'other equipment' specifically to legionaries. There is every reason to suppose that auxiliary units made use of this sort of material as well.

Auxiliary equipment

Auxiliary armour and clothing was much more varied than that used by the legions because the various units were largely employed for the sake of their particular fighting skills and tactics. Part of these different ethnic identities was the retention of their traditional fighting garb. By the early second century, with the permanent garrisoning of a number of units, these regional distinctions became diluted as recruits were increasingly drawn from the offspring of the soldiers and local women. Tombstone evidence, while useful, shows idealised images of soldiers in stock postures (see Anderson, 1984). This makes the archaeological evidence complicated, and it is difficult for any kind of general picture to be drawn of auxiliary equipment.

Some recent work suggests that it may be possible to date military equipment with greater accuracy by assuming that the more developed a province became the more the army could rely on local manufacturing to supply items of equip-

ment, instead of importing it, or making it themselves. Finally, in the Late Empire, the government came to supply all such material (Oldenstein, 1985). The evidence from the frontiers in Germany has played the most important rôle in such studies.

In Britain's case the silvered heart-shaped pendants from auxiliary cavalry horse fittings (for example, fig.10) are an interesting example. It appears that these articles, when found in a military context, are only associated with a first-century date. By the early second century many forts had been consolidated in stone and it may be that the army in Britain was now able to manufacture its own version in the fort workshops instead of importing. This may explain the appearance of the plain pendants (Oldenstein, 1976).

In Roman Britain the *auxilia* were the mainstay of the frontier garrisons in the north and west. They often formed the vanguard of troops in battle which avoided risking the lives of too many citizen legionaries. For example during Agricola's battle with the Caledonians at Mons Graupius in AD 84 he sent 11,000 *auxilia* into battle while deliberately holding the legionaries in reserve (Tacitus, *Agricola,* 35). Thanks to

---

7 A scene from Trajan's Column in Rome showing a number of mounted auxiliaries (photo and copyright; the British Museum)

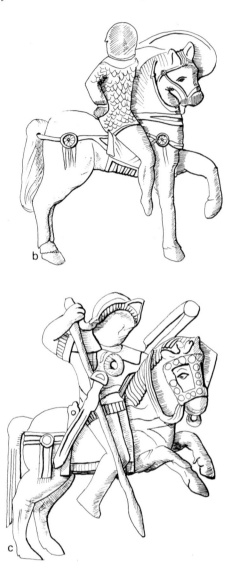

8 Military equipment from tombstones:
a figure from the tombstone of the centurion Marcus
Favonius Facilis, centurion with the *legio* XX at
Colchester who died before it was moved west in
c. AD 47. Found in 1868 to the west of Colchester;
was probably thrown over during the Boudican sack
in AD 60. Facilis is shown in full military dress minus
helmet to denote his death (*RIB* 200).
b tombstone of Longinus, a *duplicarius* with the *ala* I
Thracum, an auxiliary cavalry unit which probably
accompanied the *legio* XX. Longinus wears scale
armour and is shown mowing down a foe – a stock
pose. Like Facilis, Longinus must have died by
AD 49, his stone suffering a similar fate in that year.
It was found in 1928 in the same area (*RIB* 201).
c Sextus Valerius Genialis from his tombstone at
Cirencester, a trooper also with the *ala* I *Thracum*.
He carries a plumed standard, wields a spear, carries
a sword, *spatha*, and wears an imperial Gallic-style
sports helmet. Probably Neronian in date (*RIB* 109)

Cavalry armour and clothing

The men
Being so varied no two auxiliary units were alike
and this applies equally to cavalry. At one
extreme both horse and rider might be equipped
with armour; at the other both might go into
battle equipped with no more than a sword. The
only literary description which survives is
Arrian's corrupt and difficult *Tactica*. He was
describing the ceremonial activities of auxiliary
forces in the Eastern Empire in the early second
century. But the auxiliaries in the West were
mostly of Celtic origin and this is reflected in the
equipment they used and their love of display.

The auxiliary cavalryman's helmet is known

inscriptions and a late Roman military document,
the *Notitia Dignitatum*, we know the names of
many of the units distributed in Britain.

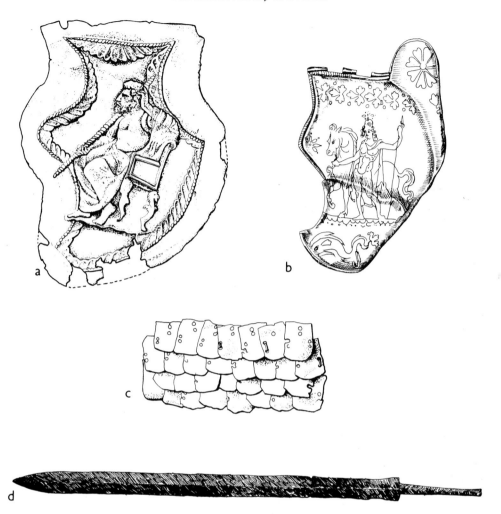

9 Auxiliary equipment:

a copper cheekpiece from an auxiliary cavalryman's helmet from Kingsholm, Gloucester. It depicts a seated figure of Jupiter and was originally attached to an iron backing. Mid-first century. Height 16cm (after Hurst, 1986, pl.96 and fig.10)

b bronze cheekpiece from an auxiliary cavalryman's helmet from South Shields, *Arbeia*, decorated with a figure of one of either Castor or Pollux performed with finely-punched lines. Probably second or third century. Height 20cm

c fragment of scale armour, *lorica squamata*, from Caerleon (after Zienkiewicz, 1986, 186, no. 155)

d cavalry *spatha* from Newstead. Length 79cm

from a number of different examples, some of which have been found in Britain dating to the first century. They seem to have been based on an iron skull-cap and neck-guard which was sheathed, all or in part, by bronze. The sports helmet from Witcham Gravel, Ely, in Cambridgeshire, has a bronze band around the iron skull-cap with punched decoration (fig.12). Bronze bosses were attached to the neck-guard and, probably, the band too. The cheek-pieces from Kingsholm (fig.9 a) and South Shields (fig.9 b) are probably from such helmets. Continental examples of later date suggest that reinforcing crests were added to the skull-caps. Like the legionaries, auxiliary cavalry used the *gladius* sword, though by the late second century the longer *spatha* was appearing (fig.9 d). Under Diocletian, a century later, it had completely superseded the *gladius*.

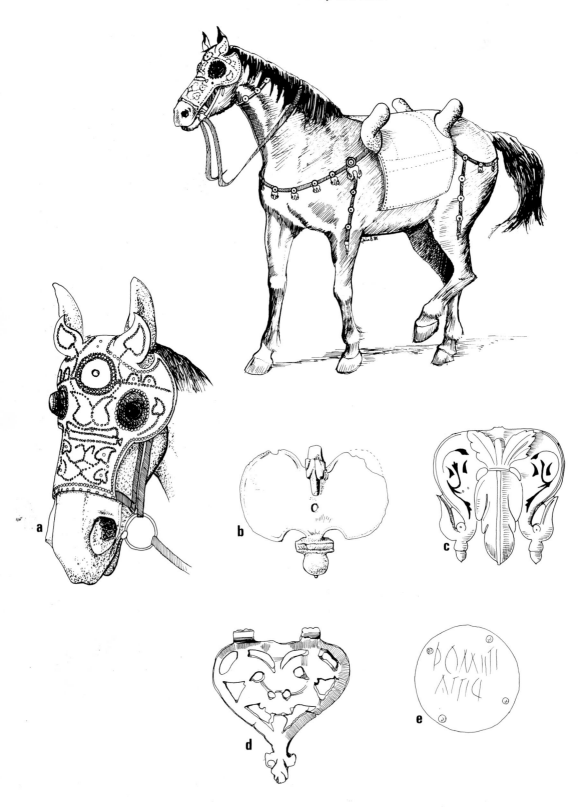

An alternative source of information is the tombstones, though, as these are rarely closely dated, it is not always possible to associate the portrayal of a soldier with a particular period. The tombstone of Longinus Sdapeze, a cavalry-man with the *ala* I *Thracum* is an exception (fig.8 b); he was based at Colchester from about AD 43-48.

Evidence for Longinus' helmet can be found on a tombstone of another member of his unit, dated to some point before AD 70. By this time the *ala* had moved west to Cirencester where Sextus Valerius Genialis died. On his tombstone he is wearing a sports helmet with neckguard and cheek pieces. In his right hand he holds a spear, in his left a hexagonal shield and standard consisting of two ribbons attached to a disc on top of the shaft (fig.8 c; *RIB* 109). Rufus Sita's tombstone from Wotton, near Gloucester, shows him with a sports helmet, the auxiliary sword and a hexagonal shield (before *c.* AD 70; *RIB* 121). Flavinus' tombstone from (probably) Red House near Corbridge is similar to these but he carries an *imago* (a standard with the image of the emperor) and wears a plumed helmet (late first century; *RIB* 1172).

It is also worth considering the evidence of Trajan's Column in Rome. The Column is decorated with a continuous narrative relief recording some of the events of Trajan's Dacian campaigns of 101 and 105 (Lepper & Frere, 1988). The most complete form of armour used by auxiliary cavalry was that used by the Sarmatians. They, and their horses, are portrayed entirely clad in scale armour (fig.9 c), though this is probably artistic licence (or ignorance) because such equipment would probably have proved a hindrance in battle. Other cavalrymen resemble those portrayed on the tombstones described above, with mail or scale armour cuirasses, oval shields and legionary-style helmets.

10 Auxiliary cavalry horse-trappings:
a studded leather head-dress from Newstead, *Trimontium*
b tinned bronze pendant from Kingsholm, two-thirds actual size (after Hurst, 1985, 27, no. 6)
c tinned bronze pendant from Newstead, two-thirds actual size (after Webster, 1985, fig.23)
d tinned bronze pendant from Vindolanda, two-thirds actual size (after Bidwell, 1985, 120, no. 16)
e tinned bronze *phalera* backing plate from Newstead, inscribed *Dometi Attici*, '[phalera] of Dometius Atticus' (9.5cm diameter)

The horses
Cavalry horses were equipped with little protection apart from those belonging to some units of eastern origin (see above and below), and instead were fitted with heavy leather saddles, the trimmings of which were decorated with various metal items such as pendants or discs known as *phalerae*. The horse also wore a leather harness, shown on the tombstone of Longinus (see above), over its whole body with these discs serving as connecting points and decoration for the various straps. These metal items are the most distinctive features of cavalry found in the ground. Like legionary belt fittings they were sometimes decorated in relief and enamelling, but their use was a Celtic tradition.

The group of horse fittings from Newstead is one of the most important British finds and includes a horse's leather frontlet (*chamfron*), decorated with incised lines and brass studs (fig.10). A more elaborate set was found at Doorwerth in Holland (Holwerda, 1931). The dating implications of some horse-fittings have been discussed above (p.25). Other distinctive metal fittings include the bronze eye guards, such as those from Ribchester and Chesters. These items are eye-shaped but include a perforated circular bulbous projection to cover the eye but allow sight. It is difficult to be certain how much of this horse armour was purely ceremonial and not intended for battle (see below).

If a horse was equipped with armour there is evidence from the third-century fort at Dura-Europos in Syria for its form. Remains of horse scale-armour show that it was a rectangular sheet laid over the horse's back with a hole for where the saddle would sit. The hole prevented the saddle from sliding round on the armour (Webster, 1985; Rostovtzeff, 1936).

Infantry armour and arms
Auxiliary infantry armour and clothing seems to have been fairly similar to that of the legionary – after all they served a similar purpose so this is only to be expected. If there was a difference then this was likely to involve either less equipment than a legionary's, or specialist equipment for a different form of fighting, such as archery and slinging. However, auxiliary infantry seem to have used oval shields in preference to the rectangular ones used by the legionaries.

The evidence from Trajan's Column indicates that the most primitive units employed by the

Roman army, such as slingers, used no armour at all, which would only have hampered them in action. If they did use armour, then it is probably safe to assume that the various different varieties known to have been used by legionaries or auxliary cavalry could have been used by the auxiliary infantry as well. However, cost and availability were probably determining factors as much as desirability. A pair of well-equipped auxiliaries on Trajan's Column seem to be clad in mail and leather trousers, legionary-style helmets and carry oval shields decorated with crescents and a laurel wreath (fig.7). The archer portrayed on a tombstone from Housesteads wears an unusual conical helmet without cheekguards, perhaps because they would have obstructed his vision as he turned his head to fire (Smith, 1968).

It is extremely difficult to differentiate between legionary and auxiliary infantry equipment as excavated artefacts. As far as helmets are concerned it seems likely that auxiliary examples were similar but much more basic. They seem to lack attachments for crests, and in the case of the 'imperial-Gallic' types also lack the embossing and bronze fittings found on legionary helmets.

Infantry units were more numerous than cavalry, and their specialities correspondingly more unusual. At one extreme there was the *cohors* I *Hamiorum sagittariorum*, raised in Syria and stationed at Carvoran on Hadrian's Wall. This unit's skilled archers were so valued that new recruits seem to have been brought from Syria rather than permit the products of marriages with local women to erase the traditional methods of fighting. On the other there is the curious *numerus barcariorum Tigrisiensium*, based at South Shields. Their name means 'Tigris boatmen' and they were presumably employed as a service unit for their navigational skills in shallow waters.

In general, then, auxiliary arms are likely to involve swords and daggers similar to those of the legionary but also the long swords, *spatha* (fig.9 d), used by cavalry; and traces of other equipment such as bone stiffeners from bows (for example, that from Prysg Field at Caerleon, Nash-Williams, 1952), or iron arrow-heads (at Vindolanda, Bidwell, 1985, 136 no.26ff). Other weapons found include the lead sling-shots used by slingers, for example, at Burnswark north of Hadrian's Wall in Dumfriesshire where a siege camp sits below an Iron Age hillfort.

Cavalry parade armour

All units of the Roman army went on parade for military and religious reasons. The remains of a number of forts in Britain include parade areas; probably the most imposing is that close to the auxiliary fort at Hardknott, *Mediobogdum*, in the Lake District, built at the beginning of the second century. Above the fort, which sits high in the hills, and to the east, is a flat area of ground used for parades. Arrian, writing in the second century, described such a parade (*Tactica*, 34; see Webster, 1985), and stressed the special helmets used for such occasions by the best horsemen and the emphasis on ceremony.

The cavalry *alae* of the Roman army seem to have regarded parades as the opportunity for particularly flamboyant display. They staged mock shows of the Trojan War which had become associated with the birth of Rome – the Trojan hero Aeneas was reputed to have been responsible for choosing the site. Some of their parade armour was both too expensive and unsuitable for warfare. The most elaborate and complete example of a helmet comes from the auxiliary cavalry fort at Ribchester,

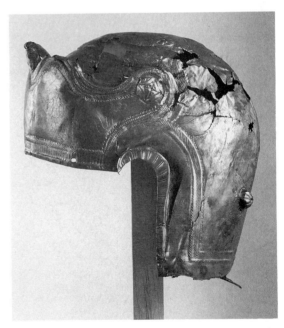

11 A bronze cavalry sports helmet from Guisborough, Yorkshire, lacking the visor, and bearing repoussé and chased decoration of figures of Mars, Minerva and a Victory. The helmet is 'gilded' with brass to give a golden appearance (photo and copyright; the British Museum)

12 A bronze cavalry sports helmet from Witcham Gravel, Ely, Cambridgeshire. The skull cap is a separate piece, and the neckguard bears three decorative bosses (photo and copyright: the British Museum)

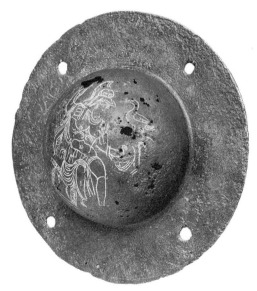

13 A bronze shield boss from Kirkham, Lancashire, with incised decoration. In the centre is a seated figure of Mars (?), and on the border, figures, shields, trophies, and altars. Diameter 19cm (photo and copyright: the British Museum)

Bremetennacum, in Lancashire (plate 2). The helmet is thought to be of first or early second century date. The helmet resembles a jockey cap rather than any of the more conventional helmets already encountered. It is remarkable not only for the embossed decoration of combat scenes on the skull cap but also the modelling of the visor in the form of a face. Other cavalry sports helmets are also known from Britain, for example from Newstead (Curle, 1911), Guisborough (fig.11), Witcham Gravel (fig.12), and Worthing, Norfolk (Toynbee, 1964, pls. 65 and 66).

Not surprisingly, such cavalrymen extended their parade armour to include their horses. An exceptionally large group of such material was found at Straubing in Bavaria (Webster, 1985; Keim and Klumbach, 1951), but a number of pieces are also known from Newstead (mentioned above). These not only include the *phalerae* which decorated the harnesses but also elaborate head-pieces which protected the eyes and face of the horse, either of lead or bronze.

The fleet

The branch of the Roman fleet in Britain was known as the *Classis Britannica*. It seems to have had a number of bases, including Dover where two forts belonging to the second century have been found, and it also participated in the construction of Hadrian's Wall, recorded on an inscription from Benwell fort (*RIB* 1340). In the context of this book the only important feature of the fleet was its apparent rôle in the extraction of iron in the Kent and Sussex weald (p. 45 and fig.23 f, g). No traces of any of its ships or docking facilities have ever been found.

Standards, decorations, awards

Throughout time armies have entrusted their destinies to talismans regarded with superstitious awe. For the Roman army victory lay with the standards. Their loss was a serious matter of disgrace. Augustus (26 BC-AD 14) was deeply shocked by the destruction of three legions in Germany and the loss of their standards in AD 9; equally the recovery of the standards lost by Crassus in Parthia was followed by public rejoicing. They were usually stored in a *sacellum* in the fort *principia*.

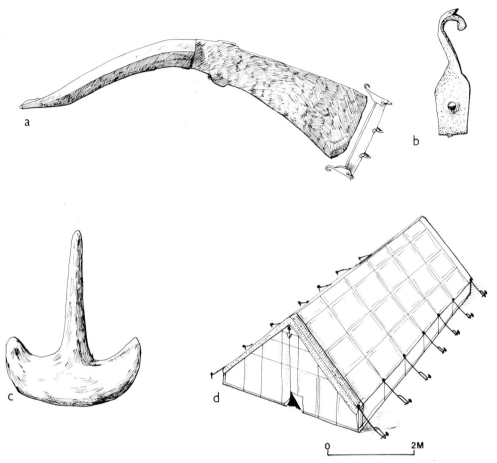

0   2M

14 Other equipment:
a *dolabrum* pick-axe from Newstead (after Curle,
  1911, pl.57) and sheath from Vindonissa,
  Switzerland (after Curle, 1911, fig.29). Length 40cm
b *dolabrum* sheath hook from Richborough. Height
  5cm (after Cunliffe, 1968, pl.34, no. 94)
c turf cutter from Great Casterton. Height 14cm
  (after Webster, 1985)
d reconstructed leather tent for an eight-man
  contubernium, forming an area of ten square Roman
  feet (after Richmond and McIntyre, 1934)

The standards

Naturally such valued items hardly ever turn up
in the ground. There were three types of
standard: the *aquila*, or eagle, normally made of
gold, which each legion carried; the *imago* which
bore the portrait of the reigning emperor; and the
individual *signa* for each century. Standards
bearing animals were peculiar to the legions and
were carried on ceremonial parades. The animals
associated with the legions in Britain can be
found on some inscriptions put up by the units,
and on some of the coinage of Carausius. The
legio II *Augusta* had a capricorn, the XX a boar.
A so-called 'standard' in the form of a horse has
been found at Vindolanda; unfortunately it is not
known to which regiment the standard belongs
(fig.15 c) and it has been argued that it is more
accurately interpreted as a chariot fitting
(Toynbee and Wilkins, 1982). Another, a bronze
hand holding an eagle found at the fleet fort in
Dover, may be part of a standard belonging to the
Classis Britannica (Williams in Philp, 1981, 148-
9). It has been suggested that a number of iron
objects resembling spearheads, but which lack
cutting edges, may be parts of standards of some
kind (fig.15 b). A number of these were found at
Vindolanda (Jackson in Bidwell, 1985, 132, no.
6ff) and it is also worth noting that a similar
example, in silver, is known from Caerleon. It
may be a ceremonial and official staff denoting
status (fig.15 a).

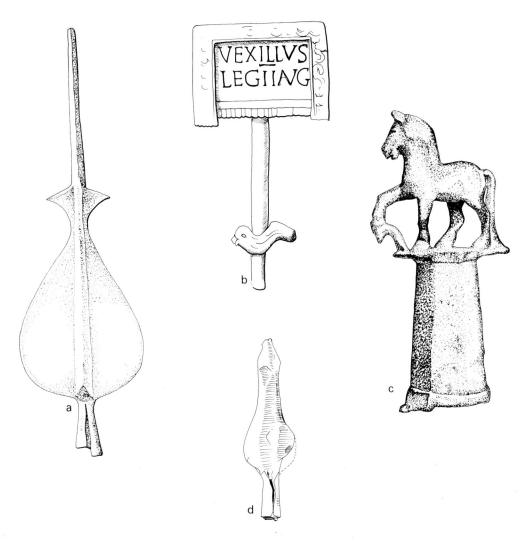

An impression of the appearance of standards can be gained from tombstones. Lucius Duccius Rufinus was a *signifer* of *legio* IX and died at York. The legion was at York from about AD 71 to the early second century when it probably left Britain. Rufinus is shown carrying a standard consisting of a shaft with a number of discs and a crescent (RCHM, York, 122, pl. 55). At the top is a hand. The tombstone of Aurelius Diogenes from Chester shows that he was an *imaginifer* probably with *legio* XX (the inscription is incomplete). In his right hand he bears a standard with an *imago* of an emperor (*RIB* 521). The emperor's face has been damaged, perhaps due to *damnatio memoriae*. Sextus Valerius Genialis,

15 Standards (not to scale):
a silver standard from Caerleon, 1928. Height 28.5cm.
b *vexillus* or *vexillum* of the *legio* II *Augusta* on a relief from Corbridge, Northumberland. The *vexillum* was a piece of cloth, probably about 50cm square, suspended from a cross-bar and decorated with a hem and fringe. The curious animal on the pole is probably supposed to represent a capricorn, this legion's emblem
c the so-called standard which has now been identified as a vehicle fitting. Found at Vindolanda (Toynbee and Wilkins, 1982). Height 6.2cm
d standard tip from Vindolanda (after Bidwell, 132, no. 6). Length 7.5cm

from Cirencester, is portrayed with a plumed standard (fig.8 c; *RIB* 109) and Flavinus' *imago* has already been mentioned (p. 29). Other evidence comes from stone reliefs (fig. 15 b).

Standards had a number of functions. Firstly, they were intended as rallying points and signals in battle (Webster, 1985, 134): each soldier could recognise the standard for his own century, maniple or cohort. This was not necessarily straightforward – in the Second Battle of Cremona during the Civil War of AD 68-9 standards changed hands quickly with confusing results (Tacitus, *Histories,* III, 22). Secondly standards were part of the organisational system of striking camp. Each part of a legion or auxiliary unit had its position within the regular marching camp plan: this was marked by the standards. Thirdly the standards were religious and superstitious talismans. As such they symbolised the purpose of battle – to fight for the pride and valour of the legion, and to defend the standards to the last.

Diplomae

Until the year 212 most auxiliary soldiers looked forward to the reward of citizenship on completion of 25 years' service (in 212 citizenship was made universal). For the sake of convenience a number of soldiers were retired simultaneously and received a record of the event, and these are occasionally found. A little under 200 are known from the whole empire but most of these are fragmentary (Roxan, 1978). They involved two leaves of inscribed bronze joined with loops. They record the date, and the names of the recipients of citizenship, or their units. These certificates are exceptionally important because they provide crucial information about the disposition of auxiliary forces at a certain point in time. One

---

16 The military diploma from Chesters, *Cilurnum*, on Hadrian's Wall, recording the grant of citizenship to eligible soldiers from 14 auxiliary regiments in Britain in the year 146. Diameter when complete, approximately 11cm (photo and copyright: the British Museum)

from Chesters fort on Hadrian's Wall is dated to the year 146 and records the award of citizenship to eligible soldiers of 14 auxiliary units in Britain (restored reading of the outside part below, after Bruce, 1885, 262).

IMP·CAESAR DIVI HADRIANI F·DIVI
TRAJANI·PART·NEPOS DIVI NERVAE PRO
NEP·T·AELIVS HADRIANVS ANTONINVS
AVG·PIVS·PONT·MAX·TR·POT·VĪĪĪĪ IMP·ĪĪ COS·ĪĪĪĪ
P·P·EQVIT·ET·PEDIT·QVI MILITAVER·IN ALIS ĪĪĪ
ET·COHORT·XI, QVAE APPELL·AVG·GALL·PROCVL·ET I
. . . . ET Ī HISP·ASTVR·ET Ī CELTIB·
ET Ī HISP·ET Ī AELIA DACOR·ET Ī AELIA
CLASSICA ET Ī FID·VARD·ET ĪĪ GALLOR·ET ĪĪ ET
VĪ NERVIORVM ET ĪĪĪ BRAC·ET ĪĪĪĪ LING·ET ĪĪĪĪ GALL·
ET SVNT IN BRITTANNIA SVB PAPIRIO AELI
ANO QVINQUE ET VIRGINTI STIPEND·EMERIT
IS DISMISSIS HONESTA MISSIONE QVORVM NOMINA
SUBSCRIPTA SVNT . . . . .

The first four lines list the titles of Antoninus Pius for the year 146, and note his 'descent' from his adoptive father Hadrian and grandfather Trajan. There then follows a list of the various units concerned, some of which can be restored from the other part of the diploma. Finally it notes that the names (*quorum nomina*) of those members of the unit with 25 years' service (*quinque et virginti stipend*) currently in Britain under the governor Papirius Aelianus, dismissed with an honourable discharge (*emeritis dismissis honesta missione*), are listed below (*subscripta sunt*).

Another, from Malpas in Cheshire, is the record of the veteran Reburrus' award of citizenship on 19 January 103, after 25 years in the *cohors* I *Pannoniorum*. He may have moved to the area to farm when he retired.

Decorations

Military decorations are extremely rare, and not a great deal is known about their precise nature. Ordinary legionaries, below the rank of centurion, were awarded either with embossed discs called *phalerae*, or torcs and bracelets, called *armillae*. The only known example from northern Britain is the Benwell torc. About 13cm (5in) in diameter, the bronze ring would have been worn on the chest. The only problem is that Benwell was an auxiliary fort and non-citizens were not usually awarded military decorations. Senior members of the legions were awarded with silver spears, *hastae purae*, *vexillae*, and crowns (*coronae*), which being made of leaves do

not survive except on stone reliefs.

As ceremonial awards these decorations were not usually worn except on special occasions, and therefore not lost – hence their rarity. However, as for so much other military material, tombstones provide an indication of how they were worn, for example the cenotaph of Marcus Caelius, centurion of *legio* XVIII who was killed in Germany in the Varian disaster of AD 9. He wears a crown of oak leaves for having saved a colleague's life, a torc on either side of his chest attached to his cuirass and at least four *phalerae* on his chest. These are decorated with deities or attributes, the most obvious of which is Hercules. On one Hercules is shown facing wearing a lion-skin head-dress, and on another a lion's head is depicted in profile (Maxfield, 1981).

The later Roman Army

The forces described above are very much those of the first and second centuries. While most of the units known in Britain at that time remained in operation, it is clear that after the disturbances of the third century the Roman army emerged as a very different kind of force. This was for the simple reason that the Empire was now on the defensive almost everywhere. The establishment of the Hadrian's Wall system anticipated this; the army had become a garrison with a number of crack mobile units which could move swiftly to a frontier disturbance. Besides this, the edict of citizenship in 212 had removed the main hierarchical difference between legionaries and auxiliaries.

It is very difficult to discuss these changes in terms of archaeological evidence in Britain. Firstly, material from the rest of the Empire suggests that body armour was now only consistently used by the cavalry. Helmets of the period are known as the *Intercisa* type after a site in Hungary where a number were found. The helmets consisted of simple skull-caps made of two halves joining down the middle. The neck-guard and cheek-pieces were attached to the leather lining rather than the helmet itself. An iron helmet of late date has been identified from fragments excavated at the Saxon Shore fort of Burgh Castle in Suffolk (fig.17 a). This particular example differs from continental examples in using four iron plates to form the skull-cap. Its appearance is completely different from the 'imperial-Gallic' helmets of the first and second

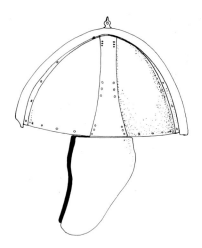

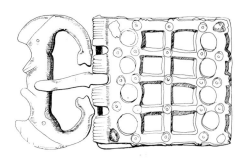

17 Late Roman military equipment:
a late Roman iron 'Intercisa-type' helmet based on Burgh Castle example (after Johnson)
b fourth-century zoomorphic belt buckle from Dorchester, Dorset. Note the opposed dolphins. length 9cm (after C.S. Green, 1984)

centuries. Armour seems to have become less regularly used in the third century, possibly as a reflection of the unsettled time – armour of all varieties requires a certain amount of maintenance. Nevertheless, a section of scale armour was found in a late-third-century context in the legionary baths at Caerleon (Brewer in Zienkiewicz, 1986, 186, no. 155). This suggests that at least some of the legionaries of that period at Caerleon were using scale armour. Manufacture may well have become much more localised; Corbridge has produced evidence of armour-making , or at least repairing, in the third and fourth centuries.

The arms used had changed also. The *spatha* (fig.9 d) was now in general use, hung from a baldric, and the dagger had been re-introduced (if it had ever fallen out of use). The metal fittings of belts suggest that these too were Germanic in form by the end of the fourth century, and possibly even in manufacture. One from Dorchester in Dorset (fig.17 b), is typical of these late fittings, though of course it would be unwise to argue the presence of a unit of German mercenaries purely on the evidence of a buckle. The various forms of javelins had also undergone design changes, principally in shortening the length of the iron head. The limited evidence available suggests that shields were now round or hexagonal.

Artillery

There are very few examples of traces of Roman artillery, or catapults, in Britain, though they were certainly used here by legions and auxiliary units. Some recent finds of artillery components are discussed by Baatz (1978), for example the metal fittings for a ballista frame from Hatra in Parthia, designed to throw stones weighing 4.5 kgm (almost 10lb). However, the remains of the equipment are far less dramatic than the earthworks designed to support them, for example at the practice camp at Burnswark, to the northwest of Hadrian's Wall; or the bolts embedded in the skeletons of British defenders at Maiden Castle in Dorset (Wheeler, 1943, 278).

Roman terminology for catapults is confusing because the names were changed at various times, depending on the literary source. These weapons were designed to propel some sort of ammunition forwards as fast and as hard as possible; lacking any form of explosive substance, and even the concept, Roman artillery designers and operators were entirely dependent on the possibilities afforded by elastic techniques. The weapons were constructed very largely of wood and rope but metal was used throughout for holding them together and other uses. Obviously it is these metal items which are most likely to be found as direct evidence, but it is the ammunition which turns up most frequently.

The largest catapults were mobile horizontal wooden frames containing a central band of twisted ropes. Into these ropes a wooden arm with a sling attachment was inserted. A mechanism of ropes and pulleys allowed this arm to be pulled back against the force of the twisted rope band. On release the arm rose and when it struck a vertical wooden frame the sling's contents, such as large stones, were sent towards the enemy. These stones could weigh in excess of 80 kgm (66lb) and have been found on a number of sites, for example Risingham and High Rochester. Metal was used for washers and other fittings. Curiously such a washer was recovered in recent excavations from the sacred spring at Bath (plate 24; Cunliffe, 1984, 82), though it is so small that it may form part of the large series of votive miniatures known from all over the Roman world.

The smaller catapults were very similar to the cross-bow both in design and the iron-headed ammunition (fig.4 f). These bolts were around 20cm (8in) in length and had either pyramid-shaped heads, or flat blades attached to wooden shafts. The power was contained in the torsion frame which used metal for a number of components, such as washers, braces and the spools for the coiled rope.

The Roman army – industry and manufacture

Introduction

The Roman army was a self-contained organisation. Josephus, the first-century Jewish historian, described a legion on the march as a mobile town. This was true in every sense of the word. The soldiers had demands, whether military or domestic, public or private, for services and goods. What they could not obtain themselves would be made by legionary or native craftsmen.

The tools and artefacts which are evidence of manufacturing in the Roman world were more or less common to the army and the civilian world. Most of these are discussed in Chapter 2, but there are some specific examples of army manufacture from Britain which are worth looking at separately. It is also important to remember that the Roman army played a vital rôle in the trading mechanisms of the Roman world, backed as it was by the financial resources of the state. Units of all sizes, whether temporarily or permanently stationed, used goods which had been acquired from sources which also supplied the civilian market. These might be local kitchen wares, Gaulish samian

pottery, food, or practically any commodity which was needed.

The period in which the army was still functioning as a major dynamic behind innovations and marketing was the first and second centuries. For much of the time parts of the army were still on the move. But by the third century, apart from the campaigns of Septimius Severus in northern Britain, the effects of permanent frontiers were being felt. Army units had now been stationed at their forts for generations. The soldiers had families, and citizenship was universal. Every permanent fort had its *vicus*, the civilian settlement which had grown up by the fort. Of course the soldiers still had to be fed, and a food surplus had to be generated to provide this, but it is no longer quite so easy to distinguish the army in terms of what it did, what it used and what it made. Romanisation had spread throughout the province of Britain and most of the civilian urban communities were equal participants in the processes of manufacture and consumption.

The fabricae

In every legion there was a body of soldiers known as *immunes*, so-called because they were immune from everyday duties. They earned that immunity through having skills which were useful to the army. The *immunes* were the manufacturing base of the Roman army, and they symbolise the Roman age simply because they were regarded as essential members of the army: they were the army's manufacturing base.

The range of crafts and skills covered almost every possible requirement. They included builders, weapons and armour makers, blacksmiths, carpenters, plumbers and tanners. And of course if these men lived to retirement age they took their skills to the civilian world, and taught their sons. In Britain this was another way through which the manufacturing skills of the Roman world were rapidly introduced. However, it is important to realise that until the province became reasonably settled, and major military bases consolidated at the beginning of the second century, much military equipment was still imported or moulded from imports (Oldenstein, 1985).

The legionary craftsmen all worked under the auspices of the *optio fabricae* who was based in the workshop of the legionary base, the *fabrica*. The best-known example in Britain is the *fabrica* at the short-lived Flavian legionary fortress of Inchtuthil in Perthshire. Apart from evidence of furnaces the building contained a deep pit into which nearly a million nails and ten iron wheel-tyres had been thrown in order to prevent their being of use to enemy tribes when the legion left in around the year AD 87 (fig.23 h and Manning, in Pitts and St Joseph, 1985, 289ff). In the third and fourth centuries armour seems to have been made, or at least repaired and altered, at Corbridge.

Depots

In certain cases a permanently-stationed legion might establish an entirely separate manufacturing compound, or depot, for certain goods. *Legio XX* had such a depot in Britain at Holt, Clwyd, about 12 km (8 miles) upriver from the fortress at Chester (Grimes, 1930). The Holt depot was established in the late first century and was only intensively used into the early second century, though the site was still active in the fourth century. It was used mainly for the making and firing of roof and building tiles (fig.23 f) though some pottery was also produced, for example *mortaria* (food mixing bowls, p.47). However, it is not clear how much of the work was actually performed by soldiers. The legionary compound at Holt included two barrack blocks which show that even if native labour was used it was under the strict supervision of two legionary centuries. Impressions of military-style *caligae* boots on tiles from Caerleon suggest soldiers were working there (fig.24).

To what extent the auxiliary units in Britain could claim such self-sufficiency is not quite so clear. Other similar examples of supply depots, though smaller, are known in the vicinity of a number of auxiliary forts, such as Ravenglass and Gelligaer. In fact most forts produce evidence of smithing, even if only the slag and ash from the furnace survives. The recently-excavated Flavian auxiliary fort at Elginhaugh, near Edinburgh, contained a 160kg (352lb) hoard of unused iron nails which may well have been manufactured on site (Hanson, 1987). The area close to the fort at Vindolanda included a building in which tanning leather was carried out (Birley, 1977, 123).

A particularly interesting site was excavated in 1970 about 0.8km (half a mile) to the north-west of Colchester at Sheepen (Niblett, 1985). While not a *fabrica* in the strict sense, the area seems to have been used as a kind of extra-mural industrial estate mostly for metal and leatherworking which was established almost as soon as the XX legion was stationed there in AD 43. It did not last beyond the Neronian period perhaps because the developing *colonia* could now supply its own needs; the legion had moved away in AD 47 and of course the whole area had been devastated by Boudica in AD 60-1. Whether or not this establishment was under direct military control is not clear, though opinion seems to favour a civilian depot working to army contracts (Webster in Niblett, 1985, 114).

A unique auxiliary shield-boss, found in London, and of first- to third-century date, bears what appears to be a maker's name, COCILLVS F[ecit], 'Cocillus made [it]'. This has raised the interesting question of civilian bronze-workers receiving military contracts, some of whom are known from their name-stamps to have made skillets and military equipment. Whether it was part of a general policy or a 'one-off' order is completely unknown (Jackson, 1984).

Building and stonework
Military inscriptions

Another class of army products was the military inscription. These were carved by the army stonemasons or appear as stamped impressions. They are invaluable sources of dating information, and of the activities of the army units, their members and their pride in their achievements. Each one is of archaeological and historical significance, even on something as mundane as a lead pipe. For example, at the legionary fortress of Chester, *Deva*, built by the XX *Valeria Victrix*, lead piping bears the name and titles of Vespasian and Titus for early in the year AD 79, and the name of the governor, Agricola (Greenstock, 1971, no. 25): IMP VESP VIIII T IMP VII COS CN IVLIO AGRICOLA LEG AVG PR PR.

Almost all the other surviving examples are on stone. Some describe the arrival of reinforcements, such as one from the Tyne at Newcastle (fig.18) dated to the year 158. The majority are religious or funerary and some of these are described in Chapters 6 and 7. Others are concerned with building work, ranging from the record of the construction of a few yards of Hadrian's Wall to the repair of dilapidated fort buildings. Many are known and they show an interesting change in style through the period.

18 Inscription from the Tyne at Newcastle on the site of the *Pons Aelius*. It records the arrival of reinforcements from the German provinces (EX GER *[manibus]* DVOBVS) for the II, VI and XX legions during the governorship of Julius Verus under Antoninus Pius in *c.* 158. The inscription is an interesting example of apparently neatly-executed work: the word *vexillato* is singular and should read *vexillari*; at the end of the fourth line it is apparent that LEG for *legio* VI had been omitted and clumsily inserted later. Diameter 66cm (*RIB* 1322; photo author; courtesy of the Newcastle Museum of Antiquities)

Construction
The army's units recorded their constructional work on prominently-displayed inscriptions. These served two purposes: firstly they indicated to any inspection which unit was responsible for what; secondly they provided a source of inspiration to some of the army's stonemasons. The result was that some inscriptions are embellished with elaborate carvings which must reflect something of the corporate pride felt by some of the troops. A monumental and elegantly carved inscription from the legionary fortress at Caerleon is a model of early imperial epigraphic style. Dedicated by the *legio* II *Augusta* (fig.21 a) it gives Trajan's titles for the year 100 but does not specify the work done – the building on which it had been placed would have made this obvious at the time.

Hadrian's Wall and the Antonine Wall have produced dozens of minor examples which show how the walls and forts were constructed by detachments from all classes of military unit. Inscriptions generally follow a similar pattern, beginning with the Emperor's name, his titles, the name of the unit, the name of the governor, and what was done. However, these can be highly abbreviated, which can make their correct interpretation rather difficult, especially if the inscription is represented by only a few fragments. Examples of obscure brevity come from Benwell (fig.19), and Halton Chesters (fig.20).

A stone from Milecastle 38 on Hadrian's Wall dates the construction of the building to the years 125-128. It also states that the *legio* II *Augusta* was responsible for the work under the governor Aulus Platorius Nepos. Two identical stones are known from the same milecastle and it seems that one was placed above the north gate, and the other over the south gate. The exact reading of the stone, which measures about 1 x 0.6m (1 x 2ft), is as follows (*RIB* 1638):

IMP CAES TRAIAN

HADRIANI AVG

LEG II AVG

A PLATORIO NEPOTE LEG PR PR

Even the construction of stretches of the Wall itself were recorded by inscriptions, for example one from west of Birdoswald and now lost (fig.21 b) which states that a century under the

19 Stone slab from the fort at Benwell, *Condercum*, on Hadrian's Wall, recording building work by the *legio* II *Augusta*. The slab depicts a legionary standard and the legion's emblems, a capricorn and Pegasus. The site is now covered by the western suburbs of Newcastle-upon-Tyne. Diameter 38cm (*RIB* 1341; photo and copyright: the British Museum)

20 Building slab from the fort at Halton Chesters, *Onnum*, on Hadrian's Wall, consisting of a simple inscription recording the work of the *legio* II *Augusta* in a wreath flanked by two pairs of juxtaposed eagles' heads. The date is uncertain, but probably *c.* 140. Diameter 84cm (*RIB* 1428; photo author; courtesy of the Newcastle Museum of Antiquities)

IMP CAES DIVI NERVAE F

NERVA TRAIANO AVG

GER PONTIF MAXIMO TRIB

POTEST · P P ·

COS $\overline{\text{III}}$

LEG $\overline{\text{II}}$ AVG

a

LEG II ING

>IVLI·TE

RTVLLIA

b

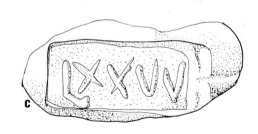

LEG XX VV

c

21 Other legionary inscriptions (not to scale):

a building inscription from Caerleon, *Isca*, recording the *legio* II *Augusta*'s work under Trajan with titles for the year 100. However, the inscription evidently had to be adapted during or after carving, as cos·II is altered to III, and therefore probably was made *c.* 98–100. This ansate slab is a particularly fine example of Roman military inscription at the height of the art. Width 1.47m (*RIB* 330)

b centurial stone from Hadrian's Wall, recording work carried out by Julius Tertullia's century from the *legio* II *Augusta*. Found at Old Wall, near Stanwix but now lost (after Collingwood-Bruce, 1885, 222). Width about 35cm (*RIB* 1970)

c *legio* XX lead-seal from Leicester, diameter 31mm (*Britannia*, 11, 1980 pl. 19)

command of the centurion Iulius Tertullianus, from the *legio* II *Augusta* was responsible for building a stretch of the Wall. In fact, like many of these stones, this example was not found on the Wall itself but had been re-used in the construction of a farmhouse. They were once displayed on the face of the Wall itself. Another, from near Milecastle 36, actually records the number of paces constructed (*RIB* 1575):

> FLORINI

P XXII

The abbreviations indicate that the century of Florinus built 22 paces of Wall length, P being short for *passūs*, 'paces'.

The building inscriptions from Hadrian's Wall are useful information for the units responsible for or involved in the huge construction works. Even the fleet participated in the work, as an

a

b

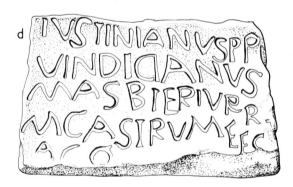

c

d

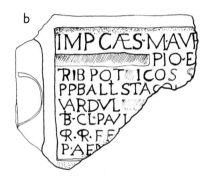

22 Later military inscriptions:

a building slab for *legio* XX *Valeria Victrix* found in 1776 at High Rochester, *Bremenium*. The inscription records that a vexillation of the legion did the work and is flanked by figures of Mars and Hercules. Beneath is a boar, the emblem of the legion. Probably third century. Width 135cm (*RIB* 1284)

b fragmentary inscription also from High Rochester recording the construction of an artillery platform (BALLIST[ARIUM]), by the *cohors* I *Vardullorum*, under Elagabalus (whose official name was *Marcus Aurelius Antoninus Pius*, here partially erased after his death) in the year 220. Diameter 61cm (*RIB* 1280)

c inscription from Birdoswald, *Banna*, on Hadrian's Wall recording rebuilding of the commandant's house which 'was covered in earth and in ruins' (QUOD ERAT HUMO COPERT ET IN LABE), the headquarters building and the bath-house, by the century of Flavius Martinus during the reign of Diocletian and Maximianus (296–300). Diameter 84cm (*RIB* 1912)

d inscription from Ravenscar, East Yorkshire, recording the building of a tower (TURR[E]M) and a fort (CASTRUM) from the ground (A SO[LO]) by Justinianus, the *praepositus* and Vindicianus, the *magister*. The coastal signal stations were build around 370 and remained in use to the beginning of the fifth century. Diameter 53cm (*RIB* 721)

inscription from the fort at Benwell, dated to *c.* 125, states (*RIB* 1340):

IMP CAES [T]RAIANO
HADRIAN ⚡ AVG
A ⚡ PLATORIO NEPOTE LEG AVG PR P
VEXILLATO CLASSIS BRITAN

The inscription gives Hadrian's name, the governor's name, and adds that the unspecified work had been carried out by a detachment, VEXILLATO, of the fleet, the CLASSIS BRITAN[NICA].

Not all inscriptions were made on stone. Part of Hadrian's Wall was built initially out of turf and wood. A fragment of a wooden inscription from Milecastle 50 on the Turf Wall bears enough letters to associate it with the governorship of Aulus Platorius Nepos, responsible for the Wall's construction (Daniels, 1978, 213).

The majority of such commemorative inscriptions are fairly simple in design. The Caerleon example is a model of early second-century imperial inscriptional style. Some of the distance slabs are no more than ordinary building blocks with relatively carelessly-formed letters – but they served the purpose of accrediting the building work to a particular group of soldiers. Some are rather more elaborate and bear sculptural embellishments which enhanced their appearance. A particularly explicit example from Bridgeness at the end of the Antonine Wall recorded the construction of four miles of the barrier by the *legio* II *Augusta*, specifying the number of paces as 4652. Flanking the inscription, which dates its erection to the year 142, are two scenes. The left-hand scene shows a single Roman cavalryman flattening four Caledonians, one of whom is decapitated. The right-hand scene shows the legion's legate offering up an animal sacrifice with an altar and some assistants. Each of the scenes is contained within a pillared frame (*RIB* 2139). The way in which the legions were split up to work on buildings is shown by an early third-century inscription from High Rochester (fig. 22 a). Another, from the same site but of slightly later date, records the building of an artillery platform (fig.22 b).

Reconstruction

So far all the inscriptions discussed record the event of the construction of new buildings or defensive boundaries. In time some of these fell into disrepair and required reconstruction work. This, too, was commemorated with inscriptions though it is clear that the art of epigraphy was not up to earlier standards. So, for example, an inscription from Birdoswald fort on Hadrian's Wall records the rebuilding of the headquarters building, the commandant's house and the bathhouse between the years 296 and 300 during the rule of Diocletian's Tetrarchy (fig. 22 c).

An undated inscription from Cawfields milecastle offers the interesting information that building work had been done here, presumably repair work in the late fourth century, by members of the Durotriges tribe from Ilchester (*RIB* 1672). They had also worked at Houseteads fort (*RIB* 1673). Clearly the needs of the times required the participation of civilians in the repair work following the disastrous invasion of the year 367. Part of this reconstruction work involved the building of signal stations on the north-east coast. One at Ravenscar yielded the latest inscription from Roman Britain (fig.22 d) which contrasts dramatically with earlier examples both in style and content.

Tombstones

Although tombstones are covered elsewhere in this book (Chapter 7) it is worth mentioning here that they can provide valuable evidence of the presence of military units. Probably the best example is that of the centurion Marcus Favonius Facilis (fig.8 a). The inscription on his tombstone (*RIB* 200) makes it a virtual certainty that *legio* XX was the legion stationed at Colchester from AD 43-49:

M·FAVON·M·F·POL·FACI
LIS·> LEG·XX·VERECVND
VS·ET·NOVICIVS·LIB·POSV
ERVNT · H · S · E ·

There are a number of similar examples from Roman Britain which indicate the presence of other military units. They are frequently accompanied by a portrayal of the dead soldier, and these can provide evidence for military equipment. The principal problem with tombstones is that they are usually undated. The Facilis example is useful because it can be used in association with closely-dated historical evidence; we know that a legion was stationed at Colchester from about AD 43 to 49, and there is no evidence to suggest that any legion was ever stationed there again. Another, from Wroxeter, has helped chart the early progress of *legio* XIV *Gemina* (fig.108 c).

Tiles

The most common form of legionary and auxiliary evidence of manufacture and building is the practice of stamping tiles for roofs, walls and hypocausts. Stamped tiles are known for most of the legions stationed in Britain, but particularly for the II *Augusta*, the IX, the VI, and the XX (fig.23 a-e). Some auxiliary units are known too, such as the *cohors* II *Asturum* at Greatchesters (Collingwood Bruce, 1885, 180), and also the fleet, the *Classis Britannica* (fig.23 f, g). This suggests that the soldiers were actually manufacturing the tiles themselves or that they were being made to order. However, the presence of military-type hob-nailed footprints on some examples suggests they were manufactured in the

23 Military building (tile-stamps a-d ½ scale):
a *legio* II *Augusta* from Caerleon
b *legio* VI *Victrix Pia Fidelis* from York
c *legio* IX *Hispana* from York
d *legio* XX *Valeria Victrix* from Chester
e tile *antefix* of *legio* XX from Holt, Clwyd. Height 12cm
f *tegula* roof tiie with the stamp of the *Classis Britannica*, from Beauport Park, East Sussex. Height 40cm
g *imbrex* roof tile, as **f**. Length 34cm
h nails from the short-lived legionary fortress at Inchtuthil, Perthshire. The nails are three of around 1,000,000 found buried in the remains of the *fabrica* of the fortress. The nails were buried when the fortress was dismantled in *c.* AD 87, and their heads distorted, to prevent them being of use to any foe. Lengths 8, 18.5 and 32cm

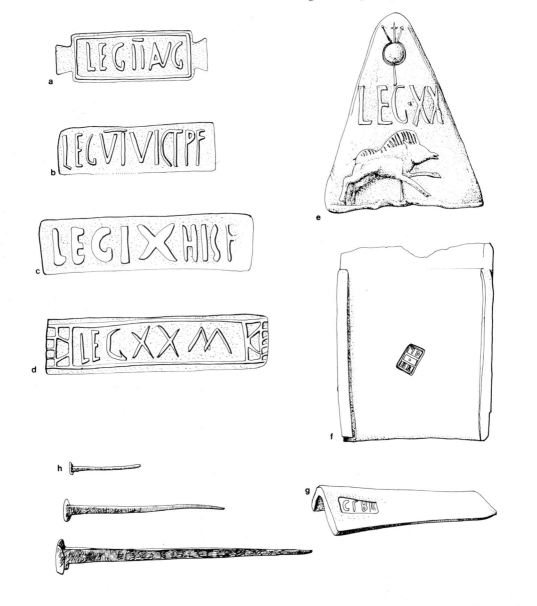

24 Fragment of *tegula* from the legionary fortress at Caerleon bearing a poorly-impressed stamp of *legio* II *Augusta* and the hob nails of a miltary boot, *caliga*. Diameter 24cm (photo: author)

military compounds (fig.24). The practice was not consistent or continuous, so for example the II *Augusta* seems only to have started stamping tiles towards the end of the first century. This may have been because once the legionary fortresses became settled it was in the army's interests to mark its possessions in case corruption led to tiles disappearing into the civilian settlements (Boon, 1984, 15 ff.). The practice seems to be related to the gradual reconstruction of major fortresses and forts in stone from *c.* AD 96.

The stamps on tiles take a large number of forms and it seems that the only brief, if there was one, was to indicate the unit's name in abbreviated form. As a result the abbreviations vary. They might be inscribed carefully into the dies – almost in inscriptional form – or casually engraved in cursive, or hand-written, form. The majority produced impressions in relief. Almost all such dies were probably made out of pieces of wood or pottery, and occasionally their impressions indicate that a nail in the centre of the die secured it to a handle. Most dies were inscribed backwards so that the impression appeared the right way round, but this was by no means always the case. Stamps created from dies which were written the right way round are known as 'retrograde stamps' (fig.24). Tile stamping was not a consistent practice – most are not stamped, even on military sites, but in some unusual cases whole buildings seem to have been roofed almost entirely with stamped tiles (see Beauport Park below). Even the antefixes, small tiles which gave the roof-edge a trim, could be stamped – those from the legionary works depot at Holt include the legion's name, LEG XX, accompanied by a boar, the legion's emblem (fig.23 e). Some examples are particularly elaborate (Boon, 1984, 9 for Caerleon).

Many of the tile-stamps of the *Classis Britannica* are associated with sites apparently unrelated to policing the seas, unlike those known from Dover, Lympne and Richborough. They are known from a number of places involved with the extraction of iron in the Weald of Kent and Sussex, for example at Cranbrook, Bodiam and, particularly, Beauport Park. The latter involves evidence of an extensive settlement, a colossal iron-slag heap and a curious bath-house whose roof, preserved in pieces by the collapse of the adjacent slag, seems to have consisted more or less entirely of tiles stamped CL.BR (fig.23 f, g and Brodribb and Cleere, 1988). This is unusual for stamped tiles which rarely formed more than a small number of the tiles used. Either the iron-working was under the supervision of the fleet or alternatively a 'job-lot' of unneeded tiles had been bought up by an enterprising administrator of the iron-works. The bath house may belong to a fort, as yet undiscovered, though there is no evidence for this. The site has not actually produced any evidence of tile-manufacture but one large tile bears the impression of a tile comb (see Chapter 2 and fig. 34 a) used for scoring the surface for the cement to grip better, which bore the stamp of the fleet (Brodribb, 1987, 106). Even if the fleet was not dealing with the iron they had certainly made or ordered the tiles.

Pottery

Fine wares

When the army arrived in Britain there was no indigenous pottery industry geared to producing Roman-style wares. Much of what the army needed was imported, including a range of fine-ware types such as samian ware, colour-coated ware, lead-glazed ware and mica-dusted ware mostly originating in central and southern Gaul (these are discussed more widely in Chapter 3). Some fine wares were also produced in Britain at an early date, though whether the potters were actually soldiers or not, we do not know. A few examples of copies of pre-Flavian Lyons ware beakers and cups were found at the Claudian-Neronian legionary fortress at Kingsholm, Gloucester (Hurst, 1985, 80). Others include copies of first-century South Gaulish samian vessels such as the Form 29 bowl and the Form 24/25 and 27 cups (fig.25 a-c). Mica-dusted ware was a popular first-century pottery imitation of bronze vessels. The soldiers were accustomed to it and by the 70s it was being manufactured at Gloucester for their use. However, it is quite possible that such early pottery manufacture in continental style was actually being performed by continental potters who had followed the army.

The short-lived (from *c.* AD 56 to the late 60s) Claudian-Neronian legionary fortress at Usk in South Wales has produced some particularly interesting evidence for how the mid-first-century army in Britain coped with pottery supply. In the first of two clear occupational phases the resident garrison, probably either the II *Augusta* or XX, used a full range of imported fine wares. The vast majority were from Lyons

25 Pottery made by or for the army (*c.* AD 50–100):

a 'Hofheim' flagon, a popular continental type introduced by the army. This example is from Kingsholm fort, near Gloucester (¼ scale; after Darling)

b bowl based on samian Form 29 but without the decoration. From Kingsholm (⅓ scale; after Darling)

c cup based on samian Form 24. From Usk (⅓ scale; after Greene)

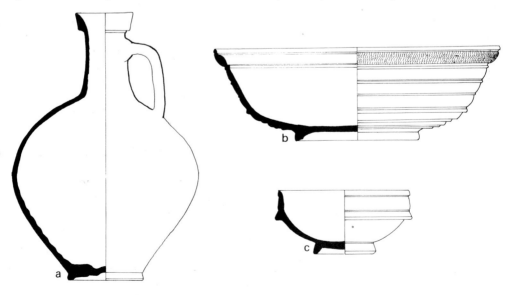

despite the fact that one of the alternatives, the Rhineland, is much closer. This may reflect the fact that potters and traders in Lyons had a long-established tradition of supplying the army. This existing trade mechanism would have been more important than the difference in distance (Greene, 1979, 139 ff.).

Coarse wares

The coarse pottery of the first phase at Usk is similar both in fabric and form to types known in the Rhineland, an area where some of the legionary garrison had originally been stationed (the II, XIV and XX). Bearing in mind that south Wales was remote and had little or native pottery tradition, this suggests that the army was manufacturing the coarse wares itself or had brought potters from the Rhineland (Greene, in Detsicas, 1973, 30 ff.).

The expediency of the arrangement is revealed by the second phase when the coarse wares used seem clearly to have been acquired from British sources, for example types from the south-east, the Gloucester area, Dorset and Somerset, and some varieties which appear to have been manufactured in the vicinity of the fortress. Clearly the army preferred to buy locally rather than waste military man-hours on potting, though whether the locals were placed under duress or awarded profitable contracts is not known. It is worth noting that the later pre-Flavian phase at Usk followed the Boudican Revolt, a time when there is thought to have been a degree of positive reconstruction going on. Part of that might have been encouraging the romanisation of native industry.

Similar evidence, either of army pottery manufacture or natives working to order, is known from other first century forts as well. The legionary vexillation fortress of Longthorpe, near Peterborough, in use from *c.* AD 47 to 60 by part of the IX and auxiliary cavalry and infantry, was associated with contemporary pottery manufacture (Dannell and Wild, 1987).

At Holt in the late first century there seems to be more evidence of direct military participation in the process of pottery making, even if it was in a supervisory capacity. However, of the eight kilns found, only two seem likely to have been for pottery, the remainder having been intended for bricks and tiles (Grimes, 1930). It has been suggested that the two pottery kilns were added at a later date as their positions suggest they were not part of the original scheme (Peacock, 1982, 139).

Unfortunately there is really very little specific evidence of pottery demonstrably made by the army in Britain. Pottery kilns are certainly known in the immediate vicinity of the forts at Carlisle, Gelligaer and South Shields. An auxiliary pottery at Brampton supplied the fort there from *c.* 105 to 125 with carinated bowls, mortaria and jars (Hogg, 1965), as did a similar operation at Muncaster near the fort at Hardknott. It is worth noting that on the continent at a few sites certain proof of legionary pottery-making is known in the form of stamps on the pottery itself but these are rare in any case, and unknown in Britain. The site at Holt has produced a die for stamping mortaria but this bears the name Julius Victor (Grimes, 1930, 131) and it is quite possible that he was a civilian. Had he been a soldier one might expect him to have said so.

Pottery manufacture by the army really seems to have been an expedient solution for times when it was otherwise unobtainable. As a result the types manufactured tend to be specific to the army unit involved. This is the case at Holt, and likewise at the legionary fortress at Kingsholm, near Gloucester (Hurst, 1985). For the most part it can be assumed that the army bought widely from civilian suppliers, perhaps showing what they wanted from examples they carried, or pattern books. When they had established a civilian supply their own potteries were closed down, as at Brampton and Muncaster, *c.* 125. This seems to have been the case with coarse pottery products known today as Black Burnished 1 and 2, from Dorset and south-east Britain respectively (see Chapter 3; fig.55). The Claudian fort at Hod Hill in Dorset occupied part of a hill-fort in the territory of the Durotriges and this early site shows that Black Burnished 1 was already being used by the Roman army.

The actual nature of the purchase arrangements is not clear, and no certain evidence exists, but it is possible that the army had long-standing contracts with some suppliers, whether local or distant. However, the nature of pottery evidence in itself does not exclude the possibility that individual units, or even individual soldiers, bought from individual traders as and when they happened to pass that way. The truth is that we do not know what the exact position was, and nor are we likely to, but one can assume that it was variable both in time and place, and that the chief criterion was whatever happened to be convenient at the time.

Leather-working

The army was undoubtedly involved in the preparation of leather and the manufacture of leather articles. These included tents (fig.14 d), shoes (figs.24 and 75), clothing and shield-covers. The fort at Catterick has produced evidence of such activities, and so has the site at Vindolanda, near Hadrian's Wall. Such deposits are associated with very large numbers of animal bones, indicating that the animals were delivered alive. The tools used in preparing the hides at Vindolanda included semi-circular pieces of wood to scrape the skins, and wooden combs. The tanning area also produced a large number of leather off-cuts (Birley, 1977, 123ff.).

Centurial dies

There is a small class of name dies known from sites, made mostly of lead, which bear a centurion's name. They clearly seem to have been used for making an impression in a material, or materials, which are unfortunately unspecified. It seems possible that they were used for stamping bread on the evidence of surviving bread loaves from Herculaneum. The stamps, known from Chester, Holt and Caerleon, have recessed or raised and mostly retrograde letters. They bear the centurion's name and also usually the name of the soldier who had made the bread (?), for example one from Caerleon (see Wright, 1984 for a summary of the evidence and references):

> > VIBI SEVE
> > SEN PAVLLIN

This means '[made by] Sentius Paullinus of the century of Vibius Severus'.

Lead seals

Although the Roman army in Britain was dispersed throughout the province, it remained a force with a centralised command and organisation. There was obviously a great deal of communication between the various units, the legionary fortresses and the governor of the province. This involved not just verbal communications but also the movement of all sorts of goods throughout the province, whether these were supplies for individual bases or raw materials whose extraction was overseen by the army.

Such material was accompanied by a lead sealing which indicated its military nature. They are extremely useful indicators of military activity. A group of seven has recently been recovered from Leicester bearing the names of a number of units including the VI and XX legions though the material they accompanied is unknown (fig.21 c). A group from South Shields bear witness to the use of the fort as a major supply base in the Severan campaigns of 209-212 because they carry the heads of Septimius Severus, Caracalla and Geta. Some of these seals bear the word AVGG. The doubling of the G was commonly used to indicate a period of joint rule. Caracalla became Augustus with his father in 198, but in 209 they were joined by his brother Geta. Had the seals belonged to after 209 they would bear the word AVGGG. Therefore the stores had arrived by 209. Amongst the stores involved were very large quantities of grain. A fort of South Shields' size (2.1 ha:5.16 acres) would normally be equipped with two granaries; instead the early third-century fort had at least twenty. Some of the same lead sealings indicate at least one of the units involved in the logistics of the campaign; they bear the name of the *cohors* V *Gallorum equitata* (Richmond, 1934, 101).

Lead sealings indicating the detail of more peaceful activities are known from Brough-under-Stainmore. Some of the 133 seals bear the word METAL for 'metallum', and the name of the *cohors* II *Nerviorum*. This unit was actually based at Whitley Castle, Alston, about 16 km (ten miles) south of the fort at Carvoran near Hadrian's Wall, and 40 km (24 miles) north of Brough by road. There was a lead-extraction area at Alston, so this suggests that lead (or silver) mined by the *cohors* II *Nerviorum* was moved southwards via Brough (Richmond, 1936). This evidence shows that the army was still involved in metal extraction in the third century. A number of other units are also represented amongst these Brough seals, including the *cohors* VII *Thracorum*, and *legio* II and *legio* VI. Their activities seem to have been different; for example a *legio* II seal carries the word EXPED for 'expedit', indicating that this legion had been responsible for despatching an unnamed commodity.

2
Crafts, Trades and Industries

Introduction

Permanently-stationed units of the Roman army tended to buy their manufactured goods from the civilian market wherever possible. The exact arrangements are unknown, but it is quite probable that contracts were arranged with major producers. As the province became increasingly romanised, the communities of Roman Britain produced a number of manufactured articles, whether made of fabric, wood, bone, stone, ceramics or metals. Production was not, of course, confined to turning out material goods. The primary industries of farming, quarrying, mining and smelting were all concerned with creating the basic necessities of living and supplying the raw materials for industry. All these categories needed tools of one sort or another. Some industries were well-established before the Roman conquest, for example agriculture – one of Julius Caesar's most important observations about the Belgae concerned their arable farming (*De Bello Gallico*, V, 12, 5) '. . . they began [i.e. were the first] to till the fields'), and an adequate range of iron tools were therefore already available. Others were entirely new and required specialist tools which eventually became taken for granted.

Crafts, trades and industries were not only a product of the towns of Roman Britain; they helped create and sustain them as well. At the heart of any successful community which takes material goods for granted is the concentration of resources and skills in a small area. This proximity creates efficiency and reduces costs both in terms of attracting supply and providing demand. Most 'towns' and settlements of Roman Britain have produced some evidence for manufacturing of some sort, for example the glass factory at Caister-by-Norwich (Atkinson, 1931), or the possible dyeing vats at Silchester (Richmond, 1966, 81); though it is not always possible to associate such evidence with specific artefacts.

One problem needs to be born in mind – many of the basic iron tools changed little from the Roman period until relatively recently, and they can be difficult to date when not associated with a firm context. This is a problem which faces museums with collections from material gathered by antiquarians in the nineteenth century.

Primary industries

Agriculture

We know from Caesar's account that the tribes of the south-east turned to agriculture and settlement in Britain after their original plans to raid had proved successful (see above). Around the end of the third century, 400 years later, a *panegyric* on the life of Constantius Chlorus described Britain as something verging on a paradise in terms of fulsome harvests, and numerous pastures (*Eumenius*, xi, 1). This was a tactful exaggeration – Constantius had recently recaptured Britain for the Empire after the usurpation of Carausius and Allectus, and clearly Britain had to be shown as having been worthy of Constantius' attention.

Nevertheless Britain was regarded by the Roman state as agriculturally valuable. Moreover, with her substantial garrison to support, there was a major forced incentive to farmers to be productive – soldiers ate before farmers. This was known as the *annona militaris* and amounted to a tax in kind. Tacitus commented on the abuse of the system by collectors in the first century (*Agricola*, 19). The distribution of arable and pastoral farming is less clear but the spread of substantial towns and rural houses indicates that surplus agricultural wealth was principally generated in the lowland zone. Sometimes the natural boundaries in an area can suggest the likely size of farms or estates, for example 800 ha (2000 acres) is a possibility for the large fourth-century estate at Bignor in Sussex.

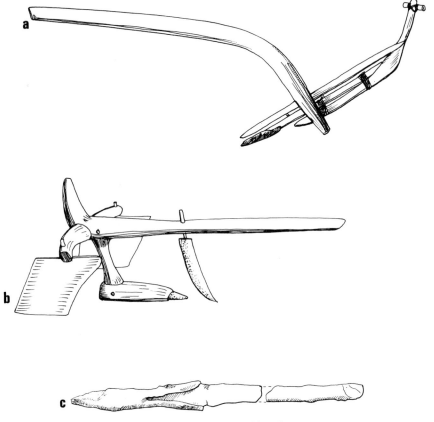

The soil

The Celtic farmers used wooden ploughs, strengthened with a pointed iron-tip to the share (the cutting point, see fig.26). The Roman invasion made two developments possible allowing heavier soils to be exploited and also to actually turn the soil over. These were: adding an iron coulter in front of the share to cut the soil, and a wood mould board behind the share. The earliest known coulter from Britain is third-century (Rees, 1979, 60). The actual process of ploughing can be seen in a small bronze statue group from Piercebridge (fig.28). Here a ploughman walks behind a pair of oxen pulling the plough, though it has been suggested that he is in fact ritually marking out the boundary of a town (Manning, 1971).

Further improvements were derived from the increased use of iron. A spade-shoe (fig.27 f), or iron toe for a wooden spade increased its cutting depth and durability. Frere (1987, 270) draws attention to the important contribution to drainage made by improved spades, and by the scythe to enable the winter feeding of livestock. In general terms this must have made agriculture

26 Ploughs

a bow ard. The main beam is pierced to allow a share beam to pass through and meet the ground at an angle. At the bottom of the share beam is an iron share, and at the top is a handle. The best-known example is from Donnerplund in Denmark. Length, about 2.8m (after Rees)

b crook ard based on the bronze model from Piercebridge. In this case the share meets the ground horizontally following behind the coulter which cuts the soil vertically. The mouldboards turn the cut soil over

c a winged bar-share from Verulamium, length 36cm (after Frere, 1972, 168, no. 17)

more of a planned activity, rather than an annual gamble with nature. Other iron tools in use include shears and mattocks, for example a set found at Chedworth in Gloucestershire (Goodburn, 1986), turf-cutters, billhooks, hoes, rakes and pitchforks. A number of fourth-century hoards of agricultural ironwork are known from Britain, for example at Silchester (Boon, 1974, 271).

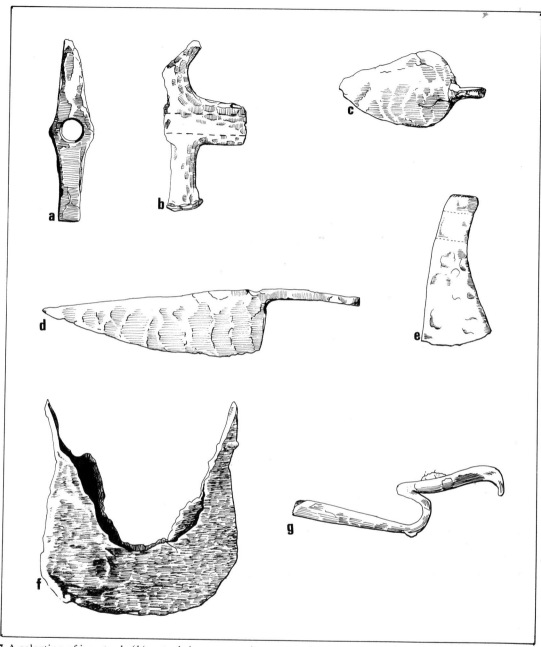

27 A selection of iron tools (⅓ actual size, except **g**) from various sites in Britain:

a & b hammers from Vindolanda and Lullingstone (Bidwell, 1986, 139, no. 52 and Meates, 1987, 97, no. 237)

c trowel from Vindolanda (Bidwell, 1986, 139, no. 56),

d curved knife from Vindolanda (after Bidwell, 1986, 143, no. 66)

e axe from Richborough (Bushe-Fox, 1947, pl.61, 341),

f spade iron from Richborough (Bushe-Fox, 1947, pl.59, 320)

g farrier's butteris with V-shaped blade (used to pare horses' hooves prior to shoeing) from the villa at Gadebridge Park (Neal, 1974, 159, 345). Length 27cm

28 Ploughman and team of ox and cow from Piercebridge, *Magis*, County Durham. The group may actually be performing the ritual marking out of a boundary. Length 5.5*cm* (Manning, 1971; photo and copyright; the British Museum)

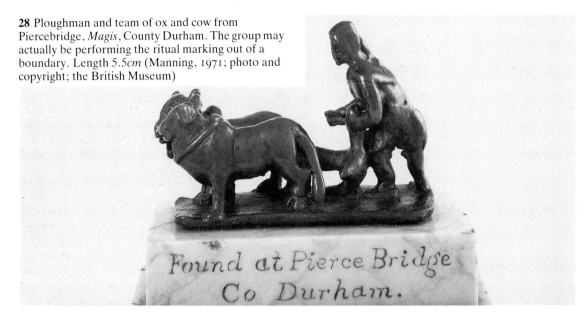

Below **29** Grinding:

a household quernstone (about ¼ scale). Quernstones required two components: a lower stationary stone and an upper stone which was turned around to provide the grinding action. They could be made of any suitable stone but Mayen lava from Germany was particularly popular. The hole at the side of the upper stone allowed a rope to be passed through to make a handle

b iron spindle from a watermill at Great Chesterford. The spindle would have been turned by a waterwheel at one end thus turning a millstone at the other. Length about 65cm

Grinding

In common use throughout the province for grinding grain were quernstones made from German volcanic lava, though many were produced in Britain itself (fig.29 a; Peacock, 1987). The lava has the properties of lightness and strength and therefore was worth importing. They vary in size, depending whether they were to be turned by hand, water or beast, but required two parts; one to stay still while the other was turned. The smaller examples sometimes have a hole drilled towards one side

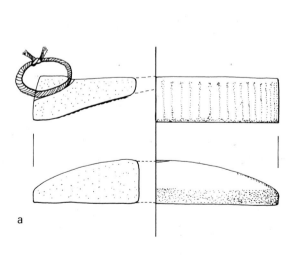

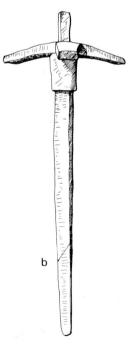

through which a rope could be passed to act as a handle and for suspending the quern from the wall when out of use (Chapman and Johnson, 1972, 51, no. 26). Water-mills were also used, as evidenced by the iron spindle from a mill wheel found at Great Chesterford (fig.29 b). The traces of a number of water-mill buildings and equipment are known at a number of sites, for example Haltwhistle Burn in the vicinity of Hadrian's Wall, and Willowford on the Wall itself.

Quarrying and mining

The knowledge that Britain contained useful mineral resources seems to have been a factor behind the invasion. Outcrops of metals, particularly iron, lead and silver, and of stone were presumably common knowledge amongst local peoples because they were rapidly exploited. Such knowledge is unlikely to be forgotten and as a result few quarries and mines now show certain traces of Roman activity, though those that do include the quarries used for Hadrian's Wall at Coombe Crag and the Gelt in Cumberland, and the Dolaucothi goldmines in Wales. Abandoned boulders in what was supposed to be the Wall's forward ditch at Limestone Corner in Northumberland show the technique of removing stones with water and wedges (fig.30).

For the same reason there are few tools which can be specifically associated with Roman quarrying and mining. The soft red stone quarries in Cumberland mentioned above show clearly the traces of chiselling on the existing rock face. Some stone was imported, for example the Carrara and Côte d'Or marble used in the Neronian 'proto-palace' at Fishbourne, but British stone was rapidly exploited too – the same building included Purbeck marble (Cunliffe, 1971, II, 1ff.) – but in the main such stone was only used for inscriptions and decoration. The first-century tombstone of the procurator Julius Classicianus from London is made of Cotswold or Northampton limestone (plate 25). The Agricolan inscription from the Verulamium forum is made of Purbeck marble (see below, p. 132).

Mines required drainage. This was sometimes achieved with a series of wooden water-wheels which lifted the water up and out of the mineshafts. A single example from Britain survives in part from the goldmines at Dolaucothi (Boon, 1966).

---

30 Wedge-holes in a large block of stone remaining in the ditch forward of Hadrian's Wall at Limestone Corner, east of Carrawburgh. The stone has been prepared for destruction by cutting holes for wooden wedges in fault-lines. The wedges would have been soaked in water to make them expand and split the block. Although substantial pieces of stone were removed here this block was abandoned and shows the technique. The coin is a ten-pence piece (photo: author)

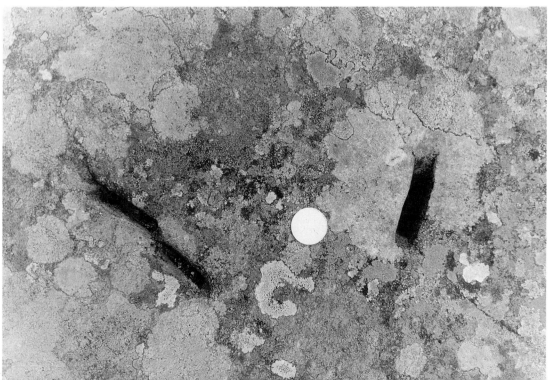

Metal production

There are a few areas in Britain which were concerned with the production of metals in pig form. Presumably this metal was then transported to where it was required. A certain number bear stamps of their owners, for example the lead pigs from the Mendips such as one bearing this stamp: TI·CLAVD·CAESAR·AVG·P·M·TR·/ P·VIIII·IMP·XVI·DE·BRITAN. The pig (now lost) can be dated to the year AD 49 and shows just how quickly Britain's metal resources were exploited. Lead is a by-product of silver extraction, or vice-versa; this and the titles on the pig suggest that this was a government concern. If so the site was probably administered on behalf of the state by a procurator. An actual stamp which may have been connected with official metal production has survived from London (see below, p.69).

Subsequently such mining concerns may have been leased to private contractors who also stamped the lead pigs, for example this one from Mansfield in Nottinghamshire: C·IVL·PROTI·BRIT· LVT·EX·ARG. This gives the name of the contractor, Caius Iulius Protius, who worked at the mines of *Lutudarum* (?) in Britain. *Lutudarum* was probably the name of a lead mine in Derbyshire. The meaning of EX·ARG is uncertain though one possibility is that it refers to the lead being a by-product of silver (*argentum*) extraction. Another is that it refers to the pig being a product 'of the silver works'. Lead was extracted in a number of other places in Britain, including North Wales and the Mendips (where its extraction seems to have been under imperial control – Whittick, 1982, and fig. 31 a), Shropshire, Clwyd, and Yorkshire. It was an essential Roman raw material, its plasticity making it ideal for lining baths and forming water pipes (fig.68). Other uses included making tanks (see Chapter 8 and fig.118), weights and coffins (see Chapter 7; figs.106 and 115), and forming part of the alloy pewter, with tin, which became increasingly popular in the third and fourth century in Roman Britain (fig.47).

Lead was not the only metal whose extraction was also leased to private contractors. A copper ingot from Anglesey is stamped: SOCIO ROMAE·NATSOL. Here *socio* indicates that a private firm, or 'association' was involved. Copper was the most essential component of a large range of alloys usually referred to now as bronze; a more accurate term is that currently in use in modern research reports 'copper alloy'. These various alloys were made up with varying amounts of tin or zinc in order to provide the raw material for the vast range of copper alloy artefacts imported to, or made in and used in, Britain.

There are a few examples of silver ingots known from Britain, but these are not necessarily new silver and may well represent melted-down material. One from Kent (fig.32) bears the workshop stamp of a private concern.

One of the areas of Roman Britain most actively involved in metal production was the Weald of Kent and Sussex (Cleere and Crossley, 1985). Though it now seems difficult to associate this rural and forested area of southern England with primary industry, it was undoubtedly once a centre for iron-making. The connection with the Fleet, the *Classis Britannica*, has already been mentioned (above p.45). A number of sites, for example Cranbrook and Bardown, have produced evidence of iron-making in the form of furnaces, slag and iron 'blooms'. 'Blooms' are pieces of raw iron created within the furnace and subsequently heated and hammered. The use of charcoal in the heating process allowed a certain amount of carbon to alloy with the iron, and the effect was to create blocks of iron parts of which were steel and therefore much harder (Cleere, 1970 and 1971). Other ironworking is known to have taken place in Northamptonshire.

---

31 Metal-working in Roman Britain (not to scale):
a lead pig from Syde, north of Cirencester. The pig bears three inscriptions, two of which are visible here. On the top are the name and titles of Vespasian for the year AD 79 and the words BRIT·EX·ARG which means it comes from the British silver mines. On the side is the abbreviated name of a company, SOC·NOVEC, probably for *Novaec·Societas*, and on the end are the initials GPC probably for the name of an agent. The pig had presumably changed hands a number of times before being lost but was evidently mined under imperial control. Length 58cm, weight 79kg
b tombstone or shrine from York of a smith at work with hammer, tongs and anvil. Height 104cm
c pair of iron tongs from Richborough from a pre-85 context (Bushe-Fox, 1949, 154, no. 335)
d mould for casting copies of the coinage of Tetricus I (270–3) found in the basilica at Silchester. About actual size (Fulford, 1985, 53)
e limestone mould from Nettleton for casting pewter bowls about 10cm in diameter (Wedlake, 1982, 71, and fig.38,6). After 340
f pottery crucible from Verulamium, *c.*150–180 (after Frere, 1984, 107, no. 2). Diameter 7.4cm
g an unfinished bronze blank for a 'Colchester' bow brooch from Baldock, Herts. First century. Height 57mm (after Stead, 1975)

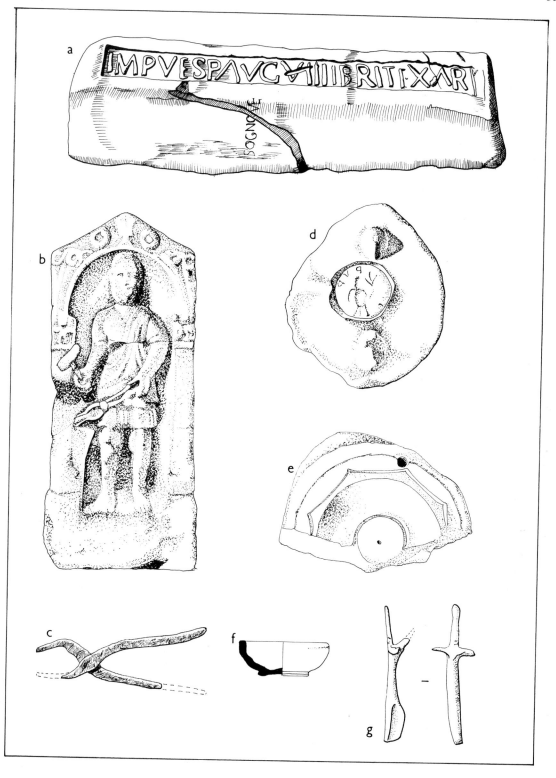

Secondary industries

Metal-working

The products of metal-working are far more numerous than evidence of the actual process of manufacture. At Verulamium traces of a bronze-smith's workshops were found in Insula XIV close to the forum. Work of this kind was evidently being carried on in the earliest phases (pre-AD 60) of a small strip of shops, and continued until the early years of the second century. The evidence for this lay not just in the pieces of scrap metal but also in the crucibles (fig.31 f), and traces of trays which had caught waste material from bronze vessels which were being finished on lathes (Frere, 1972, 11).

Traces of gold refining have been found in London, showing that metal could be transported some way from its source during the chain of production. The evidence consists of wood ash, crucibles and gold dust contained in a well and pit subsequently buried by the 'Governor's Palace' during the Flavian period. It is possible that the gold refining was under government control (Marsden, 1975, 12-13) and was only for the purposes of turning into ingots for shipping to Rome, rather than representing traces of a gold-worker's shop.

The Verulamium metal-workers of the first century operated in simple buildings. By the late third century some of the metal-workers at Silchester had moved into the basilica where scrap, a fragmentary limestone mould and a lead mould used for casting third century coin copies testify to their presence (fig.31 d). An accumulation of slag in the later fourth century suggests that iron-working had become the main activity (Fulford, 1985). A mould for a statuette is known from Gestingthorpe, north-west of Colchester (Frere, 1970). Curiously, despite the huge number of brooches – *fibulae* – that have been found in Britain, there are practically no traces of their manufacture despite confident assertions of 'British', as opposed to Continental, types. The modest settlement at Baldock, Hertfordshire, has yielded an apparently unique example of a brooch in the early stages of its manufacture (fig.31 g). The brooch, of the 'Colchester' variety (see Chapter 4), is recognisable both from the unfinished wings and catch-plate (Stead, 1975). This suggests that crude blanks were cast and then forged and worked into shape. Recent excavations at Castleford, *Lagentium*, West Yorkshire, have revealed the remains of over 800 baked clay moulds for casting spoons. The find, from a fourth-century level, is unique for the whole Roman Empire and indicates the potential for mass-production.

Although these examples of metal-working in Roman Britain can be associated with buildings in most of the towns, there was probably a large, perhaps significantly larger, metal-working industry carried on by itinerant craftsmen such as the one portrayed in a relief from York (fig.31 b). It may have been such a craftsman who deposited his recently-discovered (1985) hoard at Snettisham in Norfolk. His material included 117 unmounted gemstones and a number of pieces of scrap silver and bronze jewellery, as well as bronze and silver coins. His intention no doubt was to melt down the metal in order to make new jewellery; interestingly while the bronze coins give a *terminus post quem* of the later second century for the hoard, none of the silver coins post-date the reign of Domitian (AD 81-96), showing that this particular man had been careful to avoid the increasingly less fine silver coinage issued from the reign of Trajan onward (plates 4, 17).

In a number of cases the names of metal-

32 Silver ingot of 'double-axe' form bearing the inscription *Ex Off[icina] Curmissi*, 'from the workshop of Curmissus'. Found in Kent. Length 12cm (photo and copyright: the British Museum; *Antiq. Journ.*, 52, 1972, 84 & 87)

workers are known. A particularly fine skillet from the Isle of Ely bears the name of Boduogenus (see Chapter 3 and plate 7). The Fossdike Mars (see Chapter 6) was made by Celatus the coppersmith (*aerarius*) out of a pound of bronze (fig.88 b). Iron-workers called Basilis, Titus, Martinus, and Aprilis are known from various tools found in London. From Catterick comes a knife blade bearing the name of Victor V. The problem with these names is that they are of no help in indicating *where* these craftsmen actually worked. In some cases, especially the finer bronzework, the objects may well have been imported. The first century bronze brooches made by Aucissa (see Chapter 4 and fig.72 e) fall into this category.

In the third and fourth century pewter ware became one of the most popular types of metal plate in Roman Britain – it was a cheap substitute for silver plate and indicated a change in taste away from fine pottery as well as the cost of silver. Pewter was cast in moulds made of stone (fig.31 e). For a bowl this would require a mould for both the outer and inner faces such as pair found at Leswyn St Just in Cornwall (Brown in Strong and Brown, 1976, 34, fig.32). At Camerton in Avon three furnaces and four moulds along with slag and coal show that the settlement had a pewter industry (Wedlake, 1958). Even on the nearby complex associated with a shrine of Apollo at Nettleton a large number of mould fragments made of limestone indicate the same (Wedlake, 1982, 68 ff.) once the pagan shrine had fallen into disuse after *c.* 330.

The use of coloured 'enamelling' to decorate some metal (particularly bronze) artefacts can be mentioned here (Butcher, 1976). These artefacts were manufactured with recesses to receive coloured glass inlays, each colour being separated by a metal division. Heat caused the glass and metal to melt and therefore fuse together. It was particularly common in the northern provinces and Britain evidently had a number of craftsmen who specialised in enamelled metal-working. Amongst their products are the distinctive enamelled 'trumpet' brooches (fig.72 d) and the remarkable 'Rudge Cup' (plate 3). However, the technique could only be performed on quite small objects, and it is for this reason that brooches are the most common of the enamelled artefacts. Even so, apart from the plate brooches, these are still relatively rare (Hattatt, 1987, 127, Table III).

The cases of metal-working cited are only examples, but they indicate the kind of traces that might be expected of this craft. The workers themselves would have had a number of tools such as lathes for turning and polishing vessels, and tongs for handling the objects (fig.31 c). These, not unnaturally, were presumably removed when the business moved or was dismantled. We are left only with evidence from that which was of no further use: forgotten pieces of scrap and waste, and broken pieces of brittle stone moulds.

Ceramics

The actual products – roof-tiles and pottery – of the ceramic industry are discussed in the chapter concerned with household goods, but there were a number of tools which were used in the process of manufacture.

Tiles

In the main, roofs and heating systems were made from earthenware tiles, which, like pottery, were fired in kilns, such as that found at Hartfield in Sussex (Rudling, 1986, and McWhirr, 1979). In a number of cases we know the names of the makers, such as Arverus (fig. 33b) and Cabriabanus (fig.34 c), because they stamped their products. A number of others are known, though their names consist only of initials; for example the firm of the London area which stamped its tiles SCM, another Gloucestershire firm which stamped its tiles LLH, and a firm at Wroxeter which used a stamp for the letters LCH. Sometimes these tileries seem to have been in public ownership, for example that discovered at St Oswald's Priory in Gloucester (fig. 33 c).

Flue-tiles

Amongst the most interesting are the flue-tiles from heating systems, and for lining the walls of the hot room, *caldaria*, in a bath-house, because they carry the most useful information for tracing the manufacturers. Flue-tiles had to be secured to the walls or to their neighbours. To help the plaster gain a grip they were impressed with patterns usually made with a 'tile-comb', rather like a fork with sharp teeth (fig.34 a,b). Most are purely free-style but sometimes a tile-maker combined this with writing his name, for example one from Leicester inscribed PRIMO FECIT, which means simply 'Primo made this'.

33 Three examples of civil tile stamps (two-thirds actual size):

a the PP·BR·LON stamp indicates a tile manufactured for, or by, the procurator of the province of Britain in London

b ARVERI stamp is from Cirencester and probably indicates the name of a private firm in the ownership of *Arverus*

c The RPG stamp comes from the tile factory at St Oswald's Priory, Gloucester and indicates that the tiles were made for the *Rei Publicae Glevensium*, i.e. Gloucester, during the joint magistracy, Q Q (for *duoviri quinquennales*) of one *Iulius Florus* and another whose name is uncertain (after Heighway and Parker, 1982)

These free-style patterns are by far and away the most common but there do seem to have been a number of tile-manufacturers who impressed the patterns with a roller-die. These make an interesting subject for study because it is possible to trace the makers' activities through identifying the distribution of tiles made from the same die. In a few cases the die-pattern included the maker's name such as the Cabriabanus mentioned above, or a representational scene such as the dogs and stags from Ashtead in Surrey (fig.34 d). It appears that the practice of using roller-dies was not common, and in fact their use was predominantly in the south-east from roughly AD 75-175 (principally during three phases: 75-90, 120-125, and 155-175, Black 1985). Some of the patterns are so elaborate that the possibility that they served a decorative function cannot be discounted (Lowther 1948, and Johnston and Williams 1979).

Whether such tiles were made on site or transported is unknown. For example Cabriabanus' tiles have been found at villa sites at Darenth and Plaxtol. He may have made the tiles at each site simply using the same roller name-stamp. If he did work from a central kiln-site it has not been found. Considering how heavy and fragile tiles are it would seem that by far the easiest method would have been to manufacture them on site, unless this was close to the firm's base.

Civic tile-stamps

The practice of stamping tiles by the army has already been discussed in Chapter I. The government of the province and some towns seem to have done exactly the same, though the evidence is less numerous and widespread. It is not known whether such tiles were made in kilns that belonged to the various administrative units or whether they were stamped by the manufacturers as part of a bulk order.

An early example of a tilery in imperial ownership seems to have been in operation south-west of Silchester at Little London. Here traces of a kiln, bricks and tiles were discovered in 1925 and included one bearing a circular stamp (Greenaway, 1981) which reads: NER·CL·CAE·AVG·GER·. The wording is an abbreviation of the titles of the Emperor Nero, *Nero Claudius Caesar Augustus Germanicus*, and must therefore indicate a date between AD 54 and 68. Official tile-stamps are well-known in London where they bear the abbreviated form of the provincial government: PP·BR·LON, which probably expands to read *Procurator Provinciae Britanniae Londinii*, meaning they belonged to the Procurator of the Province of Britain in London, an equivalent to a

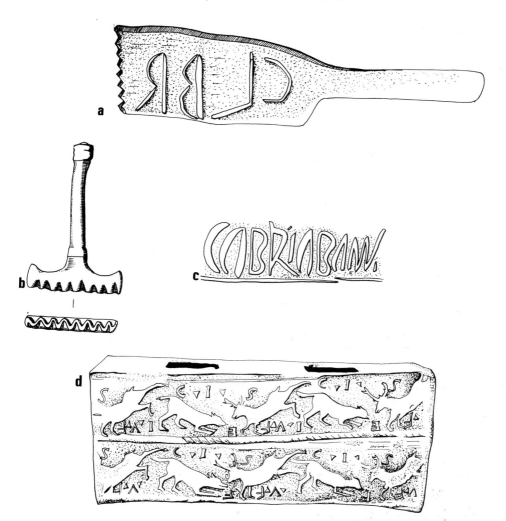

34 Tile-combs (two-thirds actual size) and roller die-stamps on box-flue tiles. Tile-combs were used mark tiles with grooves in simple patterns. This made it easier for the mortar to bind the tile to the wall. Tile-combs were usually used on box flue-tiles and voussoir tiles.

a an impression of a wooden tile-comb left on a tile from the bath-house at Beauport Park in Sussex. It bears the initials of the *Classis Britannica*, and shows that even simple tools could be imperial property

b bronze tile-comb, probably from Norfolk (private collection)

c Cabriabanus signature from Plaxtol, Kent. An example of a roller-stamp signature, which had the same effect as tile-comb grooves, on a piece of wall tile from the site at Alan's Farm, Plaxtol, Kent. The length of the name Cabriabanus is about 15cm

d box flue-tile from Ashtead villa, Surrey, where it was manufactured, bearing the impression of Lowther's Die 7. Length: about 41cm

modern stamp reading 'Property of H.M. Government' (fig.33 a, and Wright, 1985). Gloucester has produced similar examples which, like the London tiles, are found only in the vicinity of the settlement (fig.33 c, and Heighway and Parker, 1982). Some of these tiles are stamped:

RPG Q Q IVL

FLOR ET CCRSM

This stamp probably refers to the *Rei Publicae Glevensium*, i.e. the corporate administration of Gloucester, during the joint magistracy (*duoviri quinquennales*) of Iulius Florus and another man whose name is only indicated by the initials CCRSM. Other stamps are followed by the names of other magistrates, and some consist only of the letters RPG.

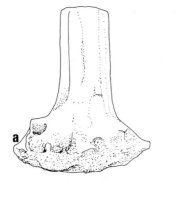

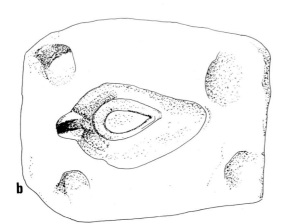

35 Pottery manufacture:

a A decorative motif, *poinçon*, used in the manufacture of mould-decorated samian ware from Colchester (Hull, 1963, 50). The view is from the side and shows the handle which allowed the motif to be pressed into the wet mould. Length 6.5cm

b lower half of lamp-mould made of fired clay from Colchester. Length 12.3cm (Hull, 1963, 109)

c impression of the Celtic sky god Taranis pottery mould from Corbridge. The mould was used to make oval plaques which could then be luted onto the site of vessels with liquid clay. The warrior attributes involve the military dress, armour and club; the god is also accompanied by the spoked wheel, symbolic of the sun. Height 12cm

Pottery

Tools used in the manufacture of pottery prior to firing are not particularly well-documented in Britain. Pottery was made both by hand and on the wheel. Wheels were presumably made mostly of wood and likewise the templates used to shape the vessels. A potter's wheel would normally have had a flywheel which could be turned by the potter's feet – such a flywheel, made of stone and about 0.75m (2ft 6in) wide was found at Stibbington in the Nene Valley in what appears to have been a potter's workshop (Wild, 1973). The potters' kiln sites at Colchester are of particular interest because some were concerned with the production of quality wares which required more tools. These included samian ware (discussed at greater length in Chapter 3), beakers and lamps. The area of the samian kiln at Colchester has produced clay moulds used to form decorated bowls, and poinçons, or decorative details, used to press into the moulds to form patterns (fig.35 a). Pottery lamps were usually made in clay moulds, and parts of these too were also found (fig.35 b). A mould for making *appliqué* plaques of the sky-god Taranis was found at Corbridge (fig.35 c).

Kilns

Pottery kilns of Roman date are well-known throughout Britain (Swan, 1984, discusses their distribution and types). Kiln structures were basic and easily constructed for the purposes of manufacturing coarse kitchen pottery. They amount to no more than ovens, usually partially below ground level, and depending on the pottery required had different types of flues and supports for the pottery. Some of the simplest were surface bonfires, or 'clamps', which have left practically no traces whatsoever. This was particularly true of the Dorset black-burnished pottery industry (known as BB1, fig.55; Farrar, 1973, 92).

Kilns contained 'kiln-furniture', various items which were distributed within kilns to help support and separate the pottery. The pottery needed to be stood on a raised floor within the kiln. This allowed the hot air to circulate evenly beneath and rise up around the assemblage. The raised floor was supported on a 'pedestal' and could either be built in as part of the structure or be made of fired-clay components. There are a large number of different types known but they all served the same purpose – those of fired-clay being portable and therefore re-usable. Essentially the parts involve supports like small columns and floors which could be made of clay plates or a large number of clay bars laid between the kiln wall and the pedestal. Probably the most elaborate example of a kiln in Britain was the

samian kiln found to the west of Colchester (Hull, 1963, 20).

It was important to stack pottery correctly within the kiln in order to allow even exposure of the clay's surface to the heat. To make this easier various forms of spacers and props were used. The military depot at Holt has produced a number of sausage-shaped clay pads used to separate mortaria, and also three pronged props which suspended lead-glazed vessels. Such spacers come in very different shapes and sizes including rings, bobbins, blocks, broken sherds from previous firings and even suitably shaped stones.

Carpentry

Wood-working was a basic industry of major importance in the Roman world. Wood was used for purposes now served in many cases by plastics and the tools are amongst the most difficult to date with certainty in their own right. Moreover, it seems that the Roman world used tools which were already well-known, and this applied to Britain as well, though clearly the needs of manufacture must have vastly increased the quantities of carpenters and their tools. Tools in use include: axes, planes, chisels, gouges/augers, borers, awls, punches, files, saws, tweezers, dividers, iron and bronze nails. The vast majority were made of iron with wood or bone handles (fig.28). Such tools are so ideally suited to their tasks that many have remained virtually unaltered to modern times. On one hand this can make Roman examples difficult to identify, but on the other they are direct testimony of skilful tool design in the Roman period.

36 Stone-workers recorded on altars to Sul at Bath:
a Sulinus altar from Bath. In the third line the dedicant Sulinus states his profession as *scultor*, a sculptor. Height 59cm (*RIB* 151)
b Priscus altar from Bath. In the third line Priscus states his profession as *lapidarius*, a stonemason. Height 53cm (*RIB* 149)

Stonemasonry

The late Neronian 'proto-palace' at Fishbourne in Sussex has produced considerable evidence for the actual manufacture of building components 'on site' (Cunliffe, 1971, I, 58). It is therefore one of the first examples of classical type stone-working in Britain, if not the first, and it seems reasonable to assume that masons must have been brought from Gaul to do the work. A fenced-off area, later buried by the Flavian palace, contained large quantities of waste stone and ironstone used to rub the stone down. The techniques also required the use of saws, hammers, bow-drills (Blagg, 1976, and Cunliffe, 1971, II, 139, 76) and chisels to rough out the stone in the first place with the assistance of the abrasive action of sand and water. Demand for stone must have been huge – the first two centuries of Roman rule saw a considerable amount of civic and domestic building in towns. This was entirely new to Britain but buildings of worked stone of some sort became relatively common. A number of rural houses in the Cotswold region, amongst others, were roofed with tiles made of the local limestone, or limestone from the Forest of Dean; some of these also had stone finials like that found at Rockbourne.

The only stonemason, a *lapidarius*, known in Roman Britain by name is Priscus, from Chartres in Gaul, though unfortunately the whereabouts of his workshop is unknown (fig.36b). It may have been in Gaul as he is only known from a dedication he made at Bath. At least three sculptors, *sculptores*, are known – Sulinus who may have worked in Bath where his dedicatory inscription to *Sulevis* (his namesake?) was found (fig.36a), Juventinus who carved a figure of Mars in a niche found near Bisley in Gloucestershire (Rhodes, 1964, 27, no. 12.i), and Searigillus, son of Searix, who carved an altar bearing a relief of Mercury dedicated by one Lovernius at the temple of Mercury at Uley in Gloucestershire (Hassall, in *Britannia*, 12, 1981, 370, no. 5).

How stonemasons and sculptors worked in Roman Britain as far as 'schools' and workshops are concerned is not clear. However, some regional variations in carving styles indicate that while the classical tradition was observed localised versions developed. Some of the column bases and Corinthian capitals from the Wroxeter forum colonnade, the Chester fortress *principia* and from Ribchester are of a distinctive type which may have been manufactured by a single craftsman and his apprentices (Blagg in Munby and Henig, 1977, I, 59). Special skills must have been developed by some 'schools' in order to deal with their own particular local material such as Kimmeridge shale which was used for furniture, and Whitby jet in Yorkshire, used for personal ornaments. Stonemasonry and sculpting were at the heart of Romano-British art and a number of examples of their products occur throughout this book, whether the temple pediment from Bath, or military inscriptions and tombstones from Hadrian's Wall.

Bone-working

Bone was a basic raw material in the Roman world. In the next chapters a number of household and personal items made of bone are described. There are few traces of bone-working in Roman Britain, though a site at Colchester has produced considerable evidence for the industry in the early fourth century. Most of the remains were partially-worked pieces of bone designed as leaves, probably intended to be decorative elements of furniture. These 'wasters' suggested that the craftsman worked from a large piece of bone for grip. Traces of working on the unfinished pieces indicated a number of tools had been used, such as knives, rasps, files, saws, drills, chisels, lathes and polishing tools (N. Crummy, 1981). However in isolation it is unlikely that any of these tools would be demonstrably different than those used in carpentry or stone-working. An interesting use of bone survives from Silchester in the form of sheep shoulder blades (fig.37 g). These have had a number of small discs removed, presumably to be used as gaming pieces or spindle whorls (see below).

Spinning and weaving

Very few examples of fabrics from Roman Britain have survived and this makes the topic a very difficult one to discuss (Wild, 1970 and 1976). However, a number of artefacts associated with the manufacture of textiles and fabrics are known. A common find on Romano-British sites is the spindle-whorl, occasionally accompanied by its bone or wooden spindle. Whorls were made of almost any appropriate material and range from about 2-5cm (¾-2in) in diameter. They are known made of stone, shale, wood,

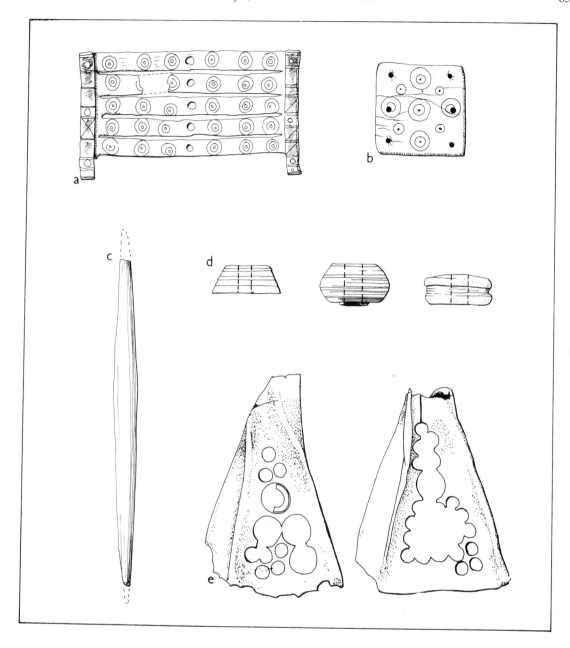

37 Textile tools:

a weaving frame from the fort at South Shields, *Arbeia*, on South Tyneside. There were originally six bone strips held by riveted bronze mounts. The threads were passed between the strips and through the holes. Width 9.2cm

b bone tablet for weaving cord and braid from Alchester. Strands were passed through each hole, then by turning the tablet a cord was formed. Using a number of tablets in a row, and a needle to pass a thread through the strands, a braid was formed. Diameter 3.75cm

c & d bone spindle and spindle whorls from Lullingstone (Meates, 1987, 150, fig.62). Two-thirds actual size

e sheep shoulder blades from Silchester. The bones have been discarded after having had a number of discs drilled out. These were presumably used for either gaming counters or spindle whorls

bone, jet, metal – even drilled coins, and pottery sherds (fig.37 c-e). Wool was combed through before it was wound on a spindle, probably by iron combs which are known from a few sites.

Fabric was woven on looms. While these were made of wood and have not survived loom weights are not uncommon. They provided the tension in the cloth and are usually reasonably substantial pieces of fired clay or lead with suspension holes. Narrow bands of cloth could be woven on small weaving frames, such as the one from South Shields made of six bone strips mounted into metal brackets at either end (fig.37 a). Braid and cord was woven with the aid of small square bone tablets drilled with holes to pass the strand through (fig.37 b).

Measuring and balancing

One of the greatest attributes of the Roman world was a comparatively well-organised system of weights and measures which was consistent throughout the Empire. Coinage, particularly the relatively consistent quality of gold coin, paralleled this, though there were some basic denominational differences which acknowledged the system already established in the Greek East. Together they symbolise the sense of order which was current. A large number of devices were used to measure and balance.

The obligation to pay tribute in the form of corn may explain a curious bronze container from the fort of Carvoran on Hadrian's Wall, shaped in the form of an inverted bucket. Bearing the name of the Emperor Domitian (AD 81-96), subsequently erased when his memory was damned by the Senate, it appears to be a corn-measure known as a *modius*, and states its capacity as 17.5 *sextarii*, or just under 9.7 litres (17 modern pints) (fig.38 b; *Archaeologia Aeliana*, 4th series, 34, 130). As a unique item we have no way of knowing if this was in common use throughout the province for measuring received tribute. Interestingly a soldier's daily grain ration was 2½ *sextarii*, so it may actually be a measure for a soldier's weekly supply assuming this was doled out every seven days (7 x 2.5 = 17.5). However, no certain evidence that soldiers ground their own corn has been found in the form of quern-stones in forts.

Roman measuring rulers were similar to their modern counterparts. A bronze example from London is made of two lengths connected by a central hinge, thus allowing it to fold away for convenience. The various divisions on it allow measurement according to Greek units of the *digitus*, and Roman units of *unciae* (fig.38 c). A more basic example from London consists of no more than an ox bone engraved with *unciae* divisions.

Weighing was achieved with one of two devices: the balance, or *libra*, and the steelyard, *statera* (fig.38 a). The balance was a simple arm bearing two pans and suspended from a central pivot. The steelyard was slightly more sophisticated, involving weights and scales, though the principle of sliding weights along the arm could be applied to balances as well. It was not uncommon for the weights to be highly ornamental – a number of examples are known where the weights were in the form of a bust of a god such as one from a hoard of instruments found in 1900 at Silchester. Such decoration of such a workaday tool may seem inappropriate – some of these weights may have been made from damaged statues. Others were simple lumps of lead, pierced for suspension, occasionally bearing simple engraved indications of weight such as 'I' for one ounce or *uncia*.

Medicine

Roman medicine was a combination of long-established Greek practices derived from the works of Hippocrates and primitive, though not necessarily less effective, homeopathy. It was performed by trained practitioners whose social status was high. Generally, doctors were Greeks and the most organised practice of medicine and surgery was in the army (a number of forts in Britain, such as Housesteads, had buildings which have been identified as hospitals). Certainly the idea that dead bodies should be dissected was current amongst serious doctors, so equally was the idea that health was to be associated with good living and not the idiosyncratic whims of the gods. Nevertheless, the numerous curses known from Britain, particularly from Bath, show that ordinary people believed that another's ill health might be secured by soliciting the help of a god. Equally it can be assumed that they thought their own good health could be secured by the same method.

It seems that medicine in Roman Britain was

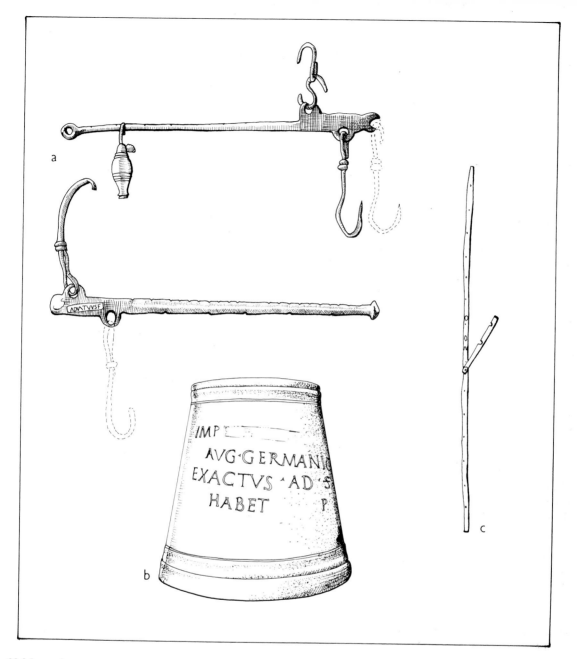

38 Measuring.

a bronze steelyards. The weight is slid along the arm until the steelyard remains horizontal, and the result read off the measures on the arm. The steelyard could be used either way up depending on the material to be weighed. The measures are frequently of debatable accuracy. The principle is expanded on by Goodburn and Grew in Frere, S.S., 1984, 57 (*Verulamium III*). Weights take many forms, some representing gods, but the majority are simple lumps of bronze with hooks for suspension, or lumps of lead pierced to take a bronze or iron hook.
upper – from Silchester
lower – from Wereham, Norfolk, stamped with the maker's name, Aduacutus (see *JRS*, 42, 105) (both about half scale).

b corn measure from Carvoran, *Magna*, on Hadrian's Wall. This is a bronze dry-measure, with a stated capacity of 17.5 *sextarii*, about 16.8 pints. Its actual capacity is nearer 20 but a missing internal gauge is probably responsible for the discrepancy. The inscription also gives the name and titles of the Emperor Domitian (AD 81–96) for the years 90–92. However, Domitian was unpopular and suffered *damnatio memoriae* after his death on the orders of the Senate; in consequence his name has been erased here as it was on public inscriptions. Height 31cm, weight about 11.5kg.

c bronze foot-rule from Princes Street, London. The rule folds in half and is held rigid when extended by a clamp. Length 29.5cm (after Wheeler, 1930, 84)

not confined to treating human beings. A small fragment of pottery from the Thames near Taplow in Berkshire bears a Greek graffito which reads: MANTIOC MYA OΦICI. This means that Mantios, who was presumably Greek, was a mule (MYA) doctor (OΦICI). The sherd may have been from his cremation urn (*Britannia*, vii, 279).

Surgical instruments

A large number of implements have been found which are traditionally associated with surgical practices, though no doubt they were also readily obtainable for domestic do-it-yourself medicine, or personal hygiene (fig.39 a-d). A large set of these tools was found in a house in Pompeii, known appropriately as the 'House of the Surgeon' – however such specialist instruments

39 'Surgical' and medical (some of these items could be, and probably usually were, used as toilet instruments):

a probe from the Walbrook, London, length 15.5cm

b *ligula* from Richborough (after Cunliffe, 1968, pl.43 172), length 15cm

c *spatula*, length 14cm

d pair of bronze forceps from the legionary baths at the Caerleon, *Isca*, fortress (after Zienkiewicz, 1986, 189, no. 188). Length 12.5cm

e oculist's tile stamp (one side of, 8cm wide) from Chester, *Deva*, reading Q·IVL·MARTINI STACTVM, 'Quintus Iulius Martinus, the unguent'; the other sides mention the oculist's anti-irritant, *diapso[ricum]*, his salve for soreness, *cro[codes] at aspri[tudinem]*, and ointments, *pencilii*. (*Britannia*, 8, 1977, 435)

f lead stopper from a jar inscribed *ex radice Britanici*, a dockleaf-derived cure for scurvy manufactured in Britain. Found in the *principia* at Haltern, Germany (Stieren, *Germania*, 12, 1928, 70, fig.1). Diameter 10.5cm

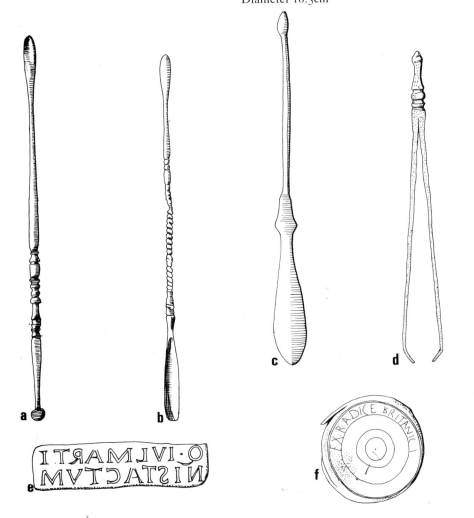

are extremely rare in Britain (see for example Allason-Jones, 1979 and Gilson, 1981).

The most basic instrument was the *spathomelae*, or spatula (fig.39 c). This was an all-purpose tool with a number of variations in the form of the blade and usually made of bronze or iron. Rounded blades were probably designed to depress the tongue, while those with points or sharp edges were probably used for making incisions. Whatever the blade form, the spatula's other end nearly always has a small swelling probably intended for use as a probe.

Scalpels were also used and have a rather more dramatic appearance, being both stouter and having larger handles as well as a number of varieties of blade. Additional cutting services were performed by cauteries, a rare example of which is known from Verulamium (Gilson, 1982). *Ligulae* were tools similar to the spatula but differ in having a small cup-shaped scoop which may have been used as a probe, an ear-scoop or for picking up small quantities of ointments out of flasks or jars (fig.39 b). They were probably used both for domestic toilet activities as well as surgery. Forceps, known as *uvulae*, made of two arms with serrated grips on a central pivot were used for gripping and extractions (fig.39 d). The larger examples might have been used during childbirth.

Small quantities of medicines could be applied with the use of glass droppers. These were shaped rather like curved drinking horns but instead of a mouth-piece they had small tips which allowed the release of droplets.

Other medical items

Eye complaints were much commoner in antiquity than now. While the Roman world had no method of treating poor eyesight, there were a number of practitioners who specialised in treating eye disease (see Pliny, *Naturalis historiae*, 28, 167-172). Their tools were probably similar to those used by surgeons, and indeed they may have been surgeons. However they are specifically testified by their use of engraved stone dies, well-known from Britain, which they pressed into their patent ointments, giving details of their names and the substances used. An example from Kenchester, Herefordshire, records the name of the oculist Vindacus Ariovistus who may have run a business in Kenchester, *Magna* (Brailsford, 1964, 73). Another, from Chester, supplied details of

medications available from Quintus Iulius Martinus (fig.39 e).

Britain was also a source of medicines. a lead jar stopper from Haltern in the Rhineland is inscribed: EX RADICE BRITANICA which probably means that the jar contained a root extract medicine called *radix Britanica* (fig.39 f). Presumably roots from Britain were regarded as the best for the purpose, which is thought to have been curing scurvy.

Transport and communications

It was in the fields of transport and communications that the Roman world differed more significantly from any other period until the invention of printing and steam locomotion. Transport and communications were at the heart of the Roman phenomenon of order, form and stability. The facts that good roads were valued, built and used, that literacy was encouraged at least amongst provincial ruling classes, meant that the basic mechanism for the transmission of romanisation existed. In this way a consciousness of participating in the Empire could be promoted, and so also could manufactured goods be dispersed.

This is one of the most interesting ways in which Roman Britain bore some resemblance to modern Britain. The roads of the province undoubtedly provided the basis of the road system we use today. Like the provincial government of Britannia modern government, national and local, maintains the roads. The roads were once accompanied by an extensive system of milestones (fig.40 e; and see Chapter 5). And through their scratched remarks and comments on pottery sherds, or metal sheets, some of the Romano-British survive the oblivion of anonymity, demonstrating that even quite humble workmen could often write their own names.

Transport

By water

Transport in the Roman world was by sea, river or road. Britain's extensive coastline may have made sea travel relatively more economic than it was elsewhere in the ancient world. However, we have little knowledge of the extent to which inland waterways were exploited but there must

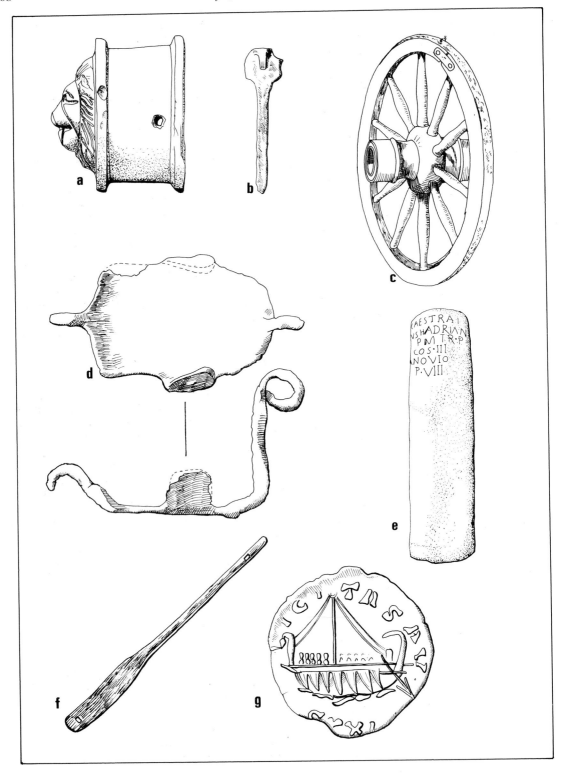

have been considerable use of such resources – the quay at the Park Street villa in Hertfordshire must have been typical; many villas are sited close to navigable rivers, such as the series of houses along the River Darenth in Kent. Some boats, or at least their fragments, have been recovered in Britain, several from London. At Blackfriars the remains of a flat-bottomed boat nearly 17m (55ft) in length suitable for sea-journeys were found in 1961, containing Kentish ragstone from near Maidstone. Across the River Thames at County Hall a round-bottomed ship with a keel in Mediterranean style was found in 1910. At Guy's Hospital in 1958 the remains of a shallow draught riverbarge were found. This kind of craft must have been the most common in Britain, suitable as it was for negotiating rivers and canals. The fleet of the *Classis Britannica* has already been mentioned (see p. 31) but no traces of its ships have ever been identified. A coin of Carausius (286-293) illustrates a galley, but it is doubtful if this is actually modelled on any of the real ships in the fleet which bore him to power

---

40 Transport:

a axle cap made of leaded bronze from the villa at Lullingstone in Kent. It was found in a level dated to *c.* 330–350. Diameter 6.3 cm (after Meates, 1987, 73, no. 148)

b iron linch-pin from Verulamium. Linch-pins were used to secure the wooden wheel to the axle. Length 17.5cm (after Frere, 1972, 174, no. 33)

c wooden cartwheel (restored) from Newstead (after Curle, 1911). This is a rare survival in Britain which was only possible because of the waterlogged conditions on the site

d iron 'hippo-sandal' from Colchester. The 'hippo-sandal' was probably fastened to the feet of horses, or more likely cattle, when journeys were being undertgaken on metalled roads. Length 21cm (after Crummy, 1983, fig.108)

e milestone found about seven miles west of the fort at Caerhun, *Kanovium* in north-west Wales. The inscription gives Hadrian's titles for the year 120–1 and states that *Kanovium* is eight [Roman] miles away. Height 2m (*RIB* 2265)

f wooden steering oar from Newstead. Length 1.6m, probably late first century

g reverse of a coin of Carausius (286–293) struck at Colchester (?) (Askew no. 221 – see bibliography for Chapter 9) with a schematic representation of a Roman galley with oars, oarsmen and a steering oar. The basic coin design dates from the reign of Hadrian (117–138) and was also used by Postumus (259–268) on whose coinage Carausius based a number of his types. Diameter 24mm

(fig.40 g). A steering oar was recovered from a well at Newstead (fig.40 f).

By road

The wreckage of ships and boats is rare enough in Britain, the traces of road transport virtually non-existent, but the roads are evidence of its importance. The fort of Newstead (*Trimontium*) north of Hadrian's Wall has produced a more or less complete wooden and iron ten-spoked cart-wheel (fig.40 c). However, the majority of wheels were probably made of no more than wooden planks strengthened with cross-bars. The components most likely to survive are the iron 'tyres', bronze or iron axlecaps (such as the bronze example in the form of a lion's head from the Lullingstone villa in Kent, fig.40 a) and linchpins (fig.40 b). Other metal fittings include bronze or iron rings known as terrets. These were used to pass a number of reins through in order to control a number of horses more easily. They were well-known in the Celtic period but these earlier versions tend to be bulkier than Roman types though their function was identical.

Horseshoes like those still in use were known as well as another variety called 'hipposandals' (fig.40 d). These were not nailed on but had protuberances which folded around the hoof. They might also have been used for driving cattle to market along the roads. Horse-bits, made of jointed rings and links, were known too, though stirrups were not invented until after the Roman period. Other bridle fittings included martin-gales. These were small metal objects often shaped like a cross which were designed to discourage a horse from throwing its head back. Horses' hooves were prepared for shoeing with a butteris (fig.28 g).

Reading and writing

Name-stamps

In a number of parts of this book the practice of name-stamping has been mentioned; for example the army's stamped tiles, the stamped mortaria or the oculists' stamps, and the stamped lead pigs. However apart from the oculists' stamps the actual dies used are virtually unknown. Two branding irons from London bear their owners' initials; c·v·c and m·m·a (Wheeler, 1929, 53). A third bears the letters MPBR, and this may stand for METALLA PROVINCIAE BRITANNIAE, and was probably used to stamp ingots of metals mined for the government.

Apart from these, and two mortaria name-stamp dies (see below), only the impressions of stamps survive. A wooden writing tablet from London bears the impression of an official branding iron. The stamp is circular and reads PROC AVG DEDERVNT around the edge and BRIT PROV in the centre, meaning 'issued by the Emperor's procurators in the province of Britain'. Military tile-stamps usually show traces of wood-grain and possibly a nail-head which suggest that the tile-stamp was 'T'-shaped, with the name carved into the head of the 'T' (Boon, 1984, 17). There seems to have been little concern for whether the name appeared the right way round on the product but the majority of stamps produced impressions in raised relief.

Some potters in Britain stamped their products. The most common examples are the first and second century mortaria potters of the south-east and at Hartshill-Mancetter (see p. 98 and Table IV). In one case it has been possible to identify a son taking his father's trade from mortarium stamps. The father was called Albinus, and worked at Brockley Hill between London and Verulamium from about AD 60–90; his son, Matugenus, worked there from about AD 80–125 (see Chapter 3, fig.57 and Table IV; K. Hartley in Frere, 1984, 286). One die used by Matugenus has survived and the die of a possible army potter called Julius Victor at Holt is known (see Wright, 1984, for a brief summary of the evidence and references). A number of mortaria dies were made and used by illiterate potters, a fact suggested by the meaningless jumble of letters or shapes in some cases. They served the same purpose, though, and must have had some use in distinguishing individuals' work, even if only at the post-firing sort-out. Potter die-stamping is also known at Colchester at the second-century samian kiln area (see Chapter 3).

Writing materials

Paper of a sort was known in the Roman world, but surviving examples are usually only found in Egypt where the exceptionally dry climate discourages decomposition. In any case paper was expensive; cheaper, and therefore more common as site finds, are the wooden writing tablets which have been found in a number of waterlogged deposits in Britain.

Wax and wood tablets consist of wooden leaves strung together, a little like a modern ring notebook, except that that the number of pages is usually no more than a handful. Alternatively, they may have been strung together in a row, folding up on top of one another like a concertina (fig.41a). Each wooden leaf was carefully worked to achieve a raised edge. The shallow recess, which amounted to most of the page, was then filled with wax which could be used as the writing surface. Some examples from London seem to have been made of imported woods, for example cedar from the Near East (Chapman and Straker in Dyson, 1986, 227). Writing can occasionally be discerned on such tablets when the *stylus* (see below) cut through the wax. One from London refers to someone called Crescens' obligation to pay money under terms of a claim (Wheeler, 1930, 54).

Wooden 'paper' tablets were made of extremely thin leaves of wood which were written on in ink, like paper. Normally the ink is no longer visible but infra-red and ultra-violet photography can reveal the contents. The bulk of the tablets from the fort at Vindolanda are of this kind. A large number have now been transcribed, and though often fragmentary, their contents have been translated, at least in part. They form a unique record of details of military life in Britain's northern frontier, ranging from details of military movements to the receipt of a gift of 40 oysters by the decurion Lucius (fig.42; see also Birley, 1977, and Bowman and Thomas, 1983).

Of course other materials were used for writing on, though these were not usually specifically designed for the purpose. The most common are fragments of pottery, especially samian, or pieces of tile and there are numerous examples known, such as an elaborate example from Silchester (fig.43). One from Billingsgate in London seems to be a fragment of a work roster – two names, Potitus and Boduacus, have been inscribed on the tile before firing and separated by a line (de la Bédoyère, 1986, 126, G7). At Carlisle a wooden army noticeboard, *tabella ansata*, has recently been found (Caruana, 1987). This is a simple wooden board but with a distinctive Roman design of 'fish-tails' on either side similar to some legionary tile-stamps (see Chapter 1). The notorious curses are discussed in Chapter 7 – usually these were sheets of lead, folded up and cast into a sacred pool or spring. Unlike their wax and wood counterparts they could not be re-used.

The Roman *stylus* was a very simple

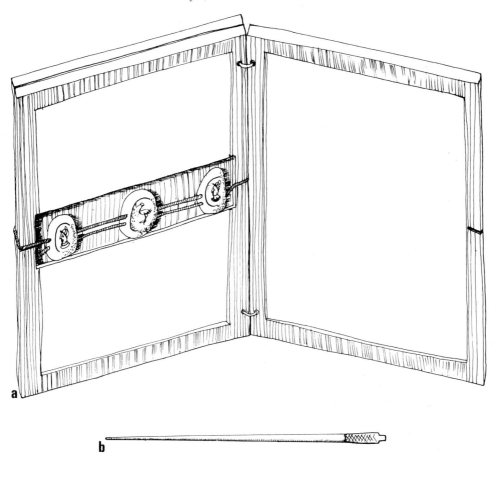

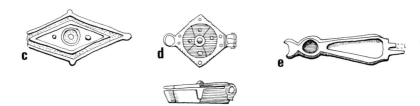

41 Written communications (two-thirds actual size except a):

a wooden triptych. These were 'books' of wood and wax writing tablets used to record contracts and transactions. However, their construction allowed a copy of the deal to be examined while allowing a sealed example to remain secure. In this way the parties could be confident that each would be unlikely to try and alter the terms of the contract in its favour. They are very rare (see Chapman in Bird *et alia*, for Southwark, volume II, 397 ff.) and the majority are simpler double-leavers, about 16cm in height

b bronze stylus from the palace at Fishbourne (after Cunliffe, 1971, 118, no. 135). The pointed end was used for writing on the wax tablets, the flattened end was used for erasing. Length 11.5cm

c bronze lozenge-shaped seal-box lid with enamelled decoration from Nettleton (after Wedlake, 1982, 207, no. 12)

d bronze rhomboid-shaped seal-box lid from Verulamium (after Frere, 1972, 206, no. 67). AD 130–150

e bronze tear-shaped seal-box lid. Unprovenanced British find

42 Vindolanda tablets:

a writing tablet from waterlogged deposits at Vindolanda, south of Hadrian's Wall. Nine fragments survive recording a letter from one Oppius Niger to one Crispinus (first line), regarding the movements of a detachment of the *cohors* I *Tungrorum* bearing letters for the governor. Their journey had probably begun at Vindolanda. The unit's name is clearly visible in at the beginning of the third line '*Ī·tungrorum . . .*'. Niger seems to have been commanding officer at *Bremetennacum* (Ribchester – mentioned in the fifth line) and had sent on the detachment; he writes to their commanding officer, Crispinus, to inform him (Bowman and Thomas, 1983, no. 30). Probably *c.* AD 95–105, diameter 18cm (photo and copyright: the British Museum)

43 Silchester tile graffito, reading *Pentacus perfidus, Campester, Lucilianus, Campanus, conticuere omnes.* The last two words open Book II of Virgil's Aeneid, so this may possibly be an exercise. However, the text is fairly meaningless, 'untrustworthy Pentacus, Campester, Lucilianus, Campanus, all fell silent'. Nevertheless, the writing is a good example of Romano-British cursive script and it is relatively easy to pick out the individual letters. The most different is 'e', which is written ' \\\'. The lower line is 8cm in length

b the back of another tablet plus two fragments, also from Vindolanda. This particular example is of exceptional interest because it appears to be a draft of a letter sent from Vindolanda and contains a reference to the provincial governor L. Neratius Marcellus. A military diploma records Marcellus as governor of Britain in *c.* 103, thus dating the tablet. The unnamed writer appears to be concerned about the conditions of his military service and writes from his winter quarters to a certain Gratius Crispinus who he believes to be in a position to intercede with the governor on his behalf. Interestingly Marcellus is also known from the letters of the Younger Pliny (Book 3, no. 8) because Pliny had obtained the post of military tribune for his friend Suetonius (the historian) from him. Towards the end of the letter the writer includes the evocative phrase '*haec tibi Vindolanda scribo*', which means 'I write this to you from Vindolanda'. The word *Vindolanda* can be read at the lower right of the main tablet, third line up, with *scribo* at the beginning of the next line on the lower left. Diameter 23cm (Bowman and Thomas, 1973, no. 37; photo and copyright: the British Museum)

---

instrument and really only consisted of a pointed tool (fig.41b). These were generally made of iron but so long as the tip was metal any suitable material could be used for the shaft, such as bone or wood. Pens, suitable for writing in ink rather than inscribing on wax, were made of reeds, quills or bronze and had split nibs. At the other end was some sort of expansion to assist in stirring ink.

Ink seems to have been carbon-based, and this is why infra-red photography will reveal traces of vanished writing (though various 'secret' inks like milk were also used). The most common form of container is an ink-pot made of samian ware (see Chapter 5). The form, Ritterling 13, is known throughout the whole period that samian ware was manufactured and imported to Britain. Essentially it is a simple pot with a small hole for inserting the pen (fig.52). However, within the pot there is a concealed lip designed to prevent spillage of ink should it be knocked over. Ink-pots of similar design and made of bronze are also known.

The small bronze seal-box, of varying shapes and often with enamelled decoration, is known from a large number of examples. The cord which fastened the document was passed through holes in the sides of the box. The wax was poured in and impressed with the seal (probably on a finger ring), the lid was closed and the seal was then protected (fig.41c, d, and e).

3

Household Life

Introduction

According to Tacitus, it was during the benign governorship of Agricola (AD 78–84), that the Romano-British were positively encouraged to enjoy the fruits of 'civilisation', *humanitas*, (*Agricola*, 21, 79). Of course this was not entirely true – Tacitus was setting out to praise his father-in-law's life and works. But there is no doubt that from the Flavian period (AD 69–96) on, the sheer quantity of household and personal items used in Roman Britain vastly increased. Nowhere is this more apparent than in London, which, as the major port of entry for imports and imigrants, received a vast quantity of goods into its warehouses (Milne, 1985). In time the rate of imports dropped in favour of Romano-British products but the contrast between the towns of late first century AD Britain and the same areas 50 years before is really very striking – it was as if a consumer revolution had taken place; in relative terms the impact on the household was as great as the one which has taken place in modern Britain when compared to the 1930s. However, it took considerably longer for this revolution to spread beyond the towns.

Food and drink

The range of vessels concerned with the consumption of food and drink extend from the very rare silver plate of treasure hoards, such as the fourth-century group from Mildenhall, to the most basic forms of coarse pottery which appear on almost every site. Broadly speaking there are three types worth considering:

1. fine tableware made in metal, glass or high quality pottery.
2. kitchen wares made of metal, glass or pottery.
3. container vessels for transportation of goods such as oil, fish-products and wine, and storage in the kitchen, such as lid-seated jars.

Distribution of vessels

Fine tablewares were made in a number of different places, but they tend to have relatively wide patterns of distribution. That is, exact parallels may occur thousands of miles apart. For example, the samian pottery products of South Gaul are found as far apart as North Africa and Scotland (figs.51 and 52). They were relatively expensive and difficult to make, so such wares as these came from a limited number of sources, requiring special raw materials and skills. They must therefore have commanded high prices which overcame the cost of transportation. The mere fact that they were expensive may have made them prestigious household possessions. We know that red-slipped fine pottery wares were highly regarded because Pliny the Elder recorded the fact in his *Naturalis historiae* (Book 35, 160), written in the first century AD.

At the other extreme each variety of coarse pottery kitchen wares may have a very restricted pattern of distribution for the simple reason that being cheap and easy to make, it was simpler and more economical to manufacture locally than transport them from a distance. Some marketing models have been developed which show this (Hodder 1974, 340ff). At Portchester, one of the 'Saxon Shore' forts mainly in use from the late third century to the late fourth, it was estimated by the excavators that the bulk of this type of pottery came from no more than 15 miles away (Fulford in Cunliffe, 1975, 301). This seems to have been the case for all Romano-British towns. However, there exist within this category a number of wares with a limited function, made by specialist potters. They have patterns of distribution which are similar to those of fine wares. In addition some manufacturers of mundane kitchen wares seem to have secured long-term contracts to supply the Roman army – this certainly appears to have been the case for the Dorset black-burnished pottery industry (see Chapter 1, p. 47, and below, p. 93). Its distribution pattern likewise resembles that of fine wares.

The map in fig.50 shows where the principal sources of domestically manufactured Romano-British pottery were sited. Some of these were far more important than others, but it is striking that almost without exception these sources were on or near rivers which ran to the south and east coasts. Most are near major towns, and a number are also on main road routes.

The pottery containers such as *amphorae* belong somewhere in between fine and coarse wares (fig.59). Not necessarily valued in themselves, they nevertheless could cross the Roman Empire for the sake of their contents. Types from the Eastern Empire and North Africa occur occasionally in Britain whilst others from Spain and Italy are relatively common.

Tableware

Roman fine tableware has always attracted more attention than the coarse kitchen wares, though in recent years coarse wares have been more intensively studied. The reasons are obvious. The metal items are frequently impressive, decorated objects. The pottery wares are sometimes decorated, the slip can have a striking appearance to the eye and the forms are consistent and relatively easy to classify. These were prestigious possessions, designed as much for display as for use. The range of forms was extensive but most belong to the main categories of bowls, vases or jugs, dishes, platters and cups.

As artefacts there are four major points of interest. Some fine tablewares are amongst the best surviving examples of Roman craftsmanship whether made in Britain or elsewhere; as such, they give an idea of contemporary aesthetic standards and material aspirations. The function of the tableware can supply some information about manners and diet. To the archaeologist the distinctive styles of different classes of tableware, particularly pottery, can provide invaluable dating information.

There are not many useful details surviving from ancient authors concerning such a day-to-day activity as eating. But it is clear that in Roman life the evening was the time for the most elaborate meal, and that was an important social occasion for the family. Known as *cena*, this could extend from being the normal main meal of the day to an outrageous all-night imperial banquet. An amusing description of a particularly vulgar gathering can be found in Petronius' *Satyricon* (31, 3 – 34, 4).

Sources of tablewares

Roman Britain was supplied with fine tablewares from the continent and the province itself. But it should be remembered that apart from towns Britain shows few signs of widespread civilian wealth in the archaeological record until well into the second century. Little of the luxurious gold and silver material described in some books concerned with Roman art and wealth came to, or at least has been found in, Britain. This was a province with a large militarised zone, insecure and unpredictable. It took time for disposable wealth to accumulate in a new, and undeveloped, province. As a result, while some exceptional pieces have been found in Britain, such as the celebrated Mildenhall treasure (plates 5, 6 and Painter, 1977), they are even rarer than elsewhere and usually of fourth-century date.

It is almost impossible to be certain of the exact origin of most metal tablewares; analysis depends on stylistic considerations and the presence or absence of continental parallels. Even if traits common to another part of the empire are identified it remains possible that the craftsman lived in Britain but had been trained elsewhere. Glass presents some similar problems, but in addition its various forms can be extremely difficult to identify in a fragmentary state; it is also prone to deterioration (fig.49, and plates 8, 9).

Pottery fine wares are easier to deal with because in many cases the actual manufacturing sites have been discovered. In addition the fabric of the pottery can indicate its origin and allow other examples to be identified. In the first and second centuries the main sources of supply were the giant samian ware manufacturing centres in Gaul though some additional types were also imported. By the third century, in response to the collapse of the Gaulish samian industries, a number of Romano-British potters, particularly those of the Oxfordshire area, developed and expanded their repertoires in response to the demand (fig.54) continuing the red-slipped fine ware tradition in Britain itself. Thereafter this source and others, such as the Nene Valley industry, dominated the market in Britain.

Problems with tablewares

Residual material

One major problem complicates an understanding of fine tablewares. As valued items they had a tendency to long life and can occur in deposits as residual sherds, though this also results from the disturbance of earlier rubbish by later occupants of a site. This means that the fine wares can be significantly, and identifiably, older than the deposits in which they are found. This is especially true of metal tablewares but also applies to pottery. At Verulamium this was believed to be the case with much of the samian (Hartley in Frere, 1972, 216). At the New Fresh Wharf in London some of the samian deposited in the third century quay fill may have represented unsold stock from demolished warehouses which may have been as much as 50 years old (Bird in Dyson, 1986, 139), though explaining this is a problem in itself.

Dated deposits

To complicate matters there is a serious lack of closely-dated deposits from the late second century onwards. Prior to this date most types of fine pottery wares, samian in particular, can be associated with levels on sites known, or thought, to be involved in specific historical events. The most notable are the Colchester shop, apparently burnt down in the Boudican Revolt of AD 60 (Hull, 1958, 152ff, and 198ff; this has been questioned recently, see Millett, 1987); the Pompeii hoard (Atkinson 1914); and the deposits from the Walls of Hadrian and Antoninus Pius (Stanfield and Simpson, 1958, various).

Selective rubbish

There is undoubtedly a difference between the relative proportions of goods in use in the Roman period and those remaining in the archaeological record. For the most part broken pottery is useless and it was discarded (except for some samian ware bowls, and occasional examples of coarse wares). Its survival is thus almost certain, and it merely waits to be found. Additional information comes from the kiln sites, when they are found, in the form of waster heaps of contemporary sherds and kiln loads which have been fired incorrectly and abandoned. Metal goods are completely different because broken, damaged or stolen vessels might be melted down. Broken glass was frequently re-used in the manufacture of new glass. It is unfortunate that while glass, silver, bronze and pewter tableware was certainly extensively used in Roman Britain the surviving examples are too few for us to be certain of estimating their real importance in relation to pottery.

Metal tablewares
Silver and gold

Most of the surviving groups of silver plate are unlikely to represent anything approaching a 'typical' well-to-do household service in Roman Britain. Many are of 'late' (i.e. third and fourth century) date and there is often an overtly religious tone to the silver plate – it may well be that these represent temple or cult collections, or they appear to have been the possessions of exceptionally wealthy people, such as the remarkable Corbridge lanx (fig.44).

The most famous Romano-British hoard of plate, from Mildenhall in Suffolk, consists of unusually fine items, including the famous Great Dish which is over 60cm (2ft) wide and weighs more than eight kgm (17 lb 10 oz) (plates 5, 6 and Painter, 1977). The Water Newton group of vessels and votive objects is more likely to be of religious significance as the earliest known Christian silver plate in the Roman world (fig.118; plate 26). The hoards of damaged silver items from Coleraine and Traprain Law (Curle, 1923), both outside the province, may represent items stolen from a number of sources within Roman Britain by raiders. Alternatively they may have been used as bribes to keep the peace, or as payment to barbarian mercenaries. At the other end of the time scale is the set of silver cups from Hockwold in Norfolk which on stylistic grounds could be as early as the beginning of the first century, perhaps a soldier's collection. However, it has been suggested that the *style* may have endured and they could be as much as a century later (fig.45; Johns, 1986). Even earlier are the silver cups of Republican date found in Celtic chieftains' graves at Welwyn (Stead, 1967, 20–3).

Bronze and pewter

Bronze (or 'copper-alloy') and pewter items are known from more mundane contexts and are more frequently found as single items – there is also a reasonable body of evidence for manufacture in Roman Britain itself (see

45 The hoard of first century silver from Hockwold. The exact date and source of the silver is unknown but the style is Augustan (26 BC–AD 14) though they may well have been made up to a century later. Heights range from 6-9cm (Johns, 1986; photo and copyright: the British Museum)

Above **44** Silver lanx, the only surviving component of a hoard of silver plate found in the 1730s in the banks of the River Tyne west of Corbridge. At least two other vessels were 'speedily committed to the melting pot' (Collingwood Bruce). The piece is one of a number of similar examples known from the late Roman Empire and forms part of the larger series of fourth-century plate including the Mildenhall treasure (plates 5, 6). Another lanx, now lost, is known from Risley Park, Derbyshire (Johns, 1981). The Corbridge lanx appears to depict Apollo, Artemis, Leto and Asteria Ortygia – deities associated with the sacred Aegean island of Delos. It has been suggested that the scene commemorates the visit to Delos by the Emperor Julian in 363 during his policy of revived official paganism. Whether the piece should be regarded as an example of fine domestic plate, or religious temple plate, is a matter for debate. Diameter 48cm.

46 A silver skillet inlaid with gold from the Backworth treasure, Northumberland. It bears an inscription reading MATR[ibus] FAB[ius] DUBIT[atus], meaning 'To the Mother Goddesses, Fabius Dubitatus'. Length 21cm (photo and copyright: The British Museum)

Below **47** Pewter tableware from various sites in Britain. Clockwise from left: jug (unprovenanced); plate (Stamford, Lincolnshire); jug (Selsey, West Sussex); cup (Cirencester); flanged bowl (Helvisick, Cornwall), cup (Lakenheath, Suffolk). All third to fourth century. Height of jugs 24–28cm

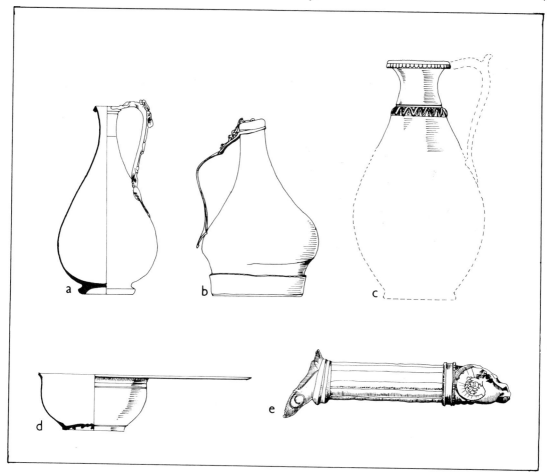

48 Bronze vessels (¼ except **e**, ½):

a jug from Verulamium, made by casting and then turning on a lathe. The handle, decorated with a stylised bovine head at the base, was made separately and then soldered on. Found in an early fourth-century level (after Frere, 1972, fig.43, no. 143)

b flagon from the 'Temple-Mausoleum' at Lullingstone villa with a cap attached by a chain. Both handle and base were made separately. Not later than *c.* AD 300 (after Meates, 1987, fig.36)

c neck of jug from the site of Christ's Hospital, London. Probably third-fourth century (after Wheeler, 1930, 117)

d simple *patera* from Bermondsey, London showing the grooves formed by turning the base on a lathe. The handle is stamped PRVFC, probably for *P[ublius] Ruf[inus] C. . . [fecit]*. Probably second century (after Wheeler, 1930, 118)

e handle from a bronze *patera*. Found at Verulamium in an unstratified level. The cast handle is hollow and decorated with a ram's head terminal (after Frere, 1972, fig.44, no. 148)

Chapter 2), for example at Camerton in Avon (Wedlake, 1958); Nettleton in Wiltshire (Wedlake, 1982; fig.31e); and Ickham in Kent (Young, in Detsicas, 1981). Typical bronze products were jugs with elaborate decorated handles, dishes and bowls (fig.48 and plate 7). Bronze items could be made by hammering and raising, suitable for dishes, bowls and jugs, or casting, suitable for jug handles and more complicated items. Cast bronze usually contains a high proportion (though not exceeding 30 per cent) of lead to help the process. Pewter, an alloy of lead and tin, is always cast and interestingly seems to be unique to fourth-century Roman Britain, where it was probably popular as a cheap substitute for the rare and expensive silver plate. A hoard of pewter tableware found at Appleshaw, Hampshire consisted of dishes, bowls, cups, and a flagon. Pewter material is also known from a number of other sites (fig.47).

Glass tableware

Glass tableware is rarely found in a condition approaching its original state because it is fragile and prone to chemical deterioration. Like metal tableware, high-quality glass was an expensive possession. The sources of glass tableware were wide and it is very difficult to be certain where any specific item originated. However, industries existed in the Rhineland, Gaul, Italy and the Eastern Empire (notably Egypt) and probably in Britain as well, for example at Mancetter, Wroxeter and Caister-by-Norwich. The supply of glass had become vastly increased by the end of the first century BC with the discovery of glass-blowing, which was much faster than casting and therefore cheaper. By the third and fourth centuries it was increasingly used in place of high-quality pottery, probably because tastes were

49 Glass (¼ scale):
a typical household bottle with separate handle from a late first-century deposit at Richborough (after Bushe-Fox, 1947, pl. 68)
b a flask found in a late first-century deposit at Richborough (after Bushe-Fox, 1947, pl. 68)
c cylindrical bottle with two separately-made handles in the form of dolphins, found in the 'Temple-Mausoleum' at the Lullingstone villa forming part of the grave goods (after Meates, 1987, fig.56)
d globular ribbed jar with turned-over rim from a late third-century deposit at Verulamium (after Frere, 1984, fig.67, 105)
e small spouted jug from a late fourth, early fifth-century deposit at Verulamium (after Frere, 1984, fig.67, 104)
f beaker with facet-cut decoration of Flavian-Trajanic date from the Antonine fire deposit at Verulamium (after Frere, 1972, fig.77, 42)
g moulded bowl with two separate handles from an unstratified level at Verulamium (after Frere, 1972, fig.74, 5)
h pillar-moulded bowl from an early second-century level at Verulamium though the type is well-known from first-century deposits (after Frere, 1972, fig.74, 4)
i beaker with zoned decoration, one of a set found sealed in a cellar level by the end of the third century at Verulamium (after Frere, 1972, fig.78, 52)
j cylindrical bowl with trailed ridge and everted rim, from a late third-, early fourth-century level at Verulamium (after Frere, 1984, fig.64, 70, text, 158, 132)

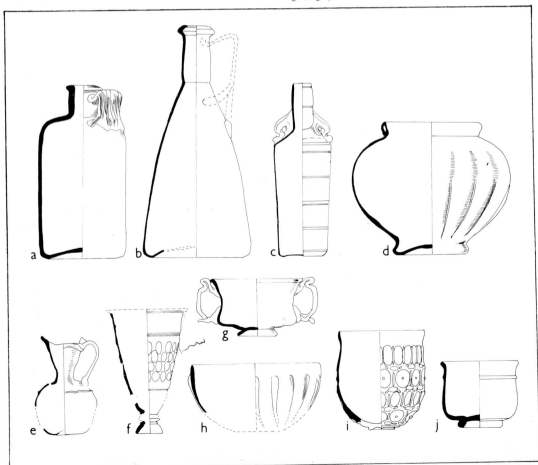

changing and it may have become cheaper as the industry became more widespread.

The typical range of vessels was not as wide as those of metal and pottery but included bottles (see below, p. 98), flagons, jugs, beakers and bowls (fig. 49, plates 8, 9). As with pottery, the majority were, however, simple storage containers. There were wide variations in the detail of shape and rim form. Colour range was also wide, including blue, amber, green, and yellow. Decoration was achieved in a number of ways including blowing the glass into a mould. The technique of casting was also used, for example to make the common pillar-moulded bowls. Other methods such as cut decoration and trailing molten glass across the surface were employed. The effects were imitated with mould, barbotine and incision decoration by samian potters (see below, Harden, 1969, and Price in Strong and Brown, 1976).

Pottery tablewares (also known as fine wares)

Table II (p. 214) shows the sources of fine pottery wares supplied to, or made in, Roman Britain according to the length of time that the various industries were in operation. The map on fig.50 shows where the Romano-British fine (and major coarse) ware industries were sited.

Samian ware

The red-slipped ware tradition

Pottery tablewares are probably best interpreted as relatively cheap substitutes for metal wares and glass vessels. Even so, the products could be of high quality both in terms of material and decoration. Throughout the Roman period there was a long-established tradition of red-gloss wares which dated back to the Hellenistic period. Pliny the Elder commented 'Among the table services samian pottery is still spoken highly of; this reputation is also retained by Arezzo in Italy . . .' (*Naturalis historiae* 35, 160, quoted in Peacock, 1982, 114). 'Samian' was the word used in antiquity to describe these wares but it is now only used in reference to the red ware products of Gaul. The origin of the word is uncertain but may relate to ceramic products of the island of Samos, and the Latin word *samiare* which means to polish. The red effect was achieved by using a clay containing iron oxide for fabric and slip and firing the pottery in an oxidising atmosphere.

Even when the Gaulish samian industries finally ceased significant production (by the mid-third century at the latest) the red-slipped ware tradition remained firmly entrenched in pottery manufacture. A number of regional industries throughout the empire continued to make similar products, especially the African red-slipped ware potters of Tunisia (Hayes, 1972). In Britain the Oxfordshire potters represented this change of source; whether the Romano-British regarded these as equivalent, we do not know.

The Arretine industry

In the Roman world the potters of the Arezzo region in Italy established themselves in the Western Empire around the end of the first century BC in this rôle (Oswald and Pryce, 1920, reprinted 1965). But by the 40s AD they had been by-passed by the samian potters of Gaul whose products are by far and away the most important fine wares found in Roman Britain, although Arretine wares are very occasionally found on early Romano-British sites (for example at Fishbourne: see G.B. Dannell, in Cunliffe, 1971, II, 260ff).

Gaulish samian

Gaulish samian is an apparently homogeneous ware but this is far from the truth. Its production lasted for over 200 years so not surprisingly there were considerable changes. For the sake of convenience scholars have identified three main geographical areas of production. In each of these there were a number of centres making the pottery. From the 30s up to around 110 the potteries of La Graufesenque in South Gaul monopolised the market in Britain, Gaul, Germany, Spain and North Africa, producing huge quantities of plain and decorated forms.

From around AD 100 to the end of the second century the factories of Central Gaul (at Les Martres-de-Veyre from about 100–125, and Lezoux from about 120–200) dominated, though the geographical spread of their products was smaller, confined mainly to Gaul and Britain. From some time in the first half of the second century up to some time in the early to mid-third century the market was shared with the disparate and individual centres of East Gaul, though as far as Britain was concerned East Gaul was only a minor source. The names and dates of some of the major potters of Central Gaul are given in Table III. The fabrics are unique to each source, but the forms are very similar though decoration,

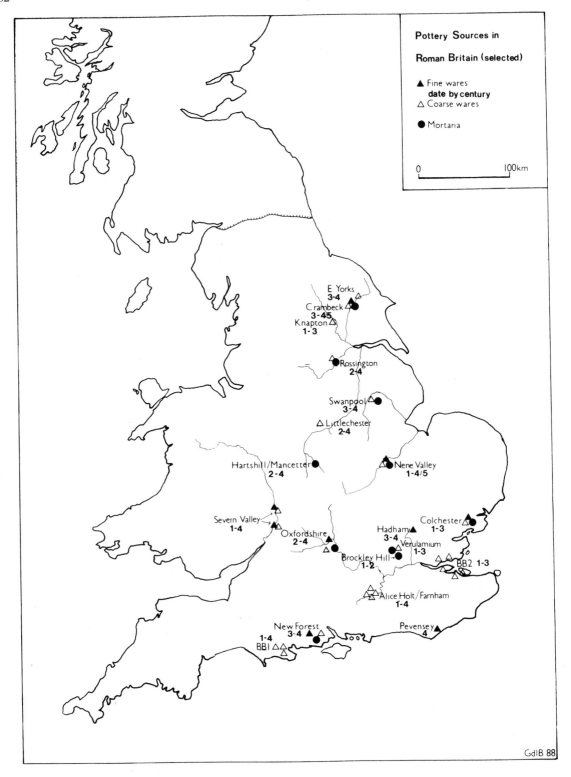

Pottery Sources in

Roman Britain (selected)

▲ Fine wares
  date by century
△ Coarse wares

● Mortaria

0   100km

E Yorks
3-4
Crambeck
3-4/5
Knapton △
1-3

△ Rossington
2-4

Swanpool △
3-4

△ Littlechester
2-4

Hartshill/Mancetter ●
2-4

▲ Nene Valley
1-4/5

Severn Valley ▲
1-4

Colchester
1-3

Oxfordshire
2-4

Hadham ▲
3-4

Verulamium
1-3

Brockley Hill
1-2

BB2 **1-3**

Alice Holt/Farnham
1-4

New Forest
3-4

Pevensey
4

1-4
BB1 △△
△△

GdIB **88**

when used, no more than related. Production was apparently not regular, each source experiencing a growth in popularity, a climax and then decline. Even those gradients were probably very erratic (Marsh in Anderson and Anderson, 1981; de la Bédoyère, 1988).

Romano-British samian

Such was the demand for samian in Roman Britain that at least two attempts were made to manufacture the ware in Britain itself. At Colchester, around the year 160, about 14 to 20 potters from East Gaul built a samian kiln and manufactured plain and decorated forms (Hull, 1958; de la Bédoyère, 1988, fig.35). At least three different, but anonymous, styles of decoration are known. As might be expected the products bear close resemblance to East Gaulish samian. The project was not apparently sucessful and very few products of these kilns have been recognized outside the Colchester area. The reasons for failure are not clear but local clays were not entirely suitable, and there may have been problems with invading an already established trading network. On the face of it, Colchester samian should have been successful because of the reduced transport costs but this was evidently not the case. The failure raises interesting questions about protective practices, and the prestige of true Gaulish samian.

One other Romano-British samian potter has been identified. Known as the 'Aldgate-Pulborough potter' from two of the first sites where his products were first identified, his samian is remarkable for its poor quality (Simpson, 1952; Webster, 1975; de la Bédoyère, 1988, fig.36). The motifs are copied from Gaulish samian but are slightly smaller, indicating that he made his decorative details by moulding the decorative details (see fig.35 a) from imported bowls. However, his manufacturing process was casual and included superimposing details, scratching the bowl surface, leaving liberal traces of fingerprints and over-firing some of his products. It is possible that his name was Verianus because a plain form Dragendorff 18/31 has been found in identical fabric at Verulamium bearing this stamp (Dickinson in Frere, 1984,

180, S61) and found in a context dating to c. 140–155. Again the interest lies in the attempt to find a place in a thriving market. Although only about 15 examples of this potter's products have been found they are much more widespread than Colchester products, occurring in Bristol, Silchester and Chichester as well as London and Pulborough.

The finding of a mould fragment in York in the style of a Gaulish Trajanic samian potter known as Drusus I (known as the style 'X-3' before a signed bowl was discovered) has been considered evidence of an attempt by this potter to establish a branch factory in Britain, or the purchase of a mould by a Romano-British potter (RCHM York, Vol. I, 63b, pl.31 and Swan, 1988, 49, plate 6). In fact no associated evidence of pottery manufacture was found, nor have any bowls from the mould, and it is more likely that the mould entered Britain in more modern times.

While not usually considered a 'formal' part of the Romano-British samian industry, it is worth considering that the Oxfordshire potters undoubtedly manufactured some wares in the spirit of the red-slipped tradition. However, unlike the samian industry, the Oxfordshire industry manufactured a wider range of wares, including grey kitchen wares, but with far less sophisticated attempts at decoration and with distribution restricted to Britain (see below, p. 90).

Samian forms

Samian ware was used extensively in both civilian and military sites. The function of samian ware is self-evident in the forms which include variations of cups, dishes, bowls and vases – in other words the full range of items suitable for refined table use (figs.51 and 52, plates 10, 12), or for those who aspired to refined table manners but could not afford silver or glass. Although the range of forms was huge (Oswald and Pryce, 1920) the majority of types are rare and a small number constitute the greater part of the surviving evidence, typically Forms 18, 27, 29, 31, 33, and 37. Despite this the way in which the industry was organised varied from area to area and probably amongst the potters themselves.

The range of samian includes a number of specialist forms for more mundane activities. These range from what appears to be a child's feeding bottle (P. Webster, 1981, 249ff), the Dragendorff 45 mortaria (mixing bowl) form

50 This map shows the main, and some of the minor, sources of pottery made in Roman Britain throughout the period. However, it remains a virtual certainty that every centre of population, even small ones, would have supported at least a cottage-industry level of pottery manufacture

Gdela B87

51 Samian – principal decorated forms (about 1/3 scale). These are the principal mould-decorated forms of samian ware drawn as half bowls in order to show as much information as possible (**a-e**, South Gaulish; **f-i** and **k** – Central Gaulish; **j** – East Gaul):

a Form 29; left, Claudian-Neronian 50–65; right, early Flavian 75–85

b Form 37; left, early Flavian 70–85; right, later Flavian 85–110

c Form 30; left, Claudian-Neronian 43–60; right, Flavian 75–100

d Form 67, late first century

e Form 78, late first century

f Form 37; left, Trajanic, 100–125, Les Martres-de-Veyre, style of Drusus I; right, Hadrianic, 120–145, Quintilianus group

g Form 64, Hadrianic, 120-145, style of Libertus

h Form 37; left, Antonine 145–180, style of Servus I; right, later Antonine 160–200, style of Doeccus

i Form 72 vase with appliqué leaves and *barbotine* animals and tendrils. About 150–200

j Form 37; left, Rheinzabern, later Antonine 150–190, Cobnertus III; right, Trier, later Antonine 150-190, style of Dexter

k Form 30; left, Hadrianic 120–145, by Butrio; right, Antonine 145–180, by Cinnamus

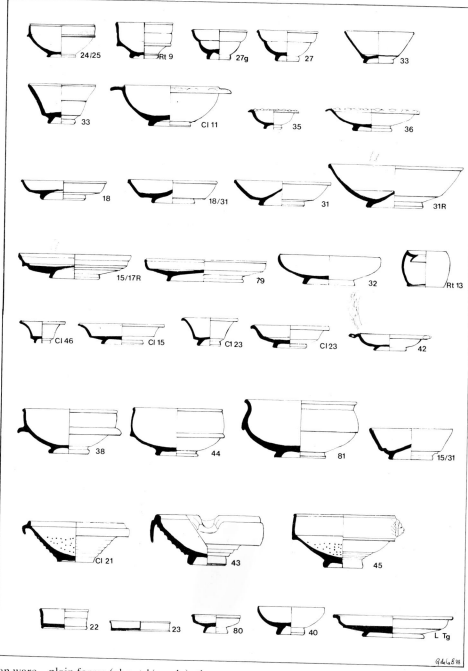

52 Samian ware – plain forms (about ¼ scale). the form numbers are mostly those of the Dragendorff-Déchelette-Knorr-Walters sequence. Others are: Cl = Curle; L = Ludowici; Rt = Ritterling. R denotes a rouletted circle on the vessel floor. All dates are approximate; the forms themselves are subject to considerable size and minor detail variation. Vessels made in East Gaul may have arrived up to the mid-third century but in general samian ceases to arrive after around 200–210: 24/25 and Rt 9 Claudian-Neronian; 27g (base groove) 1st century; 27 100–160; 33 1st century (without groove), 2nd century (with); Cl 11 70–140 (latest examples have a hooked flange); 35 and 36 throughout the period; 18 50–100; 18/31 100–140; 31 140+; 31R 160+; 15/17R 1st century; 79 160+; 32 150+; Rt 13 inkwell throughout the period; Cl 46 and 15 mostly 2nd century; Cl 23 (two types) 70+; 42 70–140; 38 125+; 44 125+; 81 120–180; 15/31 150–175; Cl 21 150+; 43 170+; 45 170+; 22 and 23 43–100; 80 160+; 40 150+; L Tg 160+

with distinctive appliqué lion's head spout (fig.52; Bird in Dyson, 1956, *New Fresh Wharf London*, 178ff) and even oil-lamps (Grew in Dyson, *op. cit.*, 204). Only the mortaria forms are at all frequent as site finds, though these are largely confined in date to the end of the second century and the third century. As items designed with a mundane purpose, it is interesting to find this kitchen activity associated with what was the best established fine tableware. This raises the question of the samian industry experiencing problems with demand and perhaps seeking new lines in order to sustain their business. Certainly these mortaria forms were largely manufactured in the late second century and third century. It has been suggested that these were purely ornamental forms, but some examples show signs of heavy grinding wear.

A number of decorative techniques were employed on some forms to imitate the effect of decoration on metal and glass, but the vast majority of samian was undecorated. Decorative techniques include mould, appliqué, barbotine, incised and rouletted decoration (figs.51 and 52). However, this subject is far too complex to enter into here, and the reader in search of more detailed information should consult some of the specialist works on the subject (for example Stanfield and Simpson, 1958; Johns, 1977, and de la Bédoyère, 1988).

Dating samian

Naturally samian does not date itself. However, there are two aspects of this ware which permit cross-dating from deposits of known date. These are the use of moulded decoration and the habit of placing the manufacturers' names on the products. This is a complex field of analysis and we are far from a complete understanding of the industry. Broadly speaking, it relies on the assumption that it is possible to break up decoration into individual styles, and separate out individual potters by their names. By associating enough products of any one individual, even if in the case of some decorated forms he is anonymous, with a number of dated sites, it should be possible to fix an approximate period for that potter's working life (see Table III). The other decorative techniques are not distinctive in this way.

Repaired and re-used samian

Proof of samian's value to the owner is evident in the fact that it was occasionally repaired when broken instead of being discarded. Very few other classes of pottery are ever found repaired. The methods of repair involved drilling holes in the parts to be joined and tying them together with strips of lead or copper-alloy; or bridging the fracture with 'X'-shaped rivets (see de la Bédoyère, 1988, 56, fig.47). The significance lies in the fact that it was clearly cheaper to go to this trouble than to replace the bowl, or that the individual bowl was considered so valuable that repair was essential.

Samian ware was sometimes re-used. This could involve adapting the form when damaged or employing the raw material to manufacture new items. Re-used forms are not uncommon. Typical of these are Dragendorff 27 cups which had had the upper lip removed and the remaining receptacle used as a miniature mortar, perhaps for grinding foodstuffs, cosmetics, medicines or paint. The Dragendorff 33 cup, a ubiquitous form, provided a useful base which might be employed as a small lid for another vessel, or perhaps as a gaming piece. Gaming pieces were also made by filing down sherds to a small circular disc. Similar sized sherds have been found in use as tesserae in mosaics. Even in the Middle Ages samian was considered to have medicinal qualities and it was ground down into compounds.

Gaulish samian ware has always dominated the study of fine wares in Britain because of its prodigious quantities and the unique information it bears in terms of individual decorative styles and potters' names. Nevertheless samian ware, though far from being an entirely homogeneous commodity, was only one type of Roman fine pottery tableware used in Roman Britain.

Other fine pottery wares in the first and second centuries

Imported fine pottery wares (fig.53)

During the period that samian was supplied to Britain, i.e. AD 43 to about 250, a number of other fine wares, usually called colour-coated wares, were also imported (plate 12). Unfortunately the number of examples is small in relation to samian, and few bear the clues of name-stamps and individual decorative styles which have helped the study of samian. For most of this time the rôle of the army was extremely important. The pre-Flavian legionary fortress at Usk in South Wales has produced some particularly

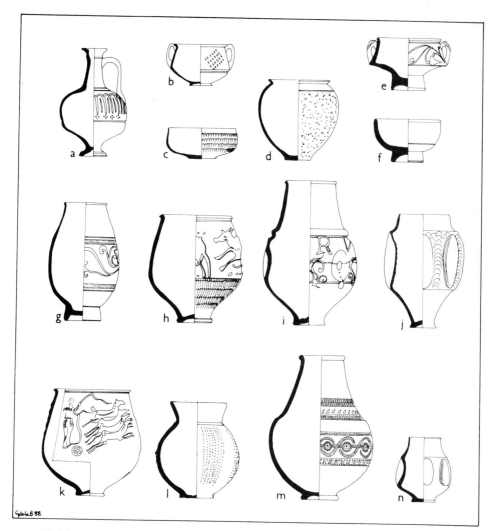

53 Fine ware drinking vessels – variations of types are considerable, and different sources manufactured many varieties. This is only a selection (about ¼ scale):

a & b Central Gaulish glazed ware made in a similar area but imported at a much earlier date, *c.* AD 43–70. They are unusual for Roman pottery in being covered with a greenish lead glaze (after Anderson)

c & d Lyons colour-coat ware, also of early date but with a more conventional brown slip. Decorative techniques include rough-cast, scaling and rustication (after Anderson)

e, f & g Central Gaulish colour-coated ware. Probably made in the same workshops that turned out colossal quantities of samian. However, the products were not stamped and bear a distinctive black-glass slip, occasionally decorated *en barbotine*. They date from *c.* 170-220 (after Richardson in Dyson, 1986 New Fresh Wharf)

h Cologne beaker with *barbotine* decoration of animals chasing one another. A blackish slip applied once after the *barbotine* work covers a white fabric. Date: 70s + for Cologne products with hunt cups appearing in the second century (after Richardson in Dyson, 1986)

i East Gaulish black colour-coated ware principally manufactured in and around Trier from about 180–250. The most common decoration was simple rouletting but occasional examples such as this one bear slogans, in this case, DA MERVM, 'Give me more wine' (after Wilson in Frere, 1972 *Verulamium* I)

j Nene Valley folded and indented beaker. The Nene Valley beakers take a number of forms including the well-known 'hunt cups' *en barbotine*. The beakers dominated the British market from *c.* 150 to the end of the period (after Wilson in Frere, 1972 *Verulamium* I)

k Colchester beaker with reddish-brown colour-coat bearing *barbotine* decoration of charioteers in a circus scene. More common are the beakers with simple rough-cast decoration. They date from *c.* 140–220

l 'Poppy beaker' manufactured at a number of sites in the vicinity of London, including Highgate Wood and Upchurch. They have a black or grey burnished surface decorated with rectangular groups of dots. About 100–160 (after Marsh and Tyers)

m Oxfordshire beaker with rouletted decoration in a number of bands, *c.* 240+ (after Wedlake, 1982)

n New Forest beaker with indented walls, late third, early fourth century (after Swan in Detsicas, 1973)

valuable evidence of early imported fine wares apart from samian (see Chapter 1). However, some of the major towns have also produced valuable deposits, particularly London, Verulamium and Colchester.

The evidence from Usk

Up until about the year AD 70 non-samian fine wares came from a number of areas in Gaul, the Rhineland and Italy. The industry at Lyons is of particular importance because of its apparent close association with the army. At Usk the majority of non-samian fine wares were from Lyons, especially the hemispherical cup forms. The cup is a useful dating tool because it seems to have passed out of use about the year AD 70 following the demise of the Lyons industry (fig.25c). This seems to have been because of a city fire, the civil war disruptions of AD 68–69 and a general change in fashions. Thereafter beakers became the normal drinking vessel in the northern provinces, which means that excavated cup forms, even if unstratified, can probably be attributed to the period AD 43–70, though the residual factor should not be forgotten (Greene, 1979).

Gaulish fine wares

One of the most distinctive early fine ware types is the lead-glazed ware from the Allier valley in Central Gaul (west of Lyons). Lead-glazing was not a common Roman ceramic practice and resembles mediaeval pottery in surface appearance (fig.53 a, b). Two other distinctively early types are fine wares manufactured in the province of *Gallia Belgica*, or modern Belgium. These are known as *terra nigra* – black-grey polished ware, and *terra rubra* – orange/brown/ buff ware. Plates, cups and dishes were made in both wares by potters who also stamped their names on some of their products, for example Julios (Rigby in Detsicas, 1973). The forms show that much inspiration had been drawn from the Arretine and samian industries, but these northern versions were not long-lived. By the 50s *terra rubra* had passed out of fashion and by the 70s *terra nigra* had suffered a similar fate while the South Gaulish samian potters went from strength to strength.

It is also worth noting that continental fine wares, particularly samian, inspired Romano-British potters in the south-east to produce copies of the most popular forms in a grey-black fabric with a polished surface. These are distinct from those manufactured by the army for its own use (see Swan, 1988, 62, fig. II, nos 117–19).

Imported and Romano-British beakers

Until the end of the second century the majority of these imported non-samian fine wares appeared in the form of beakers made in the Rhineland, particularly in the Cologne and Trier areas, and in a number of centres in the region of the Central Gaulish samian industry (fig.53 e-i). Some also originated in Britain with large industries developing at Colchester and in the Nene Valley, near Peterborough, each with their own particular styles (fig.53 j-n). Their fabrics and slips are the clues to their origin but the picture is a confused one and is only beginning to become clear with the recent publication of some important sites and studies (for example the New Fresh Wharf: Richardson in Dyson, 1986, 96ff; also Arthur and Marsh, 1978, and Anderson, 1980).

These beakers are of similar forms and may have been designed for drinking while sitting upright, instead of lying down as was the Mediterranean custom. Samian 'cup' forms, if they were indeed used for drinking, are more appropriate to Mediterranean habits, so these beakers may have satisfied a particular demand, a rare hole in a market almost comprehensively covered by the astute samian potters. The Rhenish beakers, for example those made at Trier, indicate their purpose with their enthusiastic mottos appropriate to intoxicated company – *Da merum!* (give me more wine), *Vivatis!* (long life) or *Svavis* (sweet) are amongst those known (fig.53 i). A *Svavis* beaker seems to have played an important part in the ritual concealment of previous owners' ancestor busts at the Lullingstone villa (Meates, 1979, 36, and 1987, fig.85 no. 362) and is one of a large number of contemporary beakers from that site.

Other red-slipped wares

It is also worth noting the occasional examples of so-called 'Pompeian red ware'. These appear in Britain in deposits dating from AD 43 to the end of the first century. The name implies a single industry but the only unifying factor is the range of forms of bowls, plates and lids covered with a red slip. They were made in a number of areas, notably the Pompeii region of Italy, but also including Gaul, the Eastern Empire and even in Britain at Colchester (Peacock, D.P.S. in Peacock (ed.), 1977, 157, fig.3).

Fine pottery wares in the third and fourth centuries

The contraction of markets

There were distinct changes in pottery manufacture by the mid-third century. In the first and second centuries identical samian bowls were in use across much of Britain, Germany and Gaul. By the third century, however, fine wares had become regionalised in the way that kitchen wares already were; moreover they were often being made at the same potteries. Despite this diffusion of production some well-established samian forms were still made at a number of these new sources (fig.54). This draws attention to the continuity that was current during the process of change.

Distribution of wares became more restricted – it is no exaggeration to say that in the first and second centuries identical fine pottery forms were in use thousands of miles and provinces apart. The industries at Colchester and in the Nene Valley were more concerned in this period

54 Fine ware dishes produced by Romano-British pottery industries in the third and fourth centuries (about ¼ scale):

a a product of the Oxfordshire potteries, a dish in the tradition of the samian Form 36; however, white paint has replaced the *barbotine* decoration. Fourth century (after Bushe-Fox)

b a third-century Nene Valley dish also emulating samian Form 36, though this time with *barbotine* decoration (after Hartley)

c a fourth-century flanged bowl emulating samian Form 38 made of parchment ware and decorated with red painted hooks (after Gillam)

d third-fourth-century New Forest bowl using samian Form 37 though with white painted decoration (after Swan)

e third-fourth-century New Forest bowl emulating samian Form 36 though with stamped rosette decoration on the rim (after Swan)

f third-fourth-century New Forest parchment ware bowl with internal decoration of orange-brown paint (after Swan)

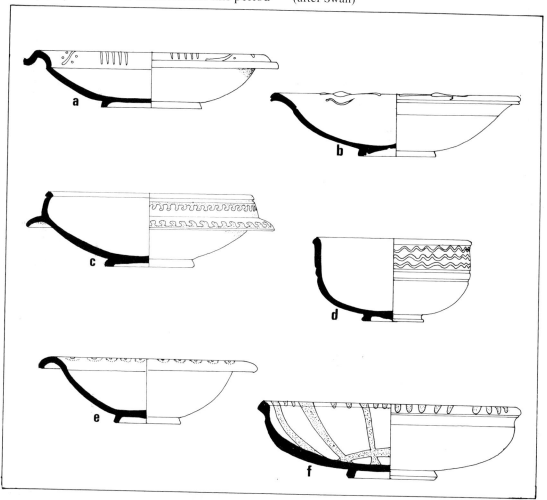

with producing forms to compete with the continental drinking vessels, rather than a full range of fine wares; typically beakers, cups and lidded bowls. The limited quantities of 'Pompeian red ware' and the unsuccessful samian enterprise at Colchester have already been mentioned. From the third century on the product range expanded, but patterns of distribution became polarised.

Decoration and even forms now belonged to the pottery tradition alone and it is much more difficult to identify a close relationship with contemporary metal and glass prototypes. The manufacturing process seems to have been simplified, perhaps because the lengthy process involved in decorated samian, for example, produced vessels that were too costly for a changing market. This may also have been due to competition from glass tableware.

New decorative styles
In the first and second centuries the domination of the fine ware market by the samian industry meant that the most frequent type of decoration was mould-decoration. This was not normally used by Romano-British potters. Appliqué decoration, used in the samian industry, was employed in Britain in the second century, for example at Colchester where a mould for casting the appliqué figure of a gladiator was found (Hull, 1963, 91). However, it was not a common practice and apart from a few instances on Oxfordshire products it had ceased to be used by the fourth century. Barbotine decoration was rather more popular, usually as scroll or floral decoration and sometimes as embellishments around an appliqué figure scene, for example in the Nene Valley and at Colchester (fig.53 k, plate 11). By the later third and fourth century the most common decorative technique was painting, typically in a colour which contrasted with the colour of the ware (fig.54). In cases where forms seem definitely to have been derived from decorated samian types an imitation was achieved by stamping the ware, for example with rosettes, or ovolos (fig.54 d).

New fine ware industries in Roman Britain
In the third century some samian was still available from the East Gaulish factories. Its quality however was poor, and supply may have been uncertain. Nevertheless demand for red-slipped fine wares still existed in Britain throughout the third and fourth centuries and in

response to this the potteries of the Oxfordshire region, already an established source of mortaria and other coarse wares, began to manufacture their own version of popular samian forms (fig.54). Some products of other red-ware industries elsewhere entered Britain, such as African red-slip ware (Hayes, 1972), or Argonne ware. However, the known number of examples is so small that no case can yet be made for any kind of significant commercial trade in these wares; they are just as likely to have been personal effects (Bird, J., in Dore and Greene, 1977, 269–78). The same applies to exports of Romano-British fine wares, for example few traces of Oxfordshire wares are known in Europe.

The fine ware potteries at Colchester continued in operation until at least the middle of the fourth century, manufacturing beakers and flagons. Decoration was distinctive and included scenes of gladiators, charioteers, possible religious rituals, rough-cast, rouletting, painted circles, dots and scrolls, many of which are reminiscent of Celtic styles (fig.53 k and plate 11).

The Nene Valley and Oxfordshire industries
The two most important sources of third- and fourth-century fine wares in Britain were the Nene Valley potteries (Hartley, 1960, Howe *et alia*, 1980) and the Oxfordshire potteries (Young, 1977), which capitalised on the demise of the samian industry by manufacturing substitute products as well as introducing their own types. Nene Valley products include an extensive range of beakers, cups, bowls (including lidded bowls (plate 27) and others based on samian forms), flagons and mortaria. Kitchen wares were also manufactured. Decorative techniques included barbotine work, painting, rouletting and scaling. The best known of these are the so-called 'hunt cups' on which animals, and sometimes men, chase one another around the vessel.

Nene Valley products were once also known as *castor ware* after the Roman town in which they were first identified. A pottery industry has been identified in association with the nearby mid-first century legionary vexillation fortress at Longthorpe. However, there is no evidence to suggest that this led directly to the later major industry. By the mid-second century the growth of the town of *Durobrivae* was paralleled by a new pottery industry which expanded massively in the late second and third centuries and continued until the end of the fourth, possibly well into the fifth. The area was close to the waterways of the Fenland, an area which was subjected to considerable drainage and development in the second century, thus providing a substantial local market and communications. *Durobrivae* itself lies on the main Roman road north from London to Lincoln and York.

The similarity of the Nene Valley colour-coat products to wares being manufactured in Germany suggests that the industry may have been started by a group of migrant potters. Distribution was across most of Britain but a recent chemical analysis has suggested that many similar products found in south-east Britain, thought originally to be Nene Valley products, in fact came from Cologne (Anderson *et alia*, 1982), and this is an important possibility to bear in mind, especially when considering sites near the east coast.

The potters of the Oxfordshire region had a tradition of manufacture stretching back into the first century. The Thames Valley was a natural area for early Roman expansion with a number of towns growing up on the routes running west and north-west from London. The earlier potters concerned themselves with kitchen wares, and in the second century increasingly with mortaria (fig.57 f and g). But from the mid-third century on there was a considerable change in production with the emphasis being placed on fine wares and mortaria.

It has been suggested that some East Gaulish potters moved to the Oxfordshire area providing investment and stimulus; however, the decorative techniques of the new red wares are very different even if the forms were similar, for example, painting, rouletting and stamping (Young, 1973, 108). Fine ware production concentrated on the most popular samian bowl forms (fig.54 a) in a red colour-coat ware, and the white parchment wares with painted decoration; other forms include beakers (fig.53 m) and flagons (fig.58 f). The products dominate late third- and fourth-century fine ware assemblages in central Britain, and are commonly found across southern Britain and Wales. They are also occasionally found in the north.

The New Forest

Less important than either of these two major sources were the potteries of the New Forest (Fulford, 1975). The products were similar to those of the Oxfordshire area in the manufacture of red-slipped samian style forms (fig.54 d), parchment wares, and other colour-coat tablewares such as beakers (fig.53 n), cups, jugs and flagons. The industry seems to belong to the mid-third century and later, achieving sporadic distribution across southern Britain, though with an apparent dependence on main communication routes. In comparison, Oxfordshire products are more generally widespread and occur even in areas close to centres of New Forest production where it might be expected that this would not be the case.

Other centres in southern Britain

Other, minor, centres of fine ware products in southern Britain are known at Pakenham and Homersfield in Suffolk, Much Hadham near Braughing in Hertfordshire, and in the area of coastal Sussex and Hampshire where it is known as Pevensey ware.

The North

Northern Britain was not so well-served by these southern fine ware industries, though Nene Valley products in particular did spread across the area in the third century (Gillam, 1973, 58, 61), for example at Vindolanda where a wide range of Nene Valley products have been recovered (Bidwell, 1985, 181). Here we have to consider the different nature of demand – this was the military area of the province, and the civil population evidently did not enjoy quite the degree of material wealth afforded some of the inhabitants of the south. This is quite clear in the very small number of 'well-appointed' country houses in the north of the kind which are relatively common in the south from the third century; there are also very few settlements which bear comparison with the towns or regional centres in the south. By the third and fourth century, whatever the original ethnic make-up of any military unit, especially the auxiliary units, the degree of inter-breeding with local inhabitants must have reached a point whereby the two were barely distinguishable.

The North was not an area which aspired quite so much to Mediterranean manners, as is clear from the even more strongly Celtic flavour of religious practice in the region. Nevertheless the army itself exercised a certain level of demand for fine ware products in its own right, but this was dependent on other factors (see the section concerned with kitchen wares below), for example the military re-organisation of the province by Count Theodosius after the disastrous tribal invasion of 367.

In the fourth century the manufacture of pottery at Crambeck (near Malton, Yorkshire) commenced. The potters here also produced parchment ware bowls with painted decoration, cream flagons and burnished versions of samian forms (fig.54 c). After 367 Crambeck became the principal source of most pottery types in the north apart from kitchen wares (Gillam, 1973, 62). At Swanpool in Lincolnshire fourth-century potters produced some colour-coated beakers and bowls with painted decoration. Second-century industries manufacturing colour-coat wares and which lasted into the third century are known at Great Casterton in Leicestershire and at South Carlton in Lincolnshire.

None of these northern industries appear to have enjoyed the wide distribution achieved by the Oxfordshire or Nene Valley centres. The picture is an enigmatic one for archaeologists because of the lack of closely dated deposits, the lack of historical records for the period, and the lack of published material.

Fine wares – conclusion

Some general points need to be born in mind: there are undoubtedly some localised Romano-British fine ware industries of the third and fourth century yet to be identified, while others need more careful study. These reinforce the fact that each assemblage is unique and based on local idiosyncracies of manufacture and marketing; on the other hand, whatever the individual nature of these industries, their products were all designed to fill and sustain the demand which had previously been almost universally supplied by the samian industries of Gaul. The diffusion of fine ware supply amongst these sources is a clue to the very different type of economy which was in operation, not only in third and fourth century Britain, but elsewhere in the late Western Empire. Even so, it is very important not to be distracted by the individual details of separate industries because this ignores the perception of the Romano-British consumer. A good example is the beaker form manufactured in the Rhine-land and the Nene Valley. They are practically indistinguishable without scientific testing. They are to all intents and purposes identical products manufactured to fulfil an identical function. They are found throughout Britain and as such they

testify to the extraordinary phenomenon of romanisation which had promoted the spread of a relatively unified culture. We have, of course, absolutely no idea to what degree a discerning customer purchased his wares on a basis of origin. In many cases, especially with beakers, not even the small-town vendor probably knew where they had come from.

It is probably more helpful to stand back and try to assess very simply what was on offer. Throughout the period red-slipped wares were available from many different sources, with a number of basic forms retaining popularity for a very long time. There were in addition beakers, and later on the parchment wares emerged. Despite the mesmerising array of sources fine wares in Roman Britain do indicate a perhaps surprising degree of continuity, and most importantly a homogeneity in types. The factors which dictated a purchase must have been availability and price as much as taste.

Kitchen wares

Function

Fine tablewares were the household's 'best china'. There was a whole series of vessels designed for the preparation and storing of food and drink. They were mostly cheaper and more easily made with the result that their pottery forms are abundant, if fragmentary, site finds. However, wealth was not so widely spread in Roman Britain that absolutely everyone used fine tablewares. We can be sure that poorer individuals and families used kitchen wares for everything associated with eating.

Kitchen wares, despite their abundance, are really amongst the least understood artefacts of Roman Britain. Studies in recent years are beginning to uncover a picture of startling complexity, though again it should be remembered that the Roman-British user would have had little interest in where his cooking jars came from so long as they were durable and cheap. While attention is readily drawn to the amphorae or stamped mortaria, it can be less easy to appreciate how much Romano-British energy was expended in the manufacture or movement of these products. Their purpose was purely functional, they were made to be used regularly and were discarded as soon as they became unserviceable. They were cheap and easy enough to make for the residents of virtually every site of Romano-British date to own some. From the point of view of this book this is their most interesting feature. The large number of local industries is purely a feature of straight-forward economics (low manufacturing costs against high transport costs) – the relatively small number of types is a feature of a social homogeneity in striking contrast to the pre-Roman period. It is worth noting that during the period many kitchen wares were probably made of wood, possibly in equal quantities to those of pottery. Naturally these rarely survive though sites such as Vindolanda and London have produced some examples from waterlogged deposits.

Cooking

Some details of Roman cooking are known from the works of 'Apicius' (probably a collection of works by different authors), who described Mediterranean dishes – not really appropriate for Roman Britain. Here cooks must have relied as much on dishes eaten before the Conquest as they did on new Roman recipes. Nevertheless the Conquest brought innovative forms of cooking as is manifest in the specialist vessels associated with Roman cooking, for example the *mortaria* or mixing bowls (fig.57).

Roman cooking seems to have taken place over gridirons (for example Meates, 1987, fig.49, no. 307) or in ovens, presumably fired by wood, though coal may have been in use in areas where it was readily obtainable. The kitchen, because of the risk of fire, would normally have been a room on the side of the house. In forts ovens have been found on the edge of the complex beside the ramparts.

Both metal and pottery vessels were used for preparing and cooking food and drink, though for the same reasons as have been mentioned before metal vessels are rarely found. In the *House of the Vettii* in Pompeii a complete set of bronze pans was found still on the oven in the kitchen.

Metal kitchen vessels

Metal vessels devised for cooking seem to take three forms; saucepans, or *paterae*, jars and 'frying-pans'. They might be made of bronze or iron (fig.48 d, e). Occasionally the makers stamped their names on the product. A *patera* from London bears the stamp P.RVF.C presumably

for Publius Rufinus C . . . . Another example bears the stamp of Lucius Ansius, whose products have also been found at Pompeii, which has the advantages of suggesting when he worked and showing how far his products spread. Not all patera-makers had such overtly Roman names; one called Boduogenus suggests he was of Celtic origin (plate 7).

Paterae quite often had elaborately-decorated handles, such as one made by the same Boduogenus, and might also have a decorative bust, perhaps of a god within the bowl of the patera. These are not really kitchen wares at all, though their basic design was no different. They were frequently used as votive objects (see Chapter 7 and plate 7) coupled with appropriate inscriptions. The jars are unelaborate vessels lacking handles and can be considered as no more than containers for heating food. The 'frying-pans' are similar to modern examples, but differ by having hinged folding handles.

Pottery cooking vessels

Pottery cooking vessels in Roman Britain were almost universally of the type loosely known as 'grey' or 'coarse' wares. The vast bulk of all Roman pottery found in Britain falls into this category – at least in excess of three-quarters. Traditionally they were discarded as site finds because they were regarded as so commonplace and typical that they held no value for dating. They are also less attractive to the eye than samian or other fine wares. At the Lullingstone villa Pollard has distinguished 80 fabric sources, 50 of which are of a 'coarse' nature originating in a number of places such as Dorset, Alice Holt near Farnham, and north Kent (Meates, 1987, 166, fig.66).

Black-burnished wares

Some of these pottery vessels are also known as 'black-burnished' wares because of the practice of polishing part of the surface with pebbles. This results in a grey-black metallic sheen, sometime criss-crossed with lattice decoration. The actual range of forms is quite restricted and variations are usually quite minor – only chemical techniques, such as heavy mineral analysis or thin-sectioning, are likely to isolate the source (Farrar, 1977). Typical forms are the tall wide-mouthed cooking pots/jars with everted rims, flat-rimmed and flanged bowls, and dishes with or without flanged rims (fig.55).

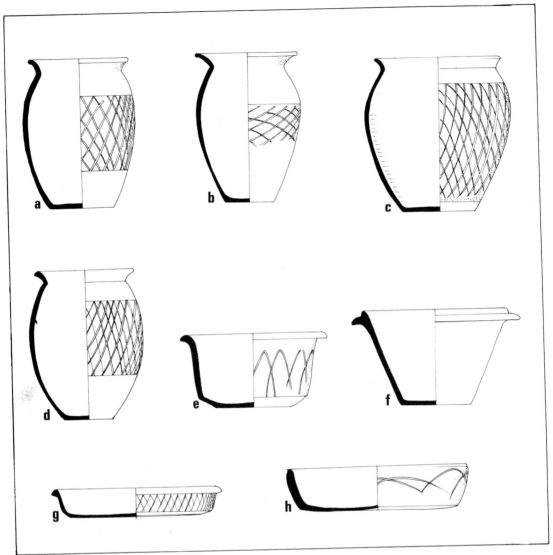

55 Various forms of black-burnished pottery (about ¼ scale):

a everted rim jar typical of the BB1 industry in the second century, with a band of acute lattice decoration (after Farrar)

b everted rim jar typical of the BB1 industry in the fourth century, the rim is now wider than the body and the lattice decoration has become obtuse (aftere Williams)

c everted rim jar typical of the BB2 industry in the second century (after Farrar)

d everted rim jar also typical of the BB2 industry (after Farrar)

e flat-rimmed BB1 bowl from the mid-second century; in time the walls became more splayed, the height of the carination dropped and eventually disappeared, the rim became flanged, and decoration changed from lattice work to a series of intersecting arcs. This example is already some way along the sequence of change (after Farrar)

f flanged bowl made by both industries in the late third and fourth centuries (after Farrar)

g flanged dish with lattice decoration typical of the BB2 industry in the fourth century (after Williams)

h BB1 'dog-dish', commonest in the second century, it could be used as a lid on flanged bowls. This is a fourth-century example (after Farrar)

Chemical and scientific techniques have only recently revealed that the military market was dominated by two major sources once the northern frontier became established at the end of the first century; the hand-made black-burnished wares from Dorset, known as BB1; and the wheel-thrown black-burnished wares made in a number of centres around the Thames Estuary from Colchester to Kent, known as BB2 (Farrar in Detsicas, 1973) (figs.50 and 55). The considerable distance involved raises the question of excessively costly transportation. There is no easy answer but a possibility is that the pottery was loaded onto shipments of vital

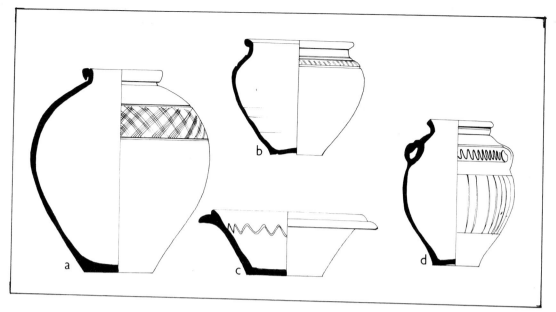

56 Alice Holt and Crambeck forms (about ⅕ scale):
a Class 1A. 13 Alice Holt jar designed probably for liquid storage, dated to *c.* 220–270 (after Lyne and Jefferies)
b Class 1. 10 Alice Holt cordoned jar. These jars belong to the later first century and first half of the second century, dominating production, (after Lyne and Jefferies)
c Crambeck flanged bowl with internal wavy line decoration. The general form is typical of the period and paralleled at a number of other centres (after Corder). Fourth century
d Crambeck cordoned cooking pot with handles (after Corder). Fourth century

goods such as food. In this way costs would have become relatively negligible because the ship would have made the journey anyway. As a result army potteries seem to have been closed down, for example at Brampton and Muncaster *c.* 125, with the effect that 'the two main categories of black-burnished kitchen wares became the commonest ware in northern Britain' being used for 'almost all the bowls, dishes and cooking pots' (Gillam, 1973, 54).

Both these black-burnished manufacturing areas had traditions of pottery-making before the Conquest, and throughout the period supplied the civilian markets in their vicinities. Both being close to the sea they were ideally placed for what seems to have been an army contract to supply their products to the northern and western military zones. From around the year 120 onward BB1 came to dominate the Hadrian's Wall area and Wales up until *c.* 367, when more local industries took over such as that of Crambeck, while BB2 was supplied to Scotland from *c.* 140,

and continued to appear in the north-east up to about the middle of the third century.

It is possible for modern scientific methods to show whether similar pottery was actually made in the same place. At the fort of Vindolanda, near Hadrian's Wall, neutron activation analysis on some third- and fourth-century material showed that most of the BB1 material came from the Poole Harbour area, and the BB2 came from a single source. The same tests indicated that the majority of the remaining kitchen, or 'grey', wares came from a single, but unknown source (Bidwell, 1985, 184). Information like this does support the idea that supply was organised, rather than random, and that army contracts may have been the reason.

Other sources

There were of course numerous other sources of similar kitchen wares, major and minor – the example of the Lullingstone villa has already been cited. In some cases coarse and fine wares were made side by side, for example in the Oxfordshire and New Forest industries. The gradual demise of the BB2 industries was matched by the expansion of the Alice Holt/Farnham grey ware pottery industry (fig.56 a, b). Starting in the late first century this industry dominated the south-east in the later third and fourth centuries, exemplifying the later domination of even coarse ware markets by relatively few major industries.

This is particularly interesting because superficially this does not make economic sense – such low-value goods should have been too costly to transport long distances. Of course what we do not know, but we may surmise, is whether these pottery industries like the black-burnished industries shared transportation with perishable goods which have left no trace. Naturally this would make the movement of low-value pottery viable, though apart from the pottery there would be no trace in the archaeological record.

Despite the domination by major sources, throughout the province a number of kitchen ware industries existed, ranging from the crude calcite-tempered products of the Knapton area to the grog-tempered products of the Wessex region. The uniqueness of local assemblages cannot be underestimated, because these wares are evidence of a complete range of types of industries, though all supplying the same basic type of demand. Almost every settlement of consequence, from villages up, would have had some kind of local coarse pottery source whether manufactured in households or local kilns, or perhaps obtained from visiting potters who used local raw materials of clay, water and tempering material to manufacture a few kiln loads before moving on. As we saw in Chapter 2 this may have been the case with tile-makers, such as Cabriabanus who worked in Kent (fig.34).

Imported coarse wares
The most common imports of coarse wares are early mortaria (see below p. 96) and up until recently it was thought that only such specialist coarse material was imported. However, at the New Fresh Wharf a small quantity of material from the Pas-de-Calais/Picardy region was identified. Dating to around the later second and early third centuries the deposit included a number of jars, bowls and dishes from an industry comparable to the BB2 industry (Richardson in Dyson, 1986, 98 & 106ff). The same deposit included a number of lid-seated jars from the Eifel/Rhine area of Germany, known as 'Eifelkeramik' ware.

Other uses
Kitchen jars were not just used for cooking. They were used widely for containing the ashes from cremations, a practice popular up until the end of the second century (see Chapter 7). Generally the jar was stoppered with a suitable dish, sometimes of samian ware. Kitchen jars were also popular containers for hoarding coin (Chapter 9). Most Romano-British coin-hoards are recovered in vessels like these.

Specialist kitchen wares

Mortaria
These are vessels of particular types designed for a specific purpose and made by specialist potters. The most important are the *mortaria*, or mixing-bowls. While their forms vary they are all designed for the Roman cooking habit of grinding food. They are very much a distinctive feature of the Roman period in Britain but some were imported before the Conquest, for example those found at Skeleton Green (Partridge, 1981).

Broadly speaking, mortaria are shallow bowls with internal gritting to aid the grinding, and have thick walls for strength and stout rims for holding and lifting (fig.57 a-j). The vast majority are made of pottery though mortaria were also carved out of single pieces of stone. In the first and second centuries many of the specialist potters stamped the products with their names

---

57 Mortaria (about ⅕ scale). The basic gritted bowl alters relatively little but the rim shows distinctive changes:
a mortaria typical of the late first, early second-century industry in southern Britain
b mortaria with angular rim, typical of the Hartshill-Mancetter industry from the mid-second century on
c Hartshill-Mancetter third-fourth-century mortaria with 'hammer-head' rim
d Nene Valley mortaria rim, 270–400 (after Hartley)
e Oxfordshire mortaria rim, 240 +
f Oxfordshire mortaria rim, 240 +
g New Forest mortaria rim, 270–350 (after Swan)
h continental first century import (after Swan)
i Soller, Kreis-Düren (Germany) mortaria rim
j the distinctive rim of the unusually large, specialist mortaria manufactured by Verecundus of Soller, Kreis-Düren
k painted signature on a mortarium from Water Newton in the Nene valley, *Sennianus Durobrivae vrit*, 'Sennianus fired [this] at Durobrivae' – date uncertain, probably late second, third century
Potters' stamps:
A number of mortaria potters' stamps are illustrated here at ½ scale (after a number of sources including K.F. Hartley, E. Birley, and the author). The numbers correspond with those given on Table IV. All those listed and illustrated are thought to have worked in Britain at some time during their careers. Mortaria stamping was almost exclusively confined to the first and second centuries, and was not even then practiced at all kiln sites. Typically the stamp is placed across the rim; many stamps have decorated borders, usually of herringbone pattern (not shown here). Some stamps were prepared the 'right way round' and thus appear backwards, 'retrograde', on the mortarium

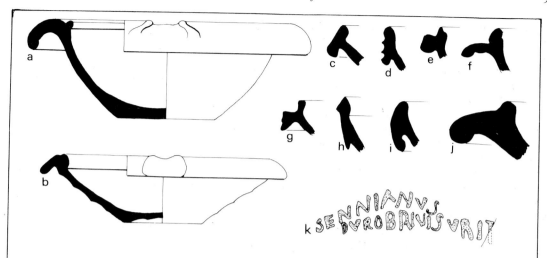

POTTERS' STAMPS (see Table IV)

ALBINV 1	XIVIISVA 2	ATICANI 3	VIDVRDIC 4
BRVCIF 5	BRVSCE 34	BVIII 42	OF·CACVMATTI 43
CANDIDVS 6	CAST 7	IIIB 7	CYNOPEC 44	DEVAL 8
DORALIVS 62	DIONNV 33	DRCCVS 12	DVBITAVS 45
OGVLER 51	IIINVI 14	VIALAT 15	LTVCENVS IVGIFFECIT 53	MARINVS 17
C.ATIVS SVDIIIVS 18	MARINAS 19	AATVGENI 20	VIIIM IIII 21
MORICAM 23	T·VIIIOM 39	MIIR 24	OASRIVS 25	RIDANVS 26
AOR 27	SAVRRI 40	SAVR NVS 28	SECNDSF 29	EXVALCF 46
SCVSF 30	SVMMACVSARO NTVIRIFECITO 56	TAAH 31	VALE 57	C·VALER SVRIAC 58
QVIIRVS VRANI 59	VNCONVSI 60	VIIIIATV 63	VONODF 65

G.de.la.B

(fig.57). This and the discovery of some kilns has helped identify a number of sources in central and south-east Britain and the continent, including Italy, Gallia Belgica, Germany, Colchester, Kent, the Verulamium/Brockley Hill area, Radlett, and Hartshill-Mancetter. In one case at Brockley Hill an actual kiln has been identified as having been used by a potter called Doinus (Table IV, and fig.57 no. 11; see Castle, 1972). The imported products generally belong to a period before about AD 60–70, thereafter Romano-British industries supplied the demand with the exception of special types of mortaria which were imported from Germany. These include the very large mortaria made and stamped by Verecundus, which date to the late second-early third century (fig.57 j).

By the third century the habit of using name stamps had died out. This is interesting in itself – presumably there had been some purpose, such as sorting out shared kiln-loads or accounting with distributors. Whatever the purpose was it had evidently ceased to exist, perhaps because manufacturing mortaria was no longer the business of autonomous potters. The Hartshill-Mancetter factories had come to dominate the market, along with mortaria products of the Oxfordshire area whose potters had commenced production in the second century (some using illiterate name-stamps), and those of the Nene Valley (where one individual signed his name on a vessel – fig.57 k). However mortaria were also made in a number of areas to supply local markets, such as those near some forts like Corbridge, or Caerleon. They serve to emphasise the fact that analysis of assemblages should not be overshadowed by the better-known large industries.

Mortars carved out of a single piece of stone are known too. They are semi-circular with a flat base but instead of having a flange or rim they usually had four projecting lugs which allowed them to be held securely (see, for example, that found at Richborough, Cunliffe, 1968, pl. 66).

Others
There were other specialist-type kitchen vessels, including strainers, cheese-presses and colanders. These are comparatively rare and difficult to recognise from pot-sherds. Swan (1988) illustrates some of these unusual vessels.

Containers

Glass bottles
Glass bottles made in Roman Britain were widely used, despite the fact that blowing glass was a relatively recent invention. Their most distinctive features are the handles made of a thick strip of drawn glass. The handle was applied to the body, folded at a right angle and then attached to the neck. The body of the bottle can be round or square, the former being free-blown, the latter mould-blown, and occasionally bears the maker's name on the base or some other motif (fig.49 a-c; Charlesworth, 1966, and in Frere, 1984, 161). Size could range widely from quite substantial examples to those more equivalent to a milk bottle or smaller. Such bottles are frequently found used in cremation burials as well (see Chapter 8). Their origin is uncertain, but as the glass is relatively impure compared to tableware examples it is possible that these bottles were made mostly in Britain, though the Rhineland and Gaul are likely alternatives. Some may have been imported for the sake of their contents.

Flagons
The flagon was the standard Roman household storage container for drinks. Typically it consists of a globular body with neck and rim and one or two handles (fig.58). They were eventually made throughout Britain in a wide range of variations on this basic form but to begin with they were imported or made by the army. The best known variety of imported flagon is the so-called 'Hofheim' flagon, named after a site in Holland where they were first identified (fig.25 a; fig.58 a). An early kiln has been found in Kent at Otford which was manufacturing flagons in the late first century, and from this period on a number of sources produced flagons (Detsicas, 1983, 157). In the first and second centuries these potteries all attempted to manufacture a similar product in terms of having a cream or off-white appearance. This was also the habit on the continent, as examples from Pompeii show. Thereafter flagons appear in the fabric of the local industry and are generally smaller in size.

Amphorae
The *amphorae* are perhaps the most distinctive ceramic products of the ancient world. Though an extremely large number of forms were made they all had the same purpose, acting as antiquity's universal packaging medium for the

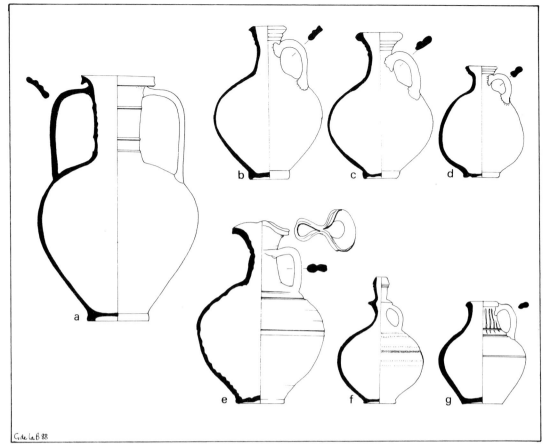

58 Flagons (about ⅕ scale):

a Hofheim-type flagon, AD 43–70. The diagnostic feature is the distinctive rim, neck and square handle. They were introduced by the army – see fig. 25a for another variety (after Anthony)

b flagon with moulded, angularly cut rings, Verulamium area, AD 70–130 (after Marsh and Tyers)

c flagon with prominent rounded upper ring, Verulamium area, 115–140 (after Marsh and Tyers)

d flagon with short, flaring rim, Verulamium area, 130–200+ (after Marsh and Tyers)

e pinched neck flagon, Verulamium area, 120–160 (after Frere, 1983, fig.127, no. 1338)

f Oxfordshire colour-coated flagon, 240–400+ (after Swan)

g Alice Holt flagon, 270+ (after Lyne and Jefferies)

long-distance transportation of perishable commodities (fig.59). Unlike the flagons and the mortaria they do occur in pre-Roman Britain, usually associated with the settlements or graves of the Celts of the first century BC. Their general form of large handles, fat necks and tapering bases was dictated by the need to be able to stack them securely on ships, but different areas used different types and occasionally the makers stamped identifying marks, or shippers wrote details of the contents and the voyage.

This kind of information has made it possible to identify a number of commodities arriving in Britain, no doubt for domestic consumption, such as fish-sauce or olive-oil from Spain, and wine from Italy and Gaul. These amphorae are useful indicators of the considerable breadth of trade that went on during the Roman period (Peacock, 1986). While amphorae and their contents suffered with the general decline in trade during the third and fourth centuries, some late examples have been found dating from the late fourth or early fifth century, shipped from Palestine. Amphorae were usually sealed with bungs of clay or wood, which when found on their own are not of immediately obvious function.

Amphorae were particularly liable to re-use, and in Roman Britain this is how they generally survive. In the Mediterranean area they are often found as part of the contents of one of the numerous wrecks. While wrecks must have been equally numerous in the English Channel and North Sea the general conditions do not make either for discovery or recovery. Amphorae were sometimes used as grave goods, or even as the containers for cremations (fig.114). Other uses include insertion into the ground as liquid containers, perhaps in a roadside tavern, or even use as structural components to save weight in

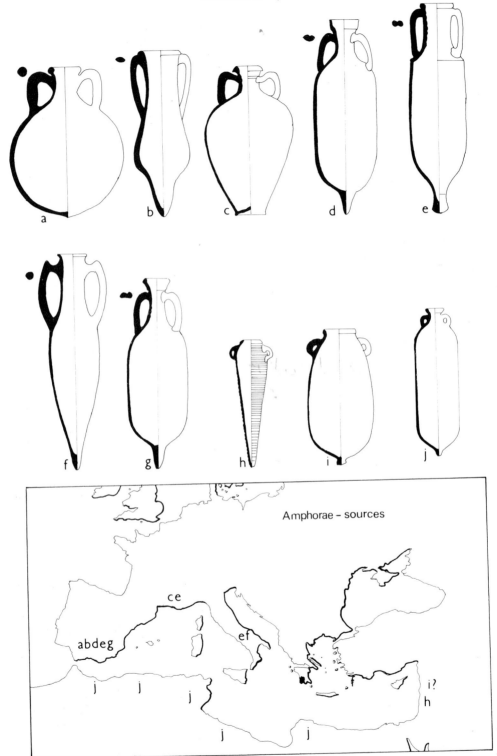

a   b   c   d   e

f   g   h   i   j

Amphorae – sources

ce

abdeg

ef

j   j   j

i?

h

j   j

walls and vaults. Mention might be made here of wooden barrels which served a similar function to amphorae in transporting wine to Britain but occasionally survive because they made handy liners for wells (McWhirr, *Roman Crafts and Industries*, 1982, 51; or at London, see Merrifield, 1965, plate 111).

Utensils

Whatever the range of bowls, plates, jars and jugs in the Romano-British household, these would have been of little use without eating utensils. In the Roman period these were knives and spoons: the fork was not invented until the mediaeval period. They are extremely hard to date because, despite being common finds, few are closely dated and it is impossible to construct a typological series similar to that for pottery types.

Spoons

Romano-British spoons seem to fall into three clear types: the small circular bowl type, or *cochlear*, with rat-tail handle, which belongs mostly to the first and second centuries; the medium-sized bowl type, of oval, pear, or fiddle shape, which occur throughout the period; and the large 'duck-handled' or zoomorphic handled form which are typically of fourth-century date (a

---

59 Some of the more typical amphora forms and their sources found in Britain (about 1/20 scale):

a Dressel 20 amphorae. Southern Spain (olive-oil). First to early third centuries. The most common amphora form in Britain

b CAM 186 amphora. Southern Spain (fish foods, e.g. sauce). First century

c Dressel 30 amphora. Southern Gaul (wine). First and second century

d Haltern 70/CAM 185A amphora. Southern Spain (sweet drink). First century

e Koan/Dressel 2–4 amphora. Originally an Island of Kos (wine) type but imitated in Central Italy which is where examples found in Britain come from. First century

f Rhodian amphora. Rhodes and Italy (wine). First century

g CAM 185 amphora. Spain

h CAM 189 amphora. Palestine. First century

i Richborough 527. East Mediterranean. First to early third centuries

j late Roman cylindrical amphora. North Africa (olive oil?). Third-fourth centuries

---

number of the spoons from the Thetford treasure were of this type, fig.95 d, e).

Spoons were made of wood, bone, bronze (which was usually tinned to give a silver appearance), and silver (fig.60 a-c). Metal spoons were cast in baked clay moulds – a unique group of over 800 fragmentary spoon moulds were found recently in a late Roman pit at the town of Castleford, *Lagentium*, in Yorkshire. Spoons made of silver frequently bear some sort of inscription, whether religious or merely the owner's name, and seem to be closely associated with religious or superstitious activities. They clearly had ritual or amuletic significance and are discussed below (figs.95, d, e and 117). Spoon handles could be quite elaborate, for example they may be twisted and bear some sort of motif at the point where the handle meets the bowl. Occasionally these resemble clasp knives in being foldable. A rare variety of spoon has a perforated bowl, presumably for straining wine, though this again may be a utensil better associated with religious activities (see plate 26).

Knives

Roman knives were made of iron or bronze, but their handles could be made of bone or wood, though examples made entirely of metal are also quite normal (fig.60 d-f). Their remains are fairly common but the range of types is almost as wide as that available today. One of the most basic variations is in the form of handle. Those of bone or wood resemble modern knives in shape and frequently carry decoration, perhaps of a series of concentric circles engraved into the material or geometric patterns. Knives made entirely of metal might have ringed handles, and some have cast handles which are designs based on animal forms; an amber knife handle from Carlisle is carved in the form of a mouse eating (McCarthy *et alia*, 1983, 267-9). Some large examples with serrated edges and substantial blades are probably to be associated with butchery, or possibly surgery. Clasp knives, with folding handles, are known too (fig.60 e).

Household equipment

This is a very large category and includes all sorts of equipment used in Romano-British houses, whether urban or rural. The subject of the actual

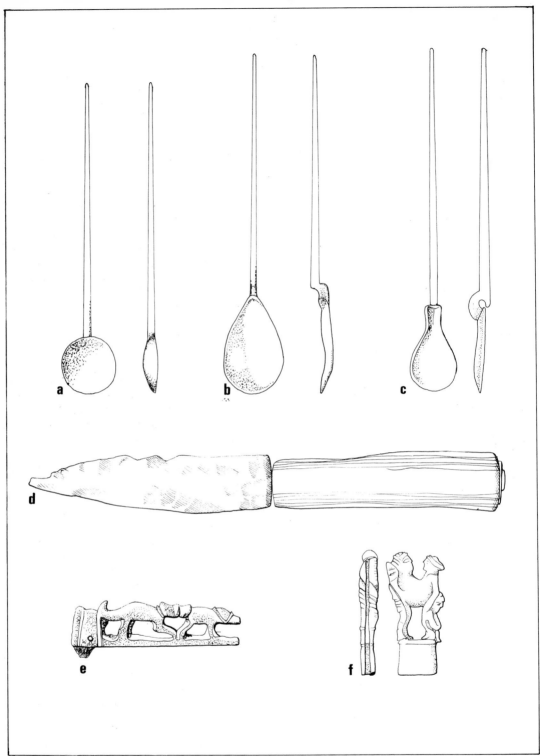

60 Utensils (⅔ scale):

a round-bowled spoon, *c.* AD 50–200

b pear-shaped bowl spoon, in use from the first half of the second century and thereafter

c mandolin bowl spoon, sometimes made of two components with a hinge joining bowl and handle

d iron knife with bone handle attached by a washer from Verulamium (after Frere, 1984, 91, no. 59)

e bronze clasp-knife handle in the form of a dog chasing a rabbit. The pivot for the iron blade is visible. Found in the Thames at Hammersmith (after Wheeler, 1930, 78, fig.19)

f bronze knife handle in the form of an erotic scene involving three athletic participants. It may have been a souvenir of entertainments at Verulamium theatre near to which it, and a similar example, were found (C. Johns in Frere, 1984, 58 no. 217)

types and structure of Romano-British houses is outside the scope of this book – but it is worth remembering that the popular impression of the lavish rural country house, or the well-appointed town house, was as much removed from the average Roman Briton as a Cotswold country house, or Chelsea town house, is from the average twentieth-century Briton. The range of houses, or perhaps 'dwellings' is a better word, was very large, with many people living in extremely simple structures that have left few traces. During motorway construction works the number of Romano-British buildings exposed along a narrow strip of land offers a revealing insight to the potential number and range of sites which remain undiscovered (Hanley, 1987, fig.1).

So, the typical impression of a well-to-do Roman Briton relaxing in his centrally-heated, painted living room with polychrome mosaic and lit with a battery of oil lamps, should be seen for what it is – a cameo portrait of affluent Roman provincial life, which was something to which the average Roman Briton could only aspire.

Lighting

In the Roman world artificial light came in two main forms; oil-lamps and candles, though lanterns were also used. In the province of *Africa Proconsularis*, now Tunisia, oil-lamps were extremely common, reflecting the extensive local production of olive-oil to fuel them. In Britain exactly the opposite is true: oil-lamps were rare because of the huge cost of shipping olive-oil from Gaul, Spain and Africa. Despite this they are still widely distributed in Britain, especially in military sites, major towns and ports, and because they can be useful for dating it is worth exploring the subject in some detail. Like most Roman pottery found in Britain, lamps are usually fragmentary. Many lamps were imported though some particularly basic types must have been made locally.

The vast majority of surviving oil-lamps are made of pottery and many came from Gaul, Italy and Africa and conform to four major types distinguished by Mortimer Wheeler (1930, 60ff.), though some classifications of lamps, for example that of Loeschcke (1911), include much more specific typological breakdowns. They all worked by filling the body, or reservoir, with olive-oil and lighting a wick inserted into the nozzle. They sometimes have at least one air-hole, and often

carry the name of the manufacturer. Lamps with multiple nozzles are not uncommon.

Lamps

1. First-century 'Volute' lamps (Wheeler's Types I and II; fig.61 a, b). These two basically similar types are distinguished firstly by their nozzles flanked by a pair of volutes. The nozzle on Type I lamps is triangular while that of Type II is rounded. Both forms were in production by the beginning of the first century AD and continued to be made until the early second century. Both types commonly carry some sort of motif on the *discus* – the circular dish-shaped roof of the body – and these can be impressive and attractive examples of moulded decoration. The majority were made in Italy and Gaul.

2. *Firmalampen* or 'factory lamps' (Wheeler's Type III, fig.61 c, d). This form of lamp was the most common in Britain and the other northern provinces. There are two variants, called Type IIIa and Type IIIb, but more importantly they usually have handles or lugs, and are rarely decorated. The IIIa form (with open nozzle-channel) was introduced by the 70s AD, and the IIIb (with closed nozzle-channel) by the end of the first century. They frequently carry the name of the factory owner, for example *Strobili, Fortis, Optati,* and *Eucarpi.* Lugs were originally pierced for suspension, but they became a purely decorative feature. Many *firmalampen* were made in Gaul, the German provinces and some in Britain, for example in the Verulamium area. The *firmalampen* were still in production at least into the third century, and probably later in some cases.

3. Circular, short-nozzled lamps (Wheeler's Type IV; fig.61 e). This type is the simplest and commonest in the Mediterranean area of the main forms of pottery oil-lamps, and was introduced as early as the mid-first century AD, remaining in production throughout the period. The nozzle is no more than a protuberance and all the emphasis is on the body and *discus*, which is frequently decorated. However, there are variations – some examples which probably originated in North Africa have nozzles based on those of Types I and II, but these are not usually found in Britain. This is a point worth bearing in mind as in recent years a very large quantity of Roman lamps have been imported to Britain particularly from North Africa as part of the antiquities trade. These sometimes find their way

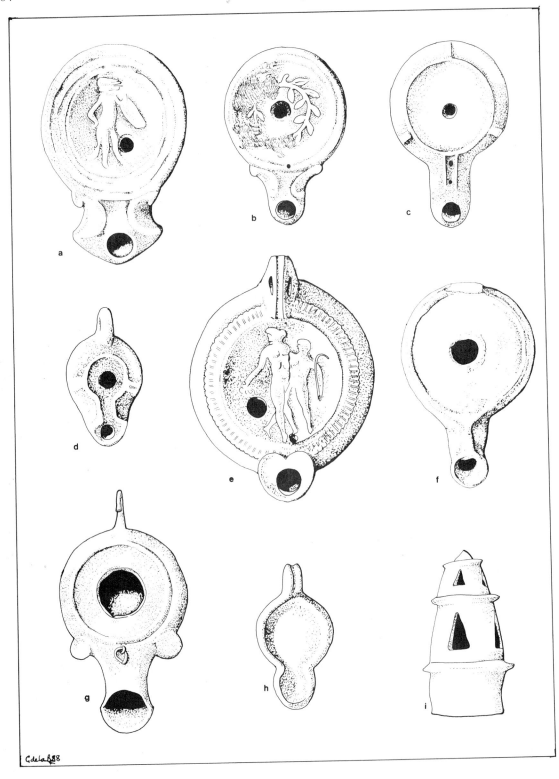

into museum collections and are described as local finds. They may even be reproductions (fig.103 d).

4. Other pottery oil-lamps. Pottery is porous unless specially glazed. As a result Roman oil-lamps must have been oily, messy objects to handle. To prevent this open-topped vessels in the shape of a lamp were made as lamp-holders but these could have been used as simple lamps in their own right (fig.61 h). Those with raised sides are probably lamp-fillers. Such simple devices were probably made in Britain, and this probably applies to simple clay-bodied vessels with wick-holes, and to a rare type made of a mica-dusted ware on a potter's wheel but based on Type III. An example from the Billingsgate Lorry Park, London, had been discarded unused because its handle had prematurely broken off, and this suggests it had been made nearby (fig.61 f).

5. Metal oil-lamps. Amongst the most remarkable examples is a gold lamp from Pompeii, but very few metal lamps have been found in Britain (fig.61 g). Some bronze lamps are known from London, including an exceptionally fine example from the Thames at Greenwich (see Wheeler, 1930, pl. 25), but otherwise we can assume that the majority of those used have long since disappeared into the melting pot. Those that survive are generally similar to clay forms but display greater variation of the handle. The Greenwich lamp, besides having two nozzles, has a curved handle decorated with a ram's head. The fort at Richborough produced a bronze lamp-stand, shaped in the form of a lamp (Bushe-Fox, 1949, 156, no. 353).

Oil-lamp manufacture

Most pottery oil-lamps were made by producing a wooden or clay model, known as an *archetype* (but see 4 above). This was then used to manufacture moulds for the upper and lower halves in which the two components of the lamp were then cast (see fig.35 b for an example from Colchester). The two halves were joined in the moulds. When dry the lamp was coated in slip and fired. Of course, it was extremely easy for a less inventive lamp-maker to use an existing lamp as his archetype, and apparently as a result lamps with identical decoration appear across the Empire, the succession of pirate lamp-makers revealed only by the gradual deterioration in the quality of the discus motif and blurring of name impressions (D.M. Bailey in Strong and Brown, 1976, 93 ff.).

It is worth briefly noting some of the motifs that appear on oil-lamps, usually the pottery forms of Types I, II and IV. The range of discus decoration is huge but include energetic erotic scenes, the busts or figures of divinities, gladiatorial or beast-killing scenes from the amphitheatre, and simple floral motifs.

Occasionally lamps of all types bear the name of the maker, or the maker of the lamp which was copied. The name appears on the base and was either produced by stamping the archetype or by writing with a sharp instrument. Many names are known, including c·oppi·res for Caius Oppius Restitutus, an Italian lamp-maker who worked in the late first and early second century. The lamps of Type III are the most common bearers of names – they are called 'factory-lamps', or *Firmalampen* because the form of the name in the genitive case implies that they were made in the

---

61 Domestic lighting (²⁄₃ scale except **h** and **i**; **a-d**, **g** from Richborough, after Bushe-Fox, 1949, pl.65–6; all clay except **g**):

a Volute lamp (Wheeler Type I; Loeschcke Type I) – first century

b Volute lamp (Wheeler Type II; Loeschcke Type IV) – first century

c *Firmalampen* (Wheeler Type IIIa; Loeschcke type IX), in this case stamped ATIMETI. Handles are common for this type, but lacking on this example – after *c.* AD 70

d *Firmalampen* (Wheeler Type IIIb; Loeschcke type X) after *c.* AD 100

e Circular short-nozzled lamp (Wheeler Type IV; Loeschke Type VIII). Mid-first century and after. This example is from North Africa, the *discus* depicts Bacchus and a satyr; the heart-shaped nozzle is typical of Africa and the East – normally the nozzle is D-shaped.

f unusual wheel-turned (as opposed to moulded) mica-dusted lamp from Billingsgate, London. The lamp was probably made in London, the mica being intended to imitate the effect of bronze. The handle is missing (de la Bédoyère, 1986, 113, no. 44)

g bronze lamp, typical for its uninspired practical design. Note the hook and suspension ring. From a late first-century context

h open-lamp/lamp-holder from London (½ scale; Wheeler, 1930, pl. 29.7)

i 'lantern' chimney from Beauport Park, East Sussex. These resemble chimney pots but seem to have been used indoors. This example, though in perfect condition, seems to be unused. Height 54cm (Brodribb and Cleere, 1988)

workshop or factory 'of' so-and-so, such as OPTATI which means in effect [EX·OFFICINA]·OPTATI – 'from the workshop of Optatus'.

Lanterns

A number of objects which appear to have functioned as pottery lanterns are known from Britain. A complete example from the bath-house at Beauport Park seems to have been unused (fig.61 i). Another, from the 'Triangular Temple' at Verulamium, may have been used to supply appropriate dimmed lighting for ritual activities (see Henig, 1984, *Religion in Roman Britain*, fig.80 for an illustration).

Candlesticks and candelabra

Candlesticks were extremely simple items made of pottery or metal which can appear at first sight

to be the bases of long-since vanished vessels. They are generally no more than cylinders with splayed bases and grooves to catch melted wax (fig.62 a). A unique example from the villa at Bignor in Sussex was made of Gaulish samian fabric, but is unfortunately now lost (Frere, 1982, 184, fig.33).

Candelabra were normally made of bronze or iron and in their most extravagant form consist of a small tripod, usually in the form of animal legs and feet, supporting a tall shaft with candle-holder at the top. Such examples are extremely rare in Britain but fragments are known from London (fig.62b). More common are simple iron prongs shaped like tripods, or trees with a number of branches, with sharpened ends for inserting into candle bases (fig.62 c).

Windows

Of course no Roman artifical light could compete with natural light when it was available. Unfortunately extremely few windows have survived from Roman Britain, though a house in Dorchester and the bath-house at Beauport Park both stand high enough to preserve a window sill. Glass is more common than the structural evidence, but its remains are mostly confined to splinters. A modest winged-corridor house at Sedgebrook, Plaxtol in Kent (Cockett, R.,

62 Other lighting:

a pottery candlestick from London Wall. Height 8cm (after Wheeler, 1930)

b bronze feet from a candelabra, King William St, London. Height 11.5cm (after Wheeler)

c iron candelabra from Silchester. Height 36cm

d iron window spike from a window grill found at Vindolanda and made from two welded, double-ended spikes. About 19cm wide (after Bidwell, 1986, 150, no. 112)

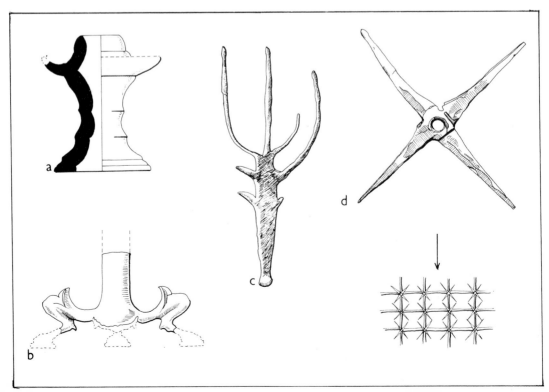

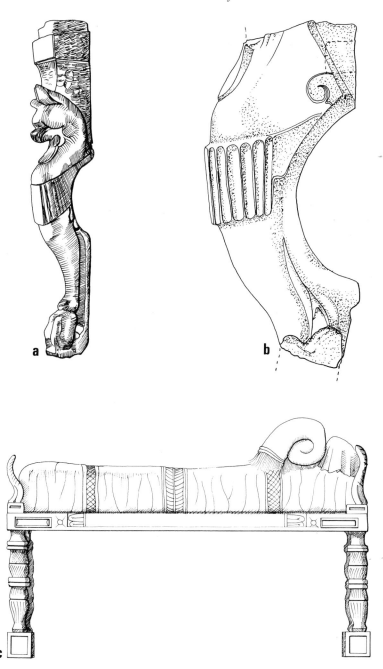

63 Furniture:
a shale table-leg, Colliton Park villa, Dorchester,
  Dorset. Height 50cm (Liversidge, 1955, 37–8)
b section of shale table-leg from Verulamium, height
  27cm (after Frere, 1984, 78)
c a four-legged couch based on that portrayed on the
  tombstone of Victor the Moor, freedman of
  Numerianus, a cavalryman in the *ala Asturum*
  stationed at South Shields, *Arbeia*, in the later
  second century (*RIB* 1064)

Archaeologia Cantiana, forthcoming) has produced most of one window pane, carefully reconstituted from fragments, but how common they were, their size, or how many such a house might have is unknown.

Window grills are known and these usually consist of an iron grid which fitted across the window space (fig.62 d). The unsuitability of such a window, combined with the high cost of glass, must surely have meant that houses had windows that were both small and few.

Furniture

The surviving houses at Herculaneum in southern Italy were preserved by a mud-flow from Vesuvius in the eruption of AD 79. This carbonised the wood so, unlike nearby Pompeii, buried by a hail of pumice, rock and ash, the wooden furniture was preserved. The houses now testify to the sparseness of the furnishing of Roman rooms in our terms, at least in the Mediterranean area. Furniture was not a major priority, though of course chairs, tables, couches and beds were all known and used (fig.63 c; Liversidge, 1955).

It almost goes without saying that Roman Britain's furniture has for the most part vanished, but some examples, mostly carved from the brittle rock called shale found at Kimmeridge in Dorset, have survived to give an impression of what might have been more widely used in wood. At Silchester a small table-top, a foot and a couch leg were recovered. Dorchester has produced a

64 Furniture (⅔ scale except **e**):

a bone hinge. A series of these cylinders were attached alternately to lid and wall of a box with dowelling. The assembly swivelled on a further length of dowel running through the cylinders (after Frere, 1972, 151, no. 186)

b bronze lion's head fitting from Fishbourne (after Frere, 1971, II, 118, no. 125)

c bronze handle with iron tang from Verulamium (after Frere, 1984, 51, no. 177)

d bronze drop handle (one side missing) with iron washer from the Sedgebrook villa, Plaxtol, Kent

e possible reconstruction of a folding stool based on a nearly complete example found at Nijmegen in Holland. Similar horizontal rods with discs were recovered from a pit at Newstead (Curle, 1911, 268–87)

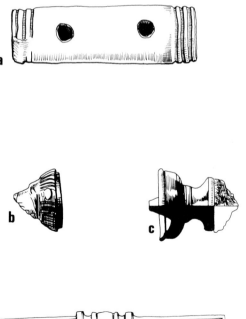

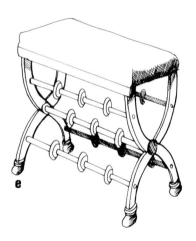

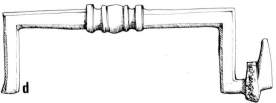

complete table-leg (fig.63 a). Small fragments of wooden table-legs have been recovered from Verulamium (fig.63 b), Billingsgate Buildings and the New Fresh Wharf in London (Chapman in Dyson and Schofield, 1980, 129, no. 670; and Weeks and Rhodes in Dyson, 1986, 231, no. 10,6) and Brough-on-Humber; but a fairly elaborate example which had been turned on a lathe was found in a well at Scole in Norfolk (Liversidge in Rogerson, 1977, 204).

---

65 A reconstructed roof with tiles exploded to show their positioning. The *tegulae* are shown with nail holes and nails but these were not always used. The finial is based on one from Norton

Similar sorts of tables were also made of metals, and finer quality stone – these are particularly well-known at Pompeii and Herculaneum, but a fragment of a table-leg made of imported marble from the island of Paros was found at the Culver Street site in Colchester. Carved with a lion's head, the piece is a unique find from Roman Britain (Crummy, P., forthcoming).

An interesting example of a folding-stool comes from a tomb at Holborough in Kent. The basic structure of the stool was made of iron but decorative features were made of bronze. Although the actual soft seating did not survive, it probably had a cushion (Liversidge, 1955).

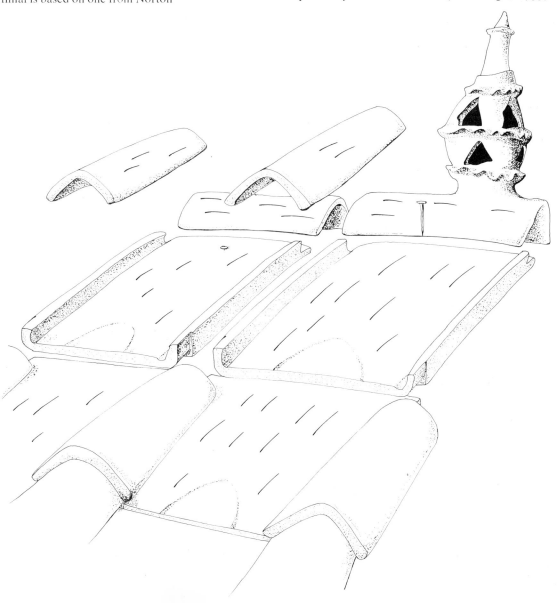

Traces of another are known from Newstead (fig.64 e; Curle, 1911, 268–87).

More important for the evidence of furniture in Roman Britain is the wide survival of metal and bone fittings to furniture. The house at Sedgebrook, Plaxtol in Kent produced a single bronze drop-handle as the only surviving remnant of furniture in use in that house. It may have come from a chest, or a drawer (fig.64 a).

Other such material known from Britain includes bone hinges for chests or caskets, bronze hinges and latches, and bronze decorative terminals and mounts or binding strips of numerous shapes and sizes (fig.64 b). Verulamium has produced a wide range of such material (fig.64 c), and at Colchester traces of the manufacture of bone fittings for furniture in the form of leaves has been found (see Chapter 2, and N. Crummy, 1981).

66 Heating tiles (about ¼ scale):

a a box flue-tile, *tubulus*, in position clamped to the wall; there would have been more tiles below, above and possibly to the side to allow circulation of warm air within the wall cavity

b a voussoir tile, *tubulus cuneatus*, which continued the passage of warm air from a stack of box tiles up and through a vaulted roof. These tiles had the useful function of relieving weight

c iron 'T'-shaped clamp probably used for securing a box flue-tile to a masonry wall. From an unstratified level at the Lullingstone villa (after Meates, 1987, 102, no. 285). Length 25cm

Heating and roofing

The Romano-British who were fortunate enough to live in well-appointed houses enjoyed the benefits afforded by roofs and heating, made from special components manufactured specially for the job (Brodribb, 1987). This aspect of Roman life is so frequently described that it has become a cliché; nevertheless it is a feature of Roman Britain which is very important. Heating and good roofing created a more comfortable domestic environment, both reflecting and promoting the desire for material improvement.

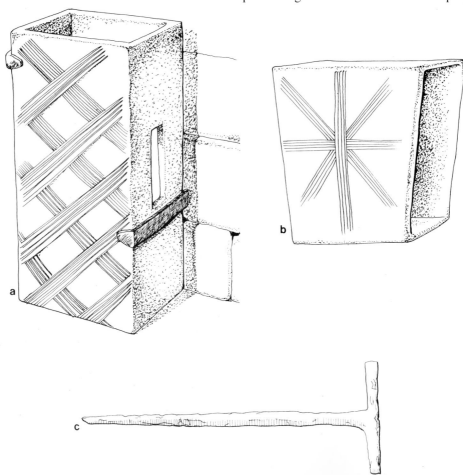

Roof-tiles

The range of tile types was huge, not just because of different functions but because they were hand-made simple items. While general types were used across Britain the variation between two sites can be quite large in terms of details of design, none of which probably affected their ability to do the job. However, as tile fragments are generally discarded on excavations this means a number of special types have gone unnoticed.

Romano-British roofs were based on a timber support structure, as are ours. None have survived, though the traces of wood if burnt can be detected on roof tile. The tiles consisted of two basic types: the *tegula*, a flat tile with flanges; and the *imbrex*, a tapering curved tile. The *tegulae* were laid side by side with flanges abutting starting from a row along the bottom of the roof. The next row slightly overlapped and was prevented from sliding forward by providing cut-outs in the flanges. Then the *imbrices* were placed over the abutted *tegulae* flanges, packed with cement. The ridge along the top of the roof was covered with ridge tiles, similar to the *imbrices*, but not tapering (fig.65). Occasionally *antefixes* were attached to the bottom row of tiles, to cover the join between the *tegulae* and *imbrex* (fig.105 a). How the *tegulae* were secured to the rafters is hotly debated. Some sites have produced certain evidence that at least some of the *tegulae* were secured with nails; at others it seems that they may have been wedged into place, secured by their own weight.

Earthenware roof tiles were not universal. Many Romano-British houses in the Cotswolds are associated with roof tiles made of the local limestone, carefully shaped in diamond form to provide an attractive overlapping pattern, and with a nail-hole in each (Brodribb, 1987, 18). The same technique is used in the area today.

Complete tiles are rare because they are brittle and heavy. However their fragments are usually the most obvious traces of a buried Roman structure on the ground surface, the *tegula* flanges being particularly distinctive.

Flue-tiles

Roman central-heating systems are well-described in many books, so this section is confined to discussing the manufactured components. The passage of hot air through the structure required ducts. This was achieved under the floor by supporting it on pillars, *pilae*, of simple square tiles known as *bessalii*. Air was circulated through the walls in pipes made of flue-tiles. These are square in section and rectangular in shape (fig.66 a). Generally they were secured to the wall with the aid of iron 'T'-shaped clamps (fig.66 c), and bear complex patterns engraved with a 'tile-comb' or roller-dies (see Chapter 2, figs.33, 34) which helped the wall plaster gain a grip. Hot air was circulated around the roof via voussoir tiles which were tapered to allow them to form a curve (fig.66 b; fig.67).

Finials

Hot air or smoke escaped through chimneys, known as *finials*. These are rare largely because they fragment into pieces undiscernible from pieces of roofing tile, and are discarded by excavators (fig. 65). There is a slight problem with interpretation because very few are definitely from the roof. Occasional examples were made in one piece with a roof-tile such as a *tegula*, or ridge-tile, and in these cases there is no doubt, for example that from Norton in Yorkshire (fig.65). Other finials seem to have no traces of roof-fittings and it is quite possible that they were used as lantern-like covers for lamps or candles such as one from the bath-house at Beauport Park (Brodribb, 1981). Finials are made of the same clay as the tiles but are shaped as cones with a number of triangular cut-outs on one or more levels. Generally each row of cut-outs is separated from the others by a flange around the outside of the chimney. The flanges were made into wavy lines by impressing fingers around the circumference. Some chimneys were made of stone, for example those from houses at Llantwit Major and Rockbourne.

Water-supply

Pipes

Few Romano-British houses enjoyed the luxury of a piped water-supply (though at least one house in Verulamium had a latrine flushed by a water-pipe – Frere, 1983, 20). When pipes are found they take two main forms: either they are made of lead, beaten into pipe shape by wrapping lead sheet around a cylindrical core and sealed with a strip of molten lead along the seam; or they were made of wooden lengths joined by iron collars, as in the case of the Verulamium pipes (fig.68).

67 A section of a hypothetical building showing the
positioning of *pilae* beneath the floor, box flue-tiles
and voussoirs

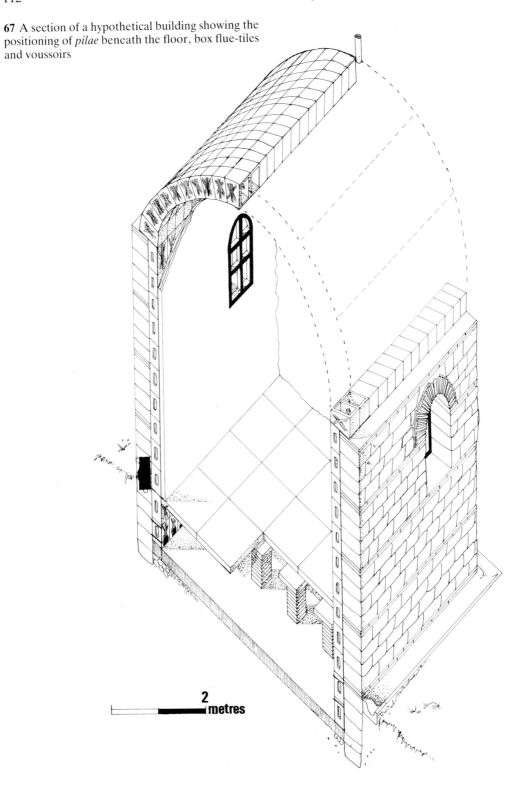

2
metres

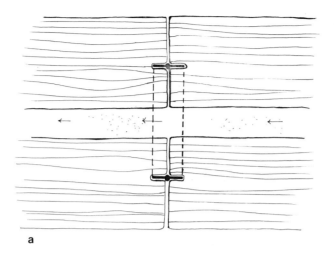

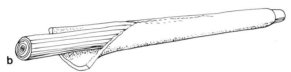

68 Water-pipes:
a section of wooden water pipes joined with an iron collar based on a Verulamium example. Diameter of collar 14.5cm (after Frere, 1984, fig.43, 112)
b being easy to work in sheet form, lead made an ideal material from which to make piping. A length of wooden pole provided a core around which to beat the lead and could be removed when the section of pipe was finished

Water-wheels
For the most part Roman water engineers exploited gravity to move water where it was needed. When this was not possible there were two alternatives; water-wheels and pumps. Water-wheels are not really domestic pieces of equipment, and in Britain the only example so far discovered is a fragment of one used to drain the goldmine at Dolaucothi in Wales (Boon, 1966).

Pumps
The best-known example of a water pump was found at Silchester. Made of wood with a pair of lead cylinders it worked on the force principle; the pump was placed in the water and two reciprocating pistons created vacuums in each cylinder – this sucked water into each cylinder in turn, from where it entered a central tank and went up through a rising pipe (Boon, 1974, 87). If nothing else the pump is interesting because it shows that some of the technology required to generate motion was available in Roman Britain, yet it would be 16 centuries before it was developed. However, the find is unique for Britain (continental examples are known) so it is unlikely that this could be regarded as common Romano-British household equipment.

Household security
The wedged-shut doors of the houses of Pompeii show that fears of inner-city violence and theft are not modern phenomena. That locks were used throughout Roman Britain is evidenced by the large number of keys that survive.

Locks
There were two main forms of lock; the tumbler lock, and the rotary, or lever lock. Tumbler locks use slide keys in order to push tumblers out of the bolt securing the door. The key has a number of projections matching the tumbler holes on the bolt (fig.69 a, b, c). Rotary locks are most commonly used today, where the key is rotated in the lock to push the bolt back. In both cases the precise design of the individual key is dependent

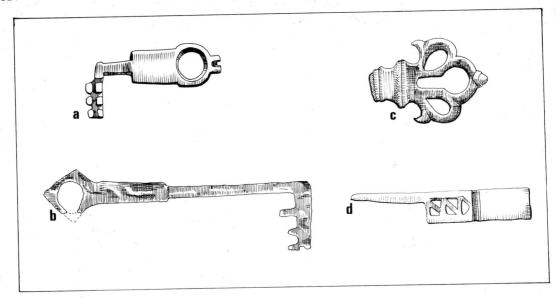

69 Keys (⅔ scale):
a bronze slide key from Richborough, length 56mm (after Cunliffe, 1968, pl. 46, 200)
b iron slide key from Richborough, length 112mm (after Cunliffe, 1968, pl. 55, 275)
c bronze key handle, iron shank decayed, unprovenanced British find
d bronze lock bolt operated by a slide key similar to **a** and **b** above. From Fishbourne Palace (after Cunliffe, 1971, II, 118, no. 136)

on the tumblers or the guards used in the lock. These vary considerably.

An iron padlock was found at the Fishbourne palace, and examples are also known from the Lullingstone villa (Meates, 1987, 95, no. 232), and the fortress at Caerleon. However, problems arise in trying to examine such mechanisms due to internal corrosion and the difficulty of access to the inside, although they seem to operate similarly to rotary locks. Such padlocks were designed to work with chains to secure some sort of door or gate, as are modern examples (Cunliffe, 1971, II, 140).

Keys

Keys were made of iron or bronze. The most elaborate combined a bronze handle with an iron shank (fig.69 c). By this means the handle could be mass-produced by casting in a mould, and then assembled to an individually-made shank. These keys are mostly known from their trifoliate bronze handles because of the susceptibility of the iron to rust away altogether.

Hooks and levers

A wide range of simple iron hooks are related to locks. These were probably straightforward levers designed to allow a door-latch to be lifted through a hole in the door from the outside. As such they are really only part of the mechanism for closing the door, rather than for locking it.

1 Bronze Coolus helmet from the Thames at London. This particular example has the names of four successive owners on the neck-guard. The cheek-pieces and crest holder are missing. It was probably lost between about AD 43 and 60. (Reproduced by courtesy of the Trustees of the British Museum.)

2 Bronze cavalry sports helmet with visor-mask from the auxiliary fort at Ribchester, *Bremetennacum*, Lancashire. The crown of the helmet is decorated with combat scenes, the mask with a mural crown. This kind of helmet was designed for theatrical effect during display battles, such as acting out the legend of the siege of Troy. Probably first or second century. (Reproduced by courtesy of the Trustees of the British Museum.)

3 The 'Rudge Cup', found at Rudge in Wiltshire in 1725. The cup, made of bronze and decorated with enamel, appears to be a souvenir of Hadrian's Wall. Round the edge of the cup are the Wall's crenellations, picked out with blue squares and a red border, and incorporating stylized shields. Above are listed some of the names of the forts: A MAIS (Bowes) ABALLA (Burgh-by-Sands) VXEL[L]ODVNVM (Stanwix) CAMBOGLANS (Castlesteads) BANNA (Birdoswald). Diameter 5 cm. (Reproduced by courtesy of the Trustees of the British Museum.)

4 Jewellery worker's hoard from Snettisham, Norfolk, before cleaning. The material includes a number of gemstones (see plate 17), rings and other pieces of jewellery as well as coins which were probably intended for melting down. They were all buried in the accompanying pot by the owner, who was prevented from recovering them. The coins indicate that the hoard was deposited in or after the late second century. (Reproduced by courtesy of the Trustees of the British Museum.)

5 The Great Dish, which formed part of the silver treasure found near Mildenhall, Suffolk, in 1942. The central theme is maritime, involving a head of Oceanus, Nereids and marine beasts; the outer frieze is a series of figures at a Bacchic revel. Fourth century. Diameter 60.5 cm, weight 8.26 kg (see bibliography for chapter 3; Painter, 1977). (Reproduced by courtesy of the Trustees of the British Museum.)

6 Silver bowl and lid from the Mildenhall treasure. The lid, or cover, was probably not originally made for the flanged bowl with which it was found as it forms a poor fit. The bowl is of a type known for the third century and earlier; stylistic considerations suggest that the cover is either third or fourth century. The cover is decorated with a frieze of animals and profile heads, above which is a leaf pattern. The 'handle' is formed by the figure of a triton blowing a conch. Diameter (bowl) 23 cm; height 19.1 cm. Weight 1.85 kg (Painter, 1977). (Reproduced by courtesy of the Trustees of the British Museum.)

7 Bronze skillet from Prickwillow, Isle of Ely, Cambridgeshire, bearing the name of its maker, Boduogenus. The Celtic name means the skillet was almost certainly made in Britain or Gaul. Probably first century. Length 24.5 cm (Toynbee, 1964, 320). (Reproduced by courtesy of the Trustees of the British Museum.)

8 Fine glassware from the Saxon Shore fort of Burgh Castle, *Gariannonum*, Norfolk. Fourth century (Reproduced by courtesy of the Trustees of the British Museum.)

Top right 9 Glass cup with mould-blown decoration of a chariot race from Colchester. The wording records the victory of a charioteer called Cresce[n]s, and in full reads *Cresces ave, Hierax vale, Olympae vale, Antiloce vale.* This means 'Hail Crescens, farewell to Hierax (and the other losers)'. It was possibly made in an East Gaulish glass factory. First century. Height 8.5 cm. (Reproduced by courtesy of the Trustees of the British Museum.)

Bottom right 10 Samian mould-decorated Form 37 made by the Antonine potter Paternus II of Lezoux in Central Gaul. Found at Wingham, Kent. The decorative design is known as 'free-style' in this case, involving a number of animals and mounted huntsmen–a popular topic. The factory name-stamp was placed in the mould and thus appears backwards, 'retrograde', on the bowl. The Paternus II factory was in operation from about 160-190. Diameter 25.5 cm. (Reproduced by courtesy of the Trustees of the British Museum.)

11 The 'Colchester vase', a beaker elaborately decorated with *barbotine* and *appliqué* motifs. In this scene two opposed gladiators are depicted, named as Memno and Valentinus. The inscription goes on to imply that they were attached to *legio* XXX, a unit based in the Rhineland. The gladiators were possibly famed in the northern provinces and had visited Colchester, though we have no means of confirming this. Probably made around 140-200. (Reproduced by courtesy of the Trustees of the British Museum.)

12 Group of typical domestic pottery from Verulamium (of varying dates) which gives an indication of the range of colour amongst Roman wares. The first and second century samian industry is represented by the mould-decorated Form 29 stamped OF-CRESTIO (*c.* AD 60-70, South Gaul, see Frere, 1972, 225, D15); the plain Forms 79, 33 and 18/31; and the *barbotine* decorated Forms 35 and 42 (see fig. 52). The beakers include the Rhenish motto beaker with the slogan DA MERVM (see fig. 53 i and Frere, 1972, 348, no. 1114) found in a late third to early fourth-century level; a Nene Valley beaker with an animal chase scene from a late third-century context (height 23 cm, Frere, 1983, 333, no. 1806); another Nene Valley beaker from the same context with indents and scales (height 20 cm, Frere, 1983, 333, no. 1812); and to the lower right a Lyons beaker with bossed decoration of late first-century date (height 13 cm, Frere, 1972, 276, no. 127). Other vessels include a black-burnished jar at upper left (see fig. 55), a third-fourth century colour coat flagon (see fig. 58 f), and a grey ware flanged dish in the foreground adjacent to a Central Gaulish colour-coated beaker with rouletted bands. This beaker is similar to those recovered from the New Fresh Wharf in London which are now dated to *c.* 180-220 (see fig. 53 e-g, and Richardson in Dyer, 1986, 118, no. 1, 114). (Reproduced by courtesy of Verulamium Museum.)

13 Bronze mirror with cover from Coddenham, Suffolk. There are repoussé medallions on the top and bottom with a bust of Nero (AD 54-68) and a sacrificial scene modelled on a coin reverse design. Diameter 6.25 cm. (Reproduced by courtesy of the Trustees of the British Museum.)

14 Gilded bronze 'bow and fantail' brooch from the fort at Greatchesters, *Aesica*, on Hadrian's Wall. The decoration is purely Celtic in the use of curvilinear motifs and trumpets. Stylistically the brooch is dated to the late first century, but it was found in the hoard of jewellery which included third-century pieces. It was probably therefore quite old when deposited. Height 11.5 cm. (Reproduced by courtesy of the Museum of Antiquities, Newcastle-upon-Tyne.)

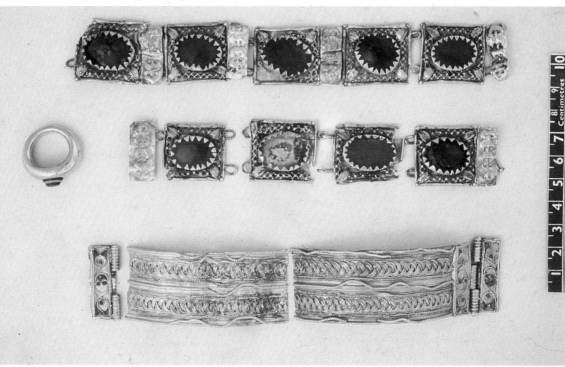

15 Gold crossbow brooch found in the Moray Firth, Scotland, in 1847. The pin is missing and the body of the brooch is hollow (most Romano-British bronze examples are solid-cast). One of the terminals was fitted with a screw thread which allowed the axis to be fitted into the wings. Fourth century. Length 7.9 cm. (Reproduced by courtesy of the Trustees of the British Museum.)

16 Gold bracelet and necklet (?) found at Rhayader, Powys, a few miles north-west from the fort at Castell Collen, Llandrindod Wells. The bracelet is decorated with gold-wire ornament, the necklet with carnelians or blue paste with filigree borders. Length of the bracelet 19 cm. (Reproduced by courtesy of the Trustees of the British Museum.)

17 Group of eight intaglios from the Snettisham hoard deposited by a jeweller who had not yet mounted them in rings (see plate 4). Various deities and motifs are depicted, including Fortuna (upper left), a *modius* containing corn (lower left), Diana (left centre), Spes (Hope, upper centre), a bird (bottom) and a dolphin (lower right). (Reproduced by courtesy of the Trustees of the British Museum.)

18 The 22 gold rings which formed part of the Thetford Treasure. Other gold jewellery included a belt buckle, four bracelets and several pendants and necklaces; the treasure also included 33 silver spoons and three silver strainers connected with the cult of the obscure Italian rural god Faunus. The jewellery appears to have been unused, though the gemstones were evidently somewhat older than the rings in which they were set. The rings appear to have been the work of a single workshop though the purpose of the deposit remains unclear. It may have been concealed for subsequent collection, or it may have been a ritual votive deposit. (Johns and Potter, 1983). (Reproduced by courtesy of the Trustees of the British Museum.)

19 Stone head of Mercury from the shrine at Uley. This was probably part of the actual cult statue which stood in the temple. Although damaged, the stumps of wings on the head can just be seen. The head is approximately life-size. (Reproduced by courtesy of the Trustees of the British Museum.)

20 Bronze figurine of Venus found at Verulamium. Probably first or second century but recovered from an early fourth-century context where it may have been intended for melting down. The statuette was probably originally used in a household *lararium* (shrine). Height 20 cm. (Frere, 1972, 140, no. 155). (Reproduced by courtesy of Verulamium Museum.)

HERCU... VENUS   MINERV... MERCURY

VULCAN   NEPTUNE

UNIDENTIFIED   UNIDENTIFIED

21 Bronze statuettes of gods and goddesses from Southbroom, Wiltshire. The figures are Romano-Celtic in style and some have unusual attributes, though it is impossible to suggest what these may signify in terms of belief. Heights 10-13 cm. (Reproduced by courtesy of the Trustees of the British Museum.)

23 Face-pot from Colchester, used as a cremation urn. This vessel may date to the later first century (see chapter 6, and Braithwaite, 1984, 105). Height 30 cm. (Reproduced by courtesy of the Trustees of the British Museum.)

Left **22** Marble portrait bust from the 'Deep Room', Lullingstone villa, Kent. Probably a portrait of a previous owner's ancestor; sealed in the room with another during the third century. The style of this bust is Hadrianic, and the marble appears to be from Greece. Height 75 cm (Meates, 1979, 36). (Reproduced by courtesy of the Trustees of the British Museum; property of Kent County Council.)

24 Some of the material recovered from the sacred spring at Bath, *Aquae Sulis*. The group includes the mask discussed in figure 99; a number of *paterae* (see Chapter 3), and bronze and pewter jugs; a pewter candlestick in the form of an animal (height 24.4 cm); bronze penannular brooch with enamelled terminals (diameter 6.8 cm); bronze washer from a model (?) catapult (diameter 8 cm); a number of gemstones; and a much larger number of coins, most of which are worn, low denominations. (Reproduced by courtesy of Bath Museums Service.)

25 Restored tombstone of Julius Alpinus Classicianus, procurator of the province of Britain in London immediately after the Boudican Revolt of AD 60. The two inscribed stones were found in 1852 (upper) and 1935 (lower), reused in the city wall near Trinity Place. Width about 2.3 m. (Reproduced by courtesy of the Trustees of the British Museum.)

26 Silver vessels and feathers from the early fourth-century Water Newton Christian treasure, discovered in 1975. Three of the feathers bearing the chi-rho symbol are shown. The jug is decorated with leaves and winding scrolls, and once had a handle (height 20.3 cm). The bowl (left) bears an inscription, indicating that it was donated by Publianus to the Lord's sacred place SANCTVM ALTARE (height 11.5 cm). The *cantharus* cup is 12.5 cm in height and uninscribed. In the foreground is a silver strainer, bearing an engraved chi-rho, of a type known from pagan religious contexts (length 20.2 cm). Strainers were used to filter wine (Painter, 1977). (Reproduced by courtesy of the Trustees of the British Museum.)

27 Hoard of 30 fourth-century gold *solidi* from Water Newton, Cambridgeshire, found in 1974. The coins, together with two folded pieces of silver plate, were placed in a bronze bowl (diameter 13.5 cm) which was inserted into a 'Romano-Saxon' pottery bowl (diameter 16 cm), and covered with a Nene Valley 'Castor Box' pottery lid (diameter 22 cm). The coins have a *terminus post quem* of 350 (see bibliography for chapter 8; Johns and Carson in Painter, 1977). (Reproduced by courtesy of the Trustees of the British Museum.)

4
The Individual

Personal hygiene

The Roman habit of regular bathing in a public or private establishment is so well-known that the details of the activity need hardly be discussed here. But it is worth noting Tacitus' comment that bathing in Britain was eagerly adopted (*Agricola*, 21), even if this probably only referred to the philo-Roman members of the Celtic upper-class. Bath-houses are amongst the earliest obviously Roman-style buildings put up in Britain. At Silchester the main bath-house preceded the late-first-century street-grid, one of whose roads subsequently covered part of the building. Bathing was only one aspect of Roman hygiene and health, and a large number of artefacts can be associated with these activities.

The Roman bather began his routine by exercising in the *palaestra*, an open area attached to the baths. Sweating brings dirt to the surface of the skin. The grime was scraped off with a *strigil* which might be made of iron or bronze, perhaps with a decorated handle, or more commonly one designed for a secure grip. The important part of the strigil was the curved blade which allowed it to be brought around the body. A unique example was found in the baths of the legionary fortress at Caerleon engraved with portrayals of six of the Twelve Labours of Hercules (fig.70 a and Zienkiewicz, 1985, 157) and indicates the possible additional significance of such decorated articles as amulets. Another bronze strigil, from Reculver in Kent, has a handle in the shape of Hercules' club (Henig, *Religion in Roman Britain*, 1984, 20).

Once the dirt was removed from the skin it was massaged with oils and perfumes. The oils were contained in small glass or pottery 'unguent' flasks. These sometimes have very small handles allowing them to be carried, perhaps on a bath attendant's belt.

Small personal hygiene sets, or *chatelaines*, made of bronze and consisting of nail-cleaners, tweezers and ear-picks seem to have been a particularly common possession. Each set was hung on a ring, perhaps so that it could be attached to a belt (fig.70 b-e). The individual components were easily lost and these are common site finds. However, their actual usefulness is more open to question, and they may have been more of a symbol of female adulthood.

Equally common are combs, though being a tool of universal cultural appeal similar examples appear from the Roman period almost up to the present day. Surviving examples are normally made of carved bone (wood was probably more common), and like the bone handles mentioned in the previous section, they might bear engraved decoration, or be carved into some sort of design. Unlike most modern combs they were double-sided (fig.70 f).

Roman mirrors served exactly the same purpose of personal vanity as they do today. In general Roman mirrors were made of metal, usually silver or silvered bronze, highly-polished on one side to achieve a reflective surface while the reverse was sometimes decorated. Glass mirrors, silvered on the back, are also known from Britain. They were secured to their frames with bitumen. Sometimes the mirror was attached to a handle, but they were also made with covers in the manner of a modern 'compact' mirror. An elaborate example from Coddenham in Suffolk made of bronze has a portrait of the Emperor Nero (AD 54–68) on one side, and a group of figures with a building on the other (plate 13). Both designs are clearly derived from coins and show that mirrors could be expensive works of art as well as purely functional items. The majority of mirrors are circular but rectangular examples are also known (Lloyd-Jones in Munby and Henig, 1977, II, 231). The most remarkable example from Roman Britain was found at Wroxeter, *Viroconium*, in Shropshire (fig.70 g).

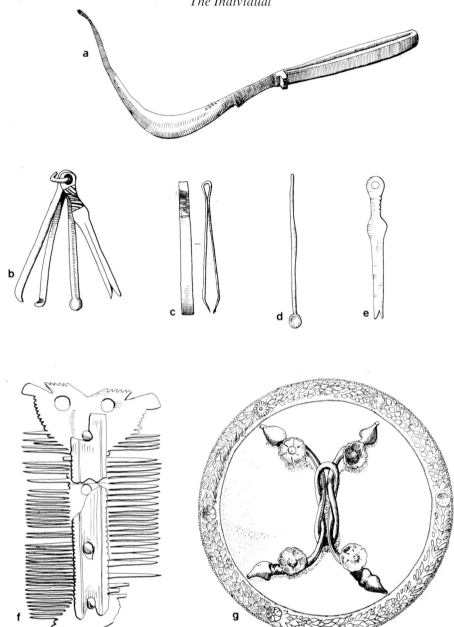

70 Personal hygiene:

a bronze strigil from the legionary bath-house at Caerleon, *Isca*, (after Zienkiewicz, 1986, 157). This is a particularly elaborate example and bears portrayals of the third to ninth of the 12 canonical Labours of Hercules. It is therefore probably one of a pair. It also bears an inscription in Greek, Καλως ελοσε, which means 'it washed you nicely'. The subject matter, the inscription and the quality of workmanship suggest that this was manufactured in the eastern Mediterranean and is correspondingly hard to date. Length 25cm

b-e bronze 'manicure set' from the Walbrook valley in London consisting of tweezers, ear-pick and nail-cleaner. Length 6cm

f double-sided bone comb from a late fourth-century inhumation burial of a woman in her fifties from Cirencester. Length 10cm (after McWhirr *et alii*, 1982)

g an unusually fine example of a silver mirror, with two entwined handles, from Wroxeter. Diameter 30 cm

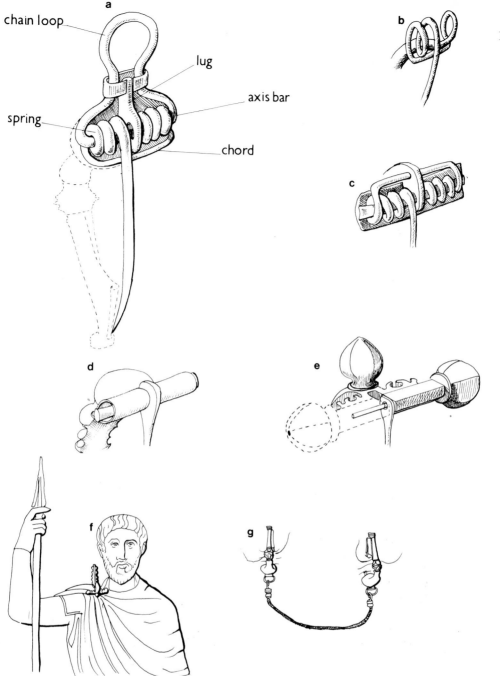

71 Brooch mechanisms (twice actual size, except **f** and **g**):

a mechanism from a sprung trumpet brooch showing how the axis bar forms the chain loop as well (see **g** below)

b the spring from a one-piece brooch showing how the bow becomes the pin

c sprung mechanism from a Colchester B brooch. Here the chord and axis bar are held by a double-pierced lug. Other similar types hold the chord in a separate lug or with a hook or claw

d hinged mechanism from a Hod Hill brooch with the axis bar held by a rolled head

e hinged mechanism from a crossbow brooch with the axis bar held in a hole passed through the arms. In this case the hole continues to the terminal through which the axis would have been passed. Sometimes one terminal was screwed in on a worm thread to hold the axis in place

f Stilicho, the Vandal general, as portrayed on a late ivory *diptych* wearing a crossbow brooch

g a pair of trumpet brooches connected by a chain

Personal decoration

Brooches (Fibulae)

Field-walking a Roman site will almost always produce large quantities of pottery. Coins are also commonly found but the third most typical finds are *fibulae*, or brooches. Their frequency and the large number of different types make them a useful archaeological tool for the Roman period in Britain.

Brooch techniques

There are so many types of brooches that it is easy to forget their purpose: Romano-British brooches had one very straightforward function – to secure clothing. This required a pin held by tension against the brooch body. There were two techniques of tensioning the pin: the sprung pin which is an extension of a coil (fig.71 a-c); and the pin which swung on an axis until restrained by a stop on its head; this is known as a hinged pin (fig.71 d, e). These two methods actually appear in a large number of different forms, frequently on the same types of brooch.

There are advantages and disadvantages of each method. The sprung pin spread the tension throughout the whole length of the coil, and therefore the metal used did not need to be as strong as that used for hinged pins. The whole spring mechanism, while complicated, did not actually require quite so much precision as the hinged method. The spring system also made it necessary for the brooch body to have large housings and lugs to hold the spring. It would have been difficult, for example, to manufacture crossbow brooches (see below) with sprung pins.

The idea of using brooches to fasten clothing was introduced to Britain by the fifth century BC at the latest. These early types were mostly simple, one-piece, bow brooches where the body, spring and pin were all made of a single piece of metal. However, hinged types of the 'involute type' were also made (see Hull and Hawkes, 1987, plates 42-3). By the period immediately preceding the Roman conquest the dominant type in the south-east was the 'Colchester' bow brooch, whose spring and pin was held to the body by a chord either secured with a hook (in the majority of cases) or passed through a pierced lug on the brooch's head. Other types included the continental 'Langton Down' brooch and 'Nauheim derivatives' (see below). Penannular brooches were also common. With a well-established domestic

tradition the brooches of the Roman period inevitably show a combination of British and continental influences. Brooches remained in use throughout the Romano-British period, but by far the greatest numbers and different types belong to the first and second centuries AD. Thereafter the range becomes relatively restricted and brooches themselves seem possibly to have become indicative of social status. The distinctive crossbow brooch form is a good example (fig.71 f).

Brooches were made almost always of bronze, occasionally tinned to give a silver appearance. Iron was also used but these are far less common, partly due to destruction by corrosion. Sometimes examples made of silver or gold are found, but these are extremely rare. A pair of silver trumpet brooches from Chorley in Lancashire is an even rarer instance which shows that some brooches were normally worn in matching pairs: in this case the chain which connected the brooches survives too. But by their very nature most brooches have come down to us singly and broken because they were easily damaged and lost.

---

72 Brooches or *fibulae*. These are specific excavated examples and therefore only broadly representative of the basic form (2/3 scale):

a one-piece 'Nauheim derivative' brooch (Fishbourne, Cunliffe, 1971, II, 100, no. 15)

b 'Polden Hill' (a 'Dolphin' variant) bow-brooch (Richborough, Bushe-Fox, 1949, 112, no. 25)

c head-stud brooch (Richborough, Bushe-Fox, 1949, 114, no. 34

d trumpet brooch with enamelled decoration (Verulamium, Frere, 1984, 25, no. 31)

e 'Aucissa' brooch (Richborough, Cunliffe, 1968, 84, no. 42)

f divided bow brooch (Chepstow, in Brailsford, 1964, 20, no. 31)

g strip bow or 'Langton Down' brooch (Richborough, Bushe-Fox, 1949, 112, no. 21)

h winged bow or 'Hod Hill' brooch (Richborough, Bushe-Fox, 1949, 111, no. 17)

i 'crossbow' or 'P-shaped' brooch (Lydney, Wheeler, 1932, 78, no. 26)

j 'thistle' brooch (Hod Hill, in Brailsford, 1964, 20 no. 33)

k 'knee' brooch (Richborough, Bushe-Fox, 1949, 118, no. 51)

l plate brooch in the form of a hare set with enamel (Richborough, Bushe-Fox, 1949, 116, no. 44)

m disc brooch set with enamel (Richborough, Bushe-Fox, 1949, 116, no. 45)

n penannular brooch (Lydney, Wheeler, 1932, 78, no. 33)

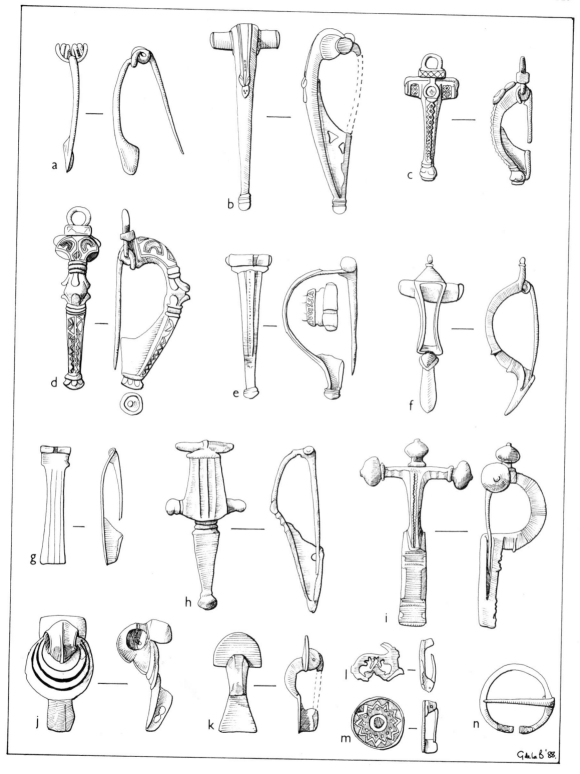

There is very little specific evidence of the manufacture of brooches in Britain, though an unfinished 'Colchester' brooch is known from Baldock (see Chapter 2, p.56, fig.31 g). This indicates that casting blanks was followed by forging and working into shape. The pins, and the simpler one-piece brooches, could be made from a piece of wire. The bodies of penannular brooches were cast or made from a bent rod, while the pins were separate and were looped around the ring. While decoration was usually achieved during the casting process a number of brooches were cast with recesses. These were subsequently filled with the coloured glass material commonly referred to as enamels (fig.72 d, and see Chapter 2 for a brief discussion of the technique).

Brooch types

The most established basic typological series of Romano-British brooches was devised by R.G. Collingwood, though his scheme is now very out of date. Nevertheless as his classifications ('Groups') are referred to in some earlier reports they are included here; it is also worth noting that Romano-British brooches can be considered as native British or continental types. It should be stressed that these basic designs are represented by a huge range of variations, and that their numbers are increasing all the time. Very few brooches are matched by duplicates. The most comprehensive record of brooch types was assembled by the late M.R. Hull in his *corpus*, much of which remains unpublished. Until this becomes available the reader is referred to R. Hattatt's three recent books which illustrate and describe around 1,400 different examples and contain useful discussions of variations.

1. One-piece brooches (fig.72 a, Group A). A very simple design known as the Nauheim type from its use in that part of Germany from about 75 BC on. The 'Nauheim derivative' or La Tène III brooches are common in Britain from the beginning of the first century AD until Neronian times, and are distinguished from the earlier examples by having a perforated catchplate.

2. Simple bow brooches (fig.72 b, Groups E, F, G, and H). This basic type has a number of variations based on the bow and transverse head with wings containing and protecting the spring; some examples have hinged pins. The bow can be decorated with a number of motifs, usually simple linear mouldings but small enamelled panels may occur. Type H, also known as the 'Dolphin', differs in the way the bow is 'humped forward over the junction of the arms' (Collingwood and Richmond, 1969, 265). These brooches were used throughout the first and second centuries and include the early 'pre-Conquest' type (Group F). Other variants include the Maxey type where the bottom of the bow expands into a fantail (later first century), the Polden Hill type which resembles the dolphin except in having lateral lugs to carry the axis bar (AD 50–70), and the T-shaped type distinguished from other bows by having hinged pins housed in tubular wings (late first century to 150).

3. Head-stud brooches (fig.72 c, Group Q). Essentially similar to the bow brooches, and usually classed as a variant of that group, this type of brooch has a head-stud at the top of the bow and a distinctive foot knob. Either sprung or hinged-pins were used. Both the stud and the bow are usually decorated with a cast pattern filled with coloured enamel. At the top of the brooch in many cases is a ring which would allow it to be connected to a pair by a chain. They were most common in the second century. Closely related are the Thealby type brooches which have the foot knob and head ring but not the stud; this variation is a distinctive northern British form.

4. Trumpet brooches (fig.72 d, Group R). This type derives its name from the expansion of the head into the shape of a trumpet which contained and protected the spring. The trumpet is a form peculiar to Britain and is found throughout the province. Many bear rings on the head, and it seems that these almost certainly formed pairs, connected by a chain. An elaborate example made of silver, over 18cm (7in) high, accompanied the Aesica brooch from Greatchesters (see below). Some second-century variations combine a trumpet head with a fantail. Trumpet brooches appeared around AD 40 and were most common in the second century.

5. Fantail or Wing-and-fanbow brooches (plate 14, Group X). In this type the bottom of the box spreads out. Derived from the continental thistle type and Maxey bow brooch type, it dates from the mid-first century up to the middle of the second century. The most impressive example was found at Greatchesters on Hadrian's Wall and is known as the 'Aesica Brooch' after the Roman name of the fort. Aesica-type brooches, though, combine the fantail foot with the arched bow of the thistle type (see below) and are best considered as a variant of both forms

which only occurred in the Claudian-Neronian period.

6. Aucissa brooches (fig.72 e, Group C). A D-shaped bow with a hinged pin on an iron axis type made in Gaul in the first half of the first century, appearing in Britain *c*. 50. Some were made by a manufacturer called Aucissa whose name appears on some brooches. They are particularly well-known from military sites. The divided bow brooch (fig.72 f, Group U) is similar to the Aucissa brooch in profile but has a longitudinal division in the bow.

7. Winged-bow/Hod Hill brooches (fig.72 h, Group P). This is a distinctive type of brooch related to the Aucissa type with three clear divisions in the bow, and a hinged-pin. The upper part carries a number, normally two, of projections, usually referred to as side knobs. The bottom part is a tapering strip connected to the upper by a small central section. The type is clearly dated to the early part of the Conquest and is often found on early military sites, such as the Claudian fort at Hod Hill in Dorset.

8. Strip and tapering bow brooches (fig.72 g, Groups K, L and M). These types are similar in having flat bows, rather than the solid bows of other varieties. There are a number of variations and they had sprung or hinged-pins. Gaulish in origin, these brooches were also imported before the Conquest, most notably the 'Langton Down' variety (Wheeler, Lydney Park, 1929, 71 ff), but were used until Flavian times.

9. Thistle or rosette brooch (fig.72 j, Group W). This brooch type belongs to the first century BC up to the late Claudian period and was made by applying a disc to a p-shaped bow.

10. Knee brooch (fig.72 k, Group V). This type, first known in Germany, appears in Britain from the later second century onwards and is predominantly distributed in the north. They tend to be relatively small, employing a squat bow in the general form of a leg and foot.

11. P-shaped/crossbow brooches (fig.72 i, Group T). The reasons for these names are obvious from the shapes. They do not occur commonly in Britain until the third century, with the elaborate examples belonging to the fourth century. Similar types appear across the Roman Empire. It is possible that this type of brooch may have indicated a high social status. In many respects the developed 'crossbow' brooch is the most complex type known. They seem to have been made from several components; the hinged pin, and the bow with leg and three terminals,

and required a hole through the arms to carry the axis bar. Although most Romano-British examples are solid they are known to have been made from hollow parts, particularly on the continent. In the most complicated examples one wing terminal was screwed into place and the upper one was usually secured with a pin passing through the top of the bow. In early examples these terminals were simply moulded extensions of the bow and wings. The bow and leg could be quite elaborately decorated with moulded and incised patterns. These include 'ring and dot', lines, chevrons and spirals; it was also not uncommon to gild examples made of bronze. Some examples had small lugs in the leg which dropped into place preventing the pin from coming out (plate 15).

12. Disc and plate brooches (fig.72 l, m). These mostly belong to the second century and resemble modern badges, rather than safety pins. The pins pivot in twin lugs on the back of the brooch, fastened into a projecting catch. Some later types were sprung. Unlike those discussed above, disc and plate brooches are often decorated with inlaid glass or enamel. Disc brooches take a number of different forms: those with peripheral lugs (second century); those with conical centres (second to third century); and those with *repoussé* decoration of horses and soldiers (second century). Plate brooches are those formed in the shape of a motif, usually a representation of an animal like a hare or cockerel – the zoomorphic type. Other types, the skeuomorphic forms, take the shape of a number of different objects such as daggers, axes, phalluses, swastikas and cornucopiae. These objects have amuletic associations and should probably be linked loosely with religion and superstition. This also applies to the 'horse and rider', possibly representing a Celtic hunter god variant on the classical Mars. This zoomorphic type is often found on religious sites (fig.101 i). There are many other types of plate brooch known, usually taking a more complicated geometric form, for example · concentric lozenges, pierced discs, conjoined discs and semi-circles, and terminals of various forms. Evidently the only restriction on design was the ingenuity of the maker.

13. Penannular brooches (fig.72 n). This extremely simple design is subject to very little variation apart from the terminals of the ring which required some sort of obstruction to prevent the pin slipping off. Most terminals are

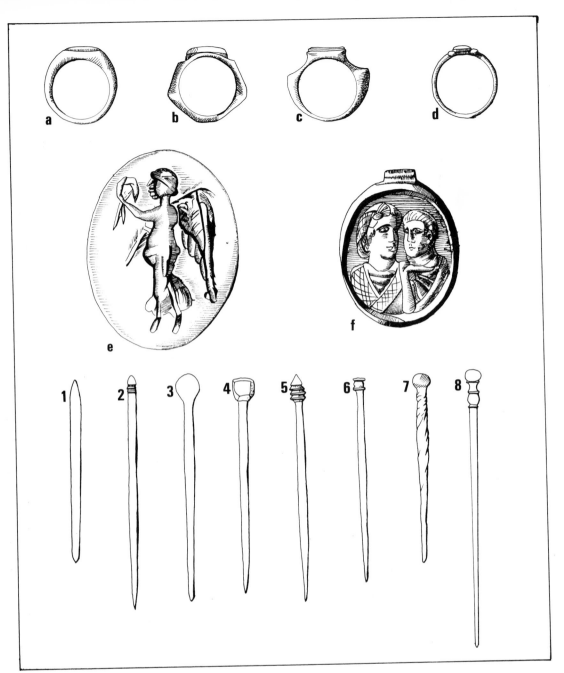

73 Jewellery (ring-types, medallions and pins):

a circular ring expanding at the bezel: a type typical of the second century

b ring with bevelled shoulders, typical of the third and fourth centuries

c ring with humped shoulders, also typical of the third and fourth centuries

d ring with four small spheres around the bezel, second century

e a stone intaglio portraying a victory. One of 88 found in the drains of the baths of the legionary fortress at Caerleon, probably because the water caused stones to work free from their mounts and were swept away before they could be recovered. Height 15.4mm (after Zienkiewicz, 1986, no. 51)

f betrothal medallion in jet from York, height 63mm (RCHM York, 1962)

Pin types (about ⅔ scale) (after N. Crummy, 1979 and 1983):

1 simple pin (throughout the period)

2 conical head with transverse grooves pin (40s/50s +)

3 bulbous head (200–400)

4 faceted head, also made in jet and metal (250+)

5 disc head (fourth century)

6 cotton reel head (200+)

7 glass pin

8 bead, reel and spool head (100–300)

simply folded over, or pinched, but others may have knobs or even animal heads, while the pins are usually simply folded over the ring. Penannular brooches were common in the pre-Conquest period (Fowler, 1960), and it is therefore difficult to date them closely. A particularly fine example made of bronze was found at Bath in the sacred spring – the terminals are decorated with animal scenes and set with red enamel (plate 24). Penannular brooches were made well into the mediaeval period.

It cannot be emphasised enough that this is a very basic breakdown of the main brooch types which have been classified. In one sense they are all drawn together by their common function, but the variations have considerable potential for identifying approximate chronologies and regional types (Table V). However, brooches are rarely found in complete form. At best they almost always lack the pin, and at worst only a small portion of the body is found. A familiarity with the basic types is useful for identifying fragmentary examples, but examination of minor detail is likely to be useful.

Unfortunately it is not possible to be sure which brooches were popular amongst specific groups of the population or even how they were normally worn. An ivory diptych of the late-Roman general Stilicho shows him wearing an elaborate crossbow brooch on his right shoulder to fasten his cloak (fig.71 f). This does draw attention to the fact that modern convention shows Roman brooches 'upside-down', a fact which becomes obvious when trying to operate examples still in working order. To some extent the distribution of certain types of brooch in northern Britain, such as 'Knee' brooches and Thealby brooches, might suggest that they were particularly favoured by the military but beyond that, one cannot say. Pairs of brooches may have been more suitable for securing female clothing. However it is perhaps surprising that brooches do not appear on any Romano-British sculpture yet discovered except for a military tombstone from Chester (which depicts a centurion, M. Aurelius Nepos, wearing a 'Knee' brooch; *RIB* 491). It is therefore difficult to draw any conclusions about which sort of person wore which sort of brooch.

Jewellery

In recent years the most exciting and remarkable find of Romano-British jewellery was the Thetford treasure. Discovered with a metal detector in 1979, the circumstances of this late fourth-century hoard of jewellery and silver spoons (see Chapter 6 and fig.95 for the spoons) remain a mystery, but the find itself amounts to one of the most important late Roman collections. There were 22 gold finger rings, four gold bracelets and five gold necklaces amongst other items (plate 18 and Johns and Potter, 1983, 11). In fact much surviving Roman jewellery is of late date – this probably reflects the debasement of the coinage and the need for some other means of storing wealth with precious metals (Higgins 1980). Certainly late jewellery seems to be bulkier than earlier examples.

Romano-British precious metal jewellery is of course rare and particularly hard to date because of the residual factor. Such treasured items would be preserved in much the same way as antique jewellery is valued today, though bronze or iron examples were presumably regarded as more disposable. Even ancient jewellery in a wearable state regularly appears in antiquities sales. Four main types can be considered:

Rings

Some time in the year 395 or later two rings, pottery and coins were buried by an anonymous person in Grovely Wood in Wiltshire. One of the rings was made of silver, and bore a gold setting in the bezel. The gem was decorated with a pair of clasped hands, a typical Roman betrothal motif (Kent and Painter, 1977, 61, no. 140). The ring was clearly both an item of financial and sentimental value and symbolises the way in which Roman rings served functions beyond mere decoration.

Roman-British rings were made of gold, silver, bronze, iron, bone, jet and glass (fig.73 a-d). Bezels often contained coloured glass, or gems engraved with some sort of motif, perhaps connected with the owner's family or business, but religious or mythological motifs are common (fig.73 e). Cupids, animals, gods, personifications (such as Fortuna, or a city goddess, a 'Tyche') are all known from Britain. However, gemstones should be regarded with caution because it seems that these were often re-used, particularly as the better-quality engraving seems to belong to the first two centuries AD. The Thetford treasure seems to have included a number of engraved gems awaiting new mounts, suggesting that the hoard was deposited, at least in part, by a jeweller. There have two recent large finds of gemstones. The first consists of a hoard of 110 unset gems and silver jewellery found at Snettisham in Norfolk in 1985 (plate 17). The second consists of 88 gems lost by bathers in the legionary fortress baths of Caerleon and recovered from the *frigidarium* drains during excavations (fig.73 e).

Rings sometimes bear inscriptions. A gold ring from the Backworth treasure bears a dedication to the Celtic Mother Goddesses MATRUM·CO·COAE (Brailsford, 1964, 22). Such inscriptions also indicate a ring's use as a signet ring, for example one from the New Fresh Wharf in London bearing the intials of the owner A·P·D. These were engraved backwards to produce a correct version when impressed into a seal (Chapman in Dyson, 1986, 235, 14.1). Rings with Christian slogans, such as VIVAS·IN·DEO, engraved on them are also well-known (fig.116 e).

The two most common types of rings are those which are basically circular but expand at one point to receive the bezel, and those with bevelled shoulders which also expand to receive the bezel. The former belongs to the second century while the latter is associated with the third and fourth century – the Grovely Wood example was such a ring.

Other varieties include a type where the shoulders supporting the bezel are concave, also known as the 'humped' shoulder type; 'serpent' rings where the ring is made out of two serpents' bodies whose heads flank the bezel; a variety where the bezel is accompanied by beads at the point of meeting with the ring; wide-band rings with square bezels; and filigree rings.

It is also worth noting that keys could also be mounted on finger-rings, though clearly their function was to act as a key rather than an eccentric decoration. They are usually so small that they probably served to open boxes, such as a jewellery box, rather than doors.

Bracelets

Romano-British bracelets are typically simple items made of gold, silver, bronze, iron, jet, shale, glass or bone. Naturally they are invariably circular or oval internally though externally they may be angular producing a number of flat faces which may be decorated. More commonly they may have diagonal grooving or serrated edges. Bracelets made of metal are usually either simple wire circles, or they may be made of a number of twisted wires, though examples made of a number of links and beads are known. Sometimes the metal may be mixed, perhaps bronze and iron. The most elaborate examples are the 'snake' bracelets where the band is broken and the ends are designed as opposed snakes' heads, for example those from Dolaucothi in Wales, which may be made of gold mined there. An outstanding bracelet made of gold, and found at Rhayader in Wales, recalls Celtic craftsmanship in the use of filigree to create a design based on scrolls and intersecting arcs (plate 16; Brailsford, 1964, plate 3).

Pins

Pins were both decorative and functional, and were probably used both for securing the hair and clothing. They are extremely numerous as site finds, for example 118 in bone from Verulamium (Goodburn and Grew in Frere, 1984, 71) but extremely hard to date. As pins their shape is self-evident: pointed lengths of some appropriate material such as bone, bronze, silver or gold. However, it is the head which is most interesting. At one extreme this may be no more than another point separated from the shaft by a small number of grooves; at the other it may be a miniature work of art of the greatest skill, perhaps portraying a personification such as *Fortuna*, or god. Heads which seem to portray ordinary individuals may have an amuletic, or commemorative, significance in the manner of a modern locket photograph. Some recent work at Colchester has led to the distinction of six basic types of bone pin and a suggested chronology (fig.73).

Other jewellery

Roman jewellery also included necklaces, medallions, pendants and earrings. Naturally only a few examples can be described, but they do show that for those who could afford to pay, high-quality goods were available even in Britain.

Necklaces were made from any suitable material. One from London is made of 70 beads of Baltic amber strung on a flax string. Another from the Backworth treasure is made of gold figure-of-eight links with a wheel pendant – the wheel was a classical and Celtic religious motif, associated with the sun (Brailsford, 1964, 28, no. 1).

Medusa medallions made of Whitby jet were worn perhaps as an amulet to protect against evil, as Theseus protected himself. Some are betrothal medallions (fig. 73 f). Metal medallions might bear relief portrayals of some worthy subject such as an emperor or empress, god or goddess.

A childrens' grave at Southfleet in Kent contained a gold pendant made of a number of horizontal strips inset with stones and pearls connected by a pair of links. At the top is a suspension hook, at the bottom a square medallion carrying three filigree tassles (Brailsford, 1964, 28, no. 7).

Earrings were made in a number of different ways and types. Even so the majority are penannular; that is, they form a broken circle. Such earrings could be plain or decorated, made of one piece of metal or more, and perhaps even have beads or pendants attached. Other types involves some sort of decorated plate or motif with a kind of wire hook for inserting into the ear-lobe.

Clothing

It is hardly surprising to learn that no complete items of clothing, apart from shoes, have survived from the Roman period in Britain, for the simple reason that materials decay in most of the prevailing conditions. Some garments have survived, mostly leather, in waterlogged deposits. Such environments prevent the introduction of fresh oxygen, and therefore the survival of micro-organisms.

Garments

But Roman Britain was famous for its cloth products, as mediaeval Britain was also to be. In the year 301 the Emperor Diocletian issued an Edict on Maximum Prices in an effort to restrain the chronic inflation of the period. He included two Romano-British items which were evidently popular across the Empire: the *Birrus Britannicus*, a waterproof cloak with a hood, and the *Tapete Britannicum*, a woollen rug for draping over a couch or perhaps a saddle. In the fourth century the government was engaged in the production of clothing for its civil and military employees – one such factory is listed in the *Notitia Dignitatum* at one of the towns whose name begins with *Venta*; unfortunately we do not know which one as the name is incomplete.

The New Fresh Wharf in London produced a large quantity of fragments from leather garments. These may have been waste pieces left after the original garments were cut up for re-use (Rhodes in Dyson, 1986, 211ff.). Leather is waterproof and was apparently only popular in areas where such clothing would have practical appeal – Britain was an obvious candidate. The fragments from the site seem to have belonged to breeches (clothing which was scorned by Romans until they discovered the eminently practical reason for wearing them in Britain and the

74 A fragment of cloth from London (photo and copyright: the British Museum)

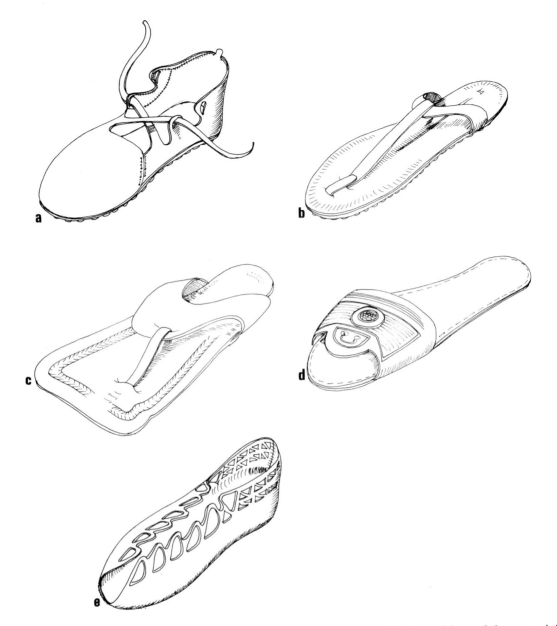

75 Shoe-types (after Rhodes and MacConnoran):
a nailed shoe, *calcei/caligae*
b stitched shoe, *socci*
c sandal, *soleae*
d ornamented stitched shoe with gilding, stamped and tooled decoration from the New Fresh Wharf, London
e one-piece shoe, *carbatinae*

north), cloaks and jackets. Most of the material had been stitched but some also bore traces of iron studs. Decoration of some sort is not uncommon – a fragment of leather from a barge at Blackfriars is decorated with a dolphin made with punched holes. A first-century well in London has also produced a pair of leather panties fastened with thongs.

The extra-mural settlement, or *vicus*, at the fort of Vindolanda near Hadrian's Wall contained a number of unique waterlogged deposits. Apart from leather a number of textile fragments were recovered and mostly belong to the late first and early second century. Many seem to have been made from local wool using Roman weaves such as two-over-two twill and in a few cases bore evidence for dying (Birley, 1977, 126). Other fragments from London are known (fig.74) amongst other places.

Shoes

Considering the general sparsity of Roman artefacts made of corruptible materials surviving in Britain, the large number of shoes known is perhaps surprising. The New Fresh Wharf in London alone produced fragments of around 150 (MacConnoran, 1986), and several hundreds more are also known from other sites in London, for example at Billingsgate Buildings (Rhodes, 1980) and the Walbrook valley. Leather shoes have been found in quantity elsewhere in Britain, most notably at Vindolanda (Birley, 1977, 124) and Newstead (Curle, 1911) but in all cases survival has depended on the shoes being buried in waterlogged deposits. In a few cases shoes bear impressions of makers' stamps, for example a stamp from Vindolanda which reads:

L AEB

THALES T F

76 Arm-purse and slave-irons:

a bronze 'arm-purse' (more likely slung on a belt) from the Roman quarry at Barcombe, south of Housesteads on Hadrian's Wall. Found in 1835 when the quarry was reopened, the purse contained three gold *aurei* and 60 silver *denarii* ending with coins of Hadrian. The purse was therefore probably lost during the construction of the Wall.

b set of slave-irons from Caister-by-Norwich, *Venta Icenorum*

This is probably an abbreviation for 'Lucius Aebutius Thales, Titi filius' – Lucius Aebutius Thales, son of Titus (*Britannia*, 4, 1973, 332). However, it seems to have been a common practice amongst the shoemakers of London to use a simple stamped motif such as an urn, a rosette or a wheel, though these are unknown elsewhere (Rhodes, 1980, 119).

There are considerable problems in classifying shoes largely because most of the surviving examples are only fragments, probably because they represent waste from manufacturing or were so damaged they were discarded. Statistical analyses based on shoe size are made more difficult by the fact that leather shoes shrink while buried, and also once recovered; this seems to be in the order of approximately 10 per cent. Nevertheless those from London at least seem to fall into four main types which correspond to classical names (fig.75). The 'nailed shoes', *calcei* or *caligae*, are distinguished by the use of nails in a variety of patterns to connect the soles to other bottom layers. The uppers were secured between the sole and the insole and usually had heel stiffeners. These shoes form the largest number of those which have survived, though it is important to realise that the 'style' of the uppers varies considerably (fig.75 a).

'Stitched shoes', *socci*, resemble nailed shoes but here the various bottom layers were secured with stitching after the uppers had been stitched to the insole. The uppers covered the instep of the foot in the manner of modern slippers (fig.75 b).

'Sandals', *soleae*, had sole units joined by nails or thonging and were held on the foot by a transverse strip of leather and a longitudinal strip

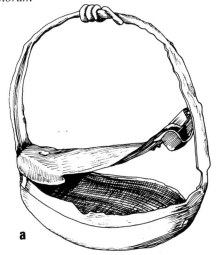

a

b

attached to the insole. Sandals were either foot-shaped or resemble flippers in having a very broad thread – these are called 'broad sandals' (fig.75 c).

'One-piece shoes', *carbatinae*, were formed of a single piece of leather wrapped around the foot and secured with thongs passed through cut-outs on the sides. Some of these shoes had quite elaborate cut-out decoration of triangles. A certain amount of stitching was necessary to form the heel (fig.75e). One other type can be mentioned; wooden-sole shoes. Known from Vindolanda, these shoes consisted of thick wooden soles and leather uppers (Birley, 1977, 125). Their purpose was presumably to allow the wearer to walk around in a bath-house without fear of burning his feet on the hot stone floors.

Others

Brief mention can be made of other items of interest. First is a set of so-called 'slave-irons' from Caister-by-Norwich (now in Norwich Castle Museum). Made from a number of iron components, these shackles were designed to allow restricted movement (fig.76 a). Slavery undoubtedly existed in Roman Britain but we have few details of individuals. A tombstone from Halton Chesters on Hadrian's Wall records the death of Hardalio and was set up by his guild of fellow slaves (*collegium conser[vorum]; RIB* 1436). The second item of interest is an 'arm-purse' from Barcombe near Hadrian's Wall (fig.76 b). These are metal containers with lids and handles generally used, as in this case, for storing coins about one's person. It seems unlikely that they were actually worn on the arm as this would have been both restrictive, and likely to result in the purse constantly sliding down. They were probably worn on belts.

5

Public and Social Life

Civic monuments

The topic of the actual structures of public buildings lie well outside the brief of this book, but it is important to consider some of the statuary, whether stone or bronze, which was produced to adorn these monuments. Virtually none of the numerous monuments which must have once existed in Roman Britain survive in any form today; the same goes for the statues and other accessories – as conspicuous and portable items (once broken) they have mostly all been carried away, re-used or melted down, and thus disappeared. Of the few survivals, most seem to have been deposited during the process of dispersal and are thus not always easily associated with their original sites.

Statues

The emperors were publicly worshipped in a religious manner through certain manifestations such as the *numen Augusti* – the spiritual power of the emperors – or as gods once they were dead, unless their memory was damned (*damnatio memoriae*). A number of dedication-slabs from Roman Britain are known, and some may have once formed part of a statue plinth, for example this inscription (now lost) from London (*RIB* 5):

NVM·C[AES·AVG]
PROV[INCIA]
BRIT[ANNIA]

This was an honorific way of acknowledging the status of the emperor and his family by erecting statues as civil dedications with a religious overtone. These must have been widespread, particularly in the forums and basilicas that were the centres of local governments in the major towns. The living emperor was not worshipped in his own right as a god except in the Eastern Empire where the idea of a ruler's divinity was already current before Rome took power.

The historian Suetonius, writing in the early second century, discussed the popularity of Titus who ruled from AD 79–81, son of Vespasian who ruled from AD 69–79. During the earlier part of his career he served as a military tribune in Britain and Germany and as a result of his efforts 'numerous statues and busts' of him were put up in both provinces (Suetonius, *Titus*, 4, 1). Apart from Titus, none of whose portrayals in Britain survive, there must have been many images of the imperial families in Roman Britain.

The only two likely surviving examples of such civic statues which are recognisable as such are bronze busts of Claudius and Hadrian, both of which probably came from full-scale figures. The Claudius bust from a river in Suffolk may have been dumped by participants in the Boudican Revolt (fig.77 a). If so it almost certainly came originally from Colchester whose official name was *Colonia Claudia Victricenisis*. The bust of Hadrian was found in the Thames at London and may well have come from the London forum, which seems to have been entirely reconstructed around the period of Hadrian's reign (117–138; fig.77 b). It is conceivable that they belonged to religious buildings concerned with worship of the deified emperors but this is far from certain (see Chapter 6). The elegant cuirassed bronze statuette of Nero, probably found at Creeting, *Combretovium*, Suffolk is more likely to have been a private possession than a public statue unless it stood in a temple (fig.78) though it gives an idea of the type of statue which would have stood in a public place.

The extensive excavations at Richborough in Kent revealed that the third-century Saxon Shore fort was preceded by a colossal monumental arch which stood across the beginning of the road to London and thus the province. The arch survives only in the form of its foundations and fragments of its marble veneer, but it must originally have been a major monument to the successful conquest of Britain. It was demolished when the Saxon Shore fort was built in the late third century. It is well-known from coins showing triumphal arches in Rome that these almost always had some sort of statue group on top,

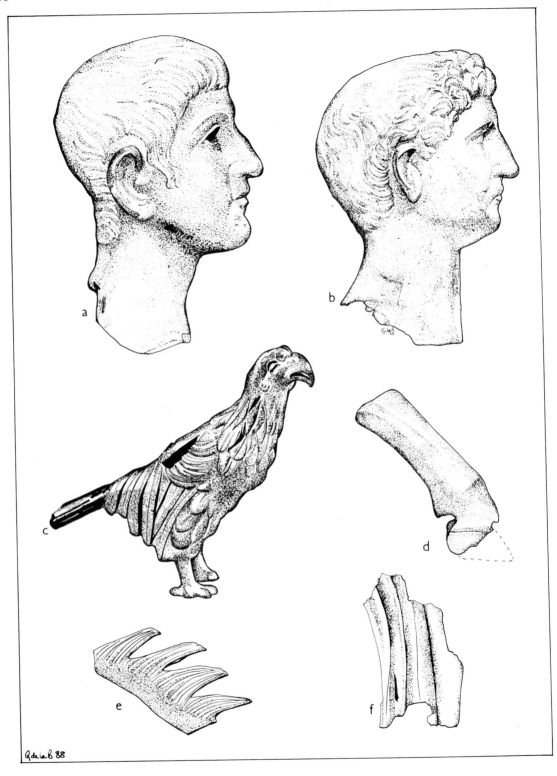

a

b

c

d

e

f

Qdelab 88

usually an emperor driving a four-horsed chariot, called a *quadriga*. The 14 fragments of bronze statuary recovered from the area of the arch include pieces of drapery (fig.77 f), a military-style cuirass and (possibly) locks of horses' hair. It seems likely on the basis of this that the arch was indeed decorated with such a chariot group; if so the most likely emperor to have been represented must be Claudius. Similar small bronze fragments from what were evidently once substantial statues are known from other sites; for example, pieces of an equestrian statue were found on the site of the forum at Gloucester (fig.77 e), and a bronze horse's foreleg from Lincoln suggests a similar statue stood there (fig.77 d).

An elegant small bronze eagle was found in the excavations of the basilica at Silchester in 1866 (fig.77c). The eagle was immortalised as the 'Eagle of the Ninth' at a time when it was believed that the *legio* IX *Hispana* marched to its destruction somewhere in Britain in the late first century. It is unlikely that it was a legionary standard if for no other reason than its find-spot is a very long way from any known legionary

78 Gilded bronze statue of the Emperor Nero (AD 54–68) from Barking Hall, Suffolk. Although it is too small to have been a 'public' statue, the figure gives an impression of the heroic posture sometimes used for such sculptures. Height 49cm (photo and copyright; the British Museum)

---

77 Public bronze statues (not to scale):

a bronze bust of the Emperor Claudius (AD 41–54) found in the River Alde at Rendham, Suffolk, in 1907. The tilt of the head suggests it formed part of an equestrian statue, probably from Colchester and perhaps removed during the Boudican Revolt of AD 60. Height 34cm (Toynbee, 1964, 46–7)

b bronze bust from a colossal statue of the Emperor Hadrian (117–138) dredged from the River Thames at London in 1834. Its original site is unknown. Hadrian certainly visited Britain in 119 and may have been involved with the construction of the second forum and basilica in London – it is possible that this was where the statue stood. Height 41cm (Toynbee, 1964, 50–1)

c the Silchester eagle. Found in the south-west part of the basilica at Silchester in 1866, where it probably formed part of an imperial statue group; it was originally identified as part of a legionary standard but this is unlikely. Made by hollow-casting with separate legs. The wings are broken off but would have been raised. Height 15cm (Toynbee, 1964, 129)

d lifesize horse foreleg from Lincoln. Found in or before 1800 (Toynbee, 1964, 52)

e fragment of horse's mane from an equestrian statue which stood in the forum at Gloucester. Length 23cm (*Antiq. Journ.*, 52, 1972, 52)

f fragment of drapery (from a military cloak?) found at Richborough. Height 29cm (Cunliffe, 1968, 70, no. 1)

fortress or camp. It is more likely that it belonged to some sort of bronze statue group, perhaps of an emperor or Jupiter, which stood originally in the basilica or in the forum.

There are a few examples of imperial stone statues known from Britain. Marble busts of Germanicus, brother of Claudius, and Trajan (98–117) are known from near Bosham in Sussex (Toynbee, 1964, 50). These are sometimes considered to have come from a centre of the imperial cult but there is not certain evidence of this. At Stonegate in York a weatherworn bust of Constantine I (306–337) was recovered before 1823 (RCHM York, 112, no. 8). If the identification is correct, the significance is straightforward – Constantine was declared emperor by the soldiers at York in 306 when his father, Constantius Chlorus, died there. The soldiers would have been enthusiastic about commemorating the success of their nominee.

Such honorific statues were not confined to members of the imperial house. A pedestal for a statue of a legionary legate has been found at the town of Caerwent, *Venta Silurum*. The statue had long since disappeared but an inscription on the pedestal records that the town community had decreed that the statue be put up in honour of Tiberius Claudius Paulinus, legate of the *legio* II *Augusta* stationed at nearby Caerleon, around the year 213 (*RIB* 311). It turned out to be a politically tactful move, for by the year 220 Paulinus had become governor of Britannia Inferior (Britain was divided into two provinces during the reign of Septimius Severus, 193–211).

Public inscriptions

Inscriptions have been discussed throughout this book where the information they contain is particularly relevant to the subject – for example military building works, tombstones and altars. These form the majority of inscriptions, which are in any case rare in Britain. There are however a number of monumental inscriptions which served a purely dedicatory and commemorative function in public places.

These inscriptions were usually composed in standard forms. They begin with the emperor's name and followed with his various titles which generally make it possible to date the inscription closely. These names and titles are comparable with those found on coin legends. After this opening the details of the event being commemorated follow, and the name of the local group or canton responsible for the inscription. Depending on the details the inscription could be composed in the *nominative* case if the emperor was responsible, or in the *dative* case if the event was being dedicated *to* the emperor. Needless to say none survive in their original setting, but those that have been recovered presumably lay where they had fallen from some prominent position relevant to their content.

The best-known of all civic inscriptions from Roman Britain is that from an entrance to the

forum at Verulamium. The inscription is very fragmentary, but the standard formulae of inscriptions have made it possible to reconstruct most of it with reasonable certainty. It was dedicated to Titus, as Emperor, shortly after his accession in AD 79 following his father's death earlier that year, and adds the name of Agricola as the current governor, the name of the town and the embellishment or donation of, presumably, a building. Of course it is not quite so straightforward – if the basilica was being dedicated in AD 79 it must have been begun several years before when Vespasian and Sextus Julius Frontinus were emperor and governor. The fragments lay close to an entrance to the forum on the north-east wall and had presumably once been placed over the entrance (R.P. Wright in Frere, 1983, 69). The wording is shown below with surviving letters underlined:

IMP·TITO·CAESARI·DIVI·VESPASIANI·F·VESPASIANO·AVG

PM·TR·P·VIIII·IMP·XV·COS·VII·DESIG·VIII·CENSORI·PATER·PATRIAE

ET·CAESARI·DIVI·VESPASIANI·F·DOMITIANO·COS·VI·DESIG·VII·PRINCIPI

IVVENTVTIS·ET·OMNIVM·COLLEGIORVM·SACERDOTI

CN·IVLIO·AGRICOLA·LEGATO·AVG·PRO·PR

MVNICIPIVM·VERVLAMIVM·BASILICA·ORNATA

Unfortunately the fragments also allow for two alternatives for the last line. These are:

CIVITAS·CATVVELLAVNORVM·FORO·EXORNATA

RESPVBLICA·VERVLAMIVM·LATIO·DONATA

A similar inscription was found at Wroxeter, *Viroconium*, also near an entrance to the forum. The wording shows that the *civitas Cornoviorum* had erected the forum and dedicated the event to Hadrian in the year 129–130 (*RIB* 288).

IMP CA[ES] · DIVI·TRAIANI·PARTHI

CI·FIL·DI[VI]·NERVAE·NEPOTI·TRA

IANO·H[A]DRIANO·AVG·PONTI[FI]

CI·MAXIMO·TRIB·POT·XIII[I]·COS·III·PP

CIVITAS·CORNOV[IORVM]

Public inscriptions were not always just attached to some tangible edifice that deserved recording, whether statue or building. It was customary for communities to go through the ritual of vowing for the Emperor's well-being – not unlike singing 'God Save the Queen' at appropriate moments, though a community is unlikely to be visited by the army for omitting to be dutiful these days. An inscription from Chichester, *Noviomagus*, recording a vow for Nero in the year AD 59, may have been such an event. After Nero's titles the abbreviation s·c·v·m for *Senatus consulto votum merito* follows. This means 'by order of the Senate [of Noviomagus] the vow was deservedly fulfilled' (*RIB* 92).

A unique inscription in Britain from Hadrian's reign seems actually to record his decision to fix the Empire's frontier. Part of this policy was the construction of his Wall. The inscription was found at Jarrow church, re-used in the church's nave, but only a fragment survived. It is possible that it came from a monument erected at the east end of Hadrian's Wall across the Tyne at Wallsend, or Tynemouth (AA², x, 195). The inscription was doubtless put up by the army but its importance is more political than military.

In the Roman world it was common for the very rich and politically ambitious to erect public buildings as part of asserting their status in a philanthropic manner. The habit has endured: Andrew Carnegie, the nineteenth-century American steel magnate, gave $45 million for building public libraries throughout the world. Across the Empire public buildings bore dedications from the wealthy local worthies who saw this as an excellent way of buying status and power. At Brough-on-Humber, *Petuaria*, a local *aedile* (= magistrate) called Marcus Ulpius Januarius presented a new stage (*proscaenium*) to the theatre and recorded the event of around 140–144 on an inscription (*RIB* 707), though the whereabouts of the theatre is still unknown. The inscription reads:

OB·HONOR[EM]
DOMVS·DIVINAE
IMP·CAES·T·AEL·H[ADRI]
ANI·ANTONINI·A[VG·PII]
PP·COS·I[II]
ET·NVMINIB·A[VG]
M·VLP·IANVARIV·
AEDILIS·VICI·PETV[AR]
PROSCAEN·****
DE·SVO·[DEDIT]

Milestones

The other most important category of civil inscriptions are the milestones. Typically these are carved cylinders of stone up to about 2m (6ft 7in) in height which bear the incumbent emperor's titles and information about the distance to the nearest settlement. Unfortunately such convenient pieces of stone must have mostly disappeared, but examples have been found throughout Britain, usually bearing information of use to travellers concerning the distance to the

nearest settlement. Thus one from near Leicester states (*RIB* 224):

IMP CAES
DIV TRAIAN PARTH F·DIV NEP
TRAIAN HADRIAN AVG PP TRB
POT IV COS III A RATIS
M II

The information about the Emperor Hadrian allows the milestone to be dated to the years 119–120, and informs the traveller that it is two miles (*M[ilia passuum]* II) from Leicester, *Ratae*. This provides additional confirmation of the Romano-British name for Leicester, information which for other places is entirely lacking. Another milestone, of similar date, supplies the name for the fort at Caerhun (fig.40 e).

Milestones were not entirely innocuous sources of information. The bearing of the Emperor's name and titles shows that they were politically sensitive objects too. A milestone from near Carlisle was erected originally under the rule of the usurper Carausius (286–293). However, following the demise of Carausius' successor Allectus, the milestone was pulled out of the ground, turned round and a new inscription carved at the other end, this time to Constantine I, as Caesar in the year 306–7. Another completely illegible inscription exists on the same stone (*RIB* 2291).

Entertainment

If Tacitus can be taken literally, Roman Britain was introduced quickly to Roman public entertainment. In the *Annals* he describes the events of the Boudican Revolt in AD 60/61, including the information that Colchester had a theatre (*Annales* xiv, 32, 55). Of course this theatre had been built for the benefit of the veteran soldiers who were settled there, but as the province became romanised so Roman pastimes became as widespread as Roman living habits. The general spread of Latin must have promoted an appreciation of Roman literary works – the villas at Farningham and nearby Lullingstone in Kent have both shown that their owners knew something of Virgil's *Aeneid*, or at least felt that it was appropriate to appear that they did. Farningham villa has a Virgilian reference on wall-painting, while the Lullingstone site has a mosaic with an elagiac couplet referring directly to a passage in the *Aeneid*. It reads:

INVIDA SI [TAVRI] VIDISSET IVNO NATATVS
IVSTIVS AEOLIAS ISSET AD VSQVE DOMOS

This means 'if jealous Juno had seen the bull swimming in this way, she might have gone to Aeolus' halls with greater justice'. In Book I of the Aeneid, Aeneas, the Trojan, is sailing to Juno's city of Carthage with Troy's sacred gods and fire. Another Trojan, Paris, had spurned Juno in favour of Helen. In her rage Juno sought the help of Aeolus, King of the Winds, to raise a storm to damage Aeneas' fleet. The point of the couplet is that this was rather unfair of Juno; if she had had to go to Aeolus she should have done so on another occasion when her husband Jupiter had disguised himself as a bull to carry off Europa (Meates, 1979, 73 ff, and plate 15 b).

It is very important to remember that many Roman 'entertainments' were inextricably linked with religious activities and that to some extent there was a shared function for associated artefacts – particularly music. The Verulamium theatre was associated with a large temple, and no doubt important religious festivals had their mythical origins acted out on the stage as part of the rituals. On the other hand there was evidently a market for more straightforward amusements such as gladiatorial bouts, or even for risqué souvenirs (fig.60 f) of possibly even more risqué displays.

Theatres and circuses

Roman public entertainments took place in theatres, amphitheatres and circuses. Theatres were semi-circular auditoria designed for the public viewing of plays, poetry and religious rituals which took place on a raised stage. Amphitheatres were elliptical auditoria devised for public viewing of contests between men, or men and beasts, which took place in the sunken central area. Circuses were elongated 'U'-shaped structures surrounding a race-track. However, it does seem that flexible use was made of such auditoria – amphitheatres, for example, could be used as theatres by the community rather than put up another expensive building.

Theatres are known in Britain from their physical remains at Verulamium, Colchester, Gosbecks (a religious temple site near Colchester), and Canterbury, and from inscriptional evidence at Brough-on-Humber (described above). Amphitheatres are known at Silchester, Cirencester, Chester, Richborough, Charterhouse, Caerleon, Caerwent, and most

recently in London on the site of the Guildhall. No circuses (for chariot-racing) are known in Britain, though large open spaces would have served quite well – these of course would leave no trace and are known to have existed elsewhere, for example the *Circus Flaminius* in Rome. The well-known theatre at Verulamium is interesting because structurally it appears to be a combination of theatre and amphitheatre – the so-called *Romano-Celtic* type; that is, the stage is built across what would otherwise be the long side of an amphitheatre, and was also associated with a temple.

By its very nature theatre requires few distinctive manufactured items, but classical theatre required the use of masks to denote mood. Caerleon, the legionary fortress of the *legio* II *Augusta* has produced an ivory mask of tragedy, but it is probably a model of the actual ones used (fig.79 a). The occurrence of similar, but life-sized items at Catterick and Baldock (fig.79 b) suggests that theatrical performances did not necessarily require a purpose-built auditorium, though London would have certainly had one (Marsh, 1979).

The practice of both indulging in and viewing fights to the death is now regarded as the most repulsive of Roman habits. The Romano-British seem to have been receptive to the idea – after all

---

79 Entertainments:

a an ivory theatre-mask from the amphitheatre at the legionary fortress at Caerleon, *Isca*, in South Wales. Such masks were commonly used in ancient drama to indicate moods and stock characters, though the size of this example suggests that it is unlikely to have been used by performers. It is also worth noting that these masks were used during religious performances. Height 10.8cm

b section of a lifesize theatrical tragic mask made of fired clay found at Baldock. Height 18cm (Stead, 1975)

c wooden reed pipe, *tibia*, from Ashton, Northamptonshire. Fourth century. Length 11.5cm (*Britannia*, 15, 1984, 300)

d iron rattle from Moorgate Street, London. Rattles may have been used in religious processions. Height 13.5cm

e gladiator's helmet of tinned bronze found in plough soil at Hawkedon, Suffolk, viewed from above. The helmet is extremely battered and has lost all its fittings such as a vizor and, possibly, a decorative crest, though it retains the broad neck-guard on which are traces of a name-stamp reading . . . OS. Probably of first century date. Weight 2.8kg, diameter 44cm (Painter, 1970)

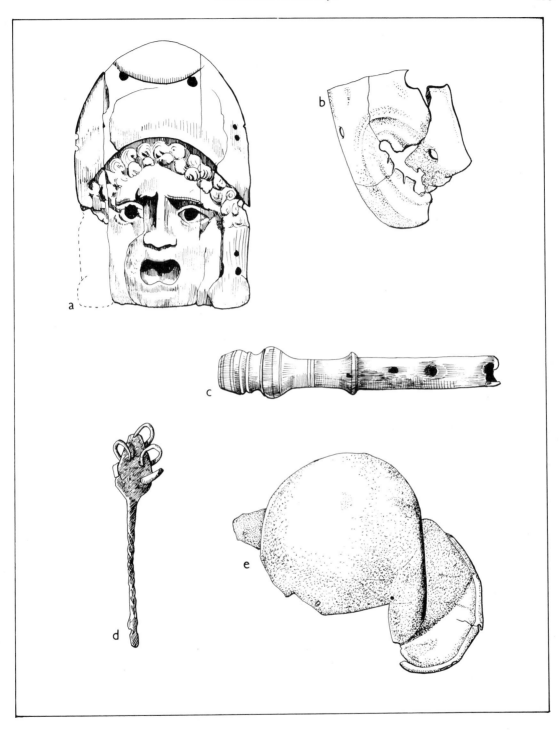

Celtic society had been as violent in its own way. One of the best-known artefacts of Roman Britain is a large beaker made at Colchester decorated with a gladiator pair accompanied by their names, Memnon and Valentinus (plate 11; Toynbee, 1964, 413–4). In fact the beaker may be a mass-production with the names incised to the purchaser's order, or with the names of current favourites. The beaker, known as 'the Colchester vase', also has scenes of bear-baiting and a dog chasing hare and deer, illustrating the range of unpleasant leisure activities open to the Romano-British.

The only artefact from Roman Britain which has been positively identified as belonging to circus activities is the 'gladiator's helmet' from Hawkedon, Suffolk (fig.79 e) recovered from plough soil in 1965. Unfortunately the helmet is badly damaged and only the rivet holes indicate that it once had an elaborate vizor. Despite limited traces of Romano-British activity in the area, Hawkedon is some way from any significant Roman settlement, and therefore from an (albeit undiscovered) amphitheatre. It has been suggested that it was stolen from Colchester and discarded or hidden by participants in the Boudican Revolt (Stead, 1970). While a possibility, this is a popular explanation for any apparently displaced artefact recovered in East Anglia and the evidence is very circumstantial. The sparsity of such material in Britain is emphasised by the fact that the recently excavated amphitheatre at Silchester produced no artefactual evidence at all of Roman entertainment activities (Fulford, 1985).

Music

The music of the ancient world is completely lost to us, but Roman Britain has produced a number of fragments of instruments. Flutes are known, the surviving examples being mostly of bone, though some fragments of bone which appear to be parts of flutes are actually sections of hinges. At Ashton in Northamptonshire the fourth-century fill of a well yielded a section of a wooden reed-pipe, *tibia* (fig.79 c). Rattles are not uncommon (fig.79 d), but known as *sistra*, they seem closely associated with religious activities, especially the rites of the Egyptian goddess Isis who certainly had a temple in London.

---

80 Gaming:

a bone dice (two-thirds actual size, exploded view)

b gaming pieces (two-thirds actual size, made of bone and pottery). The inscribed bone piece bears the word *campus*, 'field', and was found at Richborough (after Bushe-Fox, 1947, pl. 34, 82)

c hypocaust tile from Silchester, *Calleva Atrebatum*, incised with lines to form a gaming board. One of the most popular games was called *lupus latrunculorum*, which means 'Game of the brigands/ thieves'. (About half actual size)

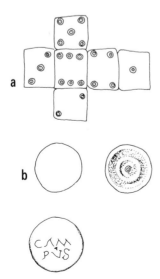

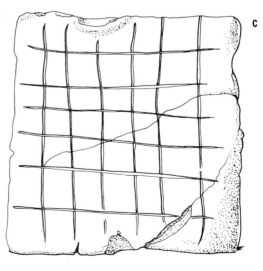

Gaming

Romano-British gaming seems to have been largely confined to dice and board-games similar to our backgammon and draughts. Dice were made usually of bone, and like ours opposing numbers added up to seven. Each number was engraved with a series of dots and circles (fig.80 a). Shakers were used and could have similar motifs as decoration. Gaming boards were made out of almost any suitable material (fig.80 c). Square tiles were particularly common, but one from a grave at the Lullingstone villa was made of wood (Meates, 1979, 129).

Gaming pieces were also made of any suitable material (fig.80 b). The Lullingstone grave included a complete set of 30 glass counters but more commonly they were made of bone or filed-down fragments of samian ware. Silchester has produced shoulder blades from sheep which had circular pieces of bone drilled out (fig.37), perhaps to be used as gaming pieces. Sometimes these gaming pieces are inscribed with numerical symbols, or even words – one from Richborough bears the word CAMPVS, which means 'field' (fig.80 b).

Religion and Superstition

Introduction

'In captured fortresses, even in the first flush of victory, they [the Romans] revere the conquered deities. They entertain the gods everywhere and adopt them as their own; they raise altars even to the unknown deities, and to the spirits of the dead . . .' (Minucius Felix, *Octavius*, 6, 23). Felix was an early third-century Christian apologist, probably from North Africa, but his observation is just as relevant to Britain. Unfortunately we have no comparable Celtic point of view, though there seems to have been a certain amount of equanimity towards Roman gods. We know from Caesar, and from Felix, that the Gauls favoured Mercury. Much later the fifth-century British chronicler Gildas alluded to the former sanctity of certain mountains, hills and rivers, though the fact that he refuses to name them suggests that they retained a little of their former status. These few sources alone indicate something of the cosmopolitan nature of the Romano-British pantheon.

A very large number of artefacts are associated with religion in Roman Britain. As we possess no literary record of what the Romano-Britons thought or believed we have to be content with the dedications they made to their gods as a basis for understanding, since at least they provide a list of names of gods. These are frequently undated, and rarely explicit.

Beliefs

It would be inappropriate in this particular study to delve deeply here into the complexities of Romano-British religious beliefs and practices; a number of excellent syntheses of the subject have been published in recent years, for example Henig (1984), Green (1986), and Webster (1986). But inevitably some discussion is needed to place the artefacts in context. Traditionally the gods of Roman Britain have been subdivided into Roman, Celtic, synthesised Roman and Celtic gods, and the oriental salvation divinities. While this is convenient it diverts attention from the basic strands of belief which remained fairly constant, almost regardless of the divinity.

In almost all cultures – our machine age is something of an exception – religious beliefs are founded on simple human concerns. Roman Britain was no different; the Britons were naturally concerned about their own well-being, and that of their families and their communities, expressed through interest in health and healing, the fertility of human beings and the land, and their personal safety and security. Even soldiers needed protection in times of war.

The protectors of all these interests were the gods. Gods in Roman Britain were recognised almost everywhere in a myriad of identities, blurred by shared powers, distinguished by parochial manifestations. These gods were of Roman and Celtic origin, separate or synthesised as considered appropriate. They were independent or associated with special places or institutions. Some of the Celtic gods were very local and therefore little-known outside their own particular area. However, such local divinities were probably very similar and it would certainly be hard to discern them under close scrutiny were such examination possible. The gods were worshipped by individuals, households, craft guilds or whole communities, depending on the occasion and place; likewise an individual god or several might be worshipped. An important point to remember is that until the Roman Conquest gods in Britain were not addressed through inscriptions or naturalistic images. The idea of an individual approach to a god was brought by Rome – the pre-Roman Celts addressed their gods as tribal groups.

Despite the very considerable range of deities available to a would-be worshipper in Roman Britain the same kinds of relationships between gods and men seem to have operated. The gods looked over the Romano-British with benign or malevolent intent. Their favours could be sought with appropriate gifts and observances, and equally their disfavour on some miscreant could be bought too. There was more to the contractual nature of the arrangement; pagan beliefs were concerned with balancing a natural equation of their duties against rights from the gods. The oriental cults, which became increasingly popular throughout the period, offered an even more intense personal relationship with a god. At its heart the relationship is a simple concept though the extraordinary range of artefacts associated with Romano-British religion is confusing.

But religion in Roman Britain did not just involve making dedications. Throughout this book the reader will have noticed that the possibility of religious connections has to be considered with some artefacts. Gods and goddesses appear as decorative motifs on numerous Roman artefacts, for example samian pottery and the intaglios on rings – but these, if religious, are only indirectly so in the sense of acting as charms or amulets. Moreover, there is the whole subject of death and burial, and of course the coming of eastern cults and their effects on the practice of religion in Roman Britain (Harris, 1965).

Religious sites

There are very few religious sites in Britain which still evoke something of the original appearance of a cult centre. Even the magnificent remains of the temple-spa at Bath require a considerable exercise of imagination to remove the over-burden of later buildings. Nevertheless, extensive excavations both here and at many other places have revealed that temples and shrines were far from rare but few were classical in style. In addition the numerous finds of altars and other dedications has shown that sacred places were just as likely to be woods, springs or other special natural features in the landscape.

For the purposes of this book we can exclude items such as structural embellishments in stone and mosaics though a few, such as the pediment from the temple at Bath (fig.82), shed some light on the nature of cults. We can also discount the mosaics found in domestic contexts which have a possible religious connection but are mainly decorative. This leaves us with statuary, altars, votive plaques and votive objects as well as some other enigmatic artefacts which appear to have played some part in religious activity.

Statues and portrayals of gods
Cult statues

Extremely few cult statues have survived from Roman Britain. The temples in which they stood were obvious targets when the official religion became Christianity and the state ceased to entertain a tolerance of beliefs. Either they were spirited away by dedicants or they were physically destroyed. Quite apart from any iconoclastic threat, statues made of bronze or stone were equally susceptible to those in search of raw materials in a less respectful age.

Those which have survived are generally classical in form even if the cults with which they are associated were synthesised cults of Roman and Celtic deities. The gilded bronze bust of Minerva from Bath is a case in point (fig.81 a). Its exact origin is unknown but it probably comes from the Temple of Sulis-Minerva which formed the religious focus of the spa of *Aquae Sulis* in Roman times. The bust exhibits all the restrained dignity and realism of classical sculpture in dramatic contrast to the powerful representation of the wild Celtic mask and its writhing hair on the temple pediment.

The temple pediment at Bath (fig.82) is a particularly interesting example of the manner in which a classical and Celtic divinity might be combined. The central feature is the fearsome gorgon's head, worn by Minerva on her shield to ward off evil (see also the goddess Brigantia, below, p.151 and fig.87 a). Unlike the classical female gorgon this example bears a Celtic warrior's face and resides within two circular wreaths, which may indicate an association with a sun-god, an assertion supported by the appearance of a possible sun or star at the apex of the pediment. Yet beside these wreaths, which are supported by two classical Victories astride globes, are a pair of Athenian helmets supporting a dolphin and an owl, two of Minerva's associates. The two sea-beasts, tritons, which appear in the corners of the pediment presumably represent water-attributes, and some have interpreted the gorgon's head as a portrayal of a Celtic water-god resembling Oceanus. Put together, all these concepts can be seen as a conflation of Minerva's attributes and the miraculous spring water and its heat, something normally associated with the sun (Cunliffe and Davenport, 1985).

The 46-cm (18-in) high bronze statue of Mercury from Gosbecks Farm, Colchester

a   b

81 Cult statues (not scale):
a life-size gilt-bronze bust of Minerva, probably from
the Temple of Sulis-Minerva at Bath, *Aquae Sulis*.
Found in 1727 during sewer-building close to the
remains of the temple. It was almost certainly part
of a life-sized statue and would have once had a
Corinthian helmet. Probably late-first, second
century
b life-size carved stone bust of the obscure Celtic god
Antenociticus from the small temple beside the fort
of Benwell, *Condercum*, on Hadrian's Wall.
Probably late second century

style is unequivocally Romano-Celtic; the god
wears a torc around his neck and the modelling of
his hair suggests an attempt at a representation of
stag's antlers.

There are a few examples of stone and bronze
busts of members of the imperial household
known from Britain. Worship of the deified
emperors and the *genius* or *numen* of the present
incumbent was one of the few religious requirements placed on a provincial population. The
bronze busts of Claudius and Hadrian (fig.77 a,
b) discussed in Chapter 5 may be from imperial
cult figures but it is more likely that they are civil
honorific statues which once stood in public
places. There must have been far more of these
than religious statues. It has been suggested that
stone busts of Trajan and Germanicus (Claudius'
brother) both found at Bosham, Sussex, are more
likely to come from an imperial cult centre –
however, there is no certain evidence of this, and
in any case the 'palace' at Fishbourne and the
cantonal capital of the Regnenses at Chichester
are not far away. Both of these are more likely
sources, where the statues would have served a
purely decorative function (Painter, 1965).

(fig.83 a; Hull, 1958), comes from a religious site
to the south of the *colonia*. It may have been a
cult statue but its size makes this unlikely. No
inscriptions have come to light naming the god or
gods worshipped here. However, like the Bath
Minerva, this statue is completely classical in its
anatomical accuracy, portraiture and attributes.
On the other hand, the stone bust of Mercury
from Uley, Gloucestershire, while superficially
classical shows much more provincial influence in
the carving (plate 19).

Part of a cult statue from the temple to a Celtic
god was found in the small building dedicated to
Antenociticus at Benwell fort on Hadrian's Wall
(fig.81 b; Simpson and Richmond, 1941). The
god is unknown elsewhere except for an altar at
Chesters fort to the west and was probably a local
deity. Only the bust of the statue survives (the
body may well have been wooden), two late-
second-century altars serving to name him. The

The remains of the cult statues from the
worship of the Persian god Mithras are the best-
known in Britain. The third-century London
mithraeum, identified in 1954, is the most
notorious of all the British mithraea known.
Others include that at Carrawburgh, still visible
in situ (fig.84). The cult would have been

Above **82** Section of the pediment from the Temple of
Sulis-Minerva at Bath, *Aquae Sulis*, showing the
Gorgon's Head in the form of a Celtic warrior.
Portions of the surrounding wreaths are visible.
Diameter of the head is about 80cm. Late first century

83 Mercury (not to scale):

a bronze statue of Mercury from the Gosbecks temple
site, south of Colchester, *Camulodunum*. The style
is purely classical and this makes it conspicuously
different from most Roman religious sculpture
found in Britain. Height 53cm

b stone relief of Mercury and his Romano-Celtic
companion Rosmerta from Gloucester. To the
lower left is a cockerel, often associated with
Mercury. Height 50cm

84 The *mithraeum* at Carrawburgh, *Brocolitia*, on Hadrian's Wall, looking north. The *mithraeum* was discovered in 1949, and was built early in the third century, reaching its present appearance in the fourth century after being destroyed in the early 300s. The far end contained a reredos with a stone relief of Mithras killing the sacred bull but this was shattered in antiquity. The three main altars were dedicated by different tribunes of the *cohors* I *Bataviorum*. The left-hand altar was pierced in order to allow a lamp to shine through. In the right foreground is the remnant of a statue of one of Mithras' attendants, Cautes. The altars and statues are modern reproductions, the originals are in Newcastle Museum of Antiquities. Length: 29m (photo: author)

---

to the large numbers of merchants and officials who worked in the provincial capital, which was also a major port. A large number of stone cult statues were excavated from this site where they had been deliberately buried. A number of other pieces found in the vicinity in the nineteenth-century were almost certainly unwittingly removed from the temple. The group from the London temple not only indicates the number of different deities who might be worshipped in any

one place, perhaps at different periods, but also the accomplished works of art that were available.

The central theme of Mithras slaying the bull is depicted on a sculpture which was donated by

---

85 Reliefs (not to scale):
a marble relief of Mithras killing the sacred bull from the Walbrook, London. The relief was found in the nineteenth century and almost certainly comes from the well-known *mithraeum* found in 1954. Mithras is accompanied by Cautes and Cautopates and surrounded by a wreath containing the Signs of the Zodiac. The inscription records the dedication by Ulpius Silvanus, a veteran of the *legio* II *Augusta*, and that the relief, or the initiation of Silvanus, was made at *Arauso*, Orange, in France. Height 42cm (*RIB* 3)
b relief of *genii cucullati* from the Police Station site in Cirencester. The three hooded figures are accompanied by a seated mother goddess. Two of them are armed with swords, perhaps to indicate their powers of victory over death. Height 27.5cm (Toynbee, 1976)
c relief, probably of Minerva, from Lower Slaughter, Gloucestershire (but not found in the well group). Height 37cm

a

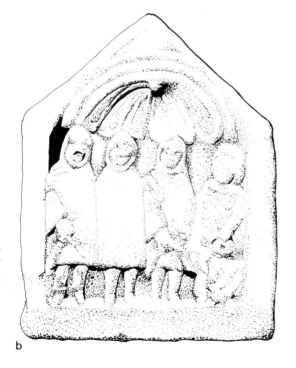

b

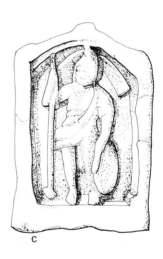

c

86 Statue variously identified as Cybele, Juno Dolichena, and Juno Regina standing on a heifer from Chesters, *Cilurnum*, on Hadrian's Wall. Height 1.6m (photo: author; courtesy of English Heritage)

came to London, perhaps as a government official. However, it should be remembered that this all hinges on independent assessments of the marbles and the pottery, neither of which date themselves. Of greater significance is the fact that so much of this material, usually so rare in Britain, is associated with one place. Whether this is truly representative of the range of quality material in Roman Britain is not so clear. The circumstance of concealment, probably during a period of zealous repression by Christians, is obviously unusual. We can probably assume that a number of other religious establishments in major centres in southern Britain would have been equipped with similar material.

The temple also produced some British limestone sculptures including another bull-slaying scene, a figure of Mithras' associate Cautopates and the Gemini, Castor and Pollux, though unlike the marble statues these were probably left *in situ* and were damaged and dispersed by the opponents of Mithraism.

A further example of oriental religious sculpture survives from Chesters fort on Hadrian's Wall, in the form of a life-sized statue of what appears to be Cybele, the great eastern mother goddess. She is shown standing on a heifer. It is possible that the statue represents Julia Mamaea as Cybele forming part of a group

Ulpius Silvanus, a veteran of the *legio* II *Augusta* (fig.85 a). A marble bust of Mithras distinguished by his Phrygian cap was also found, and may have been burnt as part of the rituals. The temple also yielded parts of marble statues of Mercury, Minerva, Serapis (a Graeco-Egyptian conflation of the Egyptian gods Osiris and Apis), and a Bacchic group. A number of other statues found in the nineteenth century nearby probably come from the same group and include a *genius* (of London?) and a river god.

All these were skilfully executed figures made from Italian marble, though their bodies may have been made of wood and plaster, and they emphasise the kind of investment the participants were prepared to make in their cult. The marbles, except for the Bacchic group, are thought to belong to the later second century, whereas the pottery evidence is thought to suggest that the mithraeum was not built until *c.* 240 (Toynbee, 1986). This may mean that the marbles were actually the long-standing property of a family, brought to Britain when one of their members

87 Local and household divinities (not to scale):

a statue of Brigantia from the fort at Birrens, *Blatobulgium*, Dumfriesshire, dedicated by the engineer, *architectus*, Amandus. Brigantia is shown in classical form in the guise of Minerva Victrix. She wears a plumed helmet, a Gorgon's head medallion, holds a spear and globe and is accompanied by a shield and omphaloid stone. Probably third century. Height 92cm (*RIB* 2091)

b statue of a *Genius loci*, 'spirit of this place' from Carlisle, *Luguvalium*, dedicated by the century of one Basilius Crescens. The inscription is incomplete and so identification is not fully certain – the piece has also been identified as the 'spirit of Basilius' century'. The figure wears a mural crown and carries a cornucopia symbol of plenty topped by a pine cone. Height 33cm (*RIB* 944)

c bronze statuette of a *Genius Paterfamilias* from Cricklade, Wiltshire. Height 11cm

d battered relief of an anonymous hunting god from the large villa at Chedworth, Gloucestershire. The villa is thought possibly to be a hostel for pilgrims to a shrine of the healing god Lenus-Mars. The figure may well therefore be Mars: it is shown with a dog and his catch, probably a rabbit. Height 43cm

a

b

c

d

which would have included her son Severus Alexander (222–235). As the statue is headless and uninscribed, identification is not possible (fig.86).

Household and local divinities

A central part of the romanised household was the worship of household divinities. In Britain, as elsewhere, surviving examples are represented by statuettes, normally made of bronze or pipeclay. Many such statuettes may have been used in the household *lararium*, which stood in a prominent place where members of the family could pay their respects to the ancestors and divinities worshipped in that house (figs.87–90). These domestic shrines are best known from Pompeii and Herculaneum, where many are still *in situ*. For the most part they are imitation temples standing on pedestals, but none survive intact in Britain, only the figures used in them; however, houses at Silchester and Verulamium respectively contain a plinth for a probable *lararium* and a subterranean niche for possibly the same purpose.

One of the best-known small statuettes is the bronze Venus from Verulamium, perhaps of

second-century date, but found in a fourth-century context where it was probably due to be melted down (plate 20). More interesting is a bronze statue of Mars from the Foss Dike in Lincolnshire (fig.88 b). Its plinth bears an inscription (*RIB* 274) to the effect that two brothers, Bruccius and Caratius Colasunius, paid 100 *sestertii* for the statue which was made by Celatus the smith out of a pound of bronze which cost three *denarii*, or 12 *sestertii*. Celatus is a Latin name but the superficially classical style is modified by the provincial traits of the figure's

89 Gilt bronze statue of Hercules from the fort at Birdoswald, *Banna*, on Hadrian's Wall. Its authenticity has recently been questioned on grounds of style and unusual state of preservation. Height 49cm (photo and copyright: the British Museum)

88 Statuettes:
a bronze statuette of Minerva from Alan's Farm, Plaxtol, Kent. The figure would have originally held a spear and owl. Height 19cm (Luard, 1859 and Toynbee, 1964, 80)
b bronze statuette of Mars from the Foss Dike, Lincolnshire, on an inscribed pedestal which details the cost of manufacture and the dedication to Mars and the spirit of the emperor. Made by Celatus the coppersmith from 3 *denarii* worth of bronze along with a contribution of 100 *sestertii* from Bruccius and Caratius Colasunius. Height 27cm (*RIB* 274)
c bronze figurine of the Celtic horse-goddess Epona. She is accompanied by two horses, ears of corn and a yoke. The group seem to form a decorative mount, perhaps from a vehicle. Said to have been found in Wiltshire but this is unverifiable. Height 7.5cm (Johns, 1971)
d lead shrine from a fourth-century level in the fort at Wallsend, *Segedunum*, containing a figure of uncertain identity. The helmet suggests Mercury, the dolphin behind his feet suggests a sea-god, the bust at the top within a semi-circle suggests a sun-god association. The shrine was probably a portable personal equivalent of the household shrine. It was accompanied by a pair of doors (not shown) which swung on the pivots. Height 7.5cm (Allason-Jones, 1984)

posture and facial features. The statue was evidently manufactured as a votive gift, hence its survival, but similar statues would not have been uncommon in well-to-do households. The Plaxtol Minerva, also superficially classical, has a similar posture (fig.88 a). Curiously the figure wears the gorgon head *aegis* on the shoulder rather than the breast. The statuette was found in association with structural remains, probably of a farmhouse, at Plaxtol, Kent, in the nineteenth century (Luard, 1859). A gilt bronze statue of Hercules said to be from Birdoswald may have belonged to the commanding officer's household, though this is purely speculation (fig.89).

An interesting recent find from the fort at Wallsend has been tentatively identified as a small shrine made of lead. Found in a fourth-century context (fig.88 d), the little shrine is shaped like a cupboard with two opening doors revealing a figure of a god, possibly Mercury, though the large number of attributes suggests that the shrines were mass-produced but that the figure of the god was selected by the customer. It is possible that this was a kind of portable *lararium*, though there are few parallels (Allason-Jones, 1984). A similar shrine, though containing a figure of Venus, has been found at Wroxeter.

While a number of classical gods are known from statuettes, there is a large category of Celtic deities which are more common. The Mother Goddesses, or *Deae Matres*, are particularly well-known. In stone they are usually carved as seated figures bearing suitable symbols of their fertility such as fish, fruit or bread. Such concerns were bound to be of great importance to a primarily agricultural community. Typically the mothers are shown in triplicate, a common way of magically strengthening the divine force paralleled in other religions; however, this is not an exclusive practice. Most of the single examples are small figurines made of a white pipeclay, and manufactured in Gaul and Germany. These single figures are usually nursing one or two babies and are known as the *dea nutrix*, literally 'nursing goddess' (fig.90 b).

The same factories also made nude female figurines which are sometimes described as the 'pseudo-Venus', because they resemble the classical Venus (fig.90 a; Jenkins, 1958). Modern opinions differ on the figures' identity and it is probably simpler just to regard them as a crude version of Venus peculiar to the north-west provinces, perhaps connected with child-birth.

---

90 Pipeclay figurines:

a 'Venus' figurine. The vast majority of these figurines are fragmentary – the illustration is restored from more than one example. Dating is uncertain, but probably Hadrianic-Antonine (see, for example, Jenkins in Dyson, ed., 1986, for the New Fresh Wharf, London). Height about 15cm

b pipeclay Mother Goddess, *Dea Nutrix*, shown here nursing a baby and seated in a wicker chair. Found at Welwyn, Hertfordshire. Height 13cm (photo and copyright: the British Museum)

a

b

These figurines have been found in religious and domestic contexts. A 'pseudo-Venus' was found in one of the temples at the religious settlement of Springhead, Roman *Vagniacae*, in Kent (Penn, 1959, 38), suggesting that perhaps such figures may have been sold at cult centres. Six examples of the *dea nutrix* were found in the settlement at Staines, Roman *Pontes* (Jenkins in Crouch and Shanks, 1984, 82). A number have been found along the Roman riverfront in London, indicating one of their ports of entry.

Much rarer in Britain than either the mothers or the Venus figurines is the Gallo-Celtic goddess Epona (fig.88 c). She is always depicted with horses, her principal associates; she is also shown with corn which indicates that she too had powers over fertility and prosperity. A small bronze group from Wiltshire shows her with a pair of foals (Johns, 1981).

An important Roman religious concept was the idea that every human being had a kind of divine alter ego, or *Genius* for men, *Juno* for women, something that we could call a soul (Alcock, 1986). The worship of the Emperor's *Genius* was an aspect of this belief. The *Genius* of an individual remained once a person was dead and was at the heart of the veneration of dead ancestors. A unique find in Britain was the recovery of two marble busts from the 'Deep Room' at the Lullingstone villa (plate 22; Meates, 1979, 36). These two busts were carved from Greek marble in a Mediterranean style of the early to mid-second century. Both are portraits of men, apparently individuals of high status, and a likeness about the faces suggests they were related. Who they were is unknown, and their connection with the modest villa in its second-century form uncertain. It is possible that the villa was a country house for an important family who lived, perhaps, in London. At any rate the villa itself was apparently unoccupied for most of the third century, but when new residents moved in *c.* 280 and discovered the busts, they treated them with a reverence that suggests they had served a religious function.

In the Roman world it was customary to revere the spirits of ancestors of the household in the *lararium*. These busts may have been portraits of ancestors of those who had lived at Lullingstone in the late second century. Why they were left is a mystery but the new owners placed them in the Deep Room, which they had redecorated, along with a beaker carefully inserted into the floor, apparently ate a ritual meal, and then sealed the

room for ever. During the next century the busts were occasionally visited to leave offerings, perhaps through a trap-door from the room above.

The Lullingstone deposit is of great interest. It not only suggests that the ancestor cult was followed in Roman Britain but it also shows the potency of the images. Clearly it was felt they could not be disposed of – but presumably the new owners had ancestors of their own, and did not wish to share their worship with those of the previous family. The tale of two families may be entirely hypothetical but the superstitions attached to the busts were clearly quite real. A small bronze statuette of a *Genius Paterfamilias* from Cricklade in Wiltshire is also part of this theme of ritual respect for the spirits of dead ancestors (fig.87 c).

Genii were not confined to being the spiritual manifestations of individuals. Places had their own *genii*, for example the *Genius loci* from Carlisle bearing a cornucopia and patera and wearing a mural crown (fig.87 b; and see Phillips, 1979 for a further example). This portrayal, while Celtic in style, is in keeping with the normal presentation of *Genii* based on the *Genius Populi Romani*, or 'Genius of the people of Rome'. However, additional features might be incorporated as appropriate. A figure of a *Genius* from the Walbrook in London (and almost certainly originally coming from the *Mithraeum*, see above, p.144) stands beside a boat's prow, no doubt reflecting the city's maritime-based prosperity. Such deities were mostly venerated in the military zone of the province, but the idea of a spiritual identity of a place was entirely in keeping with Celtic beliefs in sacred spots. *Genii* are also known as the divine identities of organisations, for example the *Genius* of the *legio* II *Augusta* at Caerleon (*RIB* 327), or the *Genius* of the Guild of Apollo at Overborough (*RIB* 611).

Stone reliefs

There are a large number of religious stone reliefs known from Britain. While these were not cult statues in the true sense of the phrase, they nevertheless acted as a visual focal point for a cult. They are generally much more Romano-Celtic in style and exhibit a great deal of variety in the manner of representation. They have been found in a very large number of different sorts of places, probably functioning as shrines. As such they recall the Celtic habit of worshipping sacred

91 Dedication slab to the goddess Coventina from 'Coventina's Well' at Carrawburgh, *Brocolitia*, on Hadrian's Wall, set up by Titus D . . . Cosconianus, *praefectus* of the *cohors* I *Bataviorum*. The unit was based at Carrawburgh in the early third century. Height 74cm (*RIB* 1534; photo: author; courtesy of English Heritage). Now in Chesters Museum

---

spots, such as woods and springs, and represent the romanisation of these loosely-defined pre-Roman spirits such as Brigantia, who appears in the guise of Minerva Victrix (fig.87 a).

A good example of such a shrine is known beside the fort at Carrawburgh on Hadrian's Wall. A spring in a hollow seems to have been sacred to Coventina and as such was the recipient of a huge number of votive goods (see below, p.164). Amongst these was a relief dedicated to Coventina, portraying the goddess reclining in a niche and holding a leaf aloft (fig.91). The relief probably once stood beside the spring, providing a naturalistic image of a goddess who may well have been no more than a vague notion before the permanent arrival of the Roman army in the vicinity in the 120s.

One relief from Gloucester is particularly interesting because it is a clear depiction of the classical Mercury in Romano-Celtic form. He is accompanied by his attributes of *caduceus* (staff), a cockerel, and a purse and wears his winged cap (fig.83 b). Beside him is a female figure, possibly Rosmerta who, like Mercury, was also a divinity associated with plenty. She is sometimes described as his Celtic consort. It is interesting to contrast the style of this relief with the classical Mercury from Gosbecks. Mercury seems to have been particularly popular in the Celtic world, equipped as he was with an ever-open purse. Caesar commented that the Gauls worshipped him above all others, believing that his power over skills, travel, commerce and enterprise was supreme (*de Bello Gallico*, 6, 17). The relief of Venus and the nymphs from High Rochester, probably of third-century date, is a similar example of a classical deity portrayed in Romano-Celtic form (fig.92).

There is an extensive range of rather more obscure reliefs of what can be conveniently

---

92 Relief from High Rochester, *Bremenium*, Northumberland showing Venus washing with the help of two water nymphs. Height 67cm (photo: author; courtesy of the Museum of Antiquities, Newcastle-upon-Tyne)

described as 'hunter-gods', for example one from Chedworth villa (fig.87 d). These gods are generally shown as single male warrior figures accompanied by weapons, dogs, and also by their victims, such as a stag. Generally anonymous, they probably belong to an extensive group of Celtic and German gods such as Cocidius, Belatucadrus and Thincsus who were associated with Mars. It has been suggested that the Chedworth villa was in fact a hostel for pilgrims visiting a shrine of Lenus-Mars, a healing god – a number of reliefs from the site appear to depict the god, one by name (Webster, 1983). Mars, like Mercury, was popular in Britain, but such reliefs tend to be found in the military part of the province where his protective powers were more likely to be appreciated. Although hardly portable, the remains of a relief known as 'Rob of Risingham' in Northumberland form an interesting example of one associated with a specific place and may represent Mars-Cocidius (fig.93).

One of the most remarkable groups of sculptures from Roman Britain is that from a well in Lower Slaughter in Gloucestershire (Rhodes, 1964, and Toynbee, 1958). The site was one of many small settlements along the Fosse Way and as such must have been typical of numerous similar small villages across the province. A number of reliefs and altars were found in a well which appears to have been sealed in the fourth century. However, as the sculptures are for the most part heavily weathered they must have been on view for a considerable time before they were buried. The facts that they were all thrown in together and that some were damaged suggests that they all belonged to a temple or shrine, now lost, and were buried by people who found their continued presence both insulting and threatening. This naturally points to Christians, but this is unproven and in this case not the point. These sculptures must represent dedications by local people or travellers which accumulated over the years at a single shrine, or group of nearby shrines (fig.85c). They are far more important than the Minerva bust from Bath, because they probably show more accurately what the Romano-British were used to in terms of religious sculpture.

The subject matter of the Lower Slaughter reliefs is overtly Celtic. Two represent the enigmatic *genii cucullati*, three hooded figures, representations of whom are known from a number of sites throughout Britain but mainly in the west and north. They were probably household spirits. Like the 'mothers', their power was strengthened by being shown in triplicate (this was peculiar to Britain) and they are sometimes actually shown with the mother goddesses (fig.85 b). This suggests related powers over fertility and prosperity, but they remain a shadowy concept.

Altars

Roman-British altars are rectangular pieces of stone which are taller than their width, though they vary considerably in size. They can be very crude, and bear a roughly-hewn inscription, like the Halton Chesters lightning memorial. The more elaborate examples have scrollwork at the top and a semi-circular depression – *focus* – in which sacrificial offerings could be burnt, or they may even carry an image of the god, such as one of the altars from the Carrawburgh mithraeum. In extremely rare cases altars were large and made of several pieces of dressed stone, but these, like that at Bath, were essentially permanent fixtures and formed part of a temple precinct, acting as the central focus of ritual. However, altars were erected wherever appropriate, at a shrine for example, or in a sacred spot such as that dedicated to Silvanus at Weardale in the Pennines (fig.94 a and *RIB* 1042). Some were designed to be portable (fig.94 e) and were equipped with iron suspension rings. Some are very crude and parochial in their dedication (fig.94 f).

Altars can sometimes be valuable evidence of the nature of a god being worshipped in any particular place, so long as they bear inscriptions. An altar found at Springhead in Kent unfortunately lacked any useful information at all despite actually being found within one of the temples (Penn, 1949, 24). However at the shrine of Apollo at Nettleton in Wiltshire a more useful

93 The remains of 'Rob of Risingham', a Romano-Celtic warrior god carved into a sandstone slab at Parkhead south of the fort at Risingham, *Habitancum*, Northumberland. The god is probably Cocidius, and was complete up until the early nineteenth century when the farmer's son began to remove it to discourage visitors. However, an earlier engraving shows the god equipped with quiver and bow. The figure was originally a little over a metre in height (photo: author)

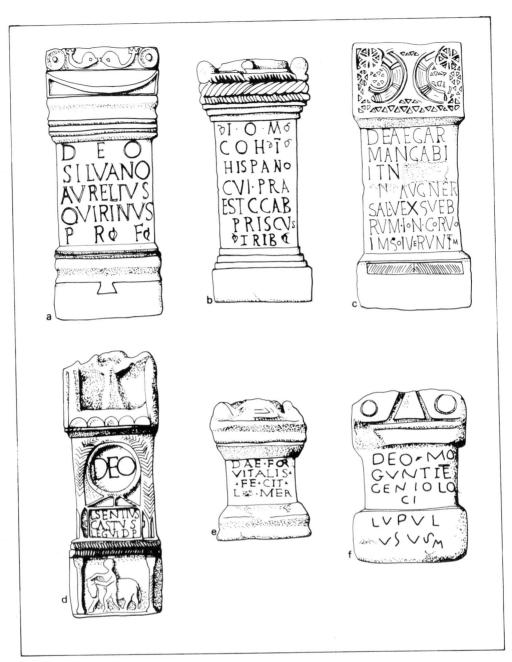

94 Altars from the northern frontier (not to scale):

a altar from Weardale, County Durham, dedicated to the god Silvanus by Aurelius Quirinius. Height 127cm (*RIB* 1042)

b altar from Maryport, *Alauna*, dedicated to Jupiter Optimus Maximus by Caius Caballius Priscus, tribune of the *cohors* I *Hispaniorum*. Height 99cm (*RIB* 817)

c altar of the goddess Garmangabis from Lanchester, *Longovicium*, County Durham. The inscription is difficult to read but the dedication was made under Gordian III (238–244), whose name has been erased, by a vexillation of the Suebians stationed at *Longovicium*. Height 137cm (*RIB* 1074)

d from the *mithraeum* at Rudchester, *Vindobala*, on Hadrian's Wall. The top is weathered but the inscription simply records a dedication 'To the God' by Lucius Sentius Castus of *legio* VI *Victrix*. At the bottom Mithras seizes the bull which is to be sacrificed. Height 125cm (*RIB* 1398)

e miniature altar dedicated to Fortuna by Vitalis from Carrawburgh, *Brocolitia*, on Hadrian's Wall. The altar had an iron ring inserted in the top with lead to make it portable. Height 36cm (*RIB* 1537)

f miniature altar dedicated to the god Moguntis and Genius of the Place by Lupulus, from Vindolanda. Height 29cm (*Britannia*, 4, 1974, 329)

example was recovered. This altar bears the inscription:

DEO APOL
LINI CVNO
MAGLO CO
ROTICA IV
TI FIL VSLM

The inscription includes the abbreviation VSLM, recording the fulfilment of a vow. This was a crucial formula because it formalised and closed the legal arrangement made with the god. The Latin words for fulfilling or paying the vow willingly and deservedly are *votum soluit libens merito*, but these are generally abbreviated, as in this case. The other words show that the dedication was to the god Apollo Cunomaglos, DEO APOLLINI CVNOMAGLO, from Corotica, son or daughter, FIL for *filius* or FILIA, of Iutus. This means that Corotica had made some promise to Apollo Cunomaglos that he/she would dedicate an altar to the god if a favour was granted. In this case we do not known what the favour was. Evidently though it had been granted and Corotica had returned the compliment, thus closing the arrangement. Such promises were also fulfilled with votive plaques. This inscription is also interesting because it introduces Apollo synthesised with a Celtic god, Cunomaglos, 'the hound-prince', otherwise unknown (Toynbee in Wedlake, 1982, 135). The same site also produced an altar dedicated to the classical hunter god Silvanus and the *numen Augusti*. Sometimes only the briefest reference was necessary – an altar from the *mithraeum* at Rudchester declares simply 'DEO', 'to the God' (fig.94 d and *RIB* 1398).

Less specific are a pair of altars from Newcastle which stood on the *Pons Aelius*, the bridge across the Tyne. Both were erected by the *legio* VI *Victrix*, which seems to have arrived in Britain with Hadrian around 119-122 when the Wall's construction was begun. One altar was dedicated to Neptune, the other to the personified god of the sea, Oceanus (*RIB* 1319 and 1320). They may refer just to the goodwill of the gods sought for the safety of the bridge, but it is perhaps more likely that they represent gratitude for the legion's safe arrival in Britain.

One soldier, perhaps a slightly eccentric individual, called Titus Irdas, set up an altar at Catterick to the unspecified god who had invented roads and paths. The altar was subsequently restored in the year 191. He appears to have been a member of the governor's guard so perhaps after a long journey from London he had good reason to give thanks for roads (*RIB* 725). The inscription reads:

DEO QVI VIAS
ET SEMITAS COM-
MENTVS EST T IR-
DAS S C F V L L M
Q VARIVS VITA-
LIS B F COS ARAM
SACRAM RESTI-
TVIT
APRONIANO ET BRA
DVA COS

In translation it reads thus: 'To the god who invented (*Deo qui . . commentus est*) roads and paths (*vias at semitas*) Titus Irdas, an old soldier on tax-collecting and police duties (S C = *singularis consularis*), gladly, willingly and deservedly (L L M = *laetus, libens, merito*) fulfilled his vow (F V = *fecit votum*)'. The inscription goes on to record that Quintus Varius Vitalis, on seconded duty by the governor (B F COS = *beneficiarius consularis*) restored the sacred altar (*aram sacram restituit*) during the consulship of Apronianus and Bradua (AD 191).

Such thanks were not necessarily preceded by vows. Thanks might be given for unexpected good luck. In this way one Tineius Longus thanked the god Anociticus (*sic*; see above, p.140 and fig.94 b) for his elevation to senatorial rank at the fort of Benwell on Hadrian's Wall in the year 180 (*RIB* 1329). The name was either incorrectly carved or the name of the god Antenociticus was not formalised with a common spelling.

Sometimes people believed (as some still do) that gods had spoken to them, requesting that certain actions be taken. Such dedications bear phrases like EX·IMPERIO which indicate that this had been done on a god's orders or commands. Sometimes there was discussion with the god on the right thing to do, usually through an intermediary such as a priest. At Ribchester fort in the early third century, Titus Floridius Natalis, the unit commander, restored a temple to Jupiter Dolichenus (probably) after having sought the god's advice (*RIB* 587). Close to Turret 22A, near Halton Chesters on Hadrian's Wall, was found the record of a lightning strike. Such a spot was turned into a precinct once sacrifices had been made. The inscription simply states FVLGVR·DIVO[RV]M, which means 'the lightning of the gods' (*RIB* 1426).

Anniversary dedications were made as a matter of routine, usually by military units or official civilian bodies. These were usually made to Jupiter Optimus Maximus and formed part of the ritual of lip-service to state cults. A particularly well-known group is the series (also dedicated to Jupiter Optimus Maximus) at the fort of Maryport, *Alauna*, in Cumbria (Jarrett, 1976). In 1870 17 altars were found buried in pits by the Roman parade ground. They are mostly dedicated to Jupiter, and it seems that on special occasions the fort's commanding officer renewed the unit's pledge of loyalty to the official religion (fig.94 b; *RIB* 817–820). The practice of deliberately burying an altar is an interesting one. This was the customary way of dealing with a religious object which was no longer required, yet retained its divine power (this recalls the treatment of the Lullingstone ancestor busts, see above p. 149).

Some altars were almost certainly prefabricated. Those which are found bearing neither inscription nor motifs may well have never been used. Alternatively, they may have been set up in an exposed place with the result that any inscription has been worn away. Some are extremely simple. One from the fort at Lanchester, *Longovicium*, in County Durham bears only a carved spoked wheel in relief. The wheel was a potent Celtic symbol of a solar god sometimes associated with Jupiter (Green, 1984, a, and 1986, b; see also fig.101 k from Felmingham Hall). Interestingly, a more elaborate altar from the same site and dedicated to the goddess Garmangabis shows how the customary scrollwork at the top of the altar has been adapted into wheels (fig.94 c).

Plaques

A cheaper, or at least more portable, way of recording the legal fulfilment of an arrangement with a god was the use of plaques, normally made of bronze or silver. Not all bear inscriptions but those that do are similar to examples on altars. They may well have been attached to gifts which were left at the sanctuary, perhaps food or objects made of perishable substances which have not survived. They are also most certain evidence of a lucrative trade carried on at shrines, probably by local craftsmen who engraved or punched in the purchaser's dedication. One of the plaques from the rural shrine of Nodens at Lydney in Gloucestershire is fairly typical of such a vow fulfilled (fig.95 b). It is an innocuous record of the day that Flavius Blandinus, an *armatura*, or drill-instructor, paid his vow to Nodens. The plaque bears a nail-hole and so it was clearly intended for public display. Flavius Blandinus was no doubt proud of his piety and concerned that Nodens and everyone else knew about it. The Lydney site and many others have also produced a number of single bronze letters, also pierced for nails (fig.101 j). These presumably performed the same function as the plaques, but whether they were nailed up in words to make full inscriptions, or as abbreviations based on initials, is not known.

Blandinus' plaque is a simple ansate form of plaque. Others are more elaborate such as that dedicated to Mars Alator at Barkway, Hertfordshire by Censorinus (fig.95 a). The slightly cramped lettering suggests that this was one of the mass-produced plaques. It is interesting to note that the habit endured to early Christian times. The Water Newton treasure of Christian silver includes a number of similar leaves, one of which bears a pagan-style inscription coupled with a chi-rho monogram (fig.116 b and see Chapter 8).

---

95 Dedicatory plaques and spoons:

a silver votive plaque/feather (restored) from Barkway, Hertfordshire, dedicated to Mars Alator by one Censorinus (after Brailsford, 1964, fig.31). Height 19cm

b bronze plaque dedicated to the god Nodens by Blandinus, the armourer, from the temple site at Lydney Park, Gloucestershire. Width 10cm (Wheeler, 1932, pl. 34)

c bronze votive plaque, originally soldered to an iron backing, depicting the head of Apollo in repoussé work. From the improvised shrine (c. 250–370) of Apollo at Nettleton Shrub, Wiltshire. Height 10.7cm (after Wedlake, 1982, 144, fig.61)

d silver duck-tailed spoon, one of 33 from the Thetford treasure, bearing an inscription, *Dei Fauni Medigeni*, recording the name of an obscure Italian rural god called Faunus and a dedicant, Medigenus. Length 8.8cm (Johns and Potter, 1983)

e silver duck-tailed spoon, one of 33, also from Thetford. The bowl of the spoon is engraved with a figure of a Triton and the word *Deinari*. Length 10.4cm (Johns and Potter, 1983)

a

b

D·M·NODONTI
ABLANDINVS
ARMATVRA
V·S·L·M

c

D·M·O
DECANVS

D·MARTI·ALATOR
DVM·CENSOR'NVS
GEMELLI·FIL
V·S·L·M

d

DEIIFAVNINEDIGENI

e

DEINARI

Curses

The altars and votive plaques described above are not uncommon. They record the conclusion of the contract with the divinity. Much rarer are the initial propositions proferred by the dedicant. A particular category of these, the curses, *defixiones*, are well-known and offer a particularly interesting insight into the trivialities and puerile concerns of human life. They are generally inscribed on pieces of metal, usually lead, which were then folded up and deposited in some suitable place such as a sacred spring or a river. However, at Uley the curses seem to have been stored by the priests in a room attached to the temple. The curse from the temple precinct of Nodens at Lydney Park is typical of many: Silvianus had lost his ring, and was fairly sure that someone called Senicianus had taken it; so,

96 *Defixio* curse tablet, 12.8cm wide, of lead/tin alloy from the spring at Bath, *Aquae Sulis*. The main inscription reads:
side a (illustrated)
Basilia donat in templum Martis ani-
lum argenteum si servus si liber [ta-]
mdiu silverit vel aliquid de hoc
noverit ut sanguin[e] liminibus ob
side b (not illustrated)
omnibus membris configatur vel et-
iam intestinis excomesis [om]nibus habe[at]
is qui anilum involavit vel qui medius
fuerit
which in translation means:
'Basilia gives to the Temple of Mars her silver ring, [and asks] that so long as [someone], whether slave or free, keeps silent or knows anything about it, he may be cursed in [his] blood and eyes [and] /
every limb, or even have all [his] intestines eaten away, if he has stolen the ring or been privy to it'
(after Hassall and Tomlin, 1983)

Silvianus asked Nodens to ensure ill-health for all those called Senicianus until the ring was recovered. In return he promised to give Nodens half the value of the ring (Collingwood in Wheeler, 1932, 100). It seems that the ring was not immediately recovered, because some time later Silvianus renewed the curse by adding the word *rediviva* to the text. The function is clear – the curse was a letter to the god asking for a service.

The degree of misery requested for the evil-doer varies quite widely, according to the victims' imagination – and sometimes they could imagine quite a lot. A curse from Pagans Hill in Somerset asks that a thief called Vassicillus, and his wife, suffer ill-health and also not be able to eat, drink, sleep or have healthy children (*Britannia*, 15, 1984, 366, 7). At Bath a woman called Basilia came to curse the thief who stole her silver ring: she asked that he suffer in every part of his body, with a final request that his intestines be eaten away (fig.96). Typically the grammar and quality of writing of these curses leave much to be desired, probably because the votary had to laboriously copy key words and phrases from standard texts available at the shrine. The cryptic dedications on altars also reflect these standard formulae – the dedicant and the god knew the terms of the contract, there was no need to do more than state the basics.

Priestly regalia

The idea of a priesthood was common to both the Roman and Celtic worlds. The emperor traditionally adopted the title of chief priests, *pontifex maximus*, and therefore was at the head of official state religion. Even so his rôle was a part-

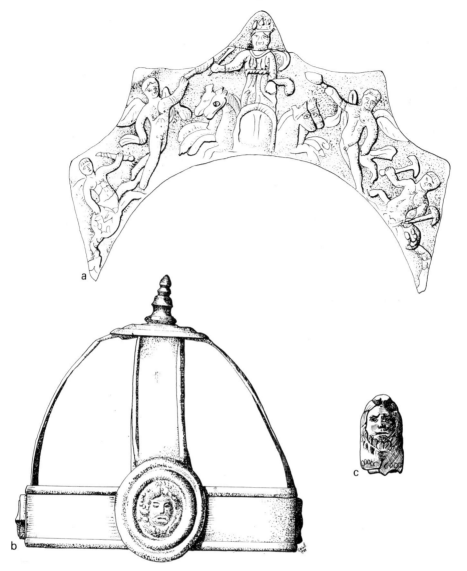

time one – in fact few pagan cults necessarily required full-time priests, though presumably the major temple sites would have needed them for administrative purposes and also to deal with visiting worshippers. Few examples of individual priests are known from Roman Britain, but they include a *haruspex* called Lucius Marcus Memor from a statue base at Bath. A *haruspex* was a soothsayer who was called on to interpret omens and the state of the entrails of sacrificial victims; such specialists belonged to mainstream Roman religious activity. Probably more typical was Gaius Calpurnius Receptus, a priest of Sulis, *sacerdos Deae Sulis*, also from Bath (*RIB* 155).

Unfortunately little is known of liturgical or

97 Priestly regalia (not to scale):

a bronze diadem from the Temple of Nodens at Lydney Park, Gloucestershire. The decoration, in repoussé work, depicts a sun-god riding in a *quadriga*, accompanied by two winged figures and two tritons. The diadem was probably worn by a priest. Diameter 19cm (Wheeler, 1932, pl. 27)

b bronze crown with repoussé medallions from Hockwold-cum-Wilton, Norfolk. The crown is adjustable for head size. Height 15.9cm

c bronze sceptre head depicting a bearded male god. Found near Amersham, Buckinghamshire. Height 3.2cm

ritual activities carried out by priests or worshippers, but there are a number of types of objects which seem to have formed part of their costume. We can assume that they probably wore togas; portrayals of priests which survive suggest that this was the case. In addition diadems, or crowns, made of bronze are known from a few sites including Hockwold-cum-Wilton (fig.97 b) in Norfolk. These simple head-dresses could be adjusted for head-size and often seem to have borne silver plaques with an appropriate motif in repoussé decoration. A bronze diadem decorated with an oriental sun-god riding a quadriga is known from Lydney (fig.97 a). More basic versions consisted of medallions connected by chains. Some retain the plaques but these also turn up on their own, for example those from Stony Stratford where they probably adorned the shrine rather than the priest. Those from Water Newton show that these were used in Christian worship as well (fig.116 a, b). Bronze sheet in the form of floral decoration found in the spring at Bath may have come from the robes of a priest of the establishment (Cunliffe, 1984, 82, fig.52).

Ritual equipment

Almost anything considered under the general subject of religion could be regarded as being part of the ritual equipment. Of course the word 'ritual' is a difficult one to define accurately in a fashion appropriate to Roman Britain. We know very little about the actual process of ceremonies, but perhaps the best way to acquire any understanding of them is to try and identify objects intended for use during the actual practice of worship on the basis of their findspots.

Some rituals seem to have involved the use of sceptres with ornamented tops. In Britain examples have been found with animals, such as a three-horned bull, and with human busts, which may have been used in rural emperor worship. However, these busts such as a so-called head of Hadrian from Worlington, Cambridgeshire, bear no more than the vaguest resemblance to the emperors they are reputed to represent by some scholars. They are just as likely to represent deities, local worthies or the priests themselves (fig.96 c). Another group from a burial at Brough bore heads of soldiers and perhaps belonged to a warrior cult with Celtic origins. The temple site at Farley Heath in Surrey produced bronze

fragments of sceptre-binding (Goodchild, 1947). These bear peculiarly primitive portrayals of stylised men and beasts that look like pin-men. Around them there are various tools and weapons. Who they were meant to represent is quite unknown, but the inclusion of a moustache on one head, which itself is surmounted on a wheel suggests a strong Celtic influence. There is nothing obviously classical about the figures at all. The spring at Bath yielded a curious larger-than-life tin mask which was probably once attached to a wooden backing (fig.99). It may have played a part in the rituals; it certainly had no practical purpose, unlike many of the other votive gifts found there. The face resembles those of face pots (see below, p.167 and fig.102). Alternatively it may simply be an anonymous votive plaque.

Ritual equipment was obviously of great amuletic importance to those who used it. It was jealously guarded and sometimes hidden. As a consequence such material is more often found as caches, secreted away for obscure reasons and

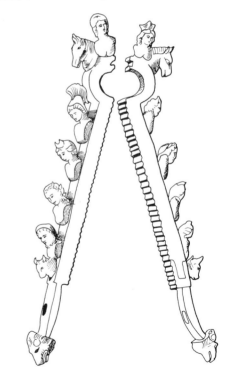

98 Bronze forceps probably used during rites associated with Cybele and Atys. Atys castrated himself after being unfaithful and this was probably the function of the forceps for committed initiates. Found in the Thames at London. Height 29cm

99 Celtic-style plaques (not to scale):
a tin mask of a male face from the spring at Bath, *Aquae Sulis*. Height 33cm
b silver plaque dedicated to Cocidius from Bewcastle, *Fanum Cocidii*, an outpost fort to the north-west of Hadrian's Wall. Height 11cm (*TCWAAS²*, 38, 1938, 195 ff, and fig.11)

never recovered. It is the kind of material that is unlikely ever to be discarded casually if for no other reason than that it was usually made of valuable materials. The Temple of Mithras in London, described above, is just such an example, but unusually the material had been deposited in the temple itself. The elaborately decorated forceps found in the Thames may have been used in the oriental cult of Cybele and Atys (fig.98). Remorseful after his infidelity to Cybele, Atys castrated himself; the more enthusiastic initiates seem to have been willing to adopt a sympathetic lifestyle. Either the forceps were thrown into the Thames because the

devotees wished to preserve them, or Christian iconoclasts wished to destroy them. Both alternatives indicate the potency of the object.

The material from the London *mithraeum* is an extremely valuable group, because not only can the objects be associated with the worship of a particular god, but also with a specific place. It has already been mentioned that the Mithras bust seems to have been regularly and deliberately burnt. The temple contained candlesticks that may have been responsible, or the use of lighted torches is a possibility. Part of the ceremony involved consumption of a meal of sacrificed animals; in this case chicken bones were found. Drinking also went on – small pottery cups were found as well as a particularly elaborate silver strainer contained within a silver drum decorated with soldiers, animals and griffins. This may have been used for straining wine or perhaps a cocktail of herbs with narcotic powers.

The shrine of Apollo at Nettleton also contained articles which may have been used at

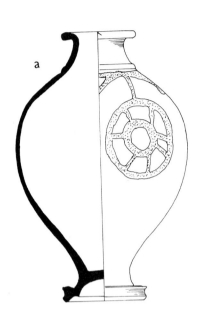

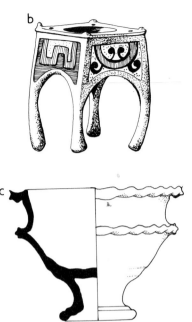

100 Other objects connected with religious activity:
a pottery jar with four painted wheels from the mid-
second century shrine of an otherwise unknown god
called Abandinus at Godmanchester, *Durovigutum*,
Cambridgeshire. Height 22cm (after H.J.M. Green,
in Henig and King, 1986, 40, fig.11)
b bronze enamelled stand or 'stool' from Farley
Heath, Surrey (after Brailsford, 1964, fig.37).
These stands are common finds at temple sites and
may have been used as supports for candles. They
sometimes occur in stacks of two, one bigger than
the other. Height 5cm
c pottery incense cup, *tazza*, from Verulamium.
These cups may also have been used as open lamps.
Probably late first century, height 10.6cm (after
Frere, 1972, 287, no. 309)

some point in the rituals. The most likely is a
bronze knife with a perforated blade attached to
a long and heavy alloy handle. It was unsuitable
for cutting and seems more likely to have been
used for piercing (Toynbee in Wedlake, 1982,
135 ff.).

More often this kind of material just seems to
have been buried in a place which is no longer of
any apparent significance. In recent years there
have been finds of great value and importance
which are thought to have had possible ritual
connections, such as the Water Newton treasure,
and most recently the Thetford treasure. It is
never very clear how many of the individual
components of these deposits are really ritual
goods, such as the Thetford spoons inscribed with
the name of the god Faunus (fig.95 d, e); or
whether they are just valued items of silver plate
or jewellery which happen to bear religious
motifs. There is frequently a mixture of material,
which serves to add confusion.

The great hoard of fourth-century silver plate
from Mildenhall in Suffolk, discovered in 1942, is
an enigma. It is a group of such exceptional value
that it can have belonged to nobody but an
extremely wealthy and important person or
family. Many of the plates and bowls bear images
of various deities. The Great Dish has a central
feature portraying the god Oceanus, which
recalls the pediment of the Temple at Bath, and
an outer frieze which shows a Bacchic revel (plate
5). These motifs raise the question of whether
the hoard is of silver plate used in religious
ceremonies. This is unlikely because there is a
mixture of Christian and pagan motifs, and it
seems that these various figures and symbols
were used for their decorative value rather than
for any religious purpose (Painter, 1977). The
hoard is almost certainly just an exceptional case
of the survival of a rich household's silver table
service. This may also be the case for the
Corbridge lanx (fig.44) though this appears to
refer to a specific religious event; unfortunately
neither of these finds bears unequivocal inscriptions of secular or religious form. This is not so
with the Water Newton treasure, which, while

containing pagan elements, is almost certainly plate from an as yet unlocated Christian church and is therefore discussed in Chapter 8.

The treasure from Thetford, also of fourth-century date, seems to have been made up rather more clearly from a mixture of secular and religious material. Much of the treasure consisted of gold jewellery in various states of completion, suggesting that the depositor was a jeweller keen to conceal his material for some pressing reason (plate 18). A number of silver spoons included with the jewellery seem to belong to rituals associated with an obscure Italian rustic god called Faunus who is hard to discern in theological terms from the better-known Pan (Johns, 1986). Inscriptions on the spoons associate Faunus with Celtic attributes such as Blotugus, 'bringer of corn', or Medugenus, 'mead-begotten', and the spoons were perhaps used during ceremonial feasts (fig.95 d, e). Little is known of Faunus in Italy in any case, which makes the appearance of such material in Norfolk very interesting. There may have been a temple on the site where it was found, but unfortunately the treasure was not revealed by the finder until after the site had been built on. A Celtic temple has been identified in the adjacent field. However, it may be that it was being hoarded for its bullion value at the time and may have come a long way from the place in which it was actually used, though the Celtic names suggest that this must have been in Britain (Johns and Potter, 1983).

Pottery incense cups, or *tazze*, are relatively common finds and may have been used during temple and domestic ritual. Typically a *tazza* is distinguished by its carinated profile, pedestal base and horizontal bands of frilled decoration, formed by pinching the clay with fingers. They may also have been used as open lamps (fig.102 c), providing light along with the candles held in miniature enamelled bronze stands (fig.100 b). Other lighting may have been supplied by pottery lanterns (fig.61 i, from a secular context); an excellent example was found in the 'Triangular Temple' at Verulamium where it no doubt supplied a suitably theatrical effect (see Henig, 1984, fig.80). Pottery is, of course, a common find on religious sites, but it is not always obvious if the vessels were directly involved in the cult. A jar from a temple to Abandinus at Godmanchester, painted with four wheels, does seem a likely candidate considering the potent symbolism of the wheel (figs.35 and 101 a; Green, M., 1984 and Green, H., in Henig

and King, 1986). The 'Triangular Temple' also contained a number of small pottery vessels which may have contained votive offerings of food and drink (Wheeler, 1936).

Votive gifts

When a dedicant, or votary, needed a service from a god a gift was sometimes promised. Some of these requests in curse form have already been discussed. Alternatively the gift might be proffered first in the hope that a favour would be forthcoming. It was a simple, straightforward and uncomplicated arrangement. Many of these votive gifts are not religious in the sense that the artefacts already discussed in this chapter undoubtedly are (plate 24). Often they are household goods, items of personal jewellery or just money. They became religiously significant when they were given to the gods; this often involved 'ritual breakage'. As personal possessions, they were closely connected with the spirit of the dedicant. For the same reason such items were sometimes buried with their owners because they were imbued with the spirit of the deceased.

In archaeological terms the result is the deposits of votive gifts and dedications. Our world exhibits exactly the same human need to work out this tit-for-tat relationship – every public fountain, pond or pool is invariably filled with coins. And of course people are chary with their gifts to the gods – the majority consists of many foreign coins, bent coins, low denomination coins and tokens. Many Roman votive gifts are the same sort of carefully-selected objects which show the spirit of giving without actually costing the giver too much. However, Roman votive or dedicatory gifts also include items of considerable value, ranging from specially-commissioned altars to expensive jewellery. Some of the images of gods described in the previous section were clearly intended as gifts, for example the Foss Dike Mars which went to the god complete with an exact tally of how much it had cost the dedicants (fig.89 b).

The discovery of a spring dedicated to the Celtic goddess Coventina at the fort of Carrawburgh (see above, p. 151) in the nineteenth century, was described by the writer of the *Handbook to the Roman Wall*, J. Collingwood Bruce:

'Covering the mouth of the well were some large stones, which had probably been taken from the upper courses of its containing walls and thrown, for the purposes of concealment, upon the mass of treasure of which the well had been made the recipient. On the removal of these stones . . . . a mass of coins, chiefly of the lower empire [i.e. third to fourth century], met the gaze of the excavators. Then carved stones, altars, coins, vases, Roman pearls, old shoes, fibulae, and other Roman remains were met with in an indiscriminate mass . . . . An extraordinary number of coins were found in the well, amounting to upwards of sixteen thousand . . .'
(Collingwood Bruce, 1885, 124 ff.)

Collingwood Bruce was of the opinion that the deposit represented a panic-stricken attempt to hide the fort's valuables in the face of some unspecified threat. We know now that the well actually represented a typical Celtic water-shrine, filled with an accumulation of votive gifts throughout the period that the fort was in occupation – and probably before (Allason-Jones and McKay, 1985). Ultimately though something untoward seems to have occurred, because some of the shrine's superstructure had been hastily thrown in on top of the well. Its contents are typical of a number of similar types of deposits known in Britain. The other best-known example is the sacred spring of Sulis-Minerva at Bath. Of course, this was not the only manner in which votive gifts might be deposited. Temple sites produce such material, whether within the temple itself, or in the surrounding area. The Temple of Nodens, at Lydney Park in Gloucestershire, is such an example.

Coins as votive gifts

Coins are an obvious choice of votive offering, though Collingwood Bruce observed that of the 16,000 or so coins in Coventina's Well, only four were gold. Money meant security and a full stomach in Roman Britain, just as it does now, so it was logical to give a little (but only a little) of what was wanted most to a god in the hope that one's prosperity would improve. At Bath the majority of the coins recovered from the spring were bronze or brass, but nevertheless a significant proportion were silver. Like many votive goods they were often the subject of deliberate damage before being given to the goddess. Four gold coins were found here too. These may seem unusually generous considering their value, but on the other hand that was all in a period of several centuries, and bearing in mind the tens of thousands of visitors who would have come to such a place perhaps four is not so striking.

The Temple of Mercury at Uley may have had an open *cella* centred around a sacred tree – the pit in which the tree may have grown produced around 500 coins during excavation (Ellison, 1988). Coins are also commonly found in rivers at crossing points where they presumably represent an offering to the river god in return for a safe crossing. One exceptionally fine example from the River Tyne at Newcastle is a mint condition *sestertius* of Hadrian with a reverse design showing a ship, perhaps chosen as a suitable offering after a sea journey. Such a coin was a rare choice for a votive gift; normally very worn coins and those of low denomination were selected.

In the late fourth century the practice of manufacturing imitation coins known as *minimi* seems to have been current (Webster, 1986, 57–64). These were token coins of insignificant value which were favoured as votive gifts. A hoard of these coins was found at the Lydney shrine of Nodens (T.V. Wheeler in Wheeler, 1932, 116 ff). Some were pieces cut down from earlier fourth-century coins.

Deposits at healing shrines

The spring at Bath was exceptional. The whole temple and bath complex was a centre of major importance; we know from inscriptions that people came from the continent to take the healing waters. Naturally then, the votive gifts apart from the coins are a large and rich group. They include metal vessels of all kinds, many of which have been discussed already in their more natural domestic context. Some were inscribed with the name of Sulis-Minerva, for example jugs, cups, candlesticks, and *paterae* (plate 24). Jewellery was also found, including a particularly fine penannular brooch with terminals decorated with enamelling in Celtic style, and 33 gemstones, perhaps thrown in all at once by a gemworker. The most curious gift was the bronze washer from a large military catapult (see Chapter 1) – it seems a curious item to donate to a divinity and the reasons for its presence can only remain an enigma. However, at only 8cm

(3.1in) in width it may in fact be a miniature in the manner of some votive tools (see below).

An interesting class of votive object are the small representations of selected parts of the body, for example an arm and hand from the temple precinct at Springhead (Penn, 1964, 170ff.). This example, known as an 'anatomical ex-voto', as well as a number of others, seems to have deliberately cut from a bronze statuette. What its exact significance was is not entirely clear, but it may be connected with the healing of that part of the dedicant's body (fig.103 g). This may explain the number of mutilated bronze statuettes from the Thames which have had various extremities removed (Merrifield in Munby and Henig, 1977, II, 388). It has been suggested that the hacking off of the bronze heads of Claudius and Hadrian (see Chapter 5), though at very different times, may be part of the Celtic head-cult, perhaps by transferring its powers to the spirit of the water. But on the other hand, shrines of the classical god of healing Aesculapius (or Asclepius), and those of Apollo and Minerva amongst others in the Mediterranean world are associated with exactly the same anatomical gifts of various appendages.

Tools and miniatures

There are some examples of weapons and tools being buried in such a way as to suggest they too were being used as votive gifts. The most certain example is from Jordan Hill in Dorset, where a succession of deposits of bent iron tools, accompanied by a coin and a bird's bones, were buried. The bird was perhaps the remains of some sort of celebratory meal but the bones were those of a raven and may have had a chthonic (pertaining to the gods of the underworld) symbolism. Each deposit was carefully separated from its predecessor by a layer of stones (Drew, 1931).

This tool deposit raises the interesting question of miniatures. Some small versions of everyday objects must have been toys but others seem certainly to have had a religious or superstitious purpose, for example the miniature tools, especially axes, or miniature military equipment such as the helmet and shields from Kirmington in South Humberside (fig.101 a-d; see also Green, 1981). Another interesting group, found in Sussex, consisted of a number of agricultural and carpentry tools (fig.101 l). Such miniatures are found as grave goods, as apparent votive gifts

on religious sites, and even as amuletic pendants. They were used from the Iron Age on, so clearly represent a well-established Celtic tradition. Rarely more than a few centimetres in length, they sometimes bear engraved symbols such as an 'X' which may have 'activated' the article (fig.101 d). In some cases the axe-head appears as a terminal on otherwise ordinary decorative pin made of bone or bronze (see Chapter 4). Of course the 'anatomical ex-votos' can be classed as miniatures as well.

What exactly these miniatures symbolised is not known, though some continental examples were dedicated to Minerva, the mother goddesses, Jupiter and Mercury. These and examples from Britain which bear symbols related to the sky such as swastikas and crescents suggests that they could be dedicated to any deity. The question then arises as to whether they indicated the craft of the dedicant – the trouble with that is that sheer numbers would mean that carpenters and woodsmen were exceptionally pious. Alternatively the axe carried a potency of its own by virtue of being an axe, the nature of which we can only guess, and this seems much more likely (Green, 1985).

The small bronze statue of a dog said to have been found in Coventina's Well may have been a toy, it may have been a votive object – we cannot be certain, though the latter is more likely in the context. At Lydney Park a number of small bronze dogs were found, and one even decorated a dedicatory plaque to the god Nodens (fig.101 f). Some connection seems to have existed with healing gods through the medium of the dog licking the affected part. This seems a singularly unlikely way of securing a rapid cure but there must have been some basis in fact. Dogs are also quite widely associated with the shrines of other healing gods, for example Asclepius. Other examples include a small bronze cockerel from the Shrine of Apollo at Nettleton, though this served the more practical purpose of supporting a candlestick, a job also apparently performed by miniature stands (see above and fig.100 b). Another bronze cockerel, from Chelmsford, is perhaps more likely to have once formed part of a Mercury group (fig.101 e), and this is an important point to consider when dealing with miniatures of animals or objects traditionally associated with specific deities. Bronze groups were made of a number of separately cast components and they rarely survive as a group.

Brooches

The 'horse and rider' plate brooches are so closely associated with temple sites that they must have had a religious connection (fig.101 i; and see Chapter 4). What this was is unknown, though they probably represent either votive gifts or souvenirs for sale to visitors. The mediaeval pilgrim badges, for example those of Thomas à Becket sold at Canterbury, may thus be part of a continuing tradition.

Face pots

One of the most interesting classes of votive goods are the so-called 'face pots'. These seem to have been introduced by the army because all known first-century examples come from a military context. Broadly speaking, they are defined by having a representation of a human face on the surface of the pot, though the actual techniques used for making the face, and the vessel forms, vary quite widely. Distribution is across Britain apart from most of Wales, the whole of the south-west and much of central southern England (fig.102, plate 23).

Unfortunately there is no documentary evidence or even a *graffito* to indicate their purposes; we can only be certain that a number were used for containing cremation burials (see below). Some others have been found in contexts which suggest a religious connection. One from Chester-le-Street bears a face and a smith's tools and formed part of a foundation deposit beneath a late gate-tower. The same area has produced an altar of a Celtic smith god. A number of others, for example from Verulamium and London, were buried in pits. However, a great many are known only from a purely household context.

Whatever the variations in vessel form and types of face, it must be the general use of the face which is the significant feature. This does not appear to have been a Celtic habit – otherwise distribution would be throughout Britain. If they were introduced by the army then the fact that much of the army of AD 43 came from the German provinces is probably of more significance. The faces may represent gods who through the faces were able to ward off evil and watch over the interests of the owner. In this broadly simple sense they could have functioned in the home as a domestic and workshop ritual vessel or shrine, as a votive gift, or as a guardian of a dead occupant. It is important to note that pots with faces on are known from the Neolithic period right up to modern times (Braithwaite, 1984).

101 Ritual miniatures and other religious material (not to scale; **a-d** from Kirmington, South Humberside, after Leahy, 1980):
a rectangular shield (4.3cm long)
b oval shield (3.6cm)
c helmet (3.1cm)
d axe (actual size)
e bronze cockerel from Chelmsford, height 4.1cm (after Drury and Wickenden, 1982)
f bronze dog from the Nodens Temple site at Lydney Park. Length 8.2cm (Wheeler, 1932, pl. 25)
g bronze arm from Lydney. Length 10.4cm (Wheeler, 1932, pl. 26)
h ritually (?) bent bronze spear from Woodeaton, Oxfordshire. Length 14.5cm
i 'horse and rider' brooch from Hayling Island, Hampshire. Length 3cm
j bronze letter 'N' with four nail holes, from Woodeaton. Height 6.2cm
k bronze wheel from Felmingham Hall, Norfolk. Part of a hoard of religious material which included a coin of Valerian (255–9). Diameter 17.8cm
l model plough found with a group of miniature tools including axes, saws and a mattock, in Sussex. Length 9.5cm

Superstition

Naturally it is rather hard to distinguish what we would call superstition from religious practices. The general idea that doing something according to a prescribed formula will achieve a desired end was common throughout Romano-British religion and is hardly less current today. The same comment applies to the idea that to veer from the prescribed formula in any way is to invite the worst to befall you. Both are superstitious attitudes and they condition much of our behaviour, whether or not we are aware of it.

There are, however, some features of Roman life which do seem better described as superstitious than religious. They involve the use of personal amulets, which were used much in the way that charm bracelets are worn nowadays. The owner wore an amulet because he or she believed it would afford some protection against the darker forces of the divine world. The principal example is the *phallus* (fig.103 b, c). The phallus in the Roman world was primarily

102 Face-pots. Three face-pots from Colchester, *Camulodunum*, used in cremation burials (the only place where this certainly occurred). The first two, probably of second century date, were almost certainly made at Colchester, the third, a face-flagon, may have been made in the Nene Valley in the fourth century. The precise significance of the features on the pots is now completely unknown. Heights about 25–28cm

associated with the god Priapus, whose generous endowment was seen as the power behind agricultural fertility (Johns, 1982, discusses the general theme of sexuality and erotica in the whole classical world). The spirit of the *phallus*, *Fascinus*, was considered to be a potent defence against the Evil Eye, *fascinatio*. They are known from house-fronts and shops in Pompeii; on pavements and bridges; and in many other places, for example on the bridge abutment at Chesters on Hadrian's Wall, or even on a quernstone from Rocester in Staffordshire (fig.104). The power of the phallus in this respect seems to be a worldwide phenomenon.

Personal *phalli* appear on rings, and on pendants such as the crude example from Verulamium (fig.103 c); they were adapted into household ornaments with bells attached to disperse evil. The concept of the phallus as an amulet appears to have been entirely new to the Celts, including those of Roman Britain, but the symbolism contained in the idea was not inappropriate to a Celtic point of view. It has been

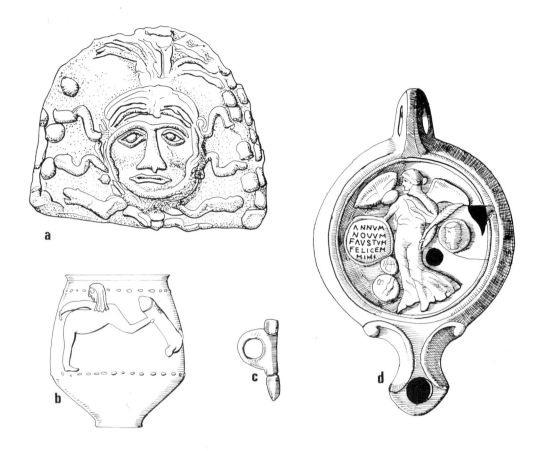

103 Superstition (not to scale):

a tile *antefix* from Colchester, *Camulodunum*, with a moulded image of a female Gorgon's head. Whether this motif was being used purely for its iconographic appeal, or because it had a superstitious power, is unknown. Width 18cm (Hull, 1958, pl. 30B)

b Nene Valley beaker of late second to early third-century date showing part of an erotic scene involving an oversized phallus and a willing recipient. Found at Horsey Toll, Cambridgeshire. Height 12.4cm

c phallus amulet from Verulamium, (after Frere, 1972, fig.33, no. 47). Length 32mm

d so-called New Year's Lamp from Ely. This lamp is a modern forgery and is a good example of an artefact with an apparently sound but erroneous provenance (personal communication: D.M. Bailey). The *discus* is decorated with a moulded figure of a Victory bearing a shield on which is inscribed *Annum novum faustum felicem mihi*, 'to me, a happy and prosperous New Year'. The figure seems to be accompanied by other New Year gifts, such as coins, cakes and nuts. Length 12.9cm

suggested that statuettes of phalluses with human bodies usefully combined the Roman force of the phallus with the Celtic force of the head. Very rare examples involve pairing the phalluses and combining them with a horse's head.

Amulets take a number of forms. A third-century grave at Colchester contained a number including pierced coins, a dog's tooth, a phallus and a bell. The group also contained an amber amulet pierced for suspension and carved as a human head in African style (Henig, 1984). The prominent nose may have also functioned as a phallus, and in this context it may be worth noting that the north and east Africa of the classical period was far wealthier and more fertile than it is today. Other amulets include pierced axes, whose powers were presumably the same as those discussed above. From Caernarvon comes a curious gold sheet inscribed with Greek letters making up magical words and symbols. It was originally rolled up, presumably so that its owner

STONE INSCRIBED WITH [275]
A PHALLIC EMBLEM.
[CILURNUM]

104 Stone inscribed with a phallus from Chesters, *Cilurnum*. Diameter 30cm. (photo: author; courtesy of English Heritage).

could carry it about with him. Occasionally amulets were made in the form of an attribute of a deity. A good example is the club of Hercules, for example one found in the Thetford treasure (Johns and Potter, 1983).

Amulets also took the form of animals. Some of the miniatures from temple sites may be parallels of personal amulets, such as the terrier from Coventina's Well (above, page 165). From Cookham in Berkshire comes a small bronze disc bearing the head of a triple-horned bull (Read *et alia*, 1986). The motif is a well-known one, the bull being a popular Celtic representation of strength and fertility, and the tripling of the horns signifying the importance of the number three.

Other examples include bronze and pipeclay figurines of bulls but this version seems to be a personal accessory.

A problem which confronts anyone concerned with the identification of ancient artefacts is that of forgeries and reproductions. Those objects concerned with religion and superstition are more subject to this than anything else because they carry a high commercial value. A so-called New Year's Lamp from Ely falls into this category, though it was originally published as a genuine Romano-British find (fig.103 d and Liversidge, 1954). Authentic ancient New Year lamps are known but this particular example combines an Italian decorative scene with a North African lamp form – a modern factory in Naples manufactured these lamps as reproductions.

7

Death and Burial

Introduction

At some time probably in the second century a man who lived at York named Quintus Corellius Fortis cremated and buried his daughter, Corellia Optata. On her tombstone (*RIB* 684) he recorded his sadness at her loss and the innocence of someone who had died so young.

Corellia Optata's grave is only one of thousands of Romano-British graves which have been found. Until Christianity became popular, burials were traditionally accompanied by a variety of grave goods. These, the tombstones and the containers of the body's physical remains, are amongst the richest sources of information for the study of Romano-British culture and society.

Except in the case of babies or miscarriages burial in Roman Britain, as everywhere else in the Empire, was legally permitted only outside the area of settlement. For this reason most of the graves that have been found are in cemeteries clustering along the roads radiating from major or minor towns. Others have been found in isolation in rural districts and probably belong to farm or country houses which have yet to be discovered. In a few cases a rural house together with its associated burials are known, for example at Lullingstone and Keston in Kent. Most such houses would have had their own cemeteries and mausolea.

Celtic burials

The idea that death is the great leveller of mankind is strenuously resisted in most cultures. This was naturally true in Roman Britain where presumably wealth and status also dictated the quality of one's tombstone and grave-goods. Nevertheless, Romano-British burials seem relatively egalitarian compared to the burials of pre-Roman Celtic Britain. Celtic society was clearly distinguished by the strict hierarchy which placed the ruling warrior class well on top. Their graves are amongst the most distinctive features of their society and are in marked contrast to those of Roman Britain.

A fairly typical example of a Celtic warrior burial was found at Owlesbury in Hampshire. Dating to around the middle of the first century BC, this inhumation burial was of an adult man accompanied by a sword, its belt, a shield and a spear (Collis, 1968, 23ff.). In northern Britain chariot burials are well-known, for example at Garton Slack where the dead man was laid on his dismantled chariot with whip and harness (Brewster, 1971 and 1976). A number of the wealthiest late Celtic burials are in south-east Britain where the Belgae lived, and show how status and wealth was now manifesting itself in the acquisition of expensive imports from the Roman world, for example amphorae, metal tableware, and quality domestic products like wrought iron hearth furniture, wine buckets and mirrors (for example at Welwyn, see Stead, 1967). These rich graves contrast with the simple graves of the majority of the population and emphasise the practice of providing the deceased with a magnificent feast. At Aylesford in Kent most of the cremated remains were placed in urns, and few were accompanied by any grave goods (Evans, 1890).

Romano-British burial practice

In Roman Britain the deceased were either cremated or buried (inhumed). In practice cremation was almost entirely confined to the first and second centuries, and even then young children were frequently inhumed in preference. Inhumation became popular in the third and fourth centuries, and as a custom it became reinforced by Christianity which promised a Day of Resurrection. Interpreted literally, this promoted a reluctance to wilfully destroy the body by cremation.

Grave-goods

Whether cremated or inhumed, the deceased was often accompanied by grave-goods. Either these were intended to sustain him or her, such as flagons which must have contained liquids, a lamp to light the way, and coins to pay passage across the River Styx to the Underworld; or they were articles which were of value to the individual such as jewellery, and other items of personal decoration. These often appear to have included shoes, the nails from which are usually the only surviving traces. They may have had a purely practical purpose for the afterlife, or they may have been symbolic of the journey the deceased would have to make to the Underworld. One of the best-known examples of personal effects is from a child's grave at Colchester, which contained a number of his toys (Hull, 1958; Toybee, 1964, 419). Sometimes these personal effects were placed in wooden chests which themselves are often represented only by their hinges, corner plates and latches (fig.106 a). Such personal possessions were probably regarded as being imbued with the deceased's persona, and therefore could not be used by anyone else. Sometimes they were 'ritually' broken in order for this spiritual presence to share the death of the deceased.

105 Grave-goods:

a bone slip from a grave at York with an inscription which means 'Lord Victor, may you have a happy win'. Victor may have been a charioteer, or gladiator. Diameter 6.8cm (RCHM York, 135, no. 149)

b bone casket fitting from a burial at York with an inscription reading *soror ave vivas in deo*, which means 'sister, may you live in God'. This may be a Christian grave good but as a casket fitting the inscription may be incidental. Length 13.7cm. (RCHM York, 135, no. 150)

c bone disc engraved with the face of a goddess or gorgon from the male inhumation in the 'Temple-Mausoleum' at Lullingstone villa. Cut down from a larger piece, possibly a plaque. Diameter 33mm (after Meates, 1987, 142, no. 392)

d colour-coated beaker (probably Oxfordshire ware; after *c.* 240, see fig.53m) from an inhumation in a cemetery at Dunstable, Bedfordshire. The beaker is inscribed *olla[m] dendrofrorum Ve[rulamiensium] Regillinus donavit*, 'Regillinus presented the pot of the *dendrophori* of Verulamium'. In the Western Empire a *dendrophorus* was a 'branch-bearer' who carried pine trees as part of the rites associated with Cybele. The *dendrophori* had guilds and it seems that this was a gift by a guild based at Verulamium (12 miles distant) to one of their number who had died, presented by Regillinus on their behalf. Height 16cm (after C.L. Matthews, *Britannia*, 11, 1980, 406)

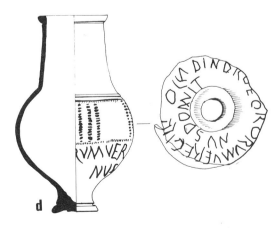

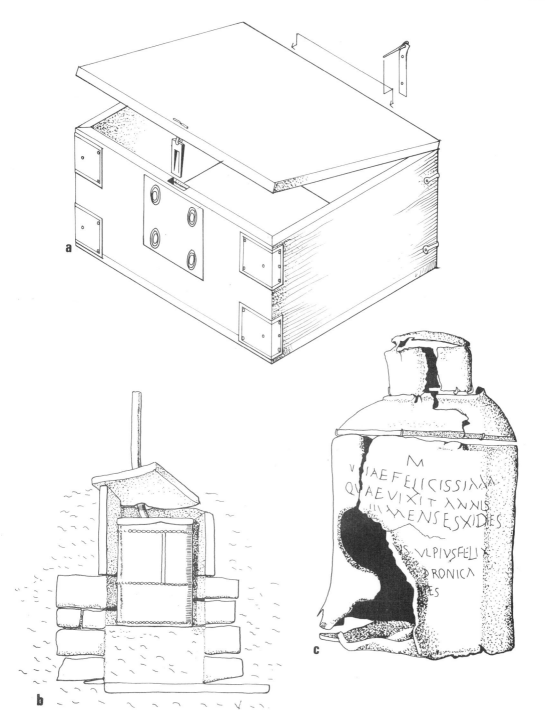

106 Cremation burial containers:

a reconstructed wooden casket, with metal fittings, from cremation burial 30 at Skeleton Green, Hertfordshire. Width approximately 30cm. The casket was accompanied by two pottery vessels, a glass beaker and a coin of Antoninus Pius (138-161), thus providing a *terminus post quem* for the burial. The coin's ritual function was to provide payment for the ferryman to take the deceased across the Styx to the underworld (after Partridge, 1981)

b Caerleon, *Isca*, pipe-burial, showing the circular lead canister as found in a stone and tile-lined pit, with a pipe leading to the former ground surface (after Wheeler, 1929). Height of canister 44cm

c lead urn from York with an inscription recording the burial of Ulpia Felicissima, aged eight years and 11 months, buried by her father and mother, Marcus Ulpius Felix and . . . . Andronica. Height 36cm

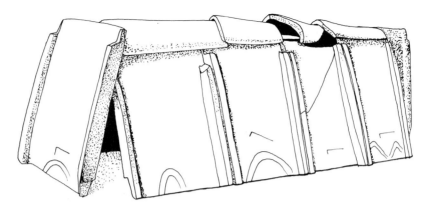

107 Tile tomb from York, *Eboracum*. Some of the tiles bear the stamp of the *legio* IX *Hispana* (RCHM York, 81, b, iv). Probably Flavian in date (the legion left in the early second century)

Valuable dating evidence can be gained from grave groups. To begin with the contents of each individual's grave were presumably deposited at the same time, which means that any datable article, such as a coin, will supply a *terminus post quem* for the burial as a whole. Secondly the goods were usually deposited intact, or even if broken all the components are likely to be there. Unlike most other archaeological deposits, grave groups were not a means of disposing of rubbish. Graves thus produce intact pottery and glass vessels and all kinds of other articles which are normally found only as they appear in refuse, fragmentary and incomplete. Unfortunately for archaeologists the coming of Christianity meant there was a marked decline in the practice of supplying the dead with grave-goods.

There are occasional examples of little messages to the dead enclosed with the burial. At York an inhumation was accompanied by a small inscribed bone slip bearing the message: 'To Lord Victor, may you have a favourable win', suggesting that Victor was a gladiator or charioteer (fig.105 a). Another, accompanied by conventional pagan grave-goods, and carved in openwork from a strip of bone, suggests the occupant had been a Christian (fig.105 b), but as the strip may have come from a casket or piece of furniture it is quite possible the slogan has no particular relevance to the dead woman. If the woman was a Christian, it is an indication of how the pagan practice of grave-goods could endure. At Dunstable a dead member of a guild probably associated with the eastern cult of Cybele received an inscribed pottery beaker from his colleagues (fig.105 d).

108 Tombstones (not to scale):

a tombstone of Regina, aged 30, of the Catuvellauni tribe, wife and freedwoman of Barates of Palmyra in Syria. Found south-west of the fort at South Shields, *Arbeia*. This remarkable monument illustrates the cosmopolitan nature of the Roman world even in north-east Britain. Regina is seated in a high-backed chair, on her right is a jewellery box, on her left a work basket. Beneath the Latin inscription is a brief equivalent in Palmyrene script. Probably early third century. Height 1.12m (*RIB* 1065). By a curious chance Barates' tombstone has also survived, found at Corbridge, *Corstopitum* (*RIB* 1171).

b tombstone of Julia Velva, who died aged 50, portrayed on a couch participating in a funerary feast and accompanied by a girl and boy (her children?), and her heir Aurelius Mercurialis who was responsible for setting up the tombstone. Found in York (RCHM York, 124, no. 82). The stone was evidently a standard, 'mass-produced' type – the spare space in the text area indicates that Mercurialis bought the stone after it had been carved. His name suggests a date in the late second, early third century. Height 1.45m (*RIB* 688)

c tombstone of Marcus Petronius, aged 38, a *signifer* with *legio* XIV *Gemina* at Wroxeter where the stone was found. Petronius was born at Vicetia (VIC) in northern Italy, and served 18 years with the legion which arrived at Wroxeter by the early 50s. The legion was awarded the titles *Martia Victrix* after putting down the Boudican Revolt in AD 60/61; these are not mentioned here so the stone was probably erected before that date. Height 1.70m (RIB 294)

d octagonal tombstone (one face only shown) of Claudia Martina, aged 19, set up by her husband Anencletus, who describes himself as a *provinc[ialis]*, a 'slave of the provincial government'. Found on Ludgate Hill in London. Stylistically dated to the late first, early second century. Height 1.19m (*RIB* 21)

e tombstone of Curatia Di[o]nysia, aged 40, portrayed in a similar fashion to Julia Velva (above, **b**), though on her own. Found in Chester. Height 119cm (*RIB* 562)

a

D M · REGINA · LIBERTA · ET · CONIVGE
BARATES · PALMYRENVS · NATIONE ·
CATVALLAVNA · AN · XXX

b

D M
IVLIE VELVE PIENTISSI
ME VIXIT AN L AVRELI
MERCVRIALIS IER FACI
VNDVM CVRAVIT VIVVS
SIBI ET SVIS FECIT

c

M PETRONIVS
L F MEN
VIC ANN
XXXVIII
MIL LEG
XIIII GEM
MILITAVIT
ANN XVIII
SIGN F VIT
H · S · E ·

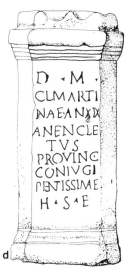

d

D · M ·
CL MARTI
NAE AN XXX
AN ENCLE
TVS
PROVINC
CONIVGI
PIENTISSIME
H · S · E

e

D M
CVRATIA DINY
SIA VIX AN XXXX
H F C

Grave-markers

A Romano-British grave might be marked in a number of ways. Probably the most common were wooden markers, shrines or tablets, and for obvious reasons these do not survive. A simple cremation grave in Kent of late-first-century date seems to have been marked by a stake (Philp, 1973, 108). Another cremation, outside the legionary fortress at Caerleon and of second-century date, appears to have been provided with a lead pipe leading to the surface. This may have been used for pouring libations down to the remains on the anniversary of the death when relatives paid their respects to their ancestors (fig.106 b).

In a few rare cases the grave might be accompanied by a substantial tomb, as was the case at the Lullingstone villa in Kent which had a building described by the excavator as 'the Temple-Mausoleum'. The structure appears to have been a temple built for the observation of rites in remembrance of two people who were inhumed below in the early fourth century, though there was no physical access to their coffins (Meates, 1979, 122 ff.). The nearby villa at Keston is accompanied by a substantial circular stone mausoleum and a smaller stone tomb. Amongst the more unusual grave-markers are the tile-tombs from York. These were constructed out of roof-tiles in order to house the deceased (fig.107).

Much the most common survivals, though, are tombstones. These range from impressive pieces of sculpture to quite simple memorial tablets. The bulk appear to have been 'mass-produced', that is, the sculptor could confidently manufacture a range of stock tombstones with appropriate motifs (fig.108 b). For example, a sculptor working near a fort would obviously manufacture tombstones bearing a military figure, legionary or auxiliary, infantry or cavalry as appropriate. Facial features and verbal details could be added later when a suitable customer had died.

Tombstones are of exceptional importance to the study of the army and Romano-British life. We have already seen their use in supplying details of military equipment. They also give evidence of artistic perceptions of the time, such as details of hairstyles and dress, and supply exact biographical details of the dead person, useful for statistical studies of population (for example Regina's tombstone, fig.108 a). It is most unfortunate that such portable pieces of stone are hardly ever found in association with the grave. They were generally carted off to use as filling for city-walls or other mundane uses, a frustrating fact, even if this did mean they were preserved.

The typical form of a gravestone begins with

109 Tombstone from Caerleon, *Isca*, recording the death of Gaius Valerius Victor from Lugdunum in Gaul, a standard-bearer, *signifer*, with *legio* II *Augusta*. He died aged 45, after 17 years' service. Width 119cm (*RIB* 365; photo and copyright; the British Museum)

110 Tombstone of Faustina and Catiotus from Lincoln. This tombstone appears to commemorate two apparently unrelated individuals. Their respective dedications are separate columns. Faustina lived 26 years, one month and 26 days and the stone was dedicated by her husband Aurelius Senecio, a town councillor, *decurio*. Claudius Catiotus has a separate dedication recording that he lived at least 60 years (*RIB* 250. Height 1.37m, photo and copyright; the British Museum)

DIS MANIBVS, or D·M. This means 'To the spirits of the departed', *manes* being those spirits, but is a kind of token statement of similar purpose to our R.I.P. Nevertheless, offerings were made at the grave to the deceased so the significance was more direct than acting as a simple slogan. There-after follows details of the dead person, usually including age, and place of origin (figs.108-110). Sometimes the person who erected the stone was recorded too. Thus we know that at Lincoln Flavius Helius 'Grecus' (a Greek) died at the age of 40 and was buried by his wife Flavia Ingenua (*RIB* 251). As with most tombstones, the date of this example is uncertain. Some military tomb-

stones can be dated when the unit is known to have moved on after a certain period (see Chapter 1 and fig.8). Otherwise dating relies on comparing carving techniques and style with examples of known date.

Some graves were adorned with particularly elaborate stonework. The tomb of Julius Classicianus from London bears enough of its inscription to identify it certainly with the man mentioned by Tacitus as helping to restore the administration of the province after the Boudican Revolt, in his rôle as *Procurator* (plate 25). The surviving parts of the tomb include a large scroll decorated with leaves from the top. The reading of the inscription is as follows (*RIB* 12):

DIS

[M]ANIBVS

[C·IVL·C·F·F]AB·ALPINI·CLASSICIANI

(at least two lines missing)

PROC·PROVINC·BRITA[NNIAE]

IVLIA·INDI·FILIA·PACATA·I[NDIANA?]

VXOR   [F]

The lower stone provides the vital information about Classicianus' career. An interesting feature is the information supplied about his wife, Julia Pacata, who had had the tomb made. She was apparently the daughter, *filia*, of Julius

111 The Colchester sphinx, almost certainly from a now lost funerary monument on the site of Essex County Hospital. The sphinx was traditionally associated with death and in this case is shown on top of various human remains, most conspicuously a head. Height 84cm (Toynbee, 1964, 112-113)

Indus, a prominent member of the Gaulish provincial aristocracy from the north-east. Classicianus' name suggests a similar provincial origin. Together they show that the Roman administration was prepared to appoint people with a potentially more sympathetic attitude towards provincial government, yet who were also committed members of the Roman ruling classes, even if this resulted in friction with the incumbent governor. Tacitus implies as much, though from his perspective provincial sympathies amounted to something approaching treachery, *bonum publicum privatis simultatibus impediebat* – 'he [Classicianus] was impeding the public good by his personal quarrels' (*Annals*, 14, 38).

The tombstone of Classicianus is of national significance because of its historical importance. Other tombs may lack this significance, but a number were evidently of even more ambitious

112 Stone head, probably from a funerary monument, found at Towcester, *Lactodurum*, Northamptonshire. Height 54cm (photo and copyright; the British Museum)

structure. The Colchester 'Sphinx' may well have come from a long-lost tomb. The sphinx was associated with death, and in this case the sphinx sits on top of a representation of human remains and a human head (fig.111; Liversidge, 1964, 112-3). The human head was of great significance to the Celts because it contained the dead man's soul. If this was the symbolism intended here, then the statue shows an interesting synthesis of Egyptian, classical and Celtic traditions. The Corbridge lion seems to have been one of four similar statues, each involving a lion killing a stag, placed at the corners of a mausoleum precinct near the fort. The lion emphasises even more strongly the whole idea of a ferocious animal, representing the potential imminence of death. The significance of the Towcester head is not quite so clear (fig.112; Liversidge, 1964, 112).

Cremation

Cremation burials are particularly valuable to the study of artefacts for the simple reason that the cremated bones and ashes required a container. The most ideal, and cheapest, were kitchen jars, of almost any variety so long as they were large enough to take the ashes. However, glass and wood was also used, and there was an industry in purpose-built containers. When used in this way containers, jars and bottles are generally referred to as 'cremation urns' (figs 106, 113, 114).

Cremations in pottery containers

A typical assemblage consists of a large grey ware jar, or amphora, containing the burnt remains, a lid or some suitable vessel substitute such as a samian Form 31 dish, and accompanying vessels, for example flagons, oil-lamps and beakers. The range of contents of such burials is obviously very wide as the following examples show:

1. Richborough fort. A cremation in a broken amphora which also contained a samian Form 31 dish, a small pottery flask and a beaker with *barbotine* decoration. By the amphora was a narrow-necked jar. The context indicated a second-century date, a conclusion assisted by the presence of the samian bowl (fig.114).
2. London, Warwick Street. A cremation of an adult and child in a Dressel 20 amphora from Spain accompanied by two lamps. The amphora was buried sideways and its opening was blocked with a tile. Two more tiles were placed facing away in order to form a kind of antechamber.

113 above Lidded lead canister which held a glass urn with cremation burial. Found in Warwick Square, London (RCHM, 1929, 154 and pl. 56). The canister is decorated with panels depicting a charioteer driving a *quadriga* and bands of *astragali*. Height of lead canister 35cm

114 below Cremation group from Richborough, *Rutupiae*, Kent (⅙ scale). The burial was placed in an amphora with its neck broken off and was accompanied by a small unguent bottle, a Nene Valley beaker, a grey ware jar, and a samian Form 31 dish. Probably late second century (after Cunliffe, 1968, pl. 52, 518–22)

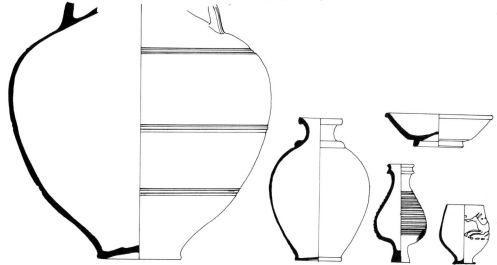

Three pot-lids were placed up against the blocking tile and in front of them, between the two flanking tiles, three pots were smashed. (Marsden, 1980, 76).

3. Skeleton Green, Braughing, Hertfordshire, burial 49. This grave was a double burial and each pottery vessel was accompanied by a duplicate except for the samian. There were two urns, two flagons, a beaker in the form of a small jar and a bag-shaped beaker, a samian Form 33 cup stamped by Tituro of Lezoux (155–190), and a samian dish Form 18/31 stamped by Suobnus of Les Martres-de-Veyre (130–155; fig.52)

(Partridge, 1981, 264). There were also fragments of a mirror. The grave had been packed in with stones, crushing the vessels of another burial below and to the side.

Cremations in glass containers
Like the pottery cremations these burials used vessels which were already available, and primarily intended to perform everyday functions:
1. London, Moorfields. A large glass jar, about 38cm (15in) high, with a single handle contained

burnt remains. The cremation was one of three contained in a wooden cist and covered with part of an amphora (RCHM, 1928, 161, 35).

2. Verulamium, St Stephen's. A child's cremation contained in a glass bottle, and accompanied by three pottery jars, a glass jar and two glass flasks. Other grave goods included a number of coins, an oil-lamp and an iron implement (?) (Gareth Davies & Saunders, *Verulamium Guide*, 1986, 28).

Cremations in purpose-made urns

Purpose-built containers for cremations were made in pottery, stone, wood, lead, and glass. Unlike the previous two groups these urns were not usually used for anything else.

1. York. A cremation in a lead container, 37cm (14.6in) high by 25cm (10in) wide, with conical lid and cylindrical cap. The container had been incised with an inscription recording the death of Ulpia Felicissima, aged 8 years and 11 months (fig.106 c).

2. London, Warwick Square. One of four lead cylindrical containers held a two-handled glass urn with lid inside which was a cremation. The lead container was decorated with panels showing a charioteer driving a quadriga (fig.113).

3. Colchester. A cremation in a face pot. Face pots are well-known in ritual contexts and one of their purposes seems to have been as cremation urns. They are found almost everywhere in Britain but with a distinct bias to the east. The exact significance of the face is unknown: they may be schematic representations of the deceased, merely symbolic of the contents, or they may have served some sort of amuletic purpose. It has been suggested that face pots were used for a particular section of society, perhaps priests, though any group is possible. The face-vase in this case was accompanied by a flagon and an oil-lamp and the group was

---

115 Coffins:

a iron hinge fitting from a wooden coffin. From burial 228 in an inhumation cemetery at Cirencester, *Corinium Dobunnorum*. The grave contained an adolescent male and was orientated east-west (after McWhirr *et alia*, 1982)

b lead coffin (reconstructed) of a young man from the early fourth-century 'Temple-Mausoleum' at Lullingstone villa, Kent. The coffin was decorated with the typical motifs of scallop shells and *astragali*. Length 2m. There were originally two burials, but grave robbers in antiquity destroyed the accompaning burial of a young woman.

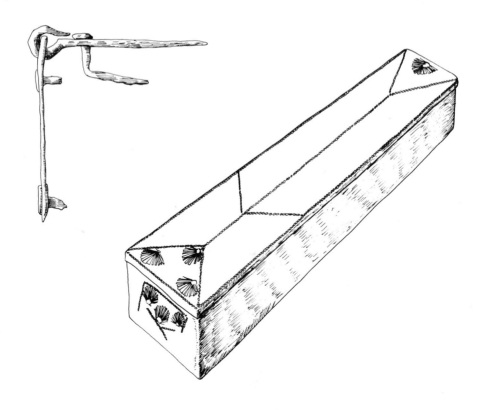

protected by being deposited in a brick-lined grave. (See Chapter 6 and fig.102; Braithwaite, 1984.)

4. Skeleton Green, Braughing, Hertfordshire, grave 35. The burnt bones had been placed in a wooden casket which had bronze and iron fittings. Inside the casket was a glass beaker, a coin of Antoninus Pius (138–161), and a cornelian intaglio. The burial was accompanied by a samian Form 42 dish stamped by Marcellinus of Les Martres-de-Veyre (115-135; fig.52), a glass bowl and a glass flagon (fig.106 a).

Inhumations

When inhumation became the norm for burial in the third century and after, the practice of re-using domestic equipment to contain the remains became far less common, though cremations did continue. Corpses were now interred in coffins, the vast majority of which must have been wood, but only the metal fittings from these usually survive (fig.115 a). Only the better-off families would have been able to afford lead or stone coffins. Sometimes inhumed bodies were covered with gypsum in order to restrict decay, and this can have the fortunate effect of supplying a cast of the body and the clothes in which it was wrapped (RCHM York, plate 33).

Inhumations in wood coffins

1. York, Trentholme Drive. A number of inhumations belonging to a later phase in the cemetery's history had been buried in wooden coffins. The coffins were represented by nails and iron corner plates though occasional fragments of wood were also found. (RCHM York, 106).

2. Richborough fort, Shepherdswell. An inhumation in a wooden coffin beneath a barrow. (Detsicas, *The Cantiaci,* 1983, 149).

Inhumations in stone coffins

1. London, Haydon Square. A stone coffin with separate lid secured by iron clamps and containing a lead coffin within which were a boy's bones. (RCHM 1928, 157).

2. London, Westminster. A stone coffin, almost certainly brought to Westminster in post-Roman times as it has a carved cross on the lid. The coffin bears an inscription recording the occupant as Valerius Amandinus, and the names of his sons, Valerius Superventor and Valerius Marcellus, who had had the coffin made. (RCHM 1928, 157 and 173).

3. York, Driffield Estate. A stone coffin inscribed for a woman called Aelia Severa, with a lid made out of the tombstone for a woman called Flavia Augustina and containing the remains of a man. (RCHM York, 99).

Inhumations in lead coffins

1. Lullingstone, Kent. One burial of two survives, both having been deposited beneath a 'Temple-Mausoleum' close to the celebrated villa *c.* AD 300. A man in his early twenties was interred wearing a shroud and leather jerkin, packed in gypsum, in a lead coffin with separate lid both of which were decorated with embossed scallop shells. He was accompanied by grave-goods including a pottery and bronze flagon, a number of glass vessels and utensils forming two sets, and a gaming board and counters. Other evidence suggested that his companion was a slightly younger woman, presumably his wife (fig.115 b).

2. Keston, Kent. A secondary burial in a lead coffin buried between two buttresses of the circular mausoleum close to a villa down a hill slope to the west (Detsicas, 1983, 101).

These selected examples of Romano-British burials serve to indicate the many different ways in which the dead were prepared for the Underworld. As with ordinary daily life one's wealth and status dictated the quality and style of the event. However, the summary removal and dismantling of Classicianus' tombstone for use as hardcore shows that the memories of the living are short, even for the mighty.

8
Christianity

Introduction

Christianity was only one of many religions with eastern origins followed in the Roman Empire. Of course it was inextricably linked with the Jews of the troubled province of Judaea, and the exclusivity of Christianity only enhanced official and popular hostility. But in the early fourth century Christianity was adopted as the official religion of the Roman Empire. Its subsequent pre-eminent status in the western world has meant that it is usually regarded as a topic in its own right, even in the history of Roman Britain (see Thomas, 1981, for a synthesis of the evidence), and so it is here.

From an archaeological point of view Christianity presents a number of problems. It was by its very nature hostile to the materialistic and acquisitive instincts of a consumer world, though this was not a trait which entirely endured. The early Christian church was a largely modest, poor and discreet organisation, quite different from the overt display of wealth and status exhibited by churchmen in the Middle Ages. This was also in contrast to the wealth of the pagan religions of the Roman Empire. Christianity was not commonly practised through the offering of votive gifts, or the deposition of curses. Christ was not portrayed with numerous stone and metal statues and statuettes, and until the religion became legitimised inscriptional evidence of any kind is scarce; even then it is never common. Fortunately there are cases where pagan customs were transferred to a Christian context – some of the contents of the Water Newton treasure are particularly noteworthy in this respect (fig.116a, b; plate 26).

All these considerations apply to Roman Britain. What they mean is that very few objects were made which specifically referred to Christianity in the first place. Those that did are not necessarily any evidence that Christianity was actually being practised. We have to be very careful how we interpret material which is apparently Christian in nature. A modern analogy is a very good way of illustrating the problem; does the person who keeps a model Buddha in his house, or wears an Egyptian 'ankh' (life) symbol around his neck, do so because he worships Buddha or the Egyptian pantheon? He may do, but he may equally like the objects for aesthetic or protective reasons.

This is the main problem with any Christian artefact from Roman Britain. Very few are definitively 'Christian' in the sense of being unequivocally associated with ritual and belief. The majority are artefacts which belong to categories already covered in this book but which happen to bear Christian symbols. While we may have the remains of *mithraea*, and various other temples in Britain where the worship of a god or gods is not in doubt, there is no absolutely certain Christian equivalent for Roman Britain. We do know that Roman Britain had an episcopal structure by the early fourth century, that is, the major cities had their own bishops, three of whom attended the Council of Arles in the year 314. Christianity may even have been introduced as early as the second century, or so the third century Christian apologist Tertullian implied (*adversus Judaeos*, vii). But the gap between the historical evidence and the archaeological evidence is a large one.

Christian symbols

Our evidence for Christianity in Roman Britain is largely dependent on the use of Christian symbols. Here again the question of function arises – does the use of Christian symbols and motifs genuinely signify use in Christian rites, or does it indicate that they were simply being used as one of the many sources of decorative details? The principal motifs and symbols concerned are the Greek letters X and P, normally referred to as the 'chi-rho' monogram, which begin the name of Christ, Χριστος. It is sometimes associated with the alpha and omega, α and ω, which symbolise

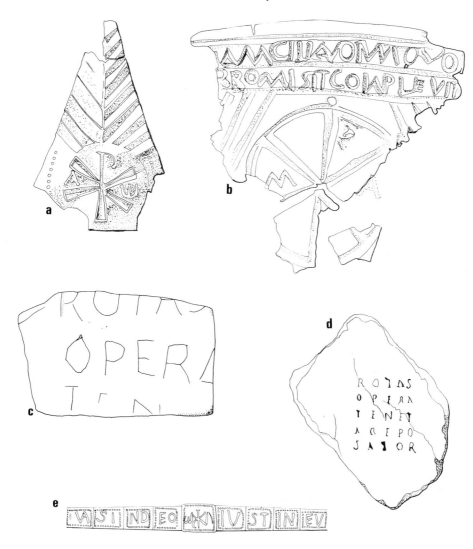

116 Finds with Christian inscriptions:

a silver plaque from the Water Newton treasure. Found in 1975 within the boundaries of *Durobrivae*, near Peterborough, along with 18 other plaques and nine vessels. The plaque bears an embossed chi-rho motif, and along with other similar examples and inscriptions make the treasure unequivocally Christian in nature. However, all other examples of plaques are pagan and this thus shows an interesting adaptation of traditional votive custom. Length 6cm

b silver plaque from the Water Newton treasure. Although fragmentary, this plaque bears an inscription reading *Anicilla votum quo[d] promisit complevit*. The inscription adds to the impression of conflated pagan and Christian votive customs because the inscription is essentially a pagan-style record of a fulfilled (*complevit*) vow (*votum promisit*), but the plaque also bears a chi-rho motif. Width 10cm

c inscribed amphora-sherd from Manchester bearing a fragment of the magic word-square which has possible, but far from certain, Christian connections. Width 18.5cm

d fragment of wall plaster, from Cirencester, bearing the complete magic word-square. The square may have been inscribed after the plaster had fallen from the wall, though how long after is a matter for debate.

e bronze finger ring (now lost) from Richborough bearing a Christian slogan, *Iustine, vivas in Deo*, 'Iustinus, may you live in God', and a chi-rho motif. Probably fourth century in date (after Cunliffe, 1968, pl. 42, 160)

Christ's statement 'I am the alpha and the omega, the beginning and the end'. There is also the use of the fish symbol, because the Greek word for a fish, ΙΧΘΥΣ, contains letters which indicate the first letters of the phrase, Ιησους Χριστος, Θεου Υιος, Σωτηρ, which means 'Jesus Christ, son of God, Saviour'.

The so-called Christian word-square is known from two sites in Britain – on a potsherd from Manchester (fig.116 c; Hassall and Tomlin in *Britannia*, 10, 353, no. 34) and as a scratching on wall-plaster from Cirencester (fig.116 d). The square is made from five Latin words which mean 'Arepo the sower holds the wheels carefully'. When re-arranged the letters made a cross from the words PATER NOSTER, or 'Our Father', and the Latin equivalents of the alpha and omega, A and O:

ROTAS
OPERA
TENET
AREPO
SATOR

and:

```
                  P
                  A
       A          T          O
                  E
                  R
  P A T E R N O S T E R
                  O
                  S
       A          T          O
                  E
                  R
```

Unfortunately the evidence of similar examples from elsewhere in the Empire (Pompeii, Budapest, and Dura-Europos) indicates that this attractive interpretation is not necessarily the only one. None are associated with other evidence of Christianity; for example Pompeii, destroyed in AD 79, has produced no supporting evidence. Moreover the letters can be arranged in a number of different ways, while the words themselves, it has been argued, are the only ones in Latin capable of being arranged in a meaningful sentence. So, while the cryptogram may have been used by Christians it was probably a well-established magical motif which proved conveniently adaptable for Christian purposes. It cannot be interpreted as necessarily 'Christian' in its own right (Hassall and Tomlin, *op. cit.*).

Problems with interpretation

All these symbols are commonly regarded as being evidence of Christianity. However, interpretation is not so straightforward. The chi-rho monogram was a political symbol as well as a religious one. Once Christianity had become adopted by the state in the early fourth century, the standard bearing the chi-rho, the appearance of which Constantine I believed had won him the Empire at the Battle of the Milvian Bridge, became the imperial banner. Its most common appearance in this form is on the coins of the House of Constantine and the House of Valentinian, some types of which are found in great numbers in fourth-century deposits in Roman Britain, for example, the bronze issues of Valentinian I (364–375) with the reverse legend GLORIA ROMANORVM around a figure of the Emperor dragging a captive and holding a standard aloft on which is the chi-rho. A rebel called Magnentius who proclaimed himself Emperor in 350 issued a bronze denomination with a reverse design consisting entirely of a chi-rho, alpha, omega and a legend referring to his own good health and that of his brother.

Clearly the chi-rho was closely tied up with the regime's claims and posture of legitimacy, righteous victory and strength and as such anticipated the political machinations of the mediaeval popes. In this form the chi-rho could obviously function as much as a conventional statement of, say, government ownership as it could refer to religious practice. There was nothing unusual about this sort of duality in the Roman world – Christianity had been adopted partly because it offered the potential for political stablility in its episcopal structures in the same way as traditionally the Capitoline Triad had been used. Moreover, the possibility of a more overt pagan interpretation of Christian symbols should not be discounted. The chi-rho contained within a circle may be related to wheel and solar cults, well-known features of Celtic religion (figs.35 b, 101 k). In this form it may have proved an attractive addition to the array of symbols already employed. It is as well to note that Constantine I commonly associated himself with *soli invicto*, 'the unconquered sun' (for example on coins, see fig.120 n).

The presence of Christian slogans does not mean that we have evidence of furtive and zealous worshippers spreading the gospel in amongst the settlements of Roman Britain. It *may* do, but on the other hand it may also represent the adoption of a suitable image when Christianity was in favour. The burial of the material may simply represent the fact that the time had returned when wise men and cowards were pagans, for example during the reign of Julian II 'the Apostate' (360–363; fig.44). It is important to remember that while the more dogmatic Christians will have adhered strictly to exclusivity, this was not usual Roman practice. It was considered quite normal to worship several gods, identify one's god with another man's if their attributes were similar or complementary, and to include Christ if it seemed convenient. Only zealous Christians would have had a problem with this idea – and the Christians had no copyright on the image of Christ and the chi-rho.

Wall-paintings

Although a few possible churches have been identified in Roman Britain, for example at Silchester, only with two rooms in the Lullingstone villa in Kent do we come close to identifying at least part of a structure where the worship of Christianity seems beyond reasonable doubt. Fourth-century wall-paintings of well-to-do figures praying, and the use of the chi-rho symbol, point to this as a chapel for the use of the villa's family and their friends (Liversidge and Weatherhead in Meates, 1987, 11ff.). Even so, this site has produced no material evidence of Christianity beyond the structure and its

paintings. The contemporary laying of mosaics with pagan subject matter in other rooms points to the possibility of syncretism here. But the fact that a Saxon church was built on the ruins of the pagan 'Temple-Mausoleum' adjacent to the villa points to a dim memory in post-Roman times that this had once been a sacred place.

Silver spoons

There is a considerable body of silver material from Britain, of fourth-century date, which bears evidence of Christian use. Some of the best-known are the silver spoons. Typically they have engravings in the bowl, usually the alpha, omega and chi-rho, such as three from the Mildenhall treasure (Painter, 1977). Others are known with Christian-type inscriptions from Thetford (Johns and Potter, 1983), and Biddulph (fig.117) amongst others. They could have been used for a number of purposes. They may have been baptism presents, or they may have been used during the ritual. The spoons from Thetford engraved with the name of the god Faunus show that the use of silver spoons in ritual was apparently not an exclusively Christian practice (fig.95 d, e). Alternatively they may have just been part of the family silver. And of course being such portable items their actual individual history is quite unknown. Whoever had them engraved may have been long since dead when they were deposited; the presence of three in the Mildenhall treasure associated with what is mainly pagan material is a case in point.

117 Silver spoon from Biddulph, Staffordshire bearing a chi-rho motif. Length 20cm (photo and copyright; the British Museum)

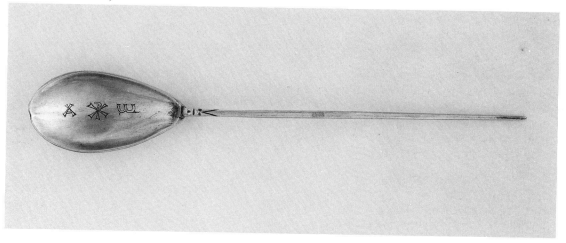

Silver and pewter plate

Of much more obviously Christian significance is the treasure from Water Newton (plate 26, and fig.116 a, b; Painter, 1977i). Of around 28 items eight were vessels of some form, one was a strainer and the remainder were plaques in the form of leaves. All are silver except for one disc of gold. The distinctive feature of this hoard is that many of the components either bear the chi-rho monogram or they bear inscriptions which are even more explicitly Christian, particularly one on a bowl which associates the name Publianus with the worship of 'the Lord's shrine'. The plaques recall the pagan use of such accessories for ritual furniture or clothing, and probably indicate that pagan ritual techniques were happily enduring even if the god had changed.

The Water Newton group dates to the fourth century and is the earliest collection of Christian silver plate from the whole Empire. Why it was buried is a mystery, for during most of the fourth century Christianity was completely legitimate. Even short bursts of persecution should not have prevented such a valuable treasure from being recovered unless the whole Christian community that knew of its existence was wiped out. Despite this enigma, it does show that there was a body of people in Roman Britain which was quite prepared to invest heavily in the church and endow it with worldly wealth. Nevertheless it is unique, and whether it is representative of Christian silver plate in use at the time is not clear.

Also worthy of consideration is the hoard of pewter plate which was deliberately buried in a late fourth-century pit in a villa floor at Appleshaw in Hampshire. However, of 32 vessels only one bears a scratched chi-rho, while another bears a more carefully-drawn fish (Brailsford, 1964 fig.19). A pewter bowl from London bears a scratched chi-rho on its base (Marsden, 1980, 146). Such 'graffiti' present a problem because they are evidently secondary to the manufacture of the plate itself, and therefore it is almost impossible to deduce any useful information about Christianity from it. The same applies to another group of pewter from Icklingham in Suffolk, consisting of nine vessels, one of which bears a stamped or incised drawing of a fish (Liversidge, 1959). Such motifs in such a context seem really to represent little more than conventional decoration on a household service – certainly there is no basis for arguing more.

Tanks

There are a number of lead tanks known which may shed light on the practice of Christianity in Roman Britain (fig.119; Guy, 1981). A number of these tanks, unique to Britain, for example one from Icklingham in Suffolk, 81cm (2ft8in) in diameter, bear the chi-rho monogram and the alpha and omega. They may well be baptismal tanks, and if so this raises the question of why none have been found associated with buildings that might have been churches. Either they were transported away as scrap, or they were actually carried around by itinerant priests who set up a church on some appropriate-looking mosaic in a friendly house. This is an interesting idea, particularly when it is considered that the 'chapel' at Lullingstone was only accessible from outside and not from within the villa itself (Meates, 1979), and it suggests a network of house churches in which a service was celebrated when a priest came that way. Certainly they are amongst the best evidence for the spread of Christianity beyond the towns.

Jewellery

All the evidence cited so far deals with artefacts which could at least have functioned at some point in Christian worship, though this is far from proven. There is also quite a lot of material which bears Christian symbols. There are a number of rings known which bear Christian slogans similar to those found on the spoons. The best-known is a gold ring from Silchester which bears the inscription SENICIANE VIVAS IIN DE, which appears to be a slightly misspelled version of VIVAS IN DEO, for 'Senicianus, may you live in God!'. The ring was originally 'pagan', bearing a bezel engraved with a bust of Venus; the inscription seems to have been a later addition. This particular ring is sometimes popularly associated with a curse from the Nodens Temple site at Lydney. The curse was made by one Silvianus who had lost a ring and cursed all those called Senicianus (Collingwood in Wheeler, 1932, 100) presumably because he knew that a Senicianus of his acquaintance had stolen it. If the Silchester ring is the same one then it says little for Senicianus' understanding of the Gospel.

Another ring, now lost, from Richborough, bore the inscription IVSTINE VIVAS IN DEO and also the chi-rho with alpha and omega (fig.116 e). Again the problem of portability arises – even if the slogan is Christian we have no guarantee

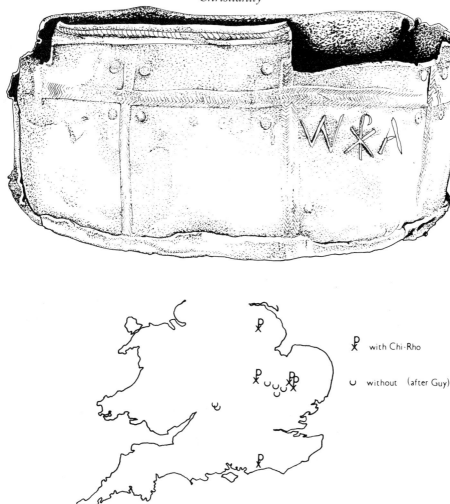

118 Lead water tank found in 1939 at Icklingham, Suffolk, with a chi-rho motif on the side, indicating that this may have been a Christian baptismal font. In 1971 a similar tank was found in the same field, and several others are known from the general area. Width: 81cm, capacity: 173 litres. The map shows other find-spots of similar tanks or fragments of tanks (after Guy, 1981)

whatsoever that the loser was a Christian, or that he lost it anywhere connected with Christianity.

Others

The other examples of possible Christian material involve the placing of Christian symbols on otherwise mundane material. A number of stones are known with the chi-rho on them, for example three from Chedworth villa (Goodburn, 1986, 28). A tile from York and a brick from Leicester also bear the chi-rho, as do a number of fragments of pottery. These may represent Christian attempts to 'de-paganise' a particular building which had non-Christian associations, or they may be idle doodles. A lead seal from Silchester is particularly interesting. It was found in the basilica, the seat of urban government, and it bears a chi-rho. It has been suggested that it came perhaps from a bishop's official document or package. On the other hand, bearing in mind the use by the imperial government of the chi-rho, it may be from a civil document (Boon, 1974, 183).

Christian burials

While a lack of grave-goods and an east-west orientation of the body is no guarantee of a Christian burial a large concentration of such graves does suggest that a Christian cemetery is likely. This is an important archaeological distinction – one of the definitions of a Christian burial is the lack of artefacts. The difference between a Roman pagan and a Christian was that the Christian hoped for a new and better life where worldly goods were quite unnecessary, while the pagan was interested in taking the best of whatever he had with him. However, beliefs were doubtless ambivalent as is evident elsewhere in the Empire – a tombstone at Maktara in Tunisia records the death of a woman called Fasiria. Above her name is the Greek Χ Ρ monogram, short for Χριστος, or Christ, but as an afterthought the pagan DMS, for *Dis Manibus* has been added.

The Christian grave-goods which appear in a few cases in Britain, discussed in the section on grave-goods above, show that this happened here too. However, the Poundbury cemetery at Dorchester, or the Bath Gate cemetery at Cirencester with 453 burials (McWhirr *et alii*, 1982), do show a transition in later burials to an east-west orientation, suggesting that Christianity was the reason, though a case has been made for arguing that better evidence lies in the so-called 'plaster-burials', the idea being that the body would be better preserved by embalming them in gypsum to greet the imminent Resurrection with an undecayed body (Green in Rees, 1977). A number of minor cemeteries with east-west oriented burials are known, for example Bradley Hill in Somerset (Leech, 1981).

Conclusion

The kind of problem presented by Christianity in Roman Britain can best be summed up by the evidence from Gloucestershire. This county contained two major towns; the *colonia* at Gloucester, and the civitas capital of the Dobunni at Cirencester. It also contained numerous minor settlements, both secular and religious, and some of the wealthiest villas known in Britain. Yet the only possible references to Christianity in the whole area consist of the three chi-rho symbols at Chedworth villa and the word-square at Cirencester. This is not untypical of Roman Britain as a whole, and a distribution map of the evidence from late Roman Britain indicates that while areas around London and Water Newton show a significant incidence of Christian material, there are whole regions, for example Wales, the south-west and Lancashire which have produced nothing at all (Thomas, 1981, 138, fig.16).

Perhaps a clue to this lack of evidence lies in the word *pagan* itself: it comes from the Latin word *pagani* which means the 'people of the countryside', indicating perhaps that Christianity met considerable resistance amongst the majority of the more traditionalist rural population. The fourth-century missionary St Martin of Tours seems to have waged a continuous battle against entrenched paganism in rural Gaul and there is no reason to assume that Roman Britain was any different.

9

Coinage in Roman Britain

Introduction

The Roman imperial coinage was an immensely important factor in the dispersal of artefacts throughout Britain, and indeed it is the most common of all Roman artefacts apart from pottery. Roman coins chart the reigns of the emperors and some of the major events of the period. As artefacts, they are also useful sources of data about metal-working techniques and artistic trends. They are also effectively unique in being the only commonplace site finds which date themselves, thus helping archaeologists to date their sites.

A number of catalogues of Roman coins now exist, making it relatively easy to research the subject (Mattingly, 1923 etc.; Mattingly and Sydenham etc., and Carson, 1962). There has also been much lively debate about the archaeological value of Roman coins. In recent years techniques have been developed which clarify the pattern of Roman coinage in Britain and ways of interpreting site finds (Casey, 1986; Reece, 1987).

The function of Celtic coinage

Coinage and a cash economy were at the heart of extensive trade in the Roman Empire. While the Celts in Britain knew and used their own coinage, its function seems to have been quite different. Roman coinage was used as currency for day-to-day transactions, but Celtic coinage was almost certainly no more than a way of storing and measuring wealth in bullion form.

Coinage was used in pre-Roman Celtic Britain from around the beginning of the first century BC (Mack, 1974; Nash, 1987). The bulk of Celtic coinage was gold and silver and it was not issued by all tribes. Distribution of coins, biased to the south and east, shows that coinage as a concept was largely derived from the Greek and Roman world. Copies of gold *staters* of Philip I of Macedonia (359–336 BC) are well-known in southern Britain.

Amongst the earliest Celtic coinage is the so-called 'Potin' coinage, made from an alloy of copper and tin. The coins circulated in south-east England, especially in the Thames Valley and Kent. As these coins were made of base metal there is some debate over whether they functioned as 'small change' in a cash economy (Allen, 1972 and Collis in Casey and Reece, 1974, 1ff.). Even if they did they are still unusual finds when compared to Roman base metal coins.

The most interesting Celtic coins are those known as the 'Dynastic' issues of the period between the invasions of Caesar and Claudius, because they bear information about the kings, or 'chiefs', in power and the names of their settlements. In most cases the coins are the only evidence we have for tribal areas and their wars of territorial conquest (though the value of this evidence is disputed). For example an issue of a king of the Atrebates called Eppillus (*c.* AD 5–10) bears on one side the abbreviation EPP, and on the other the words REX and CALLE (Mack, 1953, no. 108). The use of the word *Rex* is interesting because of the use of Latin to denote his status as 'King'. 'Calle' is short for the name 'Calleva' which survived into the Roman period as *Calleva Atrebatum* (Silchester). So the coin was struck by Eppillus, King of the Atrebates in Calleva.

Many of these later Celtic coins bear more evidence of romanisation than just a few Latin words. While Celtic motifs such as horses and boars appear on the coins, there was a trend towards semi-realistic portraiture and figures, for example on some coins of Cunobelinus (*c.* AD 10–40) of the Catuvellauni (fig. 119 a). While crude in style, inspiration had obviously been found in the portrait coins of Augustus and Tiberius, and some may even have been struck from dies engraved by continental craftsmen. But such trends are particularly concentrated in the south-east. In more remote regions such as East Anglia and the south-west, controlled by the Iceni (fig.119 b) and Durotriges respectively, coins bear Celtic designs of crescents, semi-circles, abstract horses and other beasts.

Celtic coinage was not systematically divided into denominations based on weights, though there seems to have been a tendency to make silver and gold coins in units with halves and quarters. They were almost certainly used by the Celtic aristocracy to purchase imported luxuries from the Roman world. They were also certainly used as votive gifts, because they are quite often found on sites which were subsequently used as Roman-British religious centres, for example Wanborough in Surrey which was probably the site of a Celtic shrine. A similar situation prevailed at a temple site on Hayling Island, near Portsmouth.

Roman coinage

Denominations and values

The denominations of modern coinage systems are set by governments with little relationship existing between the stated value and the actual value of the metal content. The peculiar sizes of British coins are a case in point: the 20 pence coin weighs a fraction of the 10 pence coin but is worth twice as much.

To some extent this was also true of Roman coinage, especially the brass, bronze and copper issues. However, these circulated in a theoretically fixed relationship with the silver and gold denominations on whom the credibility of the whole system depended. A silver coin, the *denarius*, was worth its value in silver (fig.119 i). If the silver coins were debased (i.e. the silver content was reduced in favour of a base metal) then problems arose. Typically people would hoard the older, good coin and prices would rise in an attempt to take in the same amount of silver as before. In an unsophisticated age the official solution was to strike more coin, but with a limited supply of silver that meant further debasement. This of course made things worse, but the process was a gradual one and it was only by the mid-third century that the consequences became serious.

It is worth briefly mentioning the plated *denarii*. Speculation on whether these were official attempts to save bullion, or outright forging, has come to no firm conclusion. However, the coins, distinguished by a worn silver coating revealing a base metal core, form a high proportion of 'silver' coin site finds – in fact up to a half (Burnett, 1987, 100). This suggests that they circulated widely as change and were therefore relatively easily lost. They were not normally hoarded and it seems that people were keen to part with them by spending them.

Despite these problems Roman coinage functioned as a largely satisfactory medium of payment and exchange. As far as Britain was concerned, the general population now had access to a universal medium of exchange. Unlike pre-Roman coinage in Britain some of the lower denomination coins were usually plentiful. The fact that such coins were essential for day-to-day transactions is proved by the episodes of local 'barbarous' issues when production of official base coinage was suspended. Such a universal currency meant that it became possible to

---

119 First- and second-century coinage – some examples (dates are for when the coin was struck) (photos: author). About actual size

a reverse of a bronze unit issued by Cunobelinus of the Trinovantes *c.* AD 10–40, showing a warrior and the legend TASCIIOVANTIS for his father (Mack 244)

b silver unit probably issued by the Iceni tribe between *c.* 10 BC to AD 60.

c silver denarius issued by Mark Antony to pay his troops *c.* 31 BC. This example shows the galley on the obverse, and legionary standards on the reverse, in this case for *legio* II. These poorer-quality coins remained in circulation for centuries and are common finds.

d & e obverse and reverse (from two coins) of barbarous *asses* of Claudius (AD 41–54). These coins were probably struck in Britain to supplement inadequate official coin right up to AD 64 when Nero resumed large-scale issues of brass and bronze coin

f *sestertius* of Claudius (AD 41–54)

g *sestertius* of Claudius (AD 41–54) countermarked NCAPR by Nero (AD 54–68) to permit it to stay in circulation despite being worn

h *sestertius* of Nero (AD 64–68)

i *denarius* of Vespasian (AD 73–79)

j *sestertius* of Titus (AD 80–81)

k *sestertius* of Domitian (AD 92–94)

l *sestertius* of Trajan (102)

m *aureus* of Hadrian (119–138)

n *sestertius* of Hadrian (early portrait, 119–128)

o *sestertius* of Hadrian (later portrait, 129–138)

p *sestertius* of Antoninus Pius (139–145)

q *sestertius* of Marcus Aurelius (175–180)

r *sestertius* of Commodus (184)

purchase imported manufactured items with cash earned from the sale of agricultural produce, or from any other produce or labour. More importantly it allowed the accumulation of wealth in a portable form. Over the first two centuries of the Roman occupation this began slowly to have an effect: houses become recognisably better built and equipped, and artefacts of Roman style became widely dispersed.

The first and second centuries

The main relationships between Roman monetary denominations are listed in Table VI but a number of general points are worth considering. Roman accounts, costs and sums were normally expressed in terms of the *sestertius* – thus the Foss Dike Mars (see Chapter 6 and fig.88 b) cost *sester[tios] n[ummos] c[entum]*, or 100 *sestertii*, to make. The silver *denarius* was the normal benchmark of value. Gold was rare, erratically minted, and even then it almost

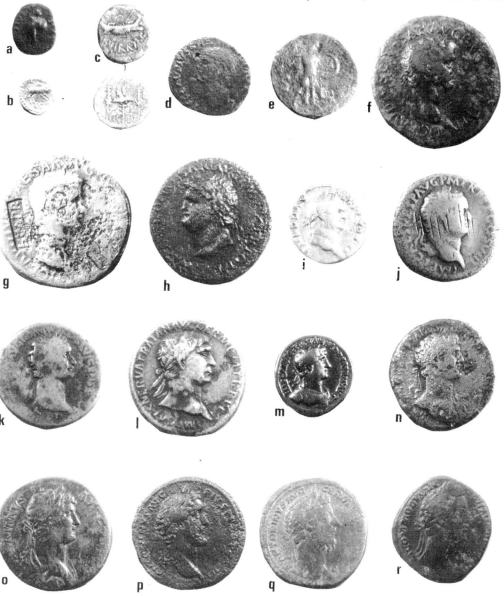

120 Third- and fourth-century coinage – some
examples (dates refer to when the coins were struck)
(photos: author). About actual size

a *denarius* of Septimius Severus (196)

b *antoninianus* of Gordian III (238–244), this coin is
said to be from the Dorchester South Street hoard

c *antoninianus* of Trajan Decius (249–251)

d *antoninianus* of Postumus, ruler of the 'Gallic
Empire' (259–268)

e 'double *sestertius*' of Postumus (259–268), very
probably overstruck on a first- or second-century
sestertius

f *antoninianus* of Probus (276–282)

g base *antoninianus* of Tetricus I (270–273).

h 'barbarous radiate' – a degenerate copy of **g**,
issued and discarded in huge quantities in Britain
c. 270–286

i base *antoninianus* of Carausius (286–293), overstruck on a 'barbarous radiate' – the radiate crown
of the earlier bust is visible across Carausius' neck

j *antoninianus* of Carausius (286–293), overstruck
on an *antoninianus* of Gallienus (253–268), the
reverse of which has survived the re-striking process

k base *antoninianus* of Carausius (286–293)

l base *antoninianus* of Carausius (286–293)

m *follis* of Maximianus (296–305), probably struck in
London

n *follis* of Constantine I (308–325), with SOLI·INVICTO·
COMITI, 'the unconquered companion Sun', and
mintmark PLN for London

o bronze coin of Constantine II, as Caesar, (330–337)

p silver *siliqua* of Constantius II (337–361)

q silver *siliqua* of Julian II (360–363), clipped down
during the succeeding decades as supplies of silver
coin dried up

r bronze *centenionalis* of Constantius II (337–361)

s bronze coin of Valens (364–378)

t bronze coin of Gratian (367–383)

u bronze 'minim' of uncertain late fourth-, early
fifth-century date

certainly circulated above face value as do modern gold coins (fig.119 m). In the first century the legionary was paid 225 *denarii* per annum before deductions for equipment and food, though in fact much of his cash in hand was probably paid in copper or brass coins. One might think of a *denarius* every three days as being sufficient to keep him in wine, women and song. However, it would be wrong to think of individuals going around with loose change consisting of all denominations. In practice base metal coins had to be changed into silver or gold via a money-changer who would naturally charge more than the notional value. Likewise he would buy back at below notional value.

The third century

In the early third century a coin identified as a double *denarius* was introduced which is known now as the *antoninianus* (fig.120 b-d). In fact it contained only about 40 per cent more silver and the purpose, if its identification is correct, was clearly to make imperial bullion go further. Some old *sestertii* were re-struck by Postumus (259–268) to make 'double sestertii' and, like the *antoninianus*, its most distinctive feature is the wearing of the radiate crown by the emperor portrayed (fig.120 e). The effect was to encourage the hoarding of older *denarii*, increase inflation and eventually to result in *antoninianii* which were no more than bronze with a silver wash (fig.120 f, g). This received a pragmatic response in Britain in the form of widespread counterfeiting (fig.120 h, and see below, p.199) and eventually the reformed coinage of the rebel emperor Carausius, though his issues only restored the standards of 15 years previously (fig.120 i-l). By the 280s the old base metal issues had become completely redundant; third-century versions are rare in Britain and demand was satisfied by the continued circulation of worn second-century coins.

The fourth century

In the fourth century the picture of Roman coinage is far more confused (Table VI). The only consistent feature was the new gold coin, called the *solidus*. Silver, when it was minted (not between 305–328 for example), was of good quality (fig.120 p, q). There were a number of silver denominations, but the most usual was one slightly smaller than the denarius, now called a *siliqua*, most of which post-date 356. The bronze coins were of denominations whose ancient names are unknown, and coins experienced episodic reforms by the government followed by inevitable debasement and reduction in size. They were often made of up to 3 per cent silver in order to enhance their appearance and to provide an illusion of value (fig.120 m-o, r-t).

It will be apparent that throughout the third and fourth century the universal medium of exchange was less consistent in its appearance and value. This may be related to the general deterioration in Empire-wide trade, though whether as cause or effect is a matter for discussion. Certainly as far as Britain was concerned there was a marked turn towards domestic production of manufactured goods in this period, particularly of fine pottery wares (see Chapter 3).

Coin-striking

The majority of early coins used in the Western Empire were struck in Rome, though in the first century a mint at Lyons was also responsible for issues up until about AD 82. In the third century Roman coins were also struck around the Empire close to the troops to whom they were paid; by the middle of the third century coin production was becoming officially dispersed, and the coins begin to bear mintmarks on the reverse. During the fourth century the system was fully established, London enjoying a brief spell as one of several centres (286–325). Fourth-century coins in Britain naturally originated mostly in the mints of the West, particularly Rome, Lyons, Arles and Trier (see Table IX for their mintmarks).

Coin blanks were prepared by hand from heated sheets of metal. The blank was then placed on top of the obverse die which was itself inserted into an anvil to take the shock. The reverse die was then placed on top of the blank and struck with a heavy hammer. The force required was so great that some of the larger base metal coins have concave reverses. Not surprisingly many first and second century *sestertii* were struck off-centre as a result – in fact very few were so well-struck that all the legend on both sides was both readable and even completely on the coin (fig.120 r). A die for the reverse of silver or gold coins of Hadrian was found in the north-east tower of the London gate at Verulamium. Made of tempered bronze, it depicts Hadrian greeted by Roma with the legend ADVENTUS AVG (Askew, 1980, 11). The general type is well-known but no coins struck from it have been identified. It is unlikely that the die is an official one because Hadrian's coinage was struck only in Rome (apart from Eastern city mints), and it almost certainly comes from a counterfeiter's equipment, nothing else of which survives.

Recognising Roman coins

The vast majority of Roman coins which have survived to modern times, and have been found, are in private collections. Even major hoards are sometimes sold off by museums for reasons of space and raising money (fig.120 b). It simply happens also to be a fact that the best place to gain familiarity with Roman coinage is through specialised commercial markets and dealers. Often these coins come from parts of the Empire where soils are relatively kind to metal; therefore they are easier to identify and learn from.

Due to the acidic nature of Britain's soils, such as the limestone of the Cotswolds and the chalk of the Downs, most base metal Roman coins, which are usually heavily worn anyway, have suffered badly. Weather and modern fertilisers add their toll. The result is that many site finds are difficult to recognise, though in practice an experienced eye can identify about three-quarters of the coins from a rural site, and from urban sites usually at least half (pers. comm. R. Reece).

Identifying the denomination is the first step. For the most part the small bronze coins, around the size of a modern penny, or smaller, belong to the third and fourth centuries. Those of the third century are almost always the base metal version of the silver antoninianus, and therefore bear the radiate crown (fig.120 b-d, f-l).

The large base metal coins mostly belong to the first and second centuries. In practice though whether they are of copper, bronze or brass is irrelevant because they will usually bear the same universal green patina unless they come from a waterlogged deposit. As these coins come from earlier in the Roman period they have a higher chance of having circulated longer, a chance increased through their greater weight and value; they are therefore very often extremely worn (fig.119 k, n).

Silver coins are all around the size of a modern penny. Their metal makes them obvious though this may be disfigured to a dull grey or black.

Plated silver coins give themselves away where the silver coating has decayed to reveal the patinated base metal core. Broadly speaking, silver coins in Britain belong mostly to the first, second and first half of the third centuries with the *denarius* giving way to the *antoninianus* in the 240s. Later silver denominations were erratically struck, and only in the fourth century were they struck again in quality metal. Even so they remained rare in Britain. Gold is always extremely rare and therefore not really worth discussing here as a site find. Only an occasional hoard will yield gold coins in quantity (plate 27).

Having established the metal and denomination the next stage with coins pre-dating 296 is to identify the ruler, or member of his family. In the first and second centuries the quality of die-engraving was sufficiently high to guarantee fairly consistent and distinctive portraits, as the illustrations on figures 119 and 121 demonstrate. In the third and fourth century the portraits began to decline in quality, partly as the art of engraving itself declined but also because the cult of the ruler's individual person was also waning. As a result it is extremely difficult to identify some of these later rulers accurately on the basis of portrait alone. Therefore the reverse types now become much more important for distinguishing various reigns. Amongst these 'anonymous' emperors the portraits of the British usurper Carausius are impressive efforts at realism. Tables VII and VIII list the main obverse legends of the emperors and the meaning of the titles.

In the next section, Roman coins are considered as historical evidence for Roman Britain. Much of the relevant information is found on the reverse legends and types. The range of variation is huge, even on the coins of some emperors with relatively short reigns. Despite this the reverse of most Roman coins bear one of a smaller number of standard reverse types. These usually refer to a deity, such as Jupiter, or a personification, such as Fortuna. Sometimes these subjects or legends were given a particular emphasis during one reign. The Emperor Domitian (AD 81-96) favoured the goddess Minerva – many of his coins bear her figure. The Emperor Trajan (AD 98–117) was declared the 'best of rulers' by the senate in 103 both for his military success and his benign rule. Many of his coins, regardless of the figures portrayed, carry a legend recording this, S·P·Q·R·OPTIMO·PRINCIPI.

It was also quite usual for some of the information concerning the emperor's various offices to be placed on the reverse. These are also accompanied by a figure, generally one favoured by the emperor. The figure, in some of these cases, is unnamed but recognisable from various attributes.

Until the chaos of the third century caused such a dispersal of coin-striking the issue of base metal coins was officially in the power of the Senate in Rome. This was indicated by a feature of the reverse which was always there: the letters s c. This is an abbreviation for SENATUS CONSULTO, and means that the coin was issued 'by decree of the Senate', though how much practical control was involved is uncertain. The impressive designs of the brass and bronze coins of Nero, for example, bear all the hall-marks of having been commissioned and controlled by Nero himself and sometimes do not bear the s c.

Dating a coin can be confused by the Roman practice of issuing coins dedicated to dead emperors who had been elevated to divine status. On such coins the dead emperor usually appears bareheaded (as on tombstones, see fig.8a) with a legend beginning DIVUS which means 'The divine . . .'. These coins are known as the posthumous issues but were not issued by all emperors. Amongst the latest of these was an extensive series struck by Trajan Decius (249–251) in memory of all his deified predecessors. Probably the most common are coins struck by Antoninus Pius (138–161) bearing the legend DIVA·FAVSTINA for his wife Faustina Senior who died in 141.

Roman coins as historical evidence

Propaganda?

Modern coinage is almost purely functional in the sense that it is a medium of exchange and little more. In an age without newspapers or any other reliable means of mass-communication Roman coins were a direct link between government and population. The image of the emperor was known to all through his coin portraits, and bore his name and titles. In some cases these portraits were of such astonishing quality that the art of Roman coin-die engraving was both admired and imitated in Renaissance Italy.

Circulating the emperor's image was probably the most important consideration in coin design. Some of the reverse designs supply considerable information about the regime's perception of itself. These include slogans which appear to promote spiritually desirable aspects of the ruling house, for example FORTVNA·AVG, the 'Fortune of Augustus' (which meant the incumbent emperor, whoever he was). More explicit are the references to provincial wars and great Roman victories. Being an unstable province, Britain features disproportionately frequently.

To what extent these coins functioned as propaganda tools is really unknown. Very few historical sources ever refer to them, and of course there is the problem of literacy. It has been suggested that the bulk of the population was illiterate and would therefore be quite immune to the information contained in coin legends; as Britain was remote the level of illiteracy may have been higher. The literate members of the population, the argument continues, would not be so simple-minded as to have their opinions formed by coin legends.

The first problem with this is the difference between intention and effect. Few people are prepared to admit that their opinions are formed by advertising and party political broadcasts; in fact the very idea is considered laughable. But the advertisements and party political broadcasts continue; presumably because their makers *believe* that they do have an effect. Whether they are right or not is irrelevant but their belief is significant. We cannot know if Roman coins were truly effective in transmitting information and opinions, but the evidence of the coins them-selves suggests that the imperial government was convinced that they did. The only alternative view is that a succession of emperors and mint officials engaged in a self-indulgent spree of artistic vanities.

A further problem is knowing what is meant by 'illiteracy'. Obviously there were few books, and therefore few people in Britain would have ever had the opportunity or inclination to read lengthy discourses. In our sense of the word they would have been 'functionally illiterate' – but day-to-day literacy is another subject altogether, and it is probably rash to assume that what we would consider illiteracy necessarily meant being completely oblivious to basic words and stock slogans.

Two good examples of coin issues in Britain support the idea that the government believed they were having an effect. The localised issue of 'Britannia' *asses* by Antoninus Pius in 154 (see below, and fig.121 c) seems to suggest very clearly that the government was making a point to the Romano-British about a recent Roman victory. The coins are rare elsewhere, but not uncommon in Britain. This suggests that they were specially distributed in Britain, and may even have been minted here. The revolt of Carausius in 286 was accompanied by immediate coin striking, even to the extent of over-striking his image on older coins (fig. 120 i, j), but more importantly the name is rarely spelt incorrectly. The extensive range of imaginative coin reverses issued by his mints, some of which were designed with obvious targets such as his legions and others on the continent, suggests that Carausius did not share modern academic reservations about the value of using coinage to communicate with ordinary people and soldiers.

Coinage referring to events in Britain

The province of Britain was a capricious place in which nearly two centuries of more or less continuous warfare were needed to sustain some sort of governable stability. For this reason Britain appears disproportionately frequently on the Roman imperial coinage, but with one exception these issues are rare everywhere. Some of this coinage is extremely important because in a number of cases it is only this secondary

121 'Britannia' coinage (photos: author)

a *as* of Hadrian (117-138) for the year 119-22 with a reverse showing the 'mourning Britannia'; this may indicate a recent Roman victory in Britain and indirectly refer to Hadrian's historically-testified visit to Britain in 122 (RIC 577a)

b *sestertius* of Antoninus Pius (138–161) for the year 143 with a reverse showing Britannia seated left with shield and spear. Other coins of the same year with the legend VICT BRIT suggest that again a Roman military success was behind the issue; it was around this time that the Antonine Wall was built (RIC 742)

c *as* of Antoninus Pius for the year 154 again bearing the 'mourning Britannia'. This coin is common in Britain, rare elsewhere; it may have been struck in Britain, or only issued in Britain – either way this indicates that some official point was being made (RIC 934)

d *sestertius* of Antoninus Pius for the year 143 with a victory and legend BRI TAN across the field

e *sestertius* of Commodus (180–192) for the year 184. Beneath the Victory is the legend VICT BRIT, again for a Roman victory in Britain (RIC 452)

f *sestertius* of Caracalla with reverse legend VICTORIAE BRITTANNICAE for the year 211–212; similar coins were issued for his father Septimius Severus, and his brother Geta

about actual size

evidence which has survived to record wars of which we would otherwise have no knowledge. Not all emperors issued coinage which referred to Britain. These are the main types (for those not illustrated here, see Askew, 1980).

Claudius, AD 41-54

Claudius issued a very rare series of *aurei* and *denarii* throughout his reign from the year AD 44 which record his victorious conquest in AD 43. The reverse design consists of a triumphal arch with a chariot and four on top coupled with the inscription DE·BRITANN. This is a direct reference to the actual triumphal arch erected in Rome in AD 44, from which a portion of the full inscription still survives.

The Greek city of Caesarea in Cappadocia issued a silver *didrachm* with the legend DE·BRITANNIS. A *didrachm* was a Greek silver denomination still commonly in use in the Eastern Empire.

It is interesting that no coins were struck by Nero to record the defeat of the Boudican Revolt in AD 60. Perhaps the event was too embarrassing though Nero seems to have exercised little or no personal control over coinage (or anything else) until AD 64. The same applies to the march north under the governorship of Agricola (AD 78–84). Agricola seems to have incurred the disfavour of the Emperor Domitian (AD 81–96), and this may be a reason for its omission from the coinage.

Hadrian, 117–138

Hadrian issued three basic types which refer to Britain. The first group includes the first known portrayal of the figure we also use as the personification of Britannia on our 50 pence piece. Those dating to the years 119–22, and struck on *asses*, bear a reverse legend PONT·MAX·TR·POT·COS·III around the figure of Britannia, beneath whom is the legend BRITANNIA (fig.121 a). This issue probably refers to Hadrian's visit to the province in that year, which was when he ordered the construction of the Wall. Similar types were issued later in the reign but bear a briefer legend of just BRITANNIA, and were struck on *asses*, *dupondii* and *sestertii*.

The visit to Britain was more directly alluded to in an issue of *sestertii* which refer to his visits to all the provinces of the Empire. They show Hadrian being greeted by Britannia who is sacrificing over an altar and bear the legend ADVENTVI·AVG·BRITANNIAE. A similar series recorded his visits to the provincial garrisons. The British version reads EXER (or EXERC)·BRITANNICVS. These later issues all date to around 134–138.

Antoninus Pius, 138–161

There seems to have been more active warfare in Britain under Pius and a large number of issues were struck referring to this. A major group, struck on *sestertii* and *asses*, belong to the years 143 to 144. They bear legends which either simply announce BRITANNIA (fig.121 b) or BRITAN, or they add IMPERATOR·II. The coins either bear a figure of Britannia or a winged victory. Britannia appears as a more confident figure now but the IMPERATOR·II and the victories (fig.121 d) are a clear indication that Antoninus Pius had taken a military acclamation for a victory in Britain that year. This may well indicate a war around the time of the building of the Antonine Wall.

The best-known coins with a figure of Britannia are examples of the huge series of 154 (fig.121 c). These are all *asses*, of poor style, bearing a mourning Britannia, accompanied by the legend BRITANNIA·COS·IIII. As Collingwood Bruce commented in his *Handbook on the Roman Wall*, 'To circulate this coin in Britain was to add insult to injury' (1885, 127). It has been suggested that this issue was struck in Britain, albeit officially, in order to make the point that another war had resulted in another defeat for Britain. This may have been so but either way the coins are far commoner in Britain than elsewhere, so it seems clear that they were struck for Britain's sake, in the interests of official propaganda. The shrine of Coventina (see Chapter 7) at Carrawburgh contained around 16,000 coins of all periods more than 300 of which were of this issue alone.

Commodus, 180–192

Commodus issued a number of *sestertii* which refer to a victory won in Britain by the year 184. We know from the historian Dio Cassius that this had involved tribes crossing a wall (but not which wall) and the apparent destruction of a legion (*Histories*, 72, 8). The coins bear reverse legends listing normal imperial titles for the years 184 and 185 but they also show a seated Victory inscribing a shield, beneath whom is the abbreviated legend VICT·BRIT (fig.121 e, and fig. 119 r). He also added the title BRIT to his obverse legend.

Septimius Severus, 193–211

Septimius Severus came to Britain in 208 to indulge in a punitive war of conquest in Scotland. He was accompanied by his sons Caracalla and Geta who succeeded him in 211. A large series of coins in all denominations were struck in the names of all three emperors in the years 210–12. They all bear reverse legends with variations on the theme VICTORIAE·BRITTANNICAE (fig.121 f), frequently abbreviated to VICT·BRIT coupled with an assortment of Victory figures. An extremely rare *as* of Caracalla dated to the year 208–9 may refer to the expedition's crossing of the rivers Tay and Forth. It shows on the reverse a bridge of boats being crossed by soldiers, and part of the legend includes the word TRAIECTVS, which means 'Crossing'.

Constantius Chlorus, 293–306

Constantius, as one of the two junior members of Diocletian's ruling tetrarchy, was sent to Britain in 296 to inflict final defeat on the usurper Allectus (see below). As part of the celebrations a gold medallion was struck at Trier shortly afterwards, probably as a commemorative award for senior military officers. It shows Constantius on horseback entering a city gate, labelled LON for Londinium, and greeted by a personification of the city. The main reverse legend reads REDDITOR·LVCIS·AETERNAE, which means 'restorer of the eternal light'. There is only one surviving specimen and it formed part of the treasure found near Arras in France in 1922.

The majority of the coins referred to are extremely rare, especially the Hadrianic issues. The coins were clearly designed to inform the population of the whole Empire about military events in Britain, and the success of the Roman armies. Defeats were omitted from the numismatic record. The rarity of the coins must have limited their propaganda effect but Roman policy on minting coins is quite unknown to us. These coins were mostly issued from the mint of Rome and form part of the Imperial series of coinage. The other coins which are of great interest to the study of Roman Britain are those which were apparently struck in Britain itself.

Coinage struck in Roman Britain

During the history of Roman Britain a certain amount of coinage was made in the island itself. Much of this seems to have belonged to a large class of semi-official, or at least officially tolerated, copies. There was also a certain amount of outright counterfeiting. However, between the years of 286 and 325 an official mint existed at London and briefly elsewhere.

Forging and copying

There is little specific evidence of forging in Britain beyond the coins themselves, but a reverse die of Hadrianic date is known from Verulamium (see above, p.193). Similarly the reverse die for a coin of the Empress Crispina, wife of Commodus, sole Emperor from 180–192, was found in South Humberside (Fox, 1983, 85). On the face of it the dies have every appearance of being official productions, but their appearance in Britain is only explicable if they were actually being used for the local striking of plated forgeries of the silver *denarius*.

During the reign of Claudius (AD 41–54), and the reign of Nero up to the year AD 64, bronze coinage was in very short supply. Why this was the case is a mystery. It may have been state policy to save money but then why did it resume striking coin in 64? In Britain this seems to have resulted in a large output of copies of official Claudian types right up to the mid-60s (fig.119 d, e). These copies range from the good to the exceptionally poor. Who was responsible is uncertain, but is very likely that they were turned out to pay soldiers with, perhaps by the army itself and possibly in Colchester (Reece, 1987, 16). The coins are certainly common but they fell out of use as soon as bronze coin was re-issued in quantity by the official mints at Rome and Lyons from AD 64 on (fig.119 h). In consequence the majority of Romano-British site finds of Claudian bronze coins fall into this class.

London has produced evidence not only for forging but also for the surreptitious disposal of mitigating evidence. A tower on the city wall contained clay moulds for casting forgeries of silver coins in silver-washed bronze of Septimius Severus (193–211) and his sons Caracalla and Geta, and also four very worn bronze and brass coins which the forger presumably intended to melt down (Marsden, 1980, 126). The small hoard has the advantage of indicating that the city wall must have been put up by *c.* 225.

In addition to these incidents there is evidence of large-scale official copying and forging in the later third century. At the time government coinage production had deteriorated to the extent that the nominal silver coin, a double denarius now called the *antoninianus*, was virtually a bronze coin containing little or no silver at all. Not only that but it was in poor supply, and the version mostly available in Britain was that struck by the rulers of the Gallic Empire who from about 259 to 273 ruled separately from the official emperors. It seems that reproductions of these coins were turned out in Britain to meet the shortfall, probably during the 270s and early 280s. They became increasingly degenerate and some of the later types seem clearly to be copies of copies.

These coins are known as 'barbarous radiates' and are found throughout Britain in huge quantities, probably because they were discarded when the coinage was reformed in the late third and early fourth century. The coins must have been produced widely in Roman Britain – a mould for the reverse of a coin of the Gallic Emperor, Tetricus I (270–273), was found at the basilica at Silchester (see Chapter 2 and fig.31 d; Fulford, 1985, 53), and shows that casting coin as well as striking was used. Extensive traces of a production centre at Whitchurch, Somerset, have been identified (Boon and Rahtz, 1965). The numbers of these coins are interesting because they demonstrate that the supply and loss of coinage was far from constant, and that therefore the numerical quantities of site finds are not valid evidence of increased or decreased occupational activity (Reece in Frere, 1984, *Verulamium* III, and see below).

Throughout the fourth century there seem to have been recurrent episodes of Romano-British coin-striking, whenever official supplies dried up. However, the whole period is a complex one, excellently summarised by John Casey (1980 and 1988), and it need only be said here that such coins are usually small and crude when compared to the coins from which they were copied (fig.120 u).

An interesting and related phenomenon was the practice of clipping down silver fourth-century coins, now known as *siliquae*. The lack of new silver coin at the beginning of the fifth century is thought to have been the cause (fig.120 q; and see Burnett, 1984).

Official coin-striking in Britain

Carausius and Allectus

The first instance of official coin striking in Britain was not regarded as such by central government. In 286 the commander of the British fleet in the Channel, Marcus Aurelius Mausaeus Carausius, usurped power in Britain. He struck an improved *antoninianus* though it was still silvered bronze (fig.40 g, fig.120 i-l), and restored a silver denomination of good quality but erratic weight based on the *denarius*. Carausius opened the first Roman mint at London and, probably, at Colchester. The mintmarks associated with these sources are listed on Table IX. The Colchester mint is by no means a certainty, only a likelihood. An alternative possibility is the small Roman maritime settlement at *Clausentum*, now Bitterne, near Southampton. Another recent suggestion (Reece, 1987) is that Gloucester may have been the second main mint, an interpretation offered on the basis that 'C' and 'G' are not distinct letter forms in Roman script. Carausius seems also to have struck coins on the continent. Distribution and style suggest that the mintmarks R and OPR refer to *Rotomagus*, modern Rouen. Many of the coins also bear sequence marks in the reverse field above the mintmark, usually two letters, for example:

$$\frac{\text{S} \quad / \quad \text{P}}{\text{MLXXI}}$$

Their precise meaning is uncertain but they probably indicate products of different departments of the mint, or different chronological issues. They may have been devised in order to discourage corruption, perhaps by making it possible to trace bad coin to the department of the mint responsible. The subject is elaborated upon by R.A.G. Carson (1959).

The range of reverse types on coins issued by Carausius show that he had not only established a competent minting system but was also using coin to help establish a positive image of himself and his regime (Askew, 1980). These include: GENIO·BRITANNI – 'the Genius of Britannia', and PAX·AVG – 'the peace of Augustus'. He commemorated the army, for example, LEG·II·AVG, and even included the Praetorian Guard in Rome, COHRT·PRAET, for good measure. Curiously the *legio* VI *Victrix* is omitted, suggesting that they had opposed his usurpation. Whatever the doubts modern authorities have about the propaganda use of Roman coins,

Carausius seems to have had none. His coins bear all the clichés appropriate to a Roman emperor. When he considered himself in alliance with the official Empire he indicated this on reverse legends with a triple G, for example COMES·AVGGG, one G for Diocletian, one G for Maximianus and one G for himself. One very rare type shows his bust alongside those of both these unwilling colleagues, with the legend CARAVSIVS·ET·FRATRES·SVI – 'Carausius and his brothers'.

Coinage in Carausius' name also includes a wide range with blundered reverse types suggesting that the strikers of the 'barbarous radiates' continued in business. If they did, their previous attempts are curiously at variance with their Carausian coins which usually bear recognisable portraits and accurately spelled obverse legends.

Carausius was murdered in 293 by his finance minister, Allectus, who, until he was killed by the army of Constantius Chlorus regaining power in Britain in 296, sustained the independent coinage. However, he abandoned Carausius' silver coin denomination but produced bronze coins with superior and more consistent flan sizes. He also introduced a small bronze coin, now referred to as a *quinarius*, but which in reality may have been an emergency *antoninianus*.

The coinage of both these reigns was rarely found until the advent of metal-detectors. It may well be that the coins were demonetised by Diocletian and were either recalled for melting, or were discarded. While few are in excellent condition very worn examples are much less usual than for almost all other Roman coins. The coinage of Carausius and Allectus is a complex subject and in many respects at an early stage of development because new types are turning up all the time. They reflect a particularly fascinating phase in Roman-British history, one for which they are the second most important source of evidence, if not *the* most important.

The Tetrarchy and Constantine I

The mints opened by Carausius were closed in 296 following the fall of Allectus, with the exception of London (fig.120 m). In the general reorganisation of the Empire under Diocletian the striking of coin became dispersed amongst the major cities of the Empire. Traditionally the eastern cities had struck their own local bronze coinage with legends in Greek, but now the coin

types became common to the whole Empire and are usually only certainly distinguished by their mint-marks. However, London coins, which were struck only in silver-washed bronze, rarely bear a mintmark (fig.120 m) until the reign of Constantine I, and their identification is based on stylistic considerations, compared to Carausian coins. Under Constantine I (306–337) mintmarks become normal once more though the London mint was permanently closed in 325. Coins with London mintmarks (Table IX) were struck in the names of Licinius I and II, Constantine I, his mother Helena, his wife Fausta, and his sons Crispus, Constantine II, and Constantius II.

Magnus Maximus

From 383 to 388 Maximus, a Spanish soldier with a senior post in Britain under the Emperor Gratian (367–383), ruled a breakaway empire consisting of Britain, Spain, Gaul and Africa. At the time London was known as *Augusta*, and it is thought that his gold coins bearing the mintmark AVG refer to London. However, this is uncertain and is likely to remain so.

Coins as archaeological evidence

There are a number of very good monographs published in recent years which discuss modern archaeological and numismatic thought about coins as site finds in detail. Unfortunately the trend towards specialisation in archaeology means that such books are left to preach to the converted and remain unread by those who regard Roman coinage as complicated, the preserve of others, and fatally branded by its association with the 'crime' of collecting. This is a pity because the subject is a fertile one. So it seems worth discussing some of these ideas here in the hope that a wider audience will become familiar with them.

It used to be assumed that single, or small groups of coins formed straightforward dating evidence. The problems involved with such an assumption have become clear as other artefacts, especially pottery, have been subjected to more analysis, demonstrating that individual coins could have very long lives. This affects the archaeological value of a single coin. In response modern attention has been focussed on the total number of coins from sites with a view to identifying patterns, and variations from these patterns.

Loss of low value coins

Coins are not usually thrown away or easily broken, and even a very worn coin has some monetary value, especially if made of silver or gold. Thus the year in which a coin was struck may be quite different from the year in which it was lost. The same applies today: a coin lost in 1988 is much more likely to bear a date from the 1970s with the 1960s and early 1980s close behind. Coins are only abandoned when they have become demonetised, or are of such low value that they are not worth picking up or looking for (coins deposited as religious votive gifts form a quite different group and are discussed above (p.164)). The consequences of these facts are that site finds of coins consist largely of worn low-value denominations; and that all the coins from a particular site are likely to represent a very small total monetary sum compared to that potentially in circulation.

A good example of the small proportion of circulating coin which ends up being lost and recovered from a site is at Corbridge. Here only 1,387 excavated coins have survived from 120 years of activity on the site (admittedly, only partially excavated). Casey (in Casey and Reece, 1974, 38) calculated that these coins add up to the value of 26 gold *aurei*. During that time the resident garrison would have been paid the equivalent of a total of about 2,000 *aurei* per year, 240,000 *aurei* over 120 years of which 26 *aurei* is a miserable 1/9000th.

Coin lists from sites are made up of coins which were lost at some unspecified date after they were struck. On the face of it, all we can do is guess from their condition whether it was a 'long' time after, or a 'short' time after. However, high value coins do not circulate quite so much as low value coins, and they may therefore have lasted a much longer time than their condition suggests. So, if a coin is found in a feature and it dates to the year AD 71, we can only really say that the feature was sealed after that year, the *terminus post quem*. Such a coin could well have been in circulation for well over a century, and all sorts of other evidence needs to be taken into account before reaching a conclusion.

This applies to all artefacts to some degree, and it is known as the *residual factor*. The residual coin may not only have been very old when it was finally sealed in a deposit; it may have been physically moved around during the digging of rubbish pits and foundation trenches. The difference with coins is that we know when they were struck, and therefore can sometimes actually demonstrate just how long they might have remained in circulation. Hoards (discussed more fully below) are a simple but biased way of showing this – a hoard of coins obviously cannot have been deposited before the date of the latest coin, but may contain coins over two centuries old; therefore any single coin may have been this old when it was lost. The silver denarii of the Roman republic which ended with the reign of Augustus are not uncommon finds in Britain. Clearly they were struck at least 70 years before the Claudian invasion, and unless they were imported before AD 43 must have been at least 70 years old when lost, depending on the site with which they are associated. Similarly a public market site, such as a forum or *macellum*, may indicate the range of coins in circulation in a particular period.

The coins from the 'palace' at Fishbourne clearly show the problem of the residual factor. The primary construction levels contain coins of Vespasian struck no later than the year AD 74. The Period 2-3 occupation levels included a coin of Hadrian (117–138) as their latest in date. It happens that the Period 2–3 occupation levels also include a worn Republican denarius which must pre-date the beginning of Augustus' reign in 26 BC. So here we have a situation in which some coins deposited in later levels actually pre-date the latest coins of earlier levels by a considerable period of time (Reece in Cunliffe, 1969, II, 93). In such a case these coins are obviously residual, if for no other reason than that they precede the Roman Conquest, but the same could apply to coins whose residual nature is less immediately clear. However, it is important to distinguish between disturbed rubbish and long life.

When we turn to low-value denominations the position is arguably easier to deal with. Lower-value coins are clearly more likely to take part in a large number of transactions than high-value coins. Therefore they become worn more quickly, and are also more likely to be lost earlier in their lives. An example is the countermarking of Claudian (AD 41–54) *sestertii* by Nero. Nero struck no copper or bronze coins from AD 54 until 64. The result was a shortage of base metal coin, and the production of copies of Claudian coins (discussed above, p.198; see fig.119 d, e). However, Nero's officials also recalled Claudian coins for examination to see if they were still up to standard; in other words it seems that Claudian sestertii were quite capable of being so worn after a maximum of 27 years that they might be withdrawn and melted down. The coins which passed, despite their wear, were countermarked NCAPR, which may stand for *Nero Caesar Augustus probavit*, or 'Nero Caesar Augustus approves' (fig.119 g). However, the picture is not quite so straightforward. The Gallic emperor Postumus (259–268) overstruck some single and double *sestertii* on old sestertii (fig.120 e); in some cases these can be identified, and include coins of Vespasian (AD 69–79) which despite being nearly 200 years old were still in circulation. It is this kind of evidence which has to be borne in mind when analysing the evidence of a single coin: a coin could have a very long life.

Nevertheless, it is still important to consider the evidence of a single coin. The construction of the second forum of Roman London is a good example. There is no literary or epigraphic evidence which supplies any information about about when this building was put up. However in the mortar of one of the piers of this building a coin of Hadrian in very good condition was found (Marsden, 1980, 103). Unfortunately the coin was lost during the Second World War, but it does seem reasonable to suggest that construction of the building was still taking place during Hadrian's reign and for several years after. This at the very least provides a pivotal point from which to work, and is better than no evidence at all.

The same considerations must necessarily apply to sites where very small numbers of coins occur, or sites with a short period of occupation. The legionary fortress at Inchtuthil is a case in point. The fortress appears to have been built during the governorship of Agricola (AD 78–84). Tacitus implies that shortly after Agricola's recall by Domitian the northern territories were given up (*Histories,* I, 2). The fact that the coin series at Inchtuthil ends with unworn coins of AD 86/7 surely suggests that the legionary fortress was abandoned then or very shortly afterwards. This is supported by the evidence for the complete dismantling of the fort (Pitts and St Joseph, 1985).

Rate of coin-loss and the coin supply

Coin production and supply was not continuous in the Roman world. The curious lack of copper and bronze coinage under Nero from AD 54 to 64 is a case in point. Studies of Domitian's coinage (AD 81–96) have shown that there was considerable fluctuation in the rate of striking silver *denarii*, with the lowest output in AD 84 and a peak in AD 92 (Burnett, 1987, 92). These fluctuations continued throughout the period. The simple result of such variations is that the average Roman handful of small change would be made up in favour of coins from years when supply was good. It follows then that a group of excavated coins would be similarly biased in favour of the years of good supply.

122 Histogram for coin-loss at Silchester, *Calleva Atrebatum,* Hampshire. It is apparent that coins struck at certain periods were more readily lost than those of other periods; this suggests that supply of coinage was correspondingly variable because a similar pattern is found across Roman Britain (after Casey)

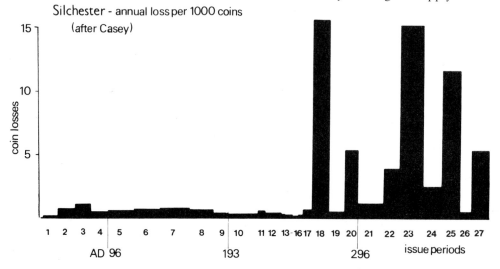

Silchester - annual loss per 1000 coins (after Casey)

From an archaeological point of view this effect runs throughout the list of coins from any site, whether the coins are excavated from sealed levels or recovered as loose surface finds. So it seems quite clear that it would be a mistake to assume that a relatively large number of coins from a particular period had a special implication for the activity on that site. We need to know how Roman coin supply to Britain fluctuated before we can start to make any assumptions.

The best way to do this is to divide up the years of Roman-British history into short periods of approximately equal length and find out how coins from each of these periods are represented in the total from a long-term site such as a town. When these figures are compared with other long-term sites in Britain, we can begin to identify the pattern of coin-supply. There are two variables: the length of the individual periods, and the site totals. A simple formula (Casey, 1980, 28) removes these, and its product is the average number of coins lost in each year of the period in question out of 1,000 coins from the site in question:

$$\frac{\text{coins per period}}{\text{length of period}} \times \frac{1000}{\text{total for site}}$$

This method and its interpretation owe much to the work of Casey and Reece, and a number of their publications are listed in the bibliography. Figure 122 shows the products of these calculations from the Silchester coin list displayed as a histogram – this is fairly typical of Romano–British town sites. There are problems; for example shorter period sites will have much higher percentages for the times when the site was occupied (though this will not affect the difference between periods); the method assumes that whatever the rate of supply it applied equally across Britain; totals below 200 are unlikely to produce accurate results. Even so, this provides a much more accurate starting point than an emotive response to different numbers of coins.

What do the figures mean? In very basic terms the Silchester list suggests that, for example, coin-supply was three times better for period 18 (260–73) than period 20 (286–96). This might suggest a greater degree of 'activity' in period 18 were it not for the fact that this same pattern is repeated elsewhere. There are other considerations: period 18 coins were generally of poor quality and low intrinsic value, therefore they would be more readily discarded; there

seem to have been far fewer coins around in periods following those with high figures – therefore coins from the earlier, high figure period would have had to serve longer, and therefore would have had more opportunity to be lost. This reminds us again: the date of a coin does not date its loss. Having established the pattern throughout the Romano-British period, we can begin to look for variations which are quite substantial before suggesting that something unusual, such as a substantial increase in the population, may have occurred.

Interpretation of coin-loss

The average patterns of coin loss which have been drawn up for Roman Britain using this method are no more than a careful use of excavated data. The method does not supply, of itself, actual information about what the coinage was being used for. A higher, or lower, incidence than the average for any period is equally devoid of such information. All such data does is to provide an indication of periods where occupation may have been of a different degree on comparable sites, taking into account the fact that all sites will vary about the mean for any period. And of course it should be remembered that the date of a coin does not date its loss.

This isolates one of the peculiar features of coinage when contrasted with other artefacts. A brooch has an obvious function, and so does most pottery. Both categories indicate the presence of human beings living and going about their business. Other artefacts may indicate what that business was, such as a quernstone. Collectively they indicate occupation, and its nature. Coinage is far less specific. It was a medium for the activities of occupation, it facilitated exchange; but all these other things would have gone on to some degree without coinage.

The presence of a Roman coin says absolutely nothing about why it was there other than that the person who lost it was familiar with Roman currency, or at least its value. Even the absence of coinage of particular periods is no guarantee that therefore occupation had ceased, especially when other evidence is taken into account, such as pottery. The fort of Housesteads is a case in point. Here no coins are known after 378, yet this is in contrast to evidence, albeit minimal (see Vindolanda below), from other sites in the north. It may simply reflect the fact that soldiers were now paid more or less exclusively in kind, instead of cash; this was called the *annona militaris* and was introduced in the fourth century as a means of transferring the obligation to pay soldiers from the government directly to the local population.

The *vicus* at Vindolanda has produced very small amounts of coinage after the late third century. Were this typical of the general area, it would probably be appropriate to assume that coin-supply to the north had deteriorated. However, the fort at Vindolanda has produced a more normal coin-list for the late third and fourth century, which suggests that virtual abandonment of the *vicus* is more likely. Here it is the *contrast*, rather than the absolute numbers, between fort and *vicus* that provides the basis for interpretation (Casey, in Bidwell, 1985, 103ff.)

So to the archaeologist Roman coinage is a class of artefact of deceptive convenience. A host of problems accompany its interpretation, and only in recent years has the subject begun to acquire real credibility. Central to this has been the development of methods by which one site can be compared with a background derived from a large number of other sites. Nevertheless it would be wrong to turn away from Roman coinage and condemn it as an unreliable witness of the world to which it belonged. It remains the only common artefact from Roman Britain which dates itself, and it cannot be ignored.

Hoards

Coin-hoards are one of the most interesting aspects of societies which use coinage. They are a particular phenomenon which supplies both historical and archaeological evidence but needs careful interpretation. The Roman Empire had no system of banking equivalent to ours. The concepts of storing cash in a bank and using credit belong to the Islamic and mediaeval worlds, and even then it has only become commonplace in the last few decades. The only possibilities for storing wealth in the ancient world were to turn cash into assets such as land, or to hoard it. The practice has been carried on from antiquity right up to modern times.

Archaeological value of hoards

Coin hoards of Roman date are well-known throughout Britain (fig.120 b). They seem generally to represent accumulations of coinage, the savings of a lifetime or several lifetimes, and were stored in some sort of suitable container. These were almost always pottery jars or vases,

though metal and glass containers are known. They were buried where they were unlikely to be found, probably near a landmark. Very few have been found actually within the confines of a known Romano-British site.

It is important to remember that a great deal of the silver and gold coinage in Roman Britain will have spent much of its time in hoards, but that most of the hoards were recovered when the cash was needed, dispersed and perhaps the individual coins were re-hoarded elsewhere. The hoards which have come to light just happen to be those which were not recovered, presumably because the hoarder was dead or was prevented from doing so. Herein lies the bias: all surviving hoards are failed hoards and we will never have an idea of actually how widespread hoarding was. On the other hand one might assume that, geographical location apart, the hoarders of Roman Britain were all equally likely to die or be killed, or even forget where they put the hoard.

Coin hoards provide dating information in two forms, but it is important to realise that their value in this respect is no better than that of a single coin. Obviously a hoard cannot have been deposited before the date of the latest coin. A hoard is given its *terminus post quem* for the latest possible date for the youngest coin in the group. This is known as the terminal date, after which the hoard was buried. But unlike a single coin a hoard was worth much more to the owner; unless the contents became worthless they were not voluntarily abandoned. It is unlikely that a hoard would have remained untouched by an owner for very long; either he would have added to it, or he would have removed it. Unless the terminal coin is worn it is probably reasonable to assume that an abandoned hoard was buried within a few years of the date of the terminal coin.

This has a certain amount of value for dating the container of the hoard. The Water Newton hoard (see below and plate 27), with a terminal date of 350, was contained in a so-called 'Romano-Saxon' bowl. This hybrid ware, made in Roman form but with 'Saxon' decoration, is difficult to date but in this case cannot have been deposited before 350, the *terminus post quem*. However, the composition of this hoard is of coins of similar date between 330 and 350. Such a fact alone makes it unlikely that the hoard was buried much after 350, perhaps only a handful of years at most. The coins are unworn and had the hoard been put together much after 350 then amongst such a closely dated group one might expect at least a single representative of the 350s. Therefore it is a reasonable assumption that the Romano-Saxon bowl must have been *made* by 350-55. The hoard has therefore provided a time before which, the *terminus ante quem*, for the objects associated with it, which also happen to include a Nene Valley pottery lid and a bronze bowl (Johns and Carson in Painter, 1977).

Hoards as historical evidence

Interpreting groups of hoards as evidence of episodic upheavals in Romano-British history is an attractive pastime. It is as well to remember though that from an archaeological standpoint there is absolutely no way in which a hoard deposited by someone subsequently killed in a Saxon raid can be distinguished from one deposited by someone who forgot where he buried it. Either are perfectly respectable possibilities, and it is an academic vanity to assume that a hoard, *per se*, is evidence of a great event. Only when trends, geographical or in terminal date, are identified can a serious case be made.

There are two examples which show different ways of interpreting such hoards. Around 70 hoards are known to end with coins of Marcus Aurelius (161–180), his wife Faustina Junior (161–175), or his designated successor Lucius Verus who predeceased Aurelius in 169. Their distribution is heavily biased to the north, and the total is higher than for preceding periods (Robertson in Casey and Reece, 1974, 31). This may possibly represent a major regional upheaval with weighty consequences for some. There is a certain amount of evidence to support this. Firstly, the author of the *Scriptores Historiae Augustae* records that war was threatening to break out in Britain during Marcus Aurelius' reign (*Scriptores Historiae Augustae*, 8, 7); and, secondly, there are the British victory coin issues of Commodus (see above p. 197) struck in 184–5. Such an incidence of hoards is at variance with coin loss for the period (see fig. 122), and makes it unlikely that the coins had somehow become not worth recovering. Even so there is no reason to suppose that the hoards are specifically related to events in geographical terms. Studies of hoards belonging to the period of the English Civil War (1641–49) show no geographical correlation between the findspots of hoards and the war's battles and sieges (Casey, 1986, 61).

In contrast there are in excess of 100 hoards from Britain which end with the 'barbarous radiates' of the Tetrici (270–73). Their distribution is general apart from a slightly higher concentration in East Anglia. The phenomenon spreads across western Europe. On one hand these could be interpreted as belonging to people involved in the general upheavals of the period and, in Britain, the rebellion of Carausius and the subsequent reconquest of the province in 296. On the other hand they may simply represent coins which had become worthless once the coinage had become reformed in the fourth century and were not worth recovering. A high loss for coins of this period is normal (see fig. 122) for the same reason, so the occurrence of a large number of unrecovered contemporary hoards may be related purely to this. Britain seems to have experienced little of the continental military activity and destruction that was taking place.

A hoard of 1,925 *denarii* from Falkirk in Scotland deposited in or after 235 is thought possibly to represent cash payments paid to Caledonian tribes in return for keeping the peace. Falkirk is near the Antonine Wall which by this date had been disused for up to 80 years. However, the hoard contains a peculiarity in its bias to earlier coins compared with contemporary hoards, which had led to the suggestion that the hoard was actually put together under Septimius Severus (193–211) and topped up later (Reece, 1987, 49ff.). This would make it less likely to be payments to tribes.

Not surprisingly we have no literary or epigraphic evidence which sheds light on the circumstances surrounding any single Romano-British hoard. Although it has been described elsewhere (Casey, 1986, 53ff), Samuel Pepys' attempt to hoard his savings in 1667 following a Dutch attack on the English fleet on the Medway, may be of interest here. Firstly Pepys sent the money with his wife and father to the family home in Huntingdonshire, that is, some way from the impending threat. Secondly the money fell off the coach and had to be recovered. Thirdly his wife and deaf father forgot where they had buried the cash. Fourthly the bags rotted in the ground dispersing the coin. Only with an iron probe was the money finally recovered with £20 abandoned. These farcical events show how ridiculous it can be to attempt to try and generalise on the reasons for hoards and the failure to recover them. Had Pepys not recovered the hoard an archaeologist would have been quite wrong to assume that a threat in Huntingdonshire was the reason for the hoard; moreover the remaining money was left for no more dramatic reason than that it could not be found.

Composition of hoards

The majority of Romano-British coin hoards consist of silver coins, or the least debased available equivalent. Hoards made up entirely of gold coins, such as those from Bredgar and Water Newton, are exceptionally rare (plate 27). Some predominantly silver hoards contain a few gold coins but its high value tended to guarantee gold a long circulation; as a result these coins are almost invariably considerably older than the majority of the silver members of the hoard. Hoards of base metal coins are not usual except in the earliest years of the Conquest and in the third and fourth centuries. This was for the same reason: during both periods silver was erratically struck, and hard to obtain in Britain.

It seems that hoards almost always contain coin of higher quality than that in circulation at the time it was buried. This shows that the Romano-British were not insensible to the government's episodic debasement of coinage, and were highly selective about the coins they chose to retain. Indeed, many hoards seem to belong to periods when debasement was taking place. The result is that hoards of the third century sometimes include Republican silver coins struck a century before the Conquest of Britain. In fact some lower quality coins, previously shunned by hoarders, were now hoarded because they were better than the new coin available at the time. Typically these include the poorer-quality silver denarii struck by Mark Antony around 31 BC to pay his troops before the battle of Actium (fig.119 c). During the early third century when the current silver issues were being debased these previously 'poor' coins became relatively 'good' coins, and therefore worth hoarding.

Sometimes, if a hoard is recovered intact and not damaged, for example by a plough, it can be possible to show how hoards were built up over a number of years – simply by dissecting the layers of coins starting with the most recent at the top. If the hoarder was being especially selective in a time of debasement the hoard may actually belong to a period somewhat later than that suggested by the date of the last coin. Others were probably made up on the spur of the moment in the face of some immediate threat, though it would be unwise, as discussed above, to attribute such instances to the nearest known military disaster.

In at least one case from Thorngrafton (Hadrian's Wall) the hoard seems to have been made up by a collector who had carefully selected coins to make sure that every one was different and that it filled an arm-purse perfectly (Collingwood Bruce, 1853, 416; for an arm-purse see fig.76a). Other savings characteristics seem to include favouring well-struck and preserved specimens. There is also a limited amount of evidence for the use of pottery vessels as 'money-boxes' in the form of a flagon-shaped pot from Lincoln with a saw-cut coin slot (White, 1981). Presumably the owner would have eventually shattered the pot to retrieve his savings (which in this case were bronze coins of the House of Constantine).

Hoards can range in size very considerably. One from the fort at Piercebridge in County Durham consisted of 128 mid-third century coins while another, from South Street, Dorchester in Dorset, was made up of 20,758 silver coins dating to between 193 and 260 (fig.120 b). However, examples of much smaller and much larger numbers are also known.

Not all groups of coins recovered from the ground necessarily constitute 'hoards' in the sense of deliberate burial. A bronze arm-purse was found in a context at the fort of Birdoswald on Hadrian's Wall which suggests that it was lost while the fort was being built in the 120s. The purse contained 28 silver *denarii*, at a time when a legionary was paid 300 a year before deductions. One might also consider coins as votive gifts (see Chapter 6).

Coins re-used in post-Roman times

One of the problems involved in dealing with Roman coins is the length of time they might have remained in use before being lost. Sometimes they were re-used long after they had ceased to have any monetary value (though of course gold and silver coins were liable to be melted down). The Anglo-Saxon peoples were particularly fond of using pierced *sestertii* as parts of jewellery, or as components of horse bridle-gear: such coins then found their way into their new owners' graves. Sometimes the use was more practical: grave 26 in the sixth- to seventh-century cemetery at Sarre in Kent contained a set of scales and weights, most of the weights being Roman coins including a *sestertius* of Commodus, and a *dupondius* of Nero.

Conclusion

In the preceding pages a very large quantity of material from Roman Britain has been covered. It will have become clear that while a great deal is known about some subjects, for example coinage, others such as religion remain a fertile source of speculation with really very little precise detail to work from.

This unsatisfactory state of affairs is bound to endure, though occasional advances may be made. This is in the nature of things and, more specifically, it is in the nature of archaeology and ancient history. The archaeologists and historians of Roman Britain have only what has chanced to survive. Even then these things have to be found, identified, recorded and published before they can be interpreted. The careful excavations at Verulamium must be contrasted with the chance discovery of the Thetford treasure by metal-detector shortly before its site was covered forever by concrete. Both are of immense value, and while the circumstances of the latter's recovery may be regretted the fact is that it would not have been found otherwise.

It is essential for the archaeologist and historian to interpret the material. A group of artefacts has no value in itself but once the components can be fitted into a framework of history and society they take on more meaning. Naturally the interpretation says as much about the interpreter as it does about the period he/she seeks to understand. The author of the *Handbook to the Roman Wall*, John Collingwood Bruce, wrote in 1885 of the Romans 'They brought all the nations of the then known world into unity, and spread the blessings of order and civilisation to the very ends of the earth'. The source of his perception of the Roman world is evident in his next statement: 'The people of England are in this respect, the successors of the Romans. Through their instrumentality vast continents . . . have obtained the advantage of a well organised government; their rude inhabitants have been induced to engage in the pursuits of peaceful industry'.

In our own age it has become more common to look at the way in which a conquering culture not only oppresses the conquered but becomes altered itself in doing so. Moreover we consume manufactured goods at a pace almost unparalleled since the Roman period. This book attempts to provide a foundation for understanding how this kind of interpretation of Romano-British society can be developed from a study of the artefacts made and used during the period. However, the character of Romano-British life is difficult to define, largely because it endured for at least four centuries. The bustling new ports and towns of the late first century, into which the manufactured products of Gaul, Italy, Germany and Spain were shipped, contrast with the great fourth-century villas of the south-west with their polychrome mosaics depicting mystery cults, and dinner services made of silver, pewter, glass and Romano-British fine wares.

But throughout the period in Britain a very particular kind of Roman life developed. Its material existence was heavily derived from the classical Roman world of the Mediterranean, whether in pottery forms or imported commodities like olive oil and fish sauce from Spain. Even the whole concept of representing gods in human form was imported. The Roman soldier, ubiquitous in Roman Britain, symbolised the sheer force with which Rome imposed herself. Throughout the book we have seen how much of what the Romano-British took for granted in their daily life was essentially Roman. The Roman world had grown not just out of military power but also out of the trading mechanisms of production and transportation. Roman Britain was brought immediately into this sphere. The injection of cash through loans and soldiers' pay supplied the Romano-British with the means to share in the Roman consumer world.

The result was the colossal amount of goods which seemed to have been shipped into Britain, particularly in the later first century; subsequently these were more or less replaced by goods made in Britain. The archaeological record is a striking contrast to that of preceding and succeeding periods: surface finds include prodigious quantities of pottery and building debris scattered with occasional coins and brooches. Excavation reveals far more.

For all this day-to-day experience of Roman living the spirit of life in Britain was deeply seated in the pre-Roman world of the British Celts. This modified the true Romanness into something unique to Britain, though there were many similarities with Gaul which shared Britain's Celtic origins. This can be seen most clearly amongst the gods of the province, for example the hunter gods, or the shadowy *genii cucullati* whose enigmatic faces peep out from beneath their robes. Their human form is Roman but they represent stronger forces and spirits which were known long before. So many Romano-British religious sites were built on places which had been sacred for centuries that there can be little doubt about the power of the Celtic gods.

This spiritual flavour of Roman Britain combined with Celtic perceptions of art and creativity. This generated remarkable works of art like the Aesica brooch and contributed to the decoration of Romano-British pottery and other products through new craft and industrial techniques brought in by Rome. It also produced sculpture which can be both naïve and attractive – the *genius* from Carlisle is a particularly good example. The Venus relief from High Rochester is an example of a less successful attempt to create a piece of classical realism in the mists and rain of frontier territory; it is no less a fusion of cultural traditions.

It is this fact of remoteness which is central to Roman Britain and it was responsible in many different ways for contributing to its very idiosyncratic variety of Roman life. It was on the edge of the known world at the beginning of the period and it remained so – the classical world remained within its Mediterranean confines. Paradoxically this fringe existence, while helping to create a kind of carpet-baggers' paradise in the first century, allowed lowland Britain to quietly develop while the rest of the Western Empire deteriorated and collapsed in on itself from the third century on. As this happened so the character of Roman Britain and Romano-British life matured in its distinctive way.

Part of this distinctive flavour was the impermanence of Roman ways, symbolised by the manner in which Celtic styles endured throughout. This is the paradox of Roman Britain: the visible remains of the Roman period, whether buildings or objects, are plentiful, yet there is a conspicuous gap from the fifth century onwards. Only in the eighth century did Anglo-Saxon society begin to manifest itself in a way which can still be seen. The Victorians and others can be forgiven for perceiving this as a 'dark age'. We know little of the sub-Roman period precisely because so much that was Roman in Roman Britain evaporated during the fifth century leaving little physical trace. It is often argued that an essentially Roman way of life did endure in the 400s and 500s; but this can never be more than an hypothesis – the sheer lack or rarity of artefacts, coins and reliable written records point to a decline in what we take for granted as features of the Roman world. The individuals may have continued to speak Latin and use Latin titles in their hierarchies but coinage had gone, manufactured goods like pottery were confined to rare instances of imports and building in stone seems to have been more or less forgotten – indeed the remains of Roman buildings were regarded with a mixture of admiration and awe. Even the new Christianity seems to have made little impact – we have barely an instance of a single church foundation of Roman date, let alone one which endured. The villa estates seem to have remained as agricultural units but the old houses were left to decay. Pottery forms of Roman type disappeared and in some places pottery fell out of use altogether.

So in historical terms the finds of Roman Britain provide a remarkable amount of evidence for a period of conspicuous consumption. The products of the Roman world are found throughout Britain – fragments of Gaulish samian can be plucked from mole-hills in Northumberland just as easily as from a ditch in Kent. Coins of the mint of Rome are equally widespread. By recognising these and all the other traces of Rome in Britain we can begin to understand something of how Roman and Celtic Britain merged to create a culture which was both rich but curiously terminal. But there is more to it than that: these finds were owned, made or bought, thrown away or buried by the Romano-British. Through their possessions and offerings we come as close to the men, women and children of Britannia as we ever can.

Appendix: Museums

In recent years many museums of all kinds in Britain have modernised the presentation of their material into exciting and stimulating displays. They are usually divided up according to context and function, in the same way as this book. This makes it much easier to understand what artefacts were used for, and the kind of person who may have used them. Museums which specialise in Romano-British material, or which have strong collections, are no exception. This appendix lists the museums which hold some of the most important Romano-British collections in Britain together with addresses and telephone numbers. However, it is not exhaustive and many interesting examples of artefacts can be found in small local museums, especially those attached to excavated villas such as Chedworth (Gloucestershire), Lullingstone (Kent), and Rockbourne (Hampshire). Would-be visitors are advised to check opening times beforehand as some are closed on one day during the week. During the winter season these opening times may be even more severely curtailed.

Bath
Roman Baths Museum, Pump Room, Stall Street, Bath, Avon – (0225) 61111.

The visitor begins his tour by descending into the remains of the huge bath and temple complex which is now largely underground. There is a particularly evocative display of inscriptions (religious and military), carved stonework and the rich collection of material recovered from the sacred spring.

Bridport
Bridport Museum, South Street, Bridport, Dorset – (03082) 22116.

Contains a fine collection of early military finds from the fort at Waddon Hill.

Caerleon
Legionary Museum, High Street, Caerleon, Gwent, Wales – (0633) 423134.

Contains material associated with the *legio* II *Augusta*, stationed here for much of the Roman period.

Cambridge
University Museum of Anthropology and Archaeology, Downing Street, Cambridge – (0223) 359714.

A large collection of Roman artefacts from sites across the county.

Canterbury
Royal Museum and Art Gallery, High Street, Canterbury, Kent – (0227) 52747.

Material from the cantonal capital *Durovernum Cantiacorum*.

Cardiff
National Museum of Wales, Cardiff – (0222) 397951.

Roman material, mostly of military origin, from across Wales.

Carlisle
Tullie House Museum, Castle Street, Carlisle, Cumbria – (0228) 34781.

As with Newcastle (see below), this museum contains important sculptures and carvings from Hadrian's Wall (western sector).

Chester
Grosvenor Museum, Grosvenor Street, Chester – (0244) 316944.

Contains material recovered from the legionary fortress of *legio* XX *Valeria Victrix*.

Chesters
Chesters Roman Fort, Chesters, Corbridge, Northumberland – (043) 471 2349.

An old-fashioned display means that a vast amount of material is packed into the two rooms of the museum. This includes many altars, including those from Coventina's Well, and the Carvoran dry-measure.

Chichester (and Fishbourne)
Chichester District Museum, 29 Little London, Chichester – (0243) 784683.

Material from the cantonal capital *Noviomagus Regnorum* and Sussex. Just to the west of Chichester on the old A27 is *Fishbourne Roman Palace and Museum*, Salthill Road, Fishbourne – (0243) 785589 – an attractive display of finds from, and part of the remains of, the palace.

Cirencester
Corinium Museum, Park Street, Cirencester, Gloucestershire GL7 2BX – (0285) 5611.

An excellent series of displays of the rich Roman material recovered from the site of Roman Britain's second city, *Corinium Dobunnorum*. Many of the objects form part of reconstructed rooms.

Colchester

Colchester and Essex Museum, The Castle, Colchester, Essex – (0206) 712222.

A more traditional display housed in the Norman Castle Keep includes some of the most important Romano-British finds. These include the pottery from the Boudican fire of AD 60, the pottery from the Colchester samian kilns and the Gosbecks Mercury. There are also a number of burial groups.

Corbridge

Corbridge Roman Station, Corbridge, Northumberland – (043) 471 2349.

A modern museum with a large display of the huge amount of Roman military and civil material excavated from the adjacent site.

Coventry

Lunt Roman Fort, Coventry Road, Baginton, Warwickshire – (0203) 303567.

Fort reconstruction and displays of finds and models (mainly military).

Devizes

Devizes Museum, 41 Long Street, Devizes, Wiltshire – (0380) 77369.

A large collection of Roman and Celtic material from Wiltshire, and see Salisbury below.

Dorchester

Dorset County Museum, High West Street, Dorchester, Dorset – (0305) 62735.

Material from Dorset, the town of *Durnovaria*, and the hill-fort at Maiden Castle destroyed by *legio* II *Augusta* in AD 43.

Edinburgh

National Museum of Antiquities, Queen Street, Edinburgh, Scotland – (031) 5511202.

Contains the important military material recovered from the fort at Newstead and the Antonine Wall.

Exeter

Royal Albert Memorial Museum, Queen Street, Exeter – (0392) 56724.

Material from the legionary fortress and later cantonal capital *Isca Dumniorum*.

Glasgow

Hunterian Museum, The University – (041) 339 8855 ext. 5431.

Military equipment and artefacts from the Antonine Wall.

Gloucester

Gloucester City Museum and Art Gallery, Brunswick Road, Gloucester – (0452) 24131.

The Roman material forms only part of the museum, but includes some important sculptures including the Lower Slaughter group, and military equipment.

Ipswich

Ipswich Museum, High Street, Ipswich, Suffolk – (0473) 213761.

Roman material from across Suffolk.

Leicester

The Jewry Wall Museum, St Nicholas Street, Leicester – (0533) 554100.

Finds from the cantonal capital *Ratae Coritanorum*.

Lincoln

Lincoln City and County Museum, Broadgate, Lincoln – (0522) 30401.

Material from the legionary fortress and later *Colonia Lindum*.

London

The British Museum, Great Russell Street, London WC1B 3DG – (01) 636 1555.

Although the Romano-British display forms only a relatively small part of this museum, it not surprisingly includes some of the major finds from the province including the Hadrian bust, the Water Newton Christian silver and coin hoard, the magnificent Thetford treasure, the Lullingstone busts and the Corbridge lanx.

Museum of London, London Wall, London EC2Y 5HN – (01) 600 3699.

An outstanding display in evocatively (but slightly frustratingly) gloomy light of some of the huge quantities of Roman objects recovered from the province's capital. The collection includes the marbles from the Temple of Mithras, and reconstructed rooms are used to display household material.

Malton

Malton Museum, Market Place, Malton, North Yorkshire – (0653) 5136.

A small collection of local finds.

Manchester

Manchester Museum, The University – (061) 273 3333 ext. 3101.

Material from Roman forts in Lancashire.

Newcastle

The University Museum of Antiquities, The Quadrangle, The University, Newcastle-upon-Tyne – (091) 2328511.

Contains a wealth of military material from the frontier zone including an exceptionally important group of inscriptions, the Aesica brooch and armour fittings.

Newport

Museum and Art Gallery, John Frost Square, Newport, Gwent, Wales – (0633) 740064.

Material from excavations at the cantonal capital of Caerwent, *Venta Silurum*.

Norwich

Castle Museum, The Castle, Norwich – (0603) 611277.

Mostly material from *Venta Icenorum*, the Roman town near Norwich, but also includes a fair quantity of military material, and religious objects from across Norfolk.

Nottingham Museum

University Museum, The University, Nottingham – (0602) 502101.

Material from the excavations at *Margidunum* and Brixstowe.

Oxford

Ashmolean Museum of Art and Archaeology, Beaumont Street, Oxford – (0865) 278000.

The collection includes objects from all over Britain, particularly pottery. For local material see *Oxfordshire County Museum*, Fletchers House, Woodstock, Oxfordshire – (0993) 811456.

Peterborough

Peterborough Museum and Art Gallery, Priestgate, Peterborough, Cambridgeshire – (0733) 43329.

Contains an important group of pottery recovered from in and around Water Newton, *Durobrivae*, the source of Nene Valley wares.

Richborough

Richborough Castle near Sandwich, Kent – (0304) 612013.

The site museum contains selected material from the excavations (other material is stored at Dover Castle).

St Albans

Verulamium Museum, St Michael's, St Albans, Hertfordshire – (0727) 54659.

The many years of excavation of *Verulamium* have produced a very large amount of material. The display of pottery at this museum is particularly valuable.

Salisbury

Salisbury and South Wiltshire Museum, The King's House, 65 The Close, Salisbury, Wiltshire – (0722) 332151.

More material from Wiltshire (see Devizes above).

Shrewsbury

Rowley House Museum, Barker Street, Shrewsbury, Shropshire – (0743) 61196.

Material from the excavations of the fort and cantonal capital at Wroxeter, *Viroconium*, and see Wroxeter below.

Silchester

Museum and Art Gallery (Silchester), Blagrave Street, Reading RG1 1QH – (0734) 55911.

A very large amount of material is displayed from the huge town site of *Calleva Atrebatum* (Silchester), mostly recovered from turn-of-the-century excavations.

South Shields

South Shields Museum and Art Gallery, Ocean Road, South Shields, Tyne and Wear – (091) 4568740.

Poorly signposted, but the museum is sited by the remains of the fort of *Arbeia* with its fine reconstructed gate-house. The collection includes the tombstones of Regina and Victor.

Taunton

Somerset County Museum, Taunton Castle, Castle Green, Taunton, Somerset – (0823) 55504.

Material from Somerset.

Vindolanda

Vindolanda Site and Museum, Chesterholm, Bardon Mill, Northumberland – (04984) 277.

An imaginative museum with a large number of the exceptionally well-preserved items on display in various reconstructions and cabinets orientated around particular themes. Much of the nearby site is open to view.

Warwick

Warwickshire County Museum, Market Place, Warwick – (0926) 493341 ext. 2500.

Material from the county.

Wroxeter

Viroconium Museum, Wroxeter Roman Site, Wroxeter, Shrewsbury, Shropshire – (074375) 330.

The site museum for *Viroconium*, and see Shrewsbury above.

York

Yorkshire Museum, Museum Gardens, York – (0904) 29745.

York, *Eboracum*, was the premier settlement of northern Britain and the museum reflects this in its rich displays of inscriptions, statues, religious, military and civil objects from the *colonia*.

Tables

I Table of Events

This table lists by date some of the principal historical and archaeological events associated with the history of Roman Britain. It is not exhaustive and is intended as a quick source of reference for use in conjunction with the rest of this book.

Date	Event
55/54 BC	Invasions of Julius Caesar.
5-10 AD	Catuvellaunian expansion begins under Cunobelinus.
42–3	Verica of the Atrebates tribe loses his kingdom to Catuvellauni and flees to Claudius.
43	Claudian invasion led by Aulus Plautius with four legions (II *Augusta*, IX *Hispana*, XIV *Gemina*, XX) and an unspecified number of auxiliaries.
47	Fosse Way 'frontier' established, with Lowland Zone province behind it.
49	Colchester established as a *colonia*. Ostorius Scapula, governor, invades southern Wales against the Deceangli.
51	Scapula continues Welsh campaign against the Ordovices and Silures.
58	Suetonius Paulinus, governor, continues Welsh campaign against the Silures.
60/61	Suetonius Paulinus invades Anglesey, Druid stronghold; meanwhile Boudican Revolt results in destruction of Colchester, London and Verulamium; revolt quelled by Paulinus; subsequent re-garrisoning of Lowlands.
71–2	Petilius Cerealis, governor, defeats Venutius, king of the Brigantes at Stanwick.

Date	Event
78–84	Governorship of Gnaeus Julius Agricola: conquest of province pursued up to north-east Scotland; dedication of Verulamium forum (79), and possibly first forum at London.
87+	Withdrawal from Agricolan conquests begins. The legionary fortress of Inchtuthil abandoned.
98–117	Establishment of Stanegate frontier under Trajan.
117	Indications of war in Britain (*Scriptores Historiae Augustae*, Hadrian, 5.2)
122	Hadrian (117–138) visits Britain; building of Hadrian's Wall begins; 'Britannia' coins issued; building of second forum at London continuing; Wroxeter forum dedicated.
143	Antonine Wall begun; 'Britannia' coins issued.
154	'Mourning Britannia' coins of Antoninus Pius issued, indicating a Roman victory.
160+	Antonine Wall given up; withdrawal to Hadrian's Wall.
184	'VICT·BRIT' coins of Commodus issued.
196/7	Clodius Albinus, governor of Britain, participates in civil war, competing for the throne. Septimius Severus, the victor, subsequently splits the province into Britannia Superior and Britannia Inferior.
209–212	Septimius Severus' campaigns in northern Britain, accompanied by his sons Caracalla and Geta. The martyrdom of Alban at Verulamium may have occurred during this period.
259–273	Britain forms part of the 'Gallic Empire' ruled by Postumus, Victorinus and Tetricus.

Date	Event
260–300	Main construction period of the Saxon Shore Forts.
286	Carausius, commander of the fleet, separates Britain from the Empire and opens the London mint.
289	Carausius negotiates peace with Diocletian and adopts the title 'Caesar'.
293	Allectus murders Carausius and seizes power.
296	Constantius Chlorus invades Britain, kills Allectus, and recovers Britain for the Empire.
306	Constantine I declared Emperor at York.
313	By this date Britain is further sub-divided into four provinces.
314	British bishops attend the Council at Arles.
326	London mint closed.
343	Constans visits Britain.
350–3	Magnentius seizes power in the Western Empire, including Britain.
367	Major invasion of Britain by a co-ordinated force of Picts, Scots and Attacotti.
369	Restoration of province by Count Theodosius well underway. A fifth province, 'Valentia', formed.
383–8	Magnus Maximus seizes power in Britain, Gaul and Spain.
396–8	Campaigns of Stilicho (Vandal general who controlled the Emperor Honorius) against Scots, Picts and Saxons.
401+	Stilicho removes Romano-British troops for a war in Gaul.
407	Additional withdrawal of troops by Constantine III further depletes the garrison.
410	Honorius instructs Britain to take care of its own defence.

II Fine Wares in Roman Britain

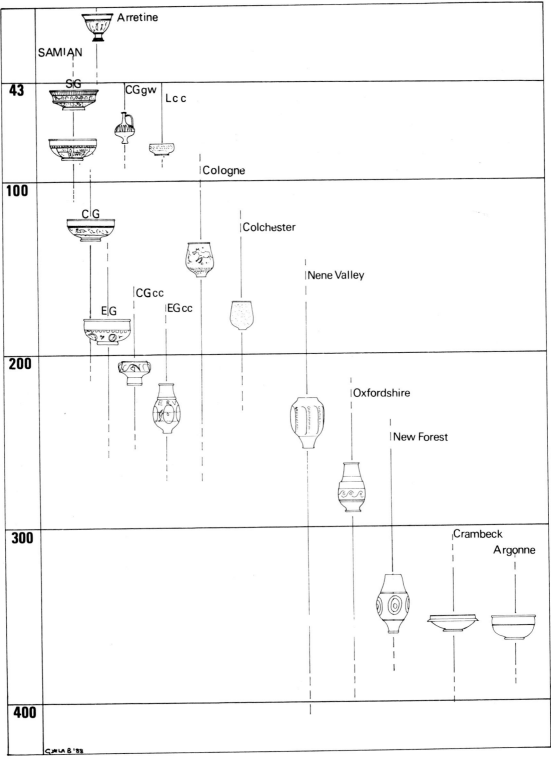

Abbreviations: SG, CG & EG = South, Central & East Gaul; L = Lyons; CC = colour-coat

III Decorated Samian potters

South Gaul

Mould-decorated samian was manufactured by large numbers of potters in South, Central and East Gaul. Some of these potters placed their names in the moulds, or stamped the finished bowls. However, it has proved difficult to associate the names of South Gaulish potters with decorative styles, because the individual motifs seem to have been widely shared. It is therefore easier to begin with bowl forms (fig.51): the South Gaulish Form 29 bowl was in use in Britain from *c.* 43–85, and the Form 37 bowl from *c.* 70–110.

Central Gaul

The Central Gaulish potters tended to restrict themselves to 'house-styles'. Even those who did not 'sign' their products can be recognised from their distinctive styles, such as the so-called 'Potter of the Rosette', and others granted 'X' numbers. Even so it is important to remember that this is the style of the *mould*, bowls from which could have been made by someone else. The essential work for these bowls is Stanfield and Simpson, *Central Gaulish Potters*, (1958). Some of the main workshops are listed below.

Trajanic potters (Les Martres-de-Veyre)

X–1	100–120
X–2	100–120
DRUSUS I (X–3)	100–125
IGOCATUS	100–125
'ROSETTE'	100–125
X–9/X–10	100–130
X–11/X–12	100–125
X–13/X–14	100–130

Hadrianic potters (Lezoux)

LIBERTUS	120–140
BUTRIO	120–140
ACAUNISSA	125–145
GEMINUS III	125–145
X–5	125–145
QUINTILIANUS GROUP	125–150
SACER-ATTIANUS	125–150
AUSTRUS	125–150

Hadrianic/early-Antonine potters (Lezoux)

X–6	130–150
CONDOLLUS	130–160
DOCILIS	130–160
LAXTUCISSA	130–160
CRICIRO	130–160
SISSVS II	135–165
CETTUS (Small 'S')	135–165

Antonine potters (Lezoux)

DIVIXTUS	145–170
PUGNUS	145–175
CINNAMUS GROUP	145–180
ADVOCISUS	150–180
ALBUCIUS	150–180
CENSORINUS	150–180
PATERNUS II GROUP	160–190
IULLINUS	160–190
CASURIUS	165–200
BANUUS	165–200
DOECCUS I	165–200

East Gaul

East Gaulish products can also often be associated with names. Unfortunately they rarely constitute more than a very small percentage of any samian assemblage in Britain. Dating mostly to the later second century and third century, they post-date much of the historically-testified activity on Britain's northern frontier. This has made it very difficult to assign periods of activity to different workshops with confidence. The most up-to-date publication of East Gaulish material in Britain can be found in Bird, J. in Dyson, T., (ed.), 1986, *The Roman Quay at St. Magnus House, London* (The New Fresh Wharf), 139 ff.

IV Mortaria potters

This table lists a number of the Romano-British mortaria potters who placed stamped impressions of their names on their products. The details are based on the work of Katharine Hartley and her specialist reports which have appeared in several major site publications. Where a potter is thought to have worked at another centre, this is indicated. Some potters used additional stamps known as 'counter-stamps', usually forming the word FECIT, 'made [this bowl]'. Dates are approximate only, and only those potters for which dates could be traced are included. A number of examples of stamps are illustrated on fig.57, indicated here *; many used more than one die-stamp though only one is illustrated.

Name	Date	Other centres
Brockley Hill (BH)/Verulamium Region (VR)		
1 ALBINUS*		
/LVGD·F/F·LVGVDV	60–90	
2 ARENTUS*	110–145	
3 ATTICATUS*	55–95	
4 AUDURDIC*	60–90	
5 BRUCCIUS	80–110	
6 CANDIDUS*	90–125	
7 CILLUS*	95–135	
8 DEVALUS*	80–100	
9 DOCCAS	85–110	
10 DOCCIUS	80–110	
11 DOINUS*	70–110	
12 DRICCIUS*	100–145	R
13 GISSUS	100–140	
14 JUNIUS (I)*	100–140	
15 LALLAIUS or		
LALLANS*	90–130	
16 L.FECIT	70–100	
17 MARINUS*	70–110	
18 G·ATTIUS·MARINUS*	95–105	R/C/H–M
19 MARTINUS*	70–110	
20 MATUGENUS*	80–125	H–M
21 MELUS*	95–135	
22 MERTUCUS	100–130	R
23 MORICAMULUS*	70–100	
24 NIDUS*	100–120	
25 OASTRIUS*/LVGD·F	65–95	
26 RIPANUS*/LVGD·F	65–95	
27 ROA*	110–150	

Name	Date	Other centres
28 SATURNINUS* (I)	100–130	
29 SECUNDUS*	65–95	
30 SOLLUS*	60–100	
31 T·M·H*	110–145	C
32 VIDEX	85–140	
Radlett, Hertfordshire (R)		
18 G·ATTIUS·MARINUS*	100–110	BH/C/H–M
33 CASTUS*	110–140	
12 DRICCIUS*	100–145	BH
22 MERTUCUS	100–130	BH
Hartshill-Mancetter (H–M)		
18 G·ATTIUS·MARINUS*	110–130	BH/C/R
34 BRUSCIUS*	140–170	
35 CARITA	160–190	
36 JUNIUS (II)	160–190	
37 MAR	160–190	
20 MATUGENUS*	100–125	BH
38 MAURUS	160–190	
39 MOSSIUS*	135–175	
40 SARRIUS*	135–174	Rossington Bridge
41 SENNIUS	160–190	
Colchester (C)		
18 G·ATTIUS·MARINUS*	90–100	R/H–M
42 BUCUS*	55–85	K
43 CRICIRO	70–100	
44 CUNOPECTUS*	160–200	
45 DUBITATUS*	150–200	
46 SEXTUS VALERIUS		
C...*	60–90	K
31 T·M·H*	110–145	VR
47 TITUS	150–200	
Kent (K)		
42 BUCUS*	55–85	C
48 CACUMATUS	65–100	
49 CAVARIUS	70–100	
50 GRACILIS	70–100	
51 C·IUL·PRI....*	70–100	
52 JUVENALIS	90–130	
53 LITUGENUS*	70–100	
54 MOTTIUS	70–100	
55 ORBISSA	55–95	Gallia Belgica
46 SEXTUS·VALERIUS·		
C...*	60–90	C
56 SUMMACHUS*	55–95	
57 VALENTINUS	110–160	

Name	Date	Other centres

Others

61	DOBALLUS*	Northampton	140–180
62	SATURNINUS II	Corbridge	160–200
63	VEDIACUS*	Nene Valley	140–180
64	CRICO	South Carlton	160–200
65	VOROCAS*	South Carlton	160+

V Brooch types in Roman Britain

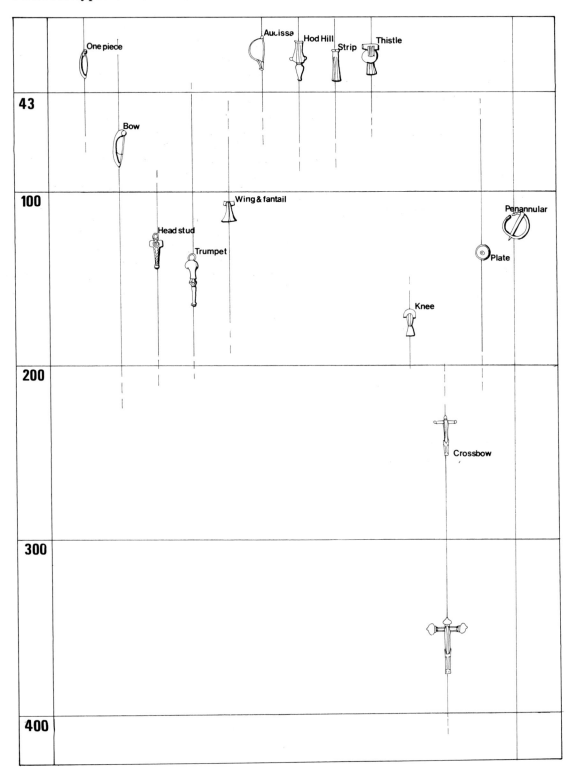

VI Coin denominations

Main units I (first to third century)

1 AUREUS (gold) (1/45 lb) = 25 *denarii (laureate crown)* (ceased regular issue 244)

1 DENARIUS (silver) (1/90 lb) = 4 *sestertii (laureate crown)* (ceased regular issue 268)

1 SESTERTIUS (brass) = 2 *dupondii (radiate crown)* (ceased regular issue 268)

1 DUPONDIUS (brass) = 2 *asses* (copper) *(laureate crown)* (ceased regular issue 268)

Occasional units

From time to time sub-units of the *as* were issued: the brass SEMIS (½ *as*), and the copper QUADRANS (¼ *as*) but they are unusual as site finds. The same applies to the gold ½ *aureus*, and silver ½ *denarius*, both called a QUINARIUS.

New units

In 215 the silver double *denarius* was issued, bearing a radiate crown, now called the ANTONINIANUS. It was withdrawn in 222 but restored in 238 and then became the staple currency unit, despite losing its silver content rapidly. In 249 the brass double *sestertius* was issued, bearing a radiate crown, and was last struck by Postumus by 268.

Main units II (fourth century)

The various reforms of Diocletian and Constantine are not fully understood, and even the names of the denominations are uncertain. Diocletian's reforms retained the AUREUS (reduced to 1/60lb) but a new silver coin was struck called the ARGENTEUS, of similar bullion value to the old *denarius*. Small change was made up of a number of base metal units of uncertain relationship, now called the FOLLIS and RADIATE. Under Constantine the gold AUREUS ceased regular issue with the introduction in 312 of the SOLIDUS at 1/72lb, and the ½ solidus SEMIS. Two main silver units were introduced: the MILIARENSE at 1/72lb, 18 to the SOLIDUS; and the SILIQUA at 1/96lb, 24 to the SOLIDUS. The base metal units which form such a huge quantity of site finds on Romano-British sites remain a mystery. They are described as bronze units (AE for 'aes' = bronze) with a number to indicate their size, for example AE 1 25mm +, AE2 25–21mm, AE3 21–17mm, AE4 16mm and below.

VII Coin legends

It would be impossible to list here all coin legends which are found on Roman coins. Instead a representative legend is listed for each emperor containing as many titles as are normally associated with the reign. In the case of long reigns one from the early and later part of the reign is listed. Offices held more than once were usually numbered – these numbers are indicated here as **, unless the emperor limited his tenure. For example Hadrian held his third and last consulship in 119 – his coins therefore almost all bear cos·III until his death in 138. The meanings of the various abbreviated details are discussed in Table VIII.

The Julio-Claudians

Augustus	(27 BC–AD 14)	CAESAR·AVGVSTVS·DIVI·F·PATER·PATRIAE
Tiberius	(14–37)	TI·CAESAR·DIVI·AVG·F·AVGVSTVS
Caligula	(37–41)	C·CAESAR·DIVI·AVG·PRON·AVG·PM·TR·P·**·PP
Claudius	(41–54)	TI·CLAVD·CAESAR·AVG·GERM·TR·P·**·IMP·**
Nero	(54–68)	IMP·NERO·CAESAR·AVG·PONT·MAX·TR·POT·PP
Galba	(68–69)	SER·SVLPI·GALBA·IMP·CAESAR·AVG·PM·TR·P
Otho	(69)	IMP·M·OTHO·CAESAR·AVG·TR·P
Vitellius	(69)	A·VITELLIVS·GERM·IMP·AVG·TR·P

The Flavians

Vespasian	(69–79)	IMP·CAES·VESPASIAN·AVG·PM·TR·P·PP·COS·***
Titus	(69–79)	T·CAES·VESPASIAN·IMP·P·TR·P·COS·** (as Caesar)
	(79–81)	IMP·T·CAES·VESP·AVG·PM·TR·P·PP·COS·***
Domitian	(69–81)	CAESAR·AVG·F·DOMITIANVS·COS·** (as Caesar)
	(81–96)	IMP·CAES·DOMIT·AVG·GERM·COS·**·CENS·PER·PP

Trajanic-Hadrianic

Nerva	(96–98)	IMP·NERVA·CAES·AVG·PM·TR·P·COS·**·PP
Trajan	(98–117)	IMP·CAES·NERVA·TRAIAN·AVG·GERM·PM (early)
		IMP·CAES·NER·TRAIANO·OPTIMO·AVG·GER·DAC· PARTHICO·PM·TR·P·COS·VI·PP (late)
Hadrian	(117–138)	IMP·CAESAR·TRAIANVS·HADRIANVS·AVG (early)
		HADRIANVS·AVG·COS·III·PP (after 129; if no PP, then 119–128)

Antonine

Antoninus Pius	(138–161)	ANTONINVS·AVG·PIVS·PP·TR·PP·COS·**
Marcus Aurelius	(139–161)	AVRELIVS·CAESAR·AVG·PII·FIL (as Caesar)
	(161–180)	M·AVREL·ANTONINVS·AVG·ARM·PARTH·MAX
Lucius Verus	(161–169)	L·VERVS·ARM·PARTH·MAX (as Caesar)
Commodus	(177–192)	IMP·L·AVREL·COMMODVS·AVG·GERM·SARM
Pertinax	(193)	IMP·CAES·P·HELV·PERTINAX·AVG
Didius Julianus	(193)	IMP·CAES·M·DID·SEVER·IVLIAN·AVG
Niger	(193–4)	IMP·CAES·C·PESC·NIGER·IVS·AVG·COS·II
Clodius Albinus	(193–5)	D·CLOD·SEPT·ALBIN·CAES (as Caesar)
	(195–7)	IMP·CAES·D·CLO·SEP·ALB·AVG

Severan

Sept. Severus	(193–211)	IMP·CAE·L·SEP·SEV·PERT·AVG
		SEVERVS·PIVS·AVG·BRIT
Caracalla	(198–217)	M·AVREL·ANTONINVS·PIVS·AVG·BRIT
Geta	(209–212)	P·SEPTIMIVS·GETA·PIVS·AVG·BRIT
Macrinus	(217–218)	IMP·C·M·OPEL·SEV·MACRINVS·AVG
Elagabalus	(218–222)	IMP·CAES·M·AVR·ANTONINVS·AVG
Sev. Alexander	(222–235)	IMP·C·M·AVR·SEV·ALEXAND·AVG

Soldier-emperors I

Maximinus I	(235–238)	IMP·MAXIMINVS·PIVS·AVG
Gordian III	(238–244)	IMP·GORDIANVS·PIVS·FEL·AVG
Philip I	(244–249)	IMP·C·M·IVL·PHILIPPVS·PF·AVG·PM
Trajan Decius	(249–251)	IMP·C·M·Q·TRAIANVS·DECIVS·AVG
Treb. Gallus	(251–253)	IMP·CAE·C·VIB·TREB·GALLVS·AVG
Volusian	(251–253)	IMP·CAE·C·VIB·VOLUSIANO·AVG
Valerian I	(253–260)	IMP·C·P·LIC·VALERIANVS·PF·AVG
Gallienus	(253–268)	IMP·C·P·LIC·GALLIENVS·PF·AVG

Gallic Empire

Postumus	(259–268)	IMP·C·POSTVMUS·PF·AVG
Victorinus	(268–270)	IMP·C·VICTORINVS·PF·AVG
Tetricus I	(270–273	IMP·C·TETRICVS·PF·AVG
Tetricus II	(270–273)	C·PIV·ESV·TETRICVS·CAES (as Caesar)

Soldier–emperors II

Claudius II	(268–270)	IMP·C·CLAVDIVS·AVG
Aurelian	(270–275)	IMP·C·AVRELIANVS·AVG
Tacitus	(275–276)	IMP·C·M·CL·TACITVS·AVG
Probus	(276–282)	IMP·C·M·AVR·PROBVS·PF·AVG

Carus	(282–283)	IMP·C·M·AVR·CARVS·PF·AVG
Numerian	(283–284)	IMP·C·NUMERIANVS·PF·AVG
Carinus	(283–285)	IMP·C·M·CARINVS·AVG

The 'British Empire'

Carausius	(286–293)	IMP·C·CARAVSIVS·PF·AVG
Allectus	(293–296)	IMP·C·ALLECTVS·PF·AVG

The Dominate (including the Tetrarchy, 293–305)

Diocletian	(284–305)	IMP·C·C·VAL·DIOCLETIANVS·AVG
Maximianus	(286–305)	IMP·C·MAXIMIANVS·PF·AVG
Constantius	(293–305)	CONSTANTIVS·NOB·CAES (as Caesar)
Galerius	(293–305)	MAXIMIANVS·NOB·CAES (as Caesar)

The Second Tetrarchy (305–306)

Constantius	(305–306)	IMP·C·CONSTANTIVS·PF·AVG
Galerius	(305–311)	IMP·C·GAL·VAL·MAXIMIANVS·PF·AVG
Severus II	(305–306)	FL·VAL·SEVERVS·NOB·CAES (as Caesar)
	(306–307)	IMP·C·SEVERVS·PF·AVG (as Aug)
Maximinus II	(305–306)	GAL·VAL·MAXIMINVS·NOB·CAE (as Caesar)
	(309–313)	IMP·C·GALER·VAL·MAXIMINVS·PF·AVG (as Aug)
Constantine I	(306–307)	CONSTANTINVS·NOB·C (as Caesar)
Maxentius	(306–312)	IMP·C·MAXENTIVS·PF·AVG
Licinius I	(308–324)	IMP·LIC·LICINIVS·PF·AVG

House of Constantine

Constantine I	(307–337)	IMP·CONSTANTINVS·PF·AVG
Crispus	(317–326)	CRISPVS·NOB·CAES
Constantine II	(317–337)	CONSTANTINVS·NOB·C (as Caesar)
	(337–340)	CONSTANTINVS·IVN·AVG
Constans	(333–337)	FL·IVL·CONSTANS·NOB·CAES (as Caesar)
	(337–350)	FL·IVL·CONSTANS·PF·AVG
Constantius II	(324–337)	FL·IVL·CONSTANTIVS·NOB·C (as Caesar)
	(337–361)	D·N·CONSTANTIVS·PF·AVG
Cons. Gallus	(351–354)	D·N·FL·CL·CONSTANTIVS·NOB·CAES (as Caesar)
Julian II	(335–360)	D·N·IVLIANVS·NOB·CAES (as Caesar)
	(360–363	D·N·FL·CL·IVLIANVS·PF·AVG
Magnentius	(350–353)	D·N·MAGNENTIVS·PF·AVG
Decentius	(351–353)	D·N·DECENTIVS·NOB·CAES (as Caesar)
Jovian	(363–364)	D·N·IOVIANVS·PF·AVG

House of Valentinian

Valentinian I	(364–375)	D·N·VALENTINIANVS·PF·AVG
Valens	(364–378)	D·N·VALENS·PF·AVG
Gratian	(367–383)	D·N·GRATIANVS·PF·AVG
Valentinian II	(375–392)	D·N·VALENTINIANVS·IVN·PF·AVG

House of Theodosius

Theodosius I	(379–395)	D·N·THEODOSIVS·PF·AVG
Arcadius	(383–408)	D·N·ARCADIVS·PF·AVG
Honorius	(393–423)	D·N·HONORIVS·PF·AVG

Revolt of Magnus Maximus

Magnus Maximus	(383–388)	D·N·MAG·MAXIMVS·PF·AVG
Flavius Victor	(387–388)	D·N·FL·VICTOR·PF·AVG

VIII Obverse titles

The legends on Roman coins followed a standardised formula of abbreviations. The main element was the emperor's name, and sometimes the name of his father, natural or adoptive. Around the name cluster a sequence of abbreviated titles. Many of these were used by most emperors and in themselves are not always distinctive. The main ones are as follows:

IMP = *Imperator*

Refers to the consular power of *imperium* which allowed the holder to raise and command an army. It was technically held on an annual basis but it was gradually absorbed into the ruler's titles under the empire as part of his name and is the origin of our word 'emperor'. It usually precedes all other parts of the legend. It was also possible for the emperor to receive a senatorial acclamation as a successful general. This was recorded by an additional IMP, and a number indication how many times the military award had been made, for example IMP·XII.

CAES = *Caesar*

Originally the family name of Julius Caesar's descendants. After 68 it became an imperial title and name. When used *without* IMP it denoted that the person concerned was the designated heir. Coins of Titus (AD 79–81) are quite common with this legend. They therefore belong to the reign of his father, Vespasian's reign (AD 69–79).

AUG = *Augustus*

Augustus was the name awarded to Octavian (26 BC–AD 14) by the Senate. Subsequently it became part of the personal name of the ruling emperor, or emperors during a joint rule. The emperor's wife was known as AUGUSTA.

COS = *Consul*

The emperor usually held one of the two annual consulships in Rome. This was a Republican office maintained under the Empire for reasons of political tact. The abbreviation cos is normally accompanied by a number indicating how many times it had been held, for example cos·III, which for the Emperor Trajan (98–117) refers to the year 100.

TR·POT = *Tribunicia Potestas*

Another of the Republican offices was the office of Tribune. Like the consulship it could be renewed. For Marcus Aurelius (161–180), who renewed his tribunician power annually on 10 December, TR·POT·XXV means that the coin was struck from a die engraved between 10 December 170 and 10 December 171.

PM = *Pontifex Maximus*

This means 'Chief Priest', a title also usually held by the emperor.

PP = *Pater Patriae*

An honorific title voted to the emperor, sometimes late in the reign. Hadrian (117–138) did not take the title until 128, a useful fact for dating his coins because he did not renew his consular power after 119. His coins therefore mostly bear the legend cos·III; but if PP is added they must date to after 128.

CENS = *Censor*

The Republican office of Censor dealt with population records and eligibility for the Senate. It was not used after Domitian's reign (AD 81–96). He adopted it in 'perpetuity' for himself and indicated so with the legend CENS·PER.

DIVUS = *Divus*

It was quite common for emperors to strike coins in the name of their popular predecessors; it was a way of enhancing one's own legitimacy. These popular predecessors were those who had been deified after death. The most frequent emperor to be honoured in this way was Augustus. Such coins bear the legend DIVUS·AUGUSTUS·PATER and were struck variously by Tiberius, Caligula, Titus, Domitian, Nerva, and Trajan Decius. Only the accompanying legend dates the coins.

Late obverse titles

DN = *Dominus Noster*

From the reign of Diocletian (286–305) on, the emperor became a much more remote figure. The Republican magistracies were rarely held, because there was no need to pay lip-service to anachronistic political machinery any longer. *Dominus Noster*, used on coins from this time on, means 'Our Lord/Master' and it symbolises the changed nature of the ruler.

NOB = *Nobilis or Nobilissimus*

Meaning no more than 'noble', this title was used from the late third century on to add to the titles of the designated heir, or 'Caesar'. So, for example, the legend CONSTANTINUS·IUN·NOB·C does not refer to Constantine I (307–337) but to one of his three sons, and designated heirs, Constantine II, during his father's reign. It dates to 317–337, rather than his period as joint ruler with his brothers from 337–340.

PF = *Pius Felix*

Introduced under Marcus Aurelius, this is an honorific religious title bestowed on an emperor to indicate his dutiful attititude towards his subjects, regardless, in fact, of whether it was in the least bit appropriate.

It was also quite common for the emperors to adopt various military epithets which refer to their various military campaigns. A general title was GERM, for Germanicus, which associated them with the famous early first-century general of that name. Trajan adopted the abbreviations DAC, and PARTH, which refer to his conquests in Dacia and Parthia. Septimius Severus and his sons Caracalla and Geta adopted BRIT to refer to their British victories and conquests (see below).

Mint-marks on coins struck in, or shipped to, Britain

Mint-marks were placed on the reverse of the coin beneath the figure or motif, the area known as the *exergue* (see fig.120 n). They should not be confused with letters placed on either side of the figure, which indicate which department of the mint the coin was struck in. In this way bad coin could be traced.

Romano-British mints

Note: under Carausius and Allectus (287–296) mint-marks were sometimes followed by the mark of value, for example XXI, in emulation of Aurelian's reforms (270–5). The precise meaning is obscure.

London (open 286–325, and possibly 383–8)
L, ML, M LL, M LN, MS L, P LN, P LON, AVG

Colchester (?, or *Clausentum*? or Gloucester?) (open 286–296)
C, CL

Continental mints

Aquileia (294 on)
AQ, AQVIL, AQ OB, AQ PS, SM AQ

Arelate (intermittently known as Constantia), modern *Arles* (313 on)
A, AR, ARL, CON, CONST, KON, KONSTAN

Lugdunum, modern *Lyons* (open variously throughout the whole period)
L, LVG, LVGD, LVG PS, PLG

Rome
R, RM, ROMA, ROM OB, SMR, VRB ROM

Siscia, modern *Sisak* in Yugoslavia
SIS, SISC, SISC PS

Ticinum, modern *Pavia* in Italy (closed 326)
T

Treveri, modern *Trier* in Germany (291 on)
SM TR, TR, TRE, TR OB, TR PS

Note: Some of the letters used in mint-marks recur in a number of different places. This was because they refer to the coinage itself. P generally means *pecunia*, money. SM or M is an abbreviation for *sacra moneta*, which refers to the coinage being a product inspired by the goddess Juno, as *Juno Moneta*. Her temple in Rome was the site of the first Roman mint. OB was short for the Greek word *obryzum*, which means 'tested by fire'; this was used on some late Roman gold. PS was short for the same thing in Latin, *pu sculatum*, and was placed on silver coins.

Bibliography and references

This is a select bibliography. The first section lists general books on Roman Britain, followed by a list of sites and their publications which are referred to throughout the book. The chapter bibliographies follow the order of the text in topics.

Abbreviations

AA^2, ^{4} = *Archaeologia Aeliana (*second, fourth series etc.,)*, Society of Antiquaries, Newcastle upon Tyne.

Antiq. Journ. = *Antiquaries Journal*, Society of Antiquaries, London.

Arch. Journ. = *Archaeological Journal*, Royal Archaeological Institute.

Arch. Camb. = *Archaeologia Cambrensis*, Cambrian Archaeological Association.

Arch. Cant. = *Archaeologia Cantiana*, Kent Archaeological Society.

B.A.R. = *British Archaeological Reports*.

BBCS = *Bulletin of the Board of Celtic Studies*, University of Wales.

CAM = Pottery forms published by C.F.C. Hawkes and M.R. Hull, *Camulodunum*, 1947, and M.R. Hull, *Roman Colchester*, 1958.

C.B.A. = Council for British Archaeology, London.

JRS = *Journal of Roman Studies*.

LAMAS = London and Middlesex Archaeological Society.

RRCSAL = *Report of the Research Committee of the Society of Antiquaries, London.*

RIB = Collingwood, R.G., and Wright, R.P. 1965.

RIC = H. Mattingly and E.A. Sydenham, *Roman Imperial Coinage*, London, 1923, etc.

TBGAS = *Transactions of the Bristol and Gloucestershire Archaeological Society.*

TCWAAS = *Transactions of the Cumberland and Westmorland Antiquarian and Archaeological Society.*

Note on classical sources

There are a number of references to classical sources in the text. The majority will be found either in translation in the Penguin Classics Series, and Mann and Penman, 1978 (see below), or with original text and translation in the Loeb Classical Library. The only exceptions are Arrian's military texts, referred to in Chapter 1. These have not been published and the reader should consult G. Webster, 1985, *The Roman Imperial Army*, for more details.

General works

Birley, A., 1979, *The People of Roman Britain*, London.

Brailsford, J.W., 1964, *Guide to the Antiquities of Roman Britain*, London.

Branigan, K., 1980, *Roman Britain, Life in an Imperial Province*, London.

Clayton, P., 1980, *A Companion to Roman Britain*, Oxford.

Collingwood, R.G., and Wright, R.P., 1965, *The Roman Inscriptions of Britain.*

Collingwood, R.G., and Richmond, I.A., 1969, *The Archaeology of Roman Britain*, London.

Frere, S.S., 1987, *Britannia*, London, third edition.

Greene, K., 1986, *The Archaeology of the Roman Economy*, London.

Greenstock, M.C., 1971, *Some Inscriptions from Roman Britain*, Lactor Series 4, London.

Kent, J.P.C., and Painter, K.S., 1977, *Wealth of the Roman World* AD *300–700*, London.

Mann, J.C., and Penman, R.G., 1978, *Literary Sources for Roman Britain*, Lactor Series 11, London.

Moore, R.W., (ed.) 1938, *The Romans in Britain*, London.

Munby, J., and Henig, M., 1977, *Roman Life and Art in Roman Britain*, B.A.R., (British Series) No. 41, Oxford.

Rivet, A.L.F., 1964, *Town and Country in Roman Britain*, London.

Salway, P., 1981, *Roman Britain*, Oxford.

Strong, D., and Brown, D., 1976, *Roman Crafts*, London, 1969.

Toynbee, J.M.C., 1962, *Art in Roman Britain*, London.

Toynbee, J.M.C., 1964, *Art in Britain under the Romans*, Oxford.

Todd, M., 1981, *Roman Britain (55 BC–AD 400)*, London.

Wacher, J.S., 1966, *The Civitas Capitals of Roman Britain*, Leicester.

Wacher, J.S., 1975, *The Towns of Roman Britain*, London.

Wheeler, R.E.M., 1930, *London in Roman Times*, London.

Sites mentioned throughout the text

BATH

Blagg, T.F.C., 1979, 'The Date of the Temple at Bath', *Britannia*, 10, 101 ff.

Cunliffe, B.W., 1984, *Roman Bath Discovered*, London, 1971, revised edition, London.

Cunliffe, B.W., 1986, 'The Sanctuary of Sulis-Minerva at Bath: a brief review' in Henig, M., and King, A., (eds), *op. cit.*

Cunliffe, B.W., (ed.) 1988, *The Temple of Sulis-Minerva at Bath: the Finds from the Sacred Spring*, Oxford.

Richmond, I.A., and Toynbee, J.M.C., 1955, 'The Temple of Sulis-Minerva at Bath', *JRS*, 45, 97 ff.

BEAUPORT PARK

Brodribb, G., and Cleere, H., 1988, 'The Classis Britannica Bath-house at Beauport Park', *Britannia*, 19.

BENWELL

Simpson, F.G., and Richmond, I.A., 1941, 'The Roman Fort on Hadrian's Wall at Benwell', *AA⁴*, 19, 37 ff.

BIGNOR

Frere, S.S., 1982, 'The Bignor Villa', *Britannia*, 13, 135–196.

CAERLEON

Boon, G.C., 1972, *Isca, The Roman Legionary Fortress at Caerleon, Monmouthshire*, Cardiff.

Nash-Williams, V.E., 1932, *The Roman Legionary Fortress at Caerleon in Monmouthshire; Report on the Excavations carried out in the Prysg Field, 1927–9, Part II – The Finds (pottery excepted)*, Cardiff, (duplicated in *Arch. Camb.*, 87, 1932, 48–104).

Nash-Williams, V.E., 1957, 'Prysg Field II', *BBCS*, 15.

Zienkiewicz, J. D., 1986, *The Legionary Fortress Baths at Caerleon, II. The Finds*, Cardiff.

CAISTER-BY-NORWICH

Atkinson, J., 1931, *Caister Excavations*, London.

CAMERTON

Wedlake, W.J., 1958, *Excavations at Camerton, Somerset*, Bath.

CARRAWBURGH

Allason-Jones, L., and McKay, B., 1985, *Coventina's Well*, Chesters.

CHEDWORTH

Goodburn, R., 1986, *The Roman Villa: Chedworth*, National Trust.

Webster, G., 1983, 'The Function of the Chedworth Roman Villa', *TBGAS*, 101, 1983, 5 ff.

CIRENCESTER

Wacher, J., and McWhirr, A., 1982, *Early Roman Occupation at Cirencester*, Cirencester Excavations I, Cirencester.

COLCHESTER

Crummy, N., 1983, *The Roman small finds from excavations in Colchester, 1971–9*, Colchester Archaeological Report No. 2, Colchester.

Crummy, P., 1984, *Excavations at Lion Walk, Balkerne Lane and Middleborough*, Colchester Archaeological Report No. 3, Colchester.

Hawkes, C., and Hull, M.R., 1947, *Camulodunum*, RRCSAL No. 14, London.

Hull, M.R., 1958, *Roman Colchester*, RRCSAL No. 20, Oxford.

Niblett, R., 1985, *Sheepen: an early Roman industrial site at Camulodunum*, C.B.A. Research Report No. 57, London.

CORBRIDGE

Bishop, M.C., and Dore, J.N., 1988, *Corbridge excavations 1947–80*, London.

DOVER

Philp, B.J., 1981, *The Excavations of the Roman Forts of the Classis Britannica at Dover, 1970–1977*, Kent Monograph Series No. 3, Dover.

EXETER

Bidwell, P.T., 1979, *The Legionary Bath-House and Basilica and Forum at Exeter*, Exeter Archaeological Report No. 1, Exeter.

Bidwell, P.T., 1980, *Roman Exeter: Fortress and Town*, Exeter.

FARLEY HEATH

Goodchild, R.G., 1947, 'Farley Heath', *Antiq. Journ.*, 27, 83.

FISHBOURNE

Cunliffe, B.W., 1971, *Excavations at Fishbourne, Vols. I & II*, RRCSAL No. 26, London, 1971.

Cunliffe, B.W., 1971a, *Fishbourne, a Roman Palace and its Garden*, London.

GADEBRIDGE

Neal, D.S., 1974, *The Excavation of the Roman Villa in Gadebridge Park, Hemel Hempstead, 1963-8*, RRCSAL No. 31, London.

GLOUCESTER

Hurst, H.R., 1985, *Kingsholm*, Gloucester Archaeological Report No. 2, Gloucester.

McWhirr, A.D., 1981, *Roman Gloucestershire*, Gloucester.

GODMANCHESTER
Green, H.J.M., 1986, 'Religious Cults at Roman Godmanchester' in Henig, M. and King, A. (eds.) *op. cit.*, 1986, 29 ff. (see bib. Chap. 6)

HADRIAN'S WALL
Collingwood Bruce, J., 1853, *The Roman Wall*, London.
Collingwood Bruce, J., 1885, *The Handbook to the Roman Wall*, London.
Daniels, C., (ed.) 1978, *Handbook to the Roman Wall*, by J. Collingwood Bruce, 13th edition, Newcastle.

HOD HILL
Brailsford, J.W., 1962, *Hod Hill, I: Antiquities from Hod Hill in the Durden Collection*, London.
Richmond, I.A., 1968, *Hod Hill II*, London.

HOLT
Grimes, W.F., 1930, *Holt, Denbighshire: The Works Depôt of the XXth Legion at Castle Lyons*, Y Cymmrodor 41, London.

INCHTUTHIL
Pitts, L., and St Joseph, J.K., 1985, *Inchtuthil, the Roman Legionary Fortress*, Britannia Monograph Series No. 6, London.

JORDAN HILL
Drew, C.D., 1931, 'Jordan Hill', *Proceedings of the Dorset Natural History and Archaeological Society*, 53, 265 ff.

KENT
Detsicas, A.P., 1983, *The Cantiaci*, Gloucester.
Philp, B.J., 1973, *Excavations in West Kent 1960–1970*, Kent Monograph Series No. 2, Dover.

LINCOLN
Petch, D.F., 1962, 'Excavations at Roman Lincoln, 1955–58' *Arch. Journ.*, 117, 40–70.
Thompson, F.H., and Whitwell, J.B., 1973, 'The Gates of Roman Lincoln', *Archaeologia*, 104, 129–207.
Webster, G., 1949, 'The Legionary Fortress at Lincoln', *JRS*, 39, 57–78.

LONDON
Bird, J., Graham, A.H., Sheldon, H. and Townend, P., (eds) 1978, *Southwark Excavations 1972–1974*, Joint Publications No. 1. LAMAS with Surrey Archaeological Society, London.
Chapman, H., and Johnson, T., 1972, *Excavations at Aldgate and Bush Lane House*, London.
de la Bédoyère, G., 1986, *The Roman Site at Billingsgate Lorry Park*, B.A.R. (British Series) No. 154, Oxford.
Dyson, T., (ed.) 1986, *The Roman Quay at St Magnus House, London: Excavations at New Fresh Wharf, London 1974–78*, Special Paper No. 8, LAMAS, London.
Jones, D.M., and Rhodes, M., 1980, *Excavations at Billingsgate Buildings 'Triangle', Lower Thames Street, 1974*, Special Paper No. 4, LAMAS, London.

Marsden, P., 1980, *Roman London*, London.
Merrifield, R., 1983, *London, City of the Romans*, London.
Milne, G., 1985, *The Port of Roman London*, London.
Royal Commission on Historical Monuments (England) 1928, *An Inventory of the Historical Monuments in London, Volume III, Roman London*, London.

LONGTHORPE
Dannell, G.B., and Wild, J.P., 1987, *Longthorpe II: the military works depot: an episode in landscape history*, Britannia Monograph Series No. 8, London.
Frere, S.S., and St Joseph, J.K., 1974, 'The Roman Fort at Longthorpe', *Britannia*, 5, 1–129.

LOWER SLAUGHTER
Rhodes, J.F., 1964, *Catalogue of Sculptures in the Gloucester City Museum*, Gloucester.
Toynbee, J.M.C., *JRS*, 48, 1958, 49 ff.

LULLINGSTONE
Meates, Lt.-Col. G.W., 1979, *The Lullingstone Roman Villa, Kent, Volume I – the Site*, Maidstone.
Meates, Lt.-Col. G.W., 1987, *The Lullingstone Roman Villa, Kent, Volume II – The Wall Paintings and Finds*, Maidstone.

LYDNEY
Wheeler, R.E.M., and Wheeler, T.V., 1932, *Report on the Excavation of the Prehistoric, Roman and Post-Roman site in Lydney Park, Gloucestershire*, RRCSAL No. 9, London.

MAIDEN CASTLE
Wheeler, R.E.M., 1943, *Maiden Castle, Dorset*, RRCSAL No. 12, Oxford.

MARYPORT
Jarrett, M.G., 1976, *Maryport, Cumbria: a Roman Fort and its Garrison*, Kendal.

NETTLETON
Wedlake, W.J., 1982, *The Excavation of the Shrine of Apollo at Nettleton, Wiltshire, 1956–1971*, RRCSAL No. 40, London.

NEWSTEAD
Curle, J., 1911, *A Roman Frontier Post and its People: The Fort of Newstead in the Parish of Melrose*, Glasgow.

PORTCHESTER
Cunliffe, B.W., 1975, *Excavations at Portchester Castle, I; Roman*, RRCSAL No. 32, London.

RICHBOROUGH
Bushe-Fox, J.P., 1949, *Fourth Report on the Excavation of the Roman Fort at Richborought, Kent*, RRCSAL No. 16, London.
Cunliffe, B.W., 1968, *Fifth Report on the Excavations of the Roman Fort at Richborough, Kent*, RRCSAL No. 23, London.

SAXON SHORE
Johnson, S., 1979, *The Roman Forts of the Saxon Shore*, London.

SILCHESTER

Boon, G.C., 1957, *Roman Silchester*, London.

Boon, G.C., 1974, *Silchester: The Roman Town of Calleva*, Newton Abbot.

Fulford, M., 1985, 'Excavations on the sites of the Amphitheatre and Forum-Basilica at Silchester, Hampshire. An Interim Report', *Antiq. Journ.*, 65, 39–81.

SKELETON GREEN

Partridge, C., 1981, *Skeleton Green. A Late Iron Age and Romano-British site*, Britannia Monograph Series 2, London.

SPRINGHEAD

Detsicas, A.P., 1983, *The Cantiaci*, Gloucester, 60 ff.

Penn, W.S., 1959, 'The Romano-British settlement at Springhead', *Arch. Cant.*, 73, 24 ff.

Penn, W.S., 1964, 'Springhead: the temple ditch site', *Arch. Cant.*, 79, 170 ff.

STAINES

Crouch, K.R., and Shanks, S.A., 1984, *Excavations in Staines 1975–76: The Friends' Burial Site*, Joint Publication No. 2, LAMAS with Surrey Archaeological Society, London.

THETFORD

Johns, C., and Potter, T., 1983, *The Thetford Treasure*, London.

ULEY

Ellison, A., 1988, *Uley shrines, Gloucestershire*, London.

VERULAMIUM (ST ALBANS)

Frere, S.S., 1972, *Verulamium Excavations I*, RRCSAL No. 28, London.

Frere, S.S., 1983, *Verulamium Excavations II*, RRCSAL No. 41, London.

Frere, S.S., 1984, *Verulamium Excavations III*, Oxford University Committee for Archaeology Monograph No. 1, Oxford.

Kenyon, K.M., 1934, 'The Roman Theatre at Verulamium' in *Transactions of the St Albans and Hertfordshire Architectural and Archaeological Society*.

Wheeler, R.E.M., and Wheeler, T.V., 1936, *Verulamium, a Belgic and two Roman Cities*, RRCSAL No. 11, Oxford.

VINDOLANDA (CHESTERHOLM)

Bidwell, P.T., 1985, *The Roman Fort of Vindolanda at Chesterholm, Northumberland*, London.

Birley, R., 1977, *Vindolanda; A Roman frontier post on Hadrian's Wall*, London.

YORK

Royal Commission on Historical Monuments (England) 1962, *An Inventory of the Historical Monuments in the City of York, Volume I, Eburacum, Roman York*, London.

WROXETER

Atkinson, J., 1942, *Excavations at Wroxeter 1923–27*, Oxford.

1 The Roman Army in Britain

General works on the Roman Army

Birley, E., *Roman Britain and the Roman Army*, Kendal.

Cheesman, G.L., 1914, *The Auxilia of the Roman Imperial Army*, Oxford.

Connolly, P., 1981, *Greece and Rome at War*, London.

Holder, P.A., 1982, *The Roman Army in Britain*, London.

Johnson, A., 1983, *Roman Forts*, London.

Lepper, F. and Frere, S.S., 1988, *Trajan's Column*, Gloucester.

Webster, G., 1985, *The Roman Imperial Army*, London (third edition).

Arms and Equipment

General works

Bishop, M.C., (ed.) 1985 *The Production and Distribution of Roman Military Equipment*, B.A.R. (International Series) No. S275, Oxford.

Farrant, N., 1980, 'The Legionary *Scutum*', *Exercitus*, 1.1, 1980, 9–10, and 1. 3, 34–6.

Hazell, P.J., 1981, 'The *pedite gladius*', *Antiq. Journ.*, 61, 73–82.

Marsden, E.W., 1969 and 1971, *Greek and Roman Artillery: Historical Development and Technical Treatises*, Oxford.

Maxfield, V., 1981, *The Military Decorations of the Roman Army*, London.

Oldenstein, J., 1976, 'Zur Ausrüstung römischer Auxiliareinheiten', *Bericht de Römisch-Germanischen Kommission*, 57, 49–284. [Auxiliary and legionary equipment of the second century.]

Oldenstein, J., 1985, 'The Manufacture and Supply of the Roman Army with bronze fittings' in Bishop, M.C., (ed.) 1985, *op. cit.*

Robinson, H. R., 1975, *The Armour of Imperial Rome*, London.

Rostovtzeff, M.I., 1946, '*Vexillum* and Victory', *JRS*, 32, 92–106.

Sander, E., 1963, 'Die Kleidung des römischen Soldaten', *Historia*, 12, 144–66. [Clothing of Roman soldiers.]

Scott, I.R., 1985, First Century Military Daggers and the Manufacture and Supply of Weapons for the Roman Army' in Bishop, M.C., (ed.) 1985, *op. cit.*

Speidel, M., 1976, 'Eagle Bearer and Trumpeter', *Bonner Jahrbuch*, 176, 124–6.

Thomas, E.B., 1971, *Helme, Schilde, Dolche*, Budapest.

Webster, G., 1958, 'The Roman Military Advance under Ostorius Scapula', *Arch. Journ.*, 115, 49 ff.

Webster, G., 1986, 'Standards and Standard-Bearers in the *Alae*', *Bonner Jahrbuch*, 186, 105–15.

Britain

Allason-Jones, L., and Miket, R., 1984, *The catalogue of small finds from South Shields Roman Fort*, Newcastle-upon-Tyne.

Allason-Jones, L., and Bishop, M.C., 1988, *Excavations at Roman Corbridge: the Hoard*, London.

Boon, G.C., 1962, 'The Roman sword from Caernarvon-Segontium', *BBCS*, 19, 85–89.

Buckland, P., 1978, 'A First-Century Shield from Doncaster', *Britannia*, 9, 247–70.

Campbell, D.B., 1984, '*Ballisteria* in first to mid-third century Britain: a reappraisal', *Britannia*, 15, 75–84.

Clay, P., and Webster, G., 1984, 'A Cheek-piece from a Cavalry Helmet found in Leicester', *Britannia* 15, 235.

Daniels, C., 1968, 'A Hoard of Iron and other Materials from Corbridge', *AA⁴*, 46, 115ff.

Densem, R., 1980, 'Pilum-heads from Roman Britain', *Exercitus*, 1.3, 27–33.

Green, C.S., 1984, 'A Late Roman Buckle from Dorchester, Dorset', *Britannia*, 15, 260.

Greep, S.J., 1987, 'Lead Sling-shot from Windridge Farm, St Albans, and the Use of the Sling by the Roman Army in Britain', *Britannia*, 18, 183.

Griffiths, N.A., 1979, 'A Gladius from Dorset, in the Ashmolean Museum', *Britannia*, 10, 259.

Jackson, R., 1984, 'A Roman stamped shield-boss from London', *Britannia*, 15, 246.

James, S., 1980, 'Two shield bosses from London', *Britannia*, 11, 320–3.

Johnson, S., 1980, 'A Late Roman Helmet from Burgh Castle', *Britannia*, 11, 303 ff.

Myres, J.N.L., 1961, 'Soldiers and Settlers in Britain, fourth to fifth century', *Medieval Archaeology*, 5, 1–70.

Richmond, I.A. and McIntyre, J., 1934, 'Tents of the Roman Army and leather from Birdoswald', *TCWAAS*, 34, 62.

Smith, D.J., 1968, 'The Archer's Tombstone from Housesteads', *AA⁴*, 46, 284ff.

Todd, M., 1981, 'A Legionary Cuirass Hinge from the Great Casterton Fort', *Britannia*, 12, 297.

Toynbee, J.M.C., and Clarke, R.R., 1948, 'A Roman decorated helmet and other objects from Norfolk', *JRS*, 38, 20–7.

Webster, G., 1971, 'A hoard of Roman military equipment from Fremington Hagg' in Butler, R.M., (ed.) 1971, *Soldier and Civilian in Roman Yorkshire*, Leicester, 107ff.

Webster, G., 1979, 'A Roman Iron Sword from Chichester', *Antiq. Journ.*, 59, 403.

Wild, J.P., 1981, 'A Find of Roman Scale Armour from Carpow', *Britannia*, 12, 305.

See also various site reports cited above, in particular: Brailsford, 1962 and Richmond, 1968 (Hod Hill); Nash-Williams, 1932 (Caerleon); Cunliffe, 1968 (Richborough); Bidwell, 1985 (Vindolanda); Hawkes and Hull, 1947, Crummy, 1983, and Niblett, 1985 (Colchester); Wacher and McWhirr, 1982 (Cirencester).

Material from other parts of the Empire

Baatz, D., 1966, 'Zur Geschützbewaffnung römischer Auxiliartruppen in der frühen und mittleren Kaiserzeit', *Bonner Jahrbuch*, 166, 194–207. [Auxiliary equipment in the early and middle principate.]

Baatz, D., 1978, 'Recent finds of ancient artillery', *Britannia*, 9, 1–17.

Baatz, D., 1980, 'Ein katapult der *Legio* IV *Macedonia* eis Cremona', *Römische Mitteilung*, 87, 283–99.

Busch, A.L., 1965, 'Die römerzeitlichen Schuhund Lederfunde der Kastelle Saalburg, Zugmantel und Kleiner Feldberg', *Saalburg Jahrbuch*, 22, 158–210. [Shoes and leather finds from Saalburg.]

Holwerda, J.J., 1931, 'Een vondst uit den Rijn bij Doorwerth', *Oudheidkundige Mededelingen*, supplement, 12, 1–26.

Jenkins, I., 1985, 'A Group of Silvered Horse-Trappings from Xanten', *Britannia*, 16, 141.

Keim, H., and Klumbach, H., 1976, *Der römische Schatzfund von Straubing*, Munich. [A find of Roman parade equipment.]

Klumbach, H., 1961, 'Ein römischer Legionarshelm aus Mainz', *Jahrbuch des Römisch-Germanischen Zentralmuseums Mainz*, 8, 96–105. [Legionary helmet from Mainz.]

Klumbach, H., 1962, 'Römische Panzerbeschläge aus Manching', Festschrift Wagner in *Schriftenreihe zur Bayerischen Landesgeschichte*, 62, 187ff. [Armour fittings from Manching.]

Oldenstein, J., 1979, 'Ein Numerum-Omnium-Beschlag aus Kreuzweingarton', *Bonner Jahrbuch*, 179, 543–52. [Metal fittings from Kreuzweingarton.]

Rostóvtzeff, M.I. (ed.), 1936, *The Excavation at Dura-Europos, VI Season* (unpublished).

Ulbert, G., 1959, *Die Römischen Donan-Kastelle Aislingen und Burghöfe*, Limesforschungen, Band 1, Berlin.

Ulbert, G., 1968, *Römische Waffen des I, Jahrhunderts n, Chr.*, Stuttgart.

Ulbert, G., 1969, 'Gladii aus Pompeii, Vorarbeiten zu einem Corpus römisches Gladii', *Germania*, 47, 97–128. [Swords from Pompeii.]

Ulbert, G., 1969a, *Das frümrömische Kastell Rheingönheim, Die Funde aus den Jahren 1912 and 1913*, Limesforschungen, Band 9, Berlin.

Ulbert, G., 1970, 'Das römische Donau-Kastell Risstissen. Die Funde aus Metall, Horn und Knocher', *Urkunden zur Vor-und Frügeschichte aus Südwürttemberg-Hohenzollern*, 4. [Finds of metal, horn and bone from the fort at Risstissen.]

Ypey, J., 1966, 'Twee Viziermaskerhelmen uit Nijmegen', *Numaga*, 13, 187–99.

Weinberg, S.S., 1979, 'A hoard of Roman armour (from Palestine)', *Antike Kunst*, 22, pt. 2, 82–6. [Includes legionary helmet and parade helmet.]

Other military material

Boon, G.C., 1984, *Laterarium Iscanum: The Antefixes, Brick & Tile Stamps of the Second Augustan Legion*, Cardiff.

Brodribb, G., 1979, 'Tile from the Roman Bath House at Beauport Park', *Britannia*, 10, 139 ff.

Caruana, I., 1987, 'A wooden ansate panel from Carlisle', *Britannia*, 18, 274.

Clay, P., 1980, 'Seven inscribed leaden sealings from Leicester', *Britannia*, 11, 317 ff.

Hogg, R., 1965, Excavations of the Roman auxiliary Tilery, Brampton', *TCWAAS (new series)*, 65, 133–68.

Richmond, I.A., 1934, 'The Roman Fort at South Shields', *AA⁴*, 11.

Richmond, I.A., and McIntyre, J., 1934, 'Tents of the Roman Army and leather from Birdoswald' in *TCWAAS*, 34, 62–90.

Richmond, I.A., 1936, 'Roman lead sealings from Brough-under-Stainmore', *TCWAAS*, 36, 104ff.

Roxan, M., 1978, *Roman Military Diplomas 1954–1977*, Institute of Archaeology Research Reports No. 2, London.

Roxan, M., 1983, 'A Roman Military Diploma from London', *Trans. LAMAS*, 34, 67.

Toynbee, J.M.C., and Wilkins, A., 1982, 'The Vindolanda Horse', *Britannia*, 13, 245 ff.

Webster, G., 1973, 'Introduction and Notes on the Pottery of the first Century AD in Use by the Roman Army' in Detsicas, A.P., (ed.) *op. cit.*

Wright, R.P., 1976, 'Tile-Stamps of the Sixth Legion found in Britain', *Britannia*, 7, 224ff.

Wright, R.P., 1984, 'The problem of the nature of pliable material to be impressed by leaden dies citing centurions in Roman Britain . . .', *Britannia*, 15, 259–6.

2 Crafts, Trades and Industries

General

Kent, J.P.C., and Painter, K.S., 1977, *Wealth of the Roman World AD 300–700*, London.

Manning, W.H. 1976, *Catalogue of Romano-British Ironwork in the Museum of Antiquities, Newcastle-upon-Tyne*, Newcastle-upon-Tyne.

McWhirr, A., 1982, *Roman Crafts and Industries*, Aylesbury.

Richmond, I.A., 1966, 'Industry in Roman Britain' in Wacher, J.S., (ed.), *The Civitas Capitals of Roman Britain*, Leicester.

Strong, D., and Brown, D., 1976 (eds), *Roman Crafts*, London.

White, K.D., 1975, *Farm Equipment of the Roman World*, Cambridge.

Agriculture

Manning, W.H., 1964, 'The Plough in Roman Britain', *JRS*, 54, 54–65.

Manning, W.H., 1970, 'Mattocks, Hoes, Spades and Related Tools in Roman Britain' in Gailey, A., and Fenton, A., (eds) *The Spade in Northern and Atlantic Europe*, Belfast, 18–29.

Manning. W.H., 1971, 'The Piercebridge Plough Group', *British Museum Quarterly*, 35, 125 ff.

Peacock, D.P.S., 1987, 'Quernstones', *Antiq. Journ.*, 67, 61–85.

Rees, S.E., 1979, *Agricultural Implements in Prehistoric and Roman Britain*, B.A.R. (British Series) No. 69, Oxford.

Rees, S., 1981, *Ancient Agricultural Implements*, Aylesbury.

Young, C., 1981, *The late Roman mill at Ickham and the Saxon Shore*, in Detsicas, A.P., (ed.) *Collectanea Historica*, Maidstone.

Quarrying and Mining

Boon, G.C., 1966, 'Dolaucothi water wheel', *JRS*, 56, 122 ff.

Whittick, G. C., 1982, 'Roman Lead-Mining on Mendip and in North Wales', *Britannia*, 13, 113 ff.

Metal-working

Blagg, T.F.C., and Read, S., 1977, 'The Roman Pewter Moulds from Silchester', *Antiq. Journ.*, 57, 270–276.

Butcher, S.A., 1976, 'Enamelling' in Strong and Brown (eds), *op. cit.*

Cleere, H.F., 1971, 'Bardown and Holbeanwood', *Sussex Archaeological Society Occasional Papers*, 1.

Cleere, H.F., 1971, 'Smelting Experiments', *Britannia*, 2.

Cleere, H., and Crossley, D., 1985, *The Iron Industry of the Weald*, Leicester.

Frere, S.S., 1970, 'A mould for a bronze statuette from Gestingthorpe', *Britannia*, 1.

Stead, I.M., 1975, 'A Roman pottery theatrical face-mask and a bronze brooch blank from Baldock, Herts', *Antiq. Journ.*, 55, 397–8.

Ceramics

Black, E.W., 1985, 'The Dating of Relief-Patterned Flue-Tiles', *Oxford Journal of Archaeology*, 4, no. 3.

Detsicas, A.P., (ed.), 1973, *Current Research in Romano-British Coarse Pottery*, C.B.A. Research Report No. 10, London.

Greenaway, J., 1981, 'The Neronian Stamped Tile from Little London, near Silchester', *Britannia*, 12, 290.

Heighway, C.M., and Parker, A.J., 1982, 'The Roman Tilery at St Oswald's Priory, Gloucester', *Britannia*, 13, 25 ff.

Lowther, A.W.G., 1948, *A study of patterns on Roman flue-tiles and their distribution*, Research Paper I of Surrey Archaeological Society.

Rudling, D., 1986, 'The Excavation of a Roman Tilery on Great Cansiron Farm, Hartfield, Sussex', *Britannia*, 17, 191, ff.

Swan, V.G., 1984, *The Pottery Kilns of Roman Britain*, London.

Wild, J.P., 1973, 'A fourth-century Potter's Workshop and Kilns at Stibbington, Peterborough' in Detsicas, A., (ed.) *op. cit.*, 135–138.

Wright, R.P., 1985, 'Official Tile-stamps from London which cite the Province of Britain', *Britannia*, 16, 193.

Carpentry

Goodman, W., 1964, *A History of Woodworking Tools*, London.

Liversidge, J., 1976, 'Woodwork' in Strong and Brown (eds), *op. cit.*

Stonemasonry

Blagg, T.F.C., 1976, 'Tools and Techniques of the Roman Stonemasons in Britain', *Britannia*, 7, 152–72.

Blagg, T.F.C., 1977, 'Schools of Stonemasons in Roman Britain', in Munby, J., and Henig, M., (eds) *op. cit.*

Bone-working

Crummy, N., 1981, 'Bone-working at Colchester', *Britannia*, 12.

Spinning and Weaving

Wild, J.P., 1970, *Textile Manufacture in the Northern Roman Provinces*, Cambridge.

Wild, J.P., 1976, 'Textiles' in Strong and Brown (eds) *op. cit.*

Medicine

Allason-Jones, L., 1979, 'Two Unrecognized Roman Surgical Instruments', *AA*[5], 7, 239–41.

Boon, G.C., 1983, 'Potters, Oculists and Eye-Troubles', *Britannia*, 14, 1 ff.

Gilson, A.G., 1981, 'A Group of Roman Medical and Surgical Instruments from Corbridge', *Saalburg-Jahrbuch*, 37, 5 ff.

Gilson, A.G., 1982, 'A Roman Iron Cautery from Verulamium', *Britannia*, 13, 303.

Name-stamps/writing

Bowman, A.K., and Thomas, J.D., 1983, *Vindolanda: the Latin Writing Tablets*, Britannia Monograph No. 4, London.

Wright, R.P., 1984, 'The problem of the nature of pliable material to be impressed by leaden dies citing centurions in Roman Britain . . .'. *Britannia*, 15, 259–6. [Discusses mortaria potters' die-stamps.]

3 Household Life

General

Many of the general works listed at the beginning of the bibliography are particularly useful for this chapter, especially Wheeler, R.E.M., 1930, Kent, J.P.C., and Painter, K.S., 1977, Strong, D., and Brown, D., 1976.

Tablewares/kitchenwares

Metal and glass ware

Bennett, J., and Young, R., 1981, 'Some New and Some Forgotten Stamped Skillets, and the Date of P. Cipius Polybius', *Britannia*, 12, 37 ff.

Charlesworth, D., 1966, 'Roman Square Bottles', *Journal of Glass Studies*, 8, 26–40.

Curle, A.O., 1923, *The Treasure of Traprain*, Glasgow.

Farley, M., Henig, M., and Taylor, J.W., 1988, 'A Hoard of Late Roman Bronze Bowls and Mounts from the Misbourne Valley, near Amersham, Bucks', *Britannia*, 19, 357 ff.

Harden, D.B., 1969, 'Ancient Glass II', *Archaeological Journal*, 126.

Johns, C.M., 1981, 'The Risley Park Silver Lanx; a Lost Antiquity from Roman Britain', *Antiq. Journ.*, 61, 53–72.

Johns, C.M., 1986, 'The Roman Silver Cups from Hockwold, Norfolk,' *Archaeologia*, 108, 1–15.

Liversidge, J., 1959, 'A New Hoard of Romano-British Pewter from Icklingham', *Proceedings of the Cambridge Antiquaries Society*, 52, 6–10.

Painter, K.S., 1977, *The Mildenhall Treasure*, London.

Stead, I.M., 1967, 'A La Tène III burial at Welwyn Garden City', *Archaeologia*, 101, 1–62.

Strong, D.E., 1966, *Greek and Roman Gold and Silver Plate*, London.

Pottery (general)

Anderson, A.C., and Anderson, A.S., 1981, *Roman Pottery Research in Britain and N.W. Europe*, B.A.R. (International Series) No. 123, Oxford.

Anderson, A.C., 1984, *Interpreting Pottery*, London.

Charleston, R.J., 1955, *Roman Pottery*, London.

Detsicas, A.P., (ed.) 1973, *Current Research in Romano-British Coarse Pottery*, C.B.A. Research Report No. 10, London.

Dore, J., and Greene, K., 1977, *Roman Pottery Studies in Britain and beyond*, B.A.R. (International Series) No. S30, Oxford.

Gillam, J.P., 1973, 'Sources of Pottery Found on Northern Military Sites' in Detsicas, A.P., (ed.) *op. cit.*

Peacock, D.P.S., (ed.) 1977, *Pottery and Early Commerce: characterisation and trade in Roman and later ceramics*, London.

Peacock, D.P.S., 1982, *Pottery in the Roman World: an ethnoarchaeological approach*, London.

Swan, V.G., 1988, *Pottery in Roman Britain*, 4th edition, Shire Archaeology Series no. 3, Aylesbury.

Samian ware

Atkinson, J., 1914, 'A hoard of samian ware from Pompeii', *JRS*, 4.

de la Bédoyère, G., 1988, *Samian Ware*, Shire Archaeology Series No. 55, Aylesbury.

Déchelette, J., 1904, *Les Vases céramiques ornés de la Gaule romaine*, Paris.

Dragendorff, H., 1895, 'Terra sigillata. Ein Beitrag zur Geschichte der griechischen und römischen Keramik', *Bonner Jahrbuch*, 96.

Hull, M.R., 1963, *The Roman Potters' Kilns of Colchester*, RRCSAL No. 21, London.

Johns, C., 1971 & 1977, *Arretine and Samian Pottery*, British Museum, London.

Knorr, R., 1919, *Töpfer und Fabriken verzierter Terra-sigillata des ersten Jahrunderts*, Stuttgart.

Knorr, R., 1952, *Terra-Sigillata-Gefässe des ersten Jahrunderts mit Töpfernamen*, Stuttgart.

Millett, M., 1987, 'Boudicca, the First Colchester Potters' Shop, and the dating of Neronian Samian', *Britannia*, 18, 93ff.

Oswald, F., 1931, *Index of potters' stamps on terra sigillata, 'samian ware'*, Margidunum (Gregg Press reprint, 1964).

Oswald, F., 1936–7 *Index of figure-types on terra sigillata, 'samian ware'*, Liverpool (Gregg Press reprint, 1964).

Oswald, F., and Pryce, T.D., 1920, *An Introduction to the Study of Terra Sigillata*, London (Gregg Press reprint, 1965).

Rogers, G.B., 1974, *Poteries Sigillées de la Gaule Centrale, I, – Les motifs non figurés*, Gallia supplement 18, Paris.

Simpson, G., 1952, 'The Aldgate Potter: a maker of Romano-British samian ware', *JRS* 42.

Stanfield, J.A., and Simpson, G., 1958, *Central Gaulish Potters*, Oxford.

Webster, P.V., 1975, 'More British samian by the Aldgate-Pulborough potter', *Britannia*, 6.

Webster, P.V., 1981, 'The feeding cup: an unusual samian form', in Anderson, A.C., and Anderson, A.S. (eds) *op. cit.*, 249 ff.

Webster, P.V., 1987, *Roman Samian Ware – Background Notes*, Cardiff.

Other fine wares

Anderson, A.C., 1980, *A Guide to Roman Fine Wares*, Vorda I.

Anderson, A.C., *et alia*, 1982, 'Chemical analysis of Hunt cups and allied forms from Britain', *Britannia*, 13.

Arthur, P., and Marsh, G., 1978, *Early fine wares in Roman Britain*, B.A.R. (British Series No. 57, Oxford.

Fulford, M.G., 1975, *New Forest Roman Pottery*, B.A.R. (British Series), No. 17, Oxford.

Greene, K.T., 1979, 'Report on the Pre-Flavian Fine Wares' in *Report on the Excavations at Usk 1965–76*, Volume I, Cardiff.

Hartley, B.R., 1960, *Notes on the Roman Pottery Industry in the Nene Valley*, Peterborough.

Hayes, J., 1972, *Late Roman Pottery*, London.

Howe, M.D., Perrin, J.R., and Mackreth, D.F., 1980, *Roman Pottery from the Nene Valley: a Guide*, Peterborough.

Rigby, V., 1973, 'Potters' Stamps on Terra Nigra and Terra Rubra found in Britain' in Detsicas, A.P. (ed.) *op. cit.*, 7-24.

Swan, V., 1973, 'Aspects of the New Forest late-Roman Pottery Industry' in Detsicas, A.P., (ed.) *op. cit.*, 117–34.

Young, C.J., 1973, 'The Pottery Industry of the Oxford Region' in Detsicas, A.P. (ed.) *op. cit.*, 105–15.

Young, C.J., 1977, *Oxfordshire Roman Pottery*, B.A.R. (British Series) No. 43, Oxford.

Coarse wares/kitchenwares/containers

Callender, M.H., 1965, *Roman Amphorae*, Oxford.

Castle, S.A., 1976, 'Roman Pottery from Brockley Hill, Middlesex, 1966 and 1972–1974', *Trans. LAMAS*, 27, 206 ff.

Catherall, P.D., 1983, 'A Romano-British Pottery Manufacturing Site at Oakleigh Farm, Higham, Kent', *Britannia*, 14, 103–142.

Corder, P., 1937, 'A pair of fourth-century Romano-British kilns near Crambeck', *Antiq. Journ.*, 17, 392–412.

Farrar, R.A.H., 1973, 'The Techniques and Sources of Romano-British black-burnished ware' in Detsicas, A.P., (ed.) *op. cit.*, 67–103.

Gillam, J.P., 1957 'Types of Roman Coarse Pottery Vessels in Northern Britain', AA^4, 35.

Hartley, K.F., 1973, 'The Marketing and Distribution of Mortaria' in Detsicas, A.P., (ed.) *op. cit.*, 39–51.

Hodder, I., 1974, 'Some marketing models for Romano-British coarse pottery', *Britannia*, 5.

Lyne, M.A.B., and Jefferies, R.S., 1979, *The Alice Holt/Farnham Roman Pottery Industry*, C.B.A. Research Report No. 30, London.

Marsh, G., and Tyers, P., 1978, 'The Roman Pottery from Southwark' in Bird *et alia., op. cit.*

Monaghan, J., 1987, *Upchurch and Thameside Roman Pottery. A ceramic typology for northern Kent, first to third centuries* AD, B.A.R. (British Series) No. 173, Oxford.

Peacock, D.P.S., and Williams, D.F., 1986, *Amphorae and the Roman Economy – an introductory guide*, London.

Webster, G., 1977, *Romano-British Coarse Pottery: a student's Guide*, C.B.A. Research Report No. 6, London.

Williams, D.F., 1977, 'The Romano-British Black-burnished Industry: An Essay on Characterisation by Heavy Mineral Analysis' in Peacock, D.P.S., (ed.), *op. cit.*

Lighting

Bailey, D.M., 1976, 'Pottery Lamps' in Strong, D., and Brown, D., *Roman Crafts*, London.

Bailey, D.M., 1980, *Catalogue of the Lamps in the British Museum 2*, London.

Loeschcke, S., *et al.*, 1911, *Beschreibung römischen Altertümer gessamelt von C.A. Niessen*, Cologne.

Wheeler, R.E.M., 1930, 'Lighting' in *London in Roman Times*, London.

Furniture

Liversidge, J., 1955, *Furniture in Roman Britain*, London.

Rogerson, A., 1975, 'Excavations at Scole, 1973', *East Anglian Archaeology Report*, No. 5, Gressenhall.

Solley, T.W.J., 1979, 'Romano-British Side-Tables and Chip-Carving', *Britannia*, 10, 169 ff.

Heating and Roofing (see bibliography for Chapter 2 as well)

Brodribb, G., 1987, *Roman Brick and Tile*, Gloucester.

Lowther, A.W.G., 1976, 'Romano-British Chimney Pots and Finials', *Antiq. Journ.*, 56, 35–48.

McWhirr, A.D. (ed.) 1979, *Roman Brick and Tile*, B.A.R. (International Series), No. S68, Oxford.

4 The Individual

Health and hygiene

Jackson, R., 1985, 'Cosmetic Sets from Late Iron Age and Roman Britain', *Britannia*, 16, 165.

Brooches

Fowler, E., 1960, 'The origins and development of the penannular brooch in Europe', *Proceedings of the Prehistoric Society*, 26, 149–77.

Hattatt, R., 1982, *Ancient and Romano-British Brooches*, Oxford.

Hattatt, R., 1985, *Iron Age and Roman Brooches*, Oxford.

Hattatt, R., 1988, *Brooches of Antiquity*, Oxford.

Hull, M.R., and Hawkes, C.F.C., 1987, *Corpus of Ancient Brooches in Britain by the late Mark Reginald Hull. Pre-Roman Bow Brooches*, B.A.R. (British Series) No. 168.

Mackreth, D., 1973, *Roman Brooches*, Salisbury and South Wiltshire Museum.

Jewellery and Clothing

Crummy, N., 1979, 'A Chronology of Romano-British Bone Pins', *Britannia*, 10, 157 ff.

Henig, M., 1978, 'Signet Rings from Roman London', *Trans. LAMAS*, 29, 113.

Henig, M., 1978, *A Corpus of Roman Engraved Gemstones from British Sites*, B.A.R. (British Series) No. 8, Oxford.

Higgins, R., 1980, *Greek and Roman Jewellery*, London (second edition).

Johns, C., and Potter, T., 1983, *The Thetford Treasure*, London.

MacConnoran, P., 1986, 'Footwear' in Dyson, T., *op. cit.* (New Fresh Wharf, London), 218 ff.

Rhodes, M., 1980, 'Leather Footwear' in Jones, D.M., *op. cit.* (Billingsgate Buildings, London), 99 ff.

5 Public Life

Marsh, G., 1979, 'Three theatre masks from London', *Britannia*, 10, 263.

Richmond, I.A., 1944, 'Three fragments of Roman official statues', *Antiq. Journ.*, 24, 1 ff.

Painter, K.S., 1970, 'A Roman bronze helmet from Hawkedon', *Proc. Suffolk Inst. Archaeol*, 31, pt, 1, 57 ff.

Stead, I., 1975, 'A Roman pottery theatrical face-mask ... from Baldock, Herts', *Antiq. Journ.*, 55, 397–8.

6 Religion and Superstition

General

Frend, W.H.C., 1955, 'Religion in Roman Britain in the Fourth Century', *Journal of the British Archaeological Association*, (third series), 18, 1ff.

Green, M.J., 1976, *The Religions of Civilian Roman Britain*, B.A.R. (British Series), No. 24, Oxford.

Green, M.J., 1983, *The Gods of Roman Britain*, Shire Archaeology Series 34, Aylesbury.

Green, M.J., 1986a, *The Gods of the Celts*, Gloucester.

Harris, J.R., and E., 1965, *Oriental Cults in Roman Britain*, Leiden.

Henig, M., 1984, *Religion in Roman Britain*, London.

Henig, M., and King, A., (eds) 1986, *Pagan Gods and Shrines of the Roman Empire*, Oxford University Committee for Archaeology Monograph No. 8, Oxford.

Johns, C.M., 1982, *Sex or Symbol – Erotic Images of Greece and Rome*, London.

Lewis, M.J.T., 1966, *Temples in Roman Britain*, Cambridge.

Rodwell, W., (ed.) 1980, *Temples, Churches and Religion in Roman Britain*, B.A.R. (British Series) No. 77 volume I, Oxford.

Ross, A., 1967, *Pagan Celtic Britain*, London.

Webster, G. 1986, *The British Celts and their Gods under Rome*, London.

Wesbster, G., 1986a, 'What the Britons required from the gods as seen through the pairing of Roman and Celtic deities and the character of votive offerings' in Henig, M., and King, A., (eds) *op. cit.*, 57 ff.

Others

Alcock, J.P., 1986, 'The Concept of Genius in Roman Britain' in Henig, M., and King, A., (eds) *op. cit.*, 134 ff.

Allason-Jones, L., 1984, 'A Lead Shrine from Wallsend', *Britannia*, 15, 231.

Allason-Jones, L., and McKay, B., 1985, *Coventina's Well*, Chesters.

Braithwaite, G., 1984, 'Romano-British Face-Pots and Head Pots', *Britannia*, 15, 99–132.

Green, M.J., 1981, 'Model Objects from Military Areas of Roman Britain', *Britannia*, 12, 253 ff.

Green, M.J., 1984a, 'Mother and Sons in Romano-Celtic religion', *Antiq. Journ.*, 64, 25–34.

Green, M.J., 1984b, *The Wheel as a Cult Symbol in the Romano-Celtic world*, Latomus, Brussels.

Green, M.J., 1985, 'A Miniature Bronze Axe from Tiddington, Warwickshire', *Britannia*, 16, 238.

Green, M.J., 1986b, 'Jupiter, Taranis and the Solar Wheel' in Henig, M., and King, A., (eds) *op. cit.*, 65.

Henig, M.J., 1984, 'Amber amulets', *Britannia*, 15, 244.

Hutchinson, V.J., *Bacchus in Roman Britain, the Evidence for His Cult*, B.A.R. (British Series) No. 151, Oxford.

Jenkins, F., 1958, 'The Cult of the "Pseudo-Venus" in Kent', *Arch. Cant.*, 72, 60–76.

Johns, C., 1971, 'A Roman bronze statuette of Epona', *British Museum Quarterly*, 36, 37–40.

Johns, C., 1986, 'Faunus at Thetford: an early Latian deity in Late Roman Britain' in Henig, M., and King, A., (eds), *op. cit.*

Leahy, K., 1980, 'Votive Models from Kirmington, South Humberside', *Britannia*, 11, 326 ff.

Liversidge, J., 1954, 'A New Year's Lamp from Ely', *Cambridge Antiquarian Society Proceedings*, 47, 40.

Luard, Major, 1859, 'On the recent discoveries of Roman remains at Plaxtol in Kent', *Arch. Cant.*, 2, 2 ff.

Oaks, L.S., 1986, 'The goddess Epona: concepts of sovereignty in a changing landscape', Henig, M., and King, A., (eds), *op. cit.*, 77.

Painter, K.S., 1965, 'A Roman Marble Head from Sussex', *Antiq. Journ.*, 45, 178.

Phillips, E.J., 1979, 'A Statue of a Genius from Burgh-by-Sands', *Britannia*, 10, 179 ff.

Read, S., Henig, M., and Cram, L., 1986, 'Three-horned Bull', *Britannia*, 17, 346.

Toynbee, J.M.C., 1976, 'Roman Sculpture in Gloucestershire' in McGrath, P., and Cannan, J., *Essays in Bristol and Gloucestershire History*, Bristol.

Toynbee, J.M.C., 1981, 'Apollo, Beasts and Seasons: Some Thoughts on the Littlecote Mosaic', *Britannia*, 12, 1 ff.

Toynbee, J.M.C., 1986, *The Roman Art Treasures from the Temple of Mithras*, Special paper no. 7, LAMAS.

7 Death and Burial

Celtic burials

Brewster, T.C.M., 1971, 'The Garton Slack chariot burial, East Yorkshire', *Antiquity*, 45.

Brewster, T.C.M., 1975, 'Garton Slack', *Current Archaeology*, 5.

Stead, I.M., 1967, 'A La Tène III burial at Welwyn Garden City', *Archaeologia*, 101.

Romano-British burials

McWhirr, A., Viner, L., and Wells, C., 1982, *Cirencester Excavations II; Romano-British Cemeteries at Cirencester*, Cirencester.

Philp, B.J., 1973, 'Site 17. A Romano-British Site at Eastwood, Fawkham, Kent' in *Excavations in West Kent 1960–1970*, Kent Monograph Series No. 2, Dover, 1973.

Reece, R., (ed.) 1977, *Burial in the Roman World*, CBA Research Report No. 22, London.

Toynbee, J.M.C., 1971, *Death and Burial in the Roman World*, London.

Wenham, L.P., 1968, *The Romano-British Cemetery at Trentholme Drive, York*, London.
Wheeler, R.E.M., 1923, 'Roman Pipe-Burial from Caerleon', *Antiq. Journ.*, 9.

8 Christianity

Barley, M.W., and Hanson, R.P.C., (eds), 1968, *Christianity in Britain 300–700*, Leicester.
Black, E.W., 1986, 'Christian and Pagan hopes of salvation in Romano-British mosaics' in Henig, M., and King, A., (eds), *op. cit.*, bibliography chapter 7, 147 ff.
Green, C., 1977, 'The significance of plaster burials for the recognition of Christian cemeteries' in Reece, R., (ed.) 1977, *op. cit.*
Guy, C.J., 1981, 'Roman Circular Lead Tanks in Britain', *Britannia*, 12, 271 ff.
Leech, R., 1981, 'The Excavation of a Romano-British Farmstead and Cemetery on Bradley Hill, Somerton, Somerset', *Britannia*, 12, 177 ff.
Liversidge, J.E.A., and Weatherhead, F.J., 1987, 'The Christian Paintings' in Meates, G.W. 1987, *Lullingstone II*.
Painter, K.S., 1966, 'The Design of the Roman Mosaic at Hinton St Mary', *Antiq. Journ.*, 56, 49–54.
Painter, K.S., 1977, *The Water Newton Early Christian Silver*, London.
Thomas, C., 1971, *Britain and Ireland in Early Christian Times AD 400–800*, London.
Thomas, C., 1981, *Christianity in Roman Britain to AD 500*, London.
Toynbee, J.M.C., 1953, 'Christianity in Roman Britain', *Journal of the British Archaeological Association*, (third series), 61, 1 ff.

9 Roman Coinage in Britain

General works

Burnett, A., 1987, *Coinage in the Roman World*, London.
Carson, R.A.G., 1970, *Coins of Greece and Rome*, London.
Casey, P.J., and Reece, R., (eds), 1974, (first edition), *Coins and the Archaeologist*, B.A.R. (British Series), no. 4, Oxford, second edition, London, 1988.
Casey, P.J., 1984, *Roman Coinage in Britain*, Aylesbury.
Casey, P.J., 1986, *Understanding Ancient Coins*, London.
Fox, J.F., 1983, *Roman Coins and How to Collect Them*, Harlow.
Greene, K., 1986, *The Archaeology of the Roman Economy*, London.
Reece, R., 1970, *Roman Coins*, London.
Sear, D., various years, *Roman Coins and their Values*, London.

Pre-Roman coinage

Allen, D.F., 1971, 'British Potin Coins: a Review' in Hill and Jesson, (eds), *op. cit.*
Collis, J., 1974, 'A functionalist approach to pre-Roman coinage' in Casey and Reece, (eds), *op. cit.*
Haselgrove, C., 1987, *Iron Age Coinage in South-East England, the Archaeological Context*, B.A.R. (British Series) No. 174, Oxford.
Mack, R.P., 1974, *The Coinage of Ancient Britain*, London.
Nash, D., 1987, *Coinage in the Celtic World*, London.

Catalogues

Askew, G., 1951, *The Coinage of Roman Britain*, London (reprinted 1980).
Carson, R.A.G., 1962, *Coins of the Roman Empire in the British Museum*, Volume VI (Severus Alexander to Balbinus and Pupienus), London.
Mattingly, H., and Sydenham, E.A., Sutherland, C.H.V., and Carson, R.A.G., (eds) 1923 etc., *The Roman Imperial Coinage*, London.
Mattingly, H., 1923 etc., *Coins of the Roman Empire in the British Museum*, Volume I (Augustus to Vitellius), 1923 and 1966; Volume II (Vespasian to Domitian), 1930 and 1966; Volume III (Nerva to Hadrian), 1936 and 1966; Volume IV (Antoninus Pius to Commodus), 1940 and 1968; and Volume V (Pertinax to Elagabalus), 1950, London.

Others

Boon, G.C. and Rahtz, P.A., 1965, 'Third-century Counterfeiting at Whitchurch, Somerset', *Arch. Journ.*, 122, 13 ff.
Brickstock, R.J., 1987, *Copies of the* Fel Temp Reparatio *Coinage in Britain*, B.A.R. (British Series) No. 176, Oxford.
Burnett, A., 1984, 'Clipped *Siliquae* and the end of Roman Britain', *Britannia*, 15, 163 ff.
Carson, R.G., 1959, 'The Mints and Coinage of Carausius and Allectus', *Journal of the British Archaeological Association*, 22, 33 ff.
White, A.J., 1981, 'A Roman Pottery Money-Box from Lincoln', *Britannia*, 12, 302.

Index

Note: a number of references are grouped under general headings, for example samian ware appears under pottery, Hadrian under emperors and so on; place-names used throughout the book are those in common usage – for example Chesterholm and St Albans which are usually referred to by their ancient names of Vindolanda and Verulamium respectively. Personal names which appear in the text have not been included with the exception of emperors, governors and sources.

Places (pottery sources appear under pottery in general index):

Alchester fig. 37
Aldgate-Pulborough potter 83
Alston 48
Amersham fig. 97
Anglesey 54
Antonine Wall 39, 76, 197, 205; fig. 121
Appleshaw 79, 186
Arles (France) 193
Arras (France) 198
Ashstead 58; fig. 34
Ashton 136; fig. 79
Autun (France) 21

Backworth 124; fig. 46
Baldock 56, 134; figs. 31, 79
Barcombe 128
Barking Hall fig. 78
Barkway 156; fig. 95
Bath (*Aquae Sulis*)
    stonemasons 62; fig. 36: cult of Sulis-Minerva 139, 158, 160, 163; figs. 36, 81, 82, 95, 99; plate 24
Beauport Park, bathhouse at 45, 58, 106, 111; figs. 23, 61
Benwell (*Condercum*)
    fort at 31, 35, 39, 43; fig. 19: temple at, 140, 155; fig. 81
Bewcastle (*Fanum Cocidii*) fig. 99
Bignor 49, 106
Birdoswald (*Banna*) 24, 39, 43, 148; figs. 22, 89, 108
Bisley 62
Bitterne (*Clausentum*) 199
Bodiam 45
Bosham 131, 140
Bradley Hill 188
Brampton 95
Bredgar 206
Bridgeness 43
Brockley Hill (*Sulloniacae*) 70, 98; fig. 57, Table IV
Brough-on-Humber (*Petuaria*) 133-4

Brough-under-Stainmore (*Verteris*) 48
Burgh Castle (*Garrianonum*) 35; fig. 17; plate 8
Burnswark 30, 36

Caerhun (*Kanovium*) 69; fig. 40
Caerleon (*Isca*) 30, 32, 36, 39, 43, 48, 114, 115, 124, 134; figs. 9, 15, 21, 39, 73
Caernarvon (*Segontium*) 169; fig. 4
Caerwent (*Venta Silurum*) 131, 134
Caister-by-Norwich (Caistor St Edmunds – *Venta Icenorum*) 49, 80
Camerton 57, 79
Canterbury (*Durovernum Cantiacorum*) 132
Carlisle (*Luguvallium*) 47, 70, 101, 133, 149; fig. 87
Carnuntum (modern Petronell – Austria) 21
Carvoran (*Magnis*) 30, 48, 60; fig. 38
Castleford (*Lagentium*) 56, 101
Catterick (*Cataractonium*) 48, 57, 134
Charterhouse (*Veb...?*) 134
Chedworth 50, 153, 187, 188; fig. 87
Chelmsford (*Caesaromagus*) fig. 101
Chester (*Deva*) 21, 38, 48, 62, 123; fig. 108
Chesters (*Cilurnum*) 35, 140, 148; figs. 16, 104
Chesterholm, *see* Vindolanda
Chester-le-Street (*Concangis*) 167
Chichester (*Noviomagus*) 83, 133, 140
Cirencester (*Corinium Dobunnorum*) 34, 188; figs. 8, 31, 85, 116
Coddenham 115; plate 9
Colchester (*Camulodunum/Colonia Claudia Victricensis*) 38, 43, 60-62, 76, 108, 124, 129, 134, 136, 169, 172, 180, 198; figs. 8, 35, 53, 103, 111; plates 9, 11
Coleraine 76
Cologne (Germany) 88, 191
Cookham 170
Corbridge (*Corstopitum/Coriosopitum*) 19, 29, 35, 37, 76, 162, 178, 201; figs. 3, 35, 44, 108
Cranbrook 45
Creeting 129
Cremona, Second Battle of 23, 24
Cricklade 149; fig. 87

Darenth, River 58, 69
Dolaucothi 53, 113
Donnerplund (Denmark) fig. 26
Doorwerth (Holland) 29
Dorchester (*Durnovaria*) 35, 106, 188, 206; fig. 120
Dunstable 174; fig. 105
Dura-Europos (Syria) 16, 23, 29, 184

Elginhaugh 38
Ely, Isle of 27, 57, 169; figs. 12, 103; plate 7

Falkirk 205
Farley Heath 160
Farningham 133
Felmingham Hall fig. 101

General